THE GREAT EVENTS

BY

FAMOUS HISTORIANS

A COMPREHENSIVE AND READABLE ACCOUNT OF THE WORLD'S
HISTORY, EMPHASIZING THE MORE IMPORTANT EVENTS, AND PRE-
SENTING THESE AS COMPLETE NARRATIVES IN THE MASTER-WORDS
OF THE MOST EMINENT HISTORIANS

NON-SECTARIAN   NON-PARTISAN   NON-SECTIONAL

ON THE PLAN EVOLVED FROM A CONSENSUS OF OPINIONS GATH-
ERED FROM THE MOST DISTINGUISHED SCHOLARS OF AMERICA
AND EUROPE, INCLUDING BRIEF INTRODUCTIONS BY SPECIALISTS
TO CONNECT AND EXPLAIN THE CELEBRATED NARRATIVES, AR-
RANGED CHRONOLOGICALLY, WITH THOROUGH INDICES, BIBLIOG-
RAPHIES, CHRONOLOGIES, AND COURSES OF READING

EDITOR-IN-CHIEF

ROSSITER JOHNSON, LL.D.

ASSOCIATE EDITORS

CHARLES F. HORNE, Ph.D.
JOHN RUDD, LL.D.

With a staff of specialists

VOLUME II

𝕿𝖍𝖊 𝕹𝖆𝖙𝖎𝖔𝖓𝖆𝖑 𝕬𝖑𝖚𝖒𝖓𝖎

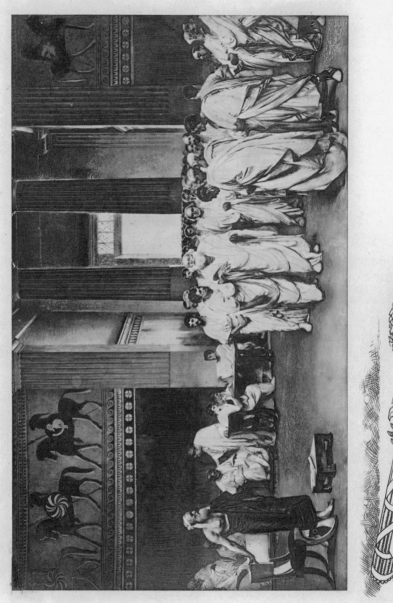

CONTENTS

VOLUME II

LIST OF ILLUSTRATIONS

VOLUME II

AN OUTLINE NARRATIVE

TRACING BRIEFLY THE CAUSES, CON-
NECTIONS, AND CONSEQUENCES OF

THE GREAT EVENTS

(FROM THE RISE OF GREECE TO THE CHRISTIAN ERA)

CHARLES F. HORNE, Ph.D.

EARTH'S upward struggle has been baffled by so many stumbles that critics have not been lacking to suggest that we do not advance at all, but only swing in circles, like a squirrel in its cage. Certain it is that each ancient civilization seemed to bear in itself the seeds of its own destruction. Yet it may be held with equal truth that each new power, rising above the ruins of the last, held something nobler, was borne upward by some truth its rival could not reach.

At no period is this more evident than in the five centuries immediately preceding the Christian era. Persia, Greece, Carthage, Rome, each in turn was with some justice proclaimed lord of the world; each in turn felt the impulse of her glory and advanced rapidly in culture and knowledge of the arts; and each in turn succumbed to the temptations that beset unlimited success. They degenerated not only in physical strength, but in moral honesty.

Let us recognize, however, that the term "world-ruler" as applied to even the greatest of these nations has but a restricted sense. When the Persian monarch called himself lord of the sun and moon, he only meant in a figurative way that he was acquainted with no other king so powerful as himself; that beyond his own dominions he heard only of feeble colonies, and beyond those the wilderness. Alexander, when he sighed for more worlds to conquer, had in reality made himself lord of less than a quarter of Asia and of about one-sixtieth part of Europe.

No man and no nation has ever yet been intrusted with the government of the entire globe. None has proved sufficiently fitted for the giant task. Each empire has been, as it were, but an experiment; and beyond the border line of seas and deserts which ringed each boastful conqueror, there were always other races developing along slower, and it may be surer, lines.

In those old days our world was in truth too big for conquest. Armies marched on foot. Provisions could not be carried in any quantity, unless a general clung to the sea-shore and depended on his ships. What Alexander might with more truth have sighed for, was some modern means of swift transportation, possessed of which he might still have enjoyed many interesting, bloody battles in more distant lands.

THE DEVELOPMENT OF THE GREEKS

Taking the idea "world power" in the restricted sense suggested, Persia lost it to Greece at Salamis. As the Asiatic hordes fled behind their panic-stricken king, the Greeks, looking round their limited horizon, could see no power that might vie with them. The idea of pressing home their success and overthrowing the entire unwieldy Persian empire was at once conceived.

But the Greeks were of all races least like to weld earth into one dominion. They could not even unite among themselves. In short it cannot be too emphatically pointed out that the work of Greece was not to consolidate, but to separate, to teach the value of each individual man. Asia had made monarchies in plenty. King after king had passed in splendid, glittering pomp across her plains, circled by a crowd of obsequious courtiers, trampling on a nameless multitude of slaves. Europe was to make democracies, or at least to try her hand at them.

It has been well said that a democracy is the strongest government for defence, the weakest for attack. Every little Greek city clung jealously to its own freedom, and to its equally obvious right to dominate its neighbors. The supreme danger of the Persian invasion united them for a moment; but as soon as safety was assured, they recommenced their bickering. Sparta with her record of ancient leadership, Athens with her new-won glory against the common foe, each tried to draw the other cities in her train. There was no one man who could dominate them all and concentrate their strength against the enemy. So for a time Persia continued to exist; she even by degrees regained something of her former influence over the divided cities.

Among these Athens held the foremost rank. She was, as we have previously seen, far more truly representative of the Greek spirit than her rival. Sparta was aristocratic and conservative; Athens democratic and progressive. The genius of her leaders gathered the lesser towns into a great naval league, in which she grew ever more powerful. Her allies sank to be dependent and unwilling vassals, forced to contribute large sums to the treasury of their overlord.

This was the age of Pericles.[1] As Athens became wealthy, her citizens became cultured. Statues, temples, theatres, made the city beautiful. Dramatists, orators, and poets made her intellectually renowned. A marvellous outburst, this of Athens! Displaying for the first time in history the full capacity of the human mind! Had there been similar flowerings of genius amid forgotten Asiatic times? One doubts it; doubts if such brilliancy could ever anywhere have passed, and left no clearer record of its triumphs.

Amid such splendor it seems captious to point out the flaw. Yet Athenian and all Greek civilization did ultimately decline. It represented intellectual, but not moral culture. The Greeks delighted intensely in the purely physical life about them; they had small conception of anything beyond. To enjoy, to be successful, that was all their goal; the means scarce counted. The Athenians called Aristides the Just; but so little did they honor his high rectitude that they banished him for a decade. His title, or it may have been his insistence on the subject, bored them.

His rival, Themistocles, was more suited to their taste, a

[1] See *Pericles Rules in Athens*, page 12.

clever scamp, who must always be dealing with both sides in every quarrel, and outwitting both. Athens was driven to banish him also at last, at his too flagrant treachery. But he was not dismissed with the scathing scorn our modern age would heap upon a traitor. He was sent regretfully, as one turns from a charming but too persistently lawless friend. The banishment was only for ten years, and he had his nest already prepared with the Persian King. If you would understand the Greek spirit in its fullest perfection, study Themistocles. Rampant individualism, seeking personal pleasure, clamorous for the admiration of its fellows, but not restrained from secret falsity by any strong moral sense—that was what the Greeks developed in the end.

Neither must Athens be regarded as a democracy in the modern sense. She was only so by contrast with Persia or with Sparta. Not every man in the beautiful city voted, or enjoyed the riches that flowed into her coffers, and could thus afford, free from pecuniary care, to devote himself to art. Athens probably had never more than thirty thousand "citizens." The rest of the adult male population, vastly outnumbering these, were slaves, or foreigners attracted by the city's splendor.

But those thirty thousand were certainly men. "There were giants in those days." One sometimes stands in wonder at their boldness. What all Greece could not do, what Persia had completely failed in, they undertook. Athens alone should conquer the world. By force of arms they would found an empire of intellect. They fought Persia and Sparta, both at once. Plague swept their city, yet they would not yield.[1] Their own subject allies turned against them; and they fought those too. They sent fleets and armies against Syracuse, the mightiest power of the West. It was Athens against all mankind!

She was unequal to the task, superbly unequal to it. The destruction of her army at Syracuse[2] was only the foremost of a series of inevitable disasters, which left her helpless. After that, Sparta, and then Thebes, became the leading city of Greece. Athens slowly regained her fighting strength; her

[1] See *Great Plague at Athens*, page 34.
[2] See *Defeat of the Athenians at Syracuse*, page 48.

intellectual supremacy she had not lost.   Socrates,[1] greatest of
her sons, endeavored to teach a morality higher than earth had
yet received, higher than his contemporaries could grasp.   Plato
gave to thought a scientific basis.

Then Macedonia, a border kingdom of ancient kinship to
the Greeks, but not recognized as belonging among them,
began to obtrude herself in their affairs, and at length won
that leadership for which they had all contended.   A hundred
and fifty years had elapsed since the Greeks had stood united
against Persia.   During all that time their strength had been
turned against themselves.   Now at last the internecine wars
were checked, and all the power of the sturdy race was directed
by one man, Alexander, King of Macedon.   Democracy had
made the Greeks intellectually glorious, but politically weak.
Monarchy rose from the ruin they had wrought.

As though that ancient invasion of Xerxes had been a crime
of yesterday, Alexander proclaimed his intention of avenging
it; and the Greeks applauded.   They understood Persia now
far better than in the elder days; they saw what a feeble mass
the huge heterogeneous empire had become.   Its people were
slaves, its soldiers mercenaries.   The Greeks themselves had
been hired to suppress more than one Persian rebellion,[2] and
to foment these also.   They had learned the enormous advantage their stronger personality gave them against the masses
of sheeplike Asiatics.

So it was in holiday mood that they followed Alexander,
and in schoolboy roughness that they trampled on the civilization of the East.   In fact, it is worth noting that the most
vigorous resistance they encountered was not from the Persians, but from a remnant of the Semites, the merchants of the
Phœnician city of Tyre.[3]   In less than eight years, B.C. 331–
323, Alexander overran the whole known world of the East,[4]
only stopping when, on the border of India, his soldiers broke
into open revolt, not against fighting, but against further wandering.

[1] See *Condemnation and Death of Socrates*, page 87.
[2] See *Retreat of the Ten Thousand Greeks*, page 68.
[3] See *Alexander Reduces Tyre*, page 133.
[4] See *The Battle of Arbela*, page 141.

If this invasion had been the mere outcome of one man's ambition, it might scarce be worth recording. But Alexander was only the topmost wave in the surging of a long imminent, inevitable racial movement. Its effect upon civilization, upon the world, was incalculably vast. Alexander and his successors were city-builders, administrators. As such they spread Greek culture, the Greek idea of individualism, over all their world.

How deep was the change, made upon the imbruted Asiatics, we may perhaps question. Our own age has seen how much of education may be lavished on an inferior race without materially altering the brute instincts within. The building-up of the soul in man is not a matter of individuals, but of centuries. Yet in at least a superficial way Greek thought became the thought of all mankind. We may dismiss Alexander's savage conquests with a sigh of pity; but we cannot deny him recognition as a most potent teacher of the world.

His empire did not last. It was in too obvious opposition to all that we have recognized as the Grecian spirit. At his death the same impulse seems to have stirred each one of his subordinates, to snatch for himself a kingdom from the confusion. Instead of one there were soon three, four, and then a dozen semi-Grecian states in Asia. The Greek element in each grew very faint.

From this time onward Asia takes a less prominent place in world affairs. Her ancient leadership in the march of civilization had long been yielded to the Greeks. Now her semblance of military power disappeared as well. Only two further happenings in all Asia seem worth noting, down to the birth of Christ. One of these was the Tartar conquest of China, an event which coalesced the Tartars, helped make them a nation.[1] It was thus fraught with most disastrous consequences for the Europe of the future. The other was the revolt of the Hebrews under Judas Maccabæus, against their Grecian rulers. This was a religious revolt, a religious war. Here for the first time we find a people who will believe, who can believe, in no god but their own, who will die sooner than give worship to another. We approach the borders of an age where the spirit

[1] See *Tartar Invasion of China*, page 126.

is more valued than the body, where the mental is stronger than the physical, where facts are dominated by ideas.[1]

Had Alexander even at the moment of his greatest strength directed his forces westward instead of east, he would have found a different world and encountered a sturdier resistance. He himself recognized this, and during his last years was gathering all the resources of his unwieldy empire, to hurl them against Carthage and against Italy. What the issue might have been no man can say. Alexander's death ended forever the impossible attempt to unite his race. Once more and until the end, Grecian strength was wasted against itself.

This gave opportunity to the growing powers of the West. Alexander is scarce gone ere we hear Carthage boasting that the Mediterranean is but a private lake in her possession. She rules all Western Africa and Spain, Sardinia and Corsica. She masters the Greeks of Sicily, against whom Athens failed. Rome is compelled to sign treaties with her as an inferior.

THE GROWTH OF ROME

Rome was only husbanding her strength; the little republic of B.C. 510 had grown much during the two centuries of Grecian splendor. Her people had become far better fitted for conquest than their eastern kinsmen. It is presumable that here too it was the difference of surroundings which had differentiated the race. The ancient Etrurian (non-Aryan) civilization on which the Latins intruded, was apparently more advanced than their own. For centuries their utmost prowess scarce sufficed to maintain their independence. Thus it was not possible for them to become too self-satisfied, to stand afar off and look down on their neighbors with Grecian scorn. The *ego* was less prominently developed; the necessity of mutual dependence and united action was more deeply taught. Their records display less of brilliancy, but more of patient persistency, than those of Greece, less of spectacular individualism, more of truly patriotic self-suppression. In Rome, even more than in Sparta, the "State" was everything. During the early days men found their highest glory in making their city glorious; their proudest boast was to be "citizens of Rome."

[1] See *Judas Maccabæus Liberates Judea*, page 245.

To trace the slow steps by which the tiny republic grew to be mistress of all Italy would take too long. She settled her internal difficulties as all such difficulties must be settled, if the race is to progress; that is, she became more democratic.[1] As the lower classes advanced in knowledge and intelligence they insisted on a share of the government. They fought their way to it. They united Rome, mastered the other Latin cities, and admitted them to partnership in her power. She conquered the Etruscans and the Samnites. For a moment we find her almost overwhelmed by an inroad of the wild Celtic tribes from the forests of Central Europe;[2] but, fortunately for her, the other Italian states were equally crushed. It was weakness against weakness, and the Romans retained their foremost place.

Not till more than a century later were they brought into serious conflict with the Greeks. In the year B.C. 280, Pyrrhus, King of Epirus, who had won a temporary leadership over a portion of the Grecian land, undertook the conquest of the West.[3] Fifty years before, Alexander with far greater power might have been victorious over a feebler Rome. Pyrrhus failed completely. If the Romans had less dash and a less wide experience of varied warfare than his followers, they had far more of true, heroic endurance. The Greeks had reached that stage of individual culture where they were much too selfishly intelligent to be willing to die in battle. Pyrrhus withdrew from Italy. Grecian brilliancy was helpless against Roman strength of union.

Then came the far more serious contest between Rome and Carthage.[4] Carthage was a Phœnician, a Semite state; and hers was the last, the most gigantic struggle made by Semitism to recover its waning superiority, to dominate the ancient world. Three times in three tremendous wars did she and Rome put forth their utmost strength against each other. Hannibal, perhaps the greatest military genius who ever lived, fought upon the side of Carthage. At one time Rome seemed

[1] See *Institution and Fall of the Decemvirate in Rome*, page 1.
[2] See *Brennus Burns Rome*, page 110.
[3] See *First Battle between Greeks and Romans*, page 166.
[4] See *The Punic Wars*, page 179.

crushed, helpless before him.[1]   Yet in the end Rome won.[2] **It** was not by the brilliancy of her commanders, not by the superiority of her resources.   It was the grim, cool courage of the Aryan mind, showing strongest and calmest when face to face with ruin.

Our modern philosophers, being Aryan, assure us that the victory of Carthage would have been an irretrievable disaster to mankind; that her falsity, her narrow selfishness, her bloody inhumanity, would have stifled all progress; that her dominion would have been the tyranny of a few heartless masters over a world of tortured slaves.   On the other hand, Rome up to this point had certainly been a generous mistress to her subjects. She had left them peace and prosperity among themselves; she had given them as much political freedom as was consistent with her sovereignty; she had wellnigh succeeded in welding all Italy into a Roman nation.   It is noteworthy that the large majority of the Italian cities clung to her, even in the darkest straits to which she was reduced by Hannibal.

Yet when the fall of her last great rival left Rome irresistible abroad, her methods changed.   It is hard to see how even Carthaginians could have been more cruel, more grasping, more corrupt than the Roman rulers of the provinces.   Having conquered the governments of the world, Rome had to face outbreak after outbreak from the unarmed, unsheltered masses of the people.   Her barbarity drove them to mad despair. "Servile" wars, slave outbreaks are dotted over all the last century of the Roman Republic.

The good, if there was any good, that Roman dominion brought the world at that period was the spreading of Greek culture across the western half of the world.   As Rome mastered the Greek states one by one, their genius won a subtler triumph over the conqueror.   Her generals recognized and admired a culture superior to their own.   They carried off the statues of Greece for the adornment of their villas, and with equal eagerness they appropriated her manners and her thought, her literature and her gods.

[1] See *Battle of the Metaurus*, page 195.
[2] See *Scipio Africanus Crushes Hannibal at Zama and Subjugates Carthage*, page 224.

But this superficial culture could not save the Roman Republic from the dry-rot that sapped her vitals from within. As a mere matter of numbers, the actual citizens of Rome or even of the semi-Roman districts close around her were too few to continue fighting over all the vast empire they controlled. The sturdy peasant population of Italy slowly disappeared. The actual inhabitants of the capital came to consist of a few thousand vastly wealthy families, who held all the power, a few thousand more of poorer citizens dependent on the rich, and then a vast swarm of slaves and foreigners, feeders on the crumbs of the Roman table.

In the battles against Carthage, the mass of Rome's armies had consisted of her own citizens or of allies closely united to them in blood and fortune. Her later victories were won by hired troops, men gathered from every clime and every race. Roman generals still might lead them, Roman laws environ them, Roman gold employ them. Yet the fact remained, that in these armies lay the strength of the Republic, no longer within her own walls, no longer in the stout hearts of her citizens.

Perhaps the world itself was slow in seeing this degeneration. The Gracchi brothers tried to stem the tide, and they were slain, sacrificed by the nation they sought to save.[1] Cornelius Sulla was the man who completed, and at the same time made plain to all, the change that had been growing up. Having bitter grievances against his enemies in the capital, he appealed for redress, not to the Roman senate, not to the votes of the populace, but to the swords of the legions he commanded. Twice he marched his soldiers against Rome. He brushed aside the feeble resistance that was offered, and entered the city like a conqueror. The blood of those who had opposed his wishes flowed in streams. Three thousand senators and knights, the flower of the Roman aristocracy, were slain at his nod. Of the common folk and of the Italians throughout the peninsula, the slaughter was immeasurable. And when his bloody vengeance was at last glutted, Sulla ruled as an extravagant, conscienceless, licentious dictator. Rome had found a fitting master.

[1] See *The Gracchi and Their Reforms*, page 259.

THE STRUGGLE OF INDIVIDUALS FOR SUPREMACY

The Roman people, the mighty race who had defied a Hannibal at their gates, were clearly come to an end. Sulla had proved the power of the Republic to be an empty shell. After his death, men used the empty forms awhile; but the surviving aristocrats had learned their awful lesson. They put no further faith in the strength of the city; they watched the armies and the generals; they intrigued for the various commands. It was an exciting game. Life and fortune were the stakes they risked; the prize—the mastery of a helpless world, waiting to be plundered.

Pompey and Cæsar proved the ablest players. Pompey overthrew what was left of the Greek Asiatic kingdoms and returned to Rome the idol of his troops, wellnigh as powerful as had been Sulla. Cæsar, looking in his turn for a place to build up an army devoted to himself, selected Gaul and spent eight years in subduing and civilizing what was in a way the most important of all Rome's conquests. In Gaul he came in contact with another, fresher Aryan race.[1] Rome received new soldiers for her legions, new brains fitted to understand and carry on the work of civilizing the world.

When Cæsar, turning away from Britain,[2] marched these new-formed legions back against Rome, even as Sulla had done, it was almost like another Gallic invasion of the South. Pompey fled. He gathered his legions from Asia; and the world resounded once more to the clash of arms.

This, then, was the third and final stage of the huge struggle for empire. War was still the business of the world. Rome had first defeated foreign nations; then she had to defeat the uprisings of the subject peoples; now her chiefs, finding her exhausted, fought among themselves for the supreme power. Armies of Asiatics, armies of Gauls, each claiming to represent Rome, battled over her helpless body.

Cæsar was victorious. But when the conquering power which had once belonged to the united nation became embodied in a single man, there was a new way by which it might be checked. The government of Rome, like that of the Greek

[1] See *Cæsar Conquers Gaul*, page 267.
[2] See *Roman Invasion and Conquest of Britain*, page 285.

and Asiatic tyrannies, became a "despotism tempered by assassination"; and Cæsar was its foremost victim.[1]

His death did not stop the fascinating gamble for empire. It only added one more move to the possible complexities of the game. The lesser players had their chance. They intrigued and they fought. Egypt, the last remaining civilized state outside of Rome, was drawn into the whirlpool also.[2] Cleopatra and Antony acted their reckless parts, and at length out of the world-wide tumult emerged "young Octavius," to assume his *rôle* as "Augustus Cæsar," acknowledged emperor of the world.[3]

Note, however, that the term "world" is still one of boast, not truth. Emperor over many men, Augustus was; but the powers of nature still shut many races safe beyond his mastery. The ocean bounded his dominion on the west; the deserts to the south and east; the German forests to the north. These last he did essay to conquer, but they proved beyond him. The wild German tribes having no cities, which they must defend at any cost, could afford to flee or hide. Choosing their own time and place they rose suddenly, smote the legions of Augustus, and melted into the wilderness again.[4]

Rome was checked at last. No civilized nation had been able to stand against her; but the wild tribes of the Germans and the Parthians did. Barbarism had still by far the larger portion of the world wherein to live and develop, and gather brain and brawn. Rome could not conquer the wilderness.

[1] See *Assassination of Cæsar*, page 313.
[2] See *Cleopatra's Conquest of Cæsar and Antony*, page 295.
[3] See *Rome Becomes a Monarchy*, page 333.
[4] See *Germans Under Arminius Revolt against Rome*, page 362.

[FOR THE NEXT SECTION OF THIS GENERAL SURVEY SEE VOLUME III.]

INSTITUTION AND FALL OF THE DECEMVIRATE IN ROME

B.C. 450

HENRY G. LIDDELL

When wars and pestilence had laid a heavy burden upon the Roman people, there appears to have been a period in which internal commotions and civil strife were stilled, and the quarrels of patricians and plebeians gave way to temporary truce. On the inevitable renewal of the old struggle the college of tribunes adopted a measure favorable to the plebeians in so far as it provided means for checking the abuse of power on the part of consuls in punishing members of that class in connection with the prosecution of suits against them.

The passage of this measure had the effect of reopening former conflicts, the patrician elements becoming greatly alarmed at what they regarded as a fresh encroachment upon their hereditary rights. The contest was long and bitter, each side either bringing forward or rejecting again and again the same measures or the same representatives.

Finally, compromises were made, and in the year B.C. 452 a commission of ten men, called *decemvirs*, constituting the *Decemvirate*, was chosen, consisting wholly of patricians, who entered with great efficiency upon the discharge of legislative duties which resulted in the production of a new code. This was approved by the senate and by the popular representatives, and was published in the form of ten copper plates or tables, which were affixed to the speaker's pulpit in the Forum. Among the new decemvirs appointed in the year B.C. 450 were several plebeians, the first official representatives of the entire people who were chosen from that class.

THE patrician burgesses endeavored to wrest independence from the "plebs" after the battle of Lake Regillus; and the latter, ruined by constant wars with the neighboring nations, being compelled to make good their losses by borrowing money from patrician creditors, and liable to become bondsmen in default of payment, at length deserted the city, and only returned on condition of being protected by tribunes of their own; they then, by the firmness of Publilius Volero and Lætorius, obtained the right of electing these tribunes at their own assembly, the "Comitia of the Tribes." Finally the great consul Spurius Cassius endeavored to relieve the commonalty by an agrarian law, so as to better their condition permanently.

The execution of the Agrarian law was constantly evaded. But on the conquest of Antium from the Volscians, in the year B.C. 468, a colony was sent thither, and this was one of the first examples of a distribution of public land to poorer citizens; which answered two purposes—the improvement of their condition, and the defence of the place against the enemy.

Nor did the tribunes, now made altogether independent of the patricians, fail to assert their power. One of the first persons who felt the force of their arm was the second Appius Claudius. This Sabine noble, following his father's example, had, after the departure of the Fabii, led the opposition to the Publilian law. When he took the field against the Volscians, his soldiers would not fight, and the stern commander put to death every tenth man in his legions. For the acts of his consulship he was brought to trial by the tribunes M. Duillius and C. Sicinius. Seeing that conviction was certain, the proud patrician avoided humiliation by suicide.

Nevertheless the border wars still continued, and the plebeians suffered much. To the evils of debt and want were added about this time the horrors of pestilential disease, which visited the Roman territory several times at that period. In one year (B.C. 464) the two consuls, two of the four augurs, and the curio Maximus, who was the head of all the patricians, were swept off—a fact which implies the death of a vast number of less distinguished persons. The government was administered by the plebeian ædiles, under the control of senatorial interreges. The Volscians and Æquians ravaged the country up to the walls of Rome; and the safety of the city must be attributed to the Latins and Hernici, not to the men of Rome.

Meantime the tribunes had in vain demanded a full execution of the Agrarian law. But in the year B.C. 462, one of the Sacred College, by name C. Terentilius Harsa, came forward with a bill, the object of which was to give the plebeians a surer footing in the state. This man perceived that as long as the consuls retained their almost despotic power, and were elected by the influence of the patricians, this order had it in its power to thwart all measures, even after they were passed, which tended to advance the interests of the plebeians. He therefore no longer demanded the execution of the Agrarian law, but proposed that a commission of ten men (*decemviri*) should be appointed to draw up constitutional laws for regulating the future relations of the patricians and plebeians.

The Reform Bill of Terentilius was, as might be supposed, vehemently resisted by the patrician burgesses. But the plebeians supported their champion no less warmly. For five consecutive years the same tribunes were reëlected and in vain endeavored to carry the bill. This was the time which least fulfils the character which we have claimed for the Roman people—patience and temperance, combined with firmness in their demands. To prevent the tribunes from carrying their law, the younger patricians thronged to the assemblies and interfered with all proceedings; Terentilius, they said, was endeavoring to confound all distinction between the orders. Some scenes occurred which seem to show that both sides were prepared for civil war.

In the year B.C. 460 the city was alarmed by hearing that the Capitol had been seized by a band of Sabines and exiled Romans, under the command of one Herdonius. Who these exiles were is uncertain. But we know, by the legend of Cincinnatus, that Cæso Quinctius, the son of that old hero, was an exile. It has been inferred, therefore, that he was among them, that the tribunes had succeeded in banishing from the city the most violent of their opponents, and that these persons had not scrupled to associate themselves with Sabines to recover their homes. The consul Valerius, aided by the Latins of Tusculum, levied an army to attack the insurgents, on condition that after success the law should be fully considered. The exiles were driven out and Herdonius was killed. But the consul fell in the assault, and the patricians, led by old Cincinnatus, refused to fulfil his promises.

Then followed the danger of the Æquian invasion, to which the legend of Cincinnatus, as given above, refers. The stern old man used his dictatorial power quite as much to crush the tribunes at home as to conquer the enemies abroad.

One of the historians tells us that in this period of seditious violence many of the leading plebeians were assassinated (as the tribune Genucius had been), and to this time only can be attributed the horrible story, mentioned by more than one writer, that nine tribunes were burned alive at the instance of their colleague Mucius. Society was utterly disorganized. The two orders were on the brink of civil war. It seemed as if Rome was to become the city of discord, not of law. Happily, there were moderate men in both orders. Now, as at the time of the secession, their voices prevailed, and a compromise was arranged.

In the eighth year after the first promulgation of the Terentilian law, this compromise was made (B.C. 454). The law itself was no longer pressed by the tribunes. The patricians, on the other hand, so far gave way as to allow three men (*triumviri*) to be appointed, who were to travel into Greece, and bring back a copy of the laws of Solon, as well as the laws and institutes of any other Greek states which they might deem good and useful. These were to be the groundwork of a new code of laws, such as should give fair and equal rights to both orders and restrain the arbitrary power of the patrician magistrates.

Another concession made by the patrician lords was a small instalment of the Agrarian law. L. Icilius, tribune of the plebs, proposed that all the Aventine hill, being public land, should be made over to the plebs, to be their quarter forever, as the other hills were occupied by the patricians and their clients. This hill, it will be remembered, was consecrated to the goddess Diana (Jana), and though included in the walls of Servius, was yet not within the sacred limits (*pomœrium*) of the patrician city. After some opposition the patricians suffered this Icilian law to pass, in hopes of soothing the anger of the plebeians. The land was parcelled out into building-sites. But as there was not enough to give a separate plot to every plebeian householder that wished to live in the city, one allotment was assigned to several persons, who built a joint house in *flats* or stories, each of which was inhabited—as in Edinburgh and in most foreign towns—by a separate family.

The three men who had been sent into Greece returned in the third year (B.C. 452). They found the city free from domestic strife, partly from the concessions already made, partly from expectation of what was now to follow, and partly from the effect of a pestilence which had broken out anew.

So far did moderate counsels now prevail among the patricians, that after some little delay they agreed to suspend the ordinary government by the consuls and other officers, and in their stead to appoint a council of ten, who were, during their existence, to be intrusted with all the functions of government. But they were to have a double duty: they were not only an administrative, but also a legislative council. On the one hand, they were to conduct the government, administer justice, and command the armies. On the other, they were to draw up a code of laws by which equal justice was to be dealt out to the whole Roman people, to patricians and plebeians alike, and by which especially the authority to be exercised by the consuls, or chief magistrates, was to be clearly determined and settled.

This supreme council of ten, or decemvirs, was first appointed in the year B.C. 450. They were all patricians. At their head stood Appius Claudius and T. Genucius, who had already been chosen consuls for this memorable year. This Appius Claudius (the third of his name) was son and grandson of those two patrician chiefs who had opposed the leaders of the plebeians so vehemently in the matter of the tribunate. But he affected a different conduct from his sires. He was the most popular man of the whole council, and became in fact the sovereign of Rome. At first he used his great power well, and the first year's government of the decemvirs was famed for justice and moderation.

They also applied themselves diligently to their great work of law-making, and before the end of the year had drawn up a code of ten tables, which were posted in the Forum, that all citizens might examine them and suggest amendments to the decemvirs. After due time thus spent, the ten tables were confirmed and made law at the Comitia of the Centuries. By this code equal justice was to be administered to both orders without distinction of persons.

At the close of the year the first decemvirs laid down their office, just as the consuls and other officers of state had been accustomed to do before. They were succeeded by a second set of ten, who, for the next year at least, were to conduct the government like their predecessors. The only one of the old decemvirs reëlected was Appius Claudius. The patricians, indeed, endeavored to prevent even this, and to this end he was himself appointed to preside at the new elections; for it was held impossible for a chief magistrate to return his own name, when he was himself presiding. But Appius scorned precedents. He returned himself as elected, together with nine others, men of no name, while two of the great Quinctian gens, who offered themselves, were rejected.

Of the new decemvirs, it is certain that three—and it is probable that five—were plebeians. Appius, with the plebeian Oppius, held the judicial office, and remained in the city; and these two seem to have been regarded as the chiefs. The other six commanded the armies and discharged the duties previously assigned to the quæstors and ædiles.

The first decemvirs had earned the respect and esteem of their fellow-citizens. The new Council of Ten deserved the hatred which has ever since cloven to their name. Appius now threw off the mask which he had so long worn, and assumed his natural character—the same as had distinguished his sire and grandsire, of unhappy memory. He became an absolute despot. His brethren in the council offered no hinderance to his will; even the plebeian decemvirs, bribed by power, fell into his way of action and supported his tyranny. They each had twelve lictors, who carried fasces with the axes in them the symbol of absolute power, as in the times of the kings; so that it was said, "Rome had now twelve Tarquins instead of one, and one hundred and twenty armed lictors instead of twelve!" All freedom of speech ceased. The senate was seldom called together. The leading men, patricians and plebeians, left the city. The outward aspect of things was that of perfect calm and peace, but an opportunity only was wanting for the discontent which was smouldering in all men's hearts to break out and show itself.

By the end of the year the decemvirs had added two more tables to the code, so that there were now twelve tables. But these two last were of a most oppressive and arbitrary kind, devoted chiefly to restore the ancient privileges of the patrician caste. Of these tables, it should be observed that they were made laws not by the vote of the people, but by the simple edict of the decemvirs.

It was, no doubt, expected that the second decemvirs also would have held *comitia* for the election of successors. But Appius and his colleagues showed no such intention, and when the year came to a close they continued to hold office as if they had been reëlected. So firmly did their power seem to be established that we hear of no endeavor being made to induce them to resign.

In the course of this next year (B.C. 449), the border wars were renewed. On the north the Sabines, and the Æquians on the northeast, invaded the Roman country at the same time. The latter penetrated as far as Mount Algidus, as in B.C. 458, when they were routed by old Cincinnatus. The decemvirs probably, like the patrician burgesses in former times, regarded these inroads not without satisfaction; for they turned away the mind of the people from their sufferings at home. Yet from these very wars sprung the events which overturned their power and destroyed themselves.

Two armies were levied, one to check the Sabines, the other to oppose the Æquians, and these were commanded by the six military decemvirs. Appius and Oppius remained to administer affairs at home. But there was no spirit in the armies. Both were defeated; and that which was opposed to the Æquians was compelled to take refuge within the walls of Tusculum.

Then followed two events which were preserved in well-known legends, and which give the popular narrative of the manner in which the power of the decemvirs was at last overthrown.

LEGEND OF SICCIUS DENTATUS.

In the army sent against the Sabines, Siccius Dentatus was known as the bravest man. He was then serving as a centurion; he had fought in one hundred and twenty battles; he had slain eight champions in single combat; had saved the lives of fourteen citizens; had received forty wounds, all in front; had followed in nine triumphal processions, and had won crowns and decorations without number. This gallant veteran had taken an active part in the civil contests between the two orders, and was now suspected, by the decemvirs commanding the Sabine army, of plotting against them. Accordingly they determined to get rid of him; and for this end they sent him out as if to reconnoitre, with a party of soldiers, who were secretly instructed to murder him. Having discovered their design, he set his back against a rock and resolved to sell his life dearly. More than one of his assailants fell and the rest stood at bay around him, not venturing to come within sword's length, when one wretch climbed up the rock behind and crushed the brave old man with a massive stone. But the manner of his death could not be hidden from the army, and the generals only prevented an outbreak by honoring him with a magnificent funeral.

Such was the state of things in the Sabine army

LEGEND OF VIRGINIA.[1]

The other army had a still grosser outrage to complain of. In this there was a notable centurion, Virginius by name. His daughter Virginia, just ripening into womanhood, beautiful as the day, was betrothed to L. Icilius, the tribune who had carried the law for allotting the Aventine hill to the plebeians. Appius Claudius, the decemvir, saw her and lusted to make her his own. And with this intent he ordered one of his clients, M. Claudius by name, to lay hands upon her as she was going to her school in the Forum, and to claim her as his slave. The man did so; and when the cries of her nurse brought a crowd round them, M. Claudius insisted on taking her before the decemvir, in order, as he said, to have the case fairly tried. Her friends consented; and no sooner had Appius heard the matter than he gave judgment that the maiden should be delivered up to the claimant, who should be bound to produce her in case her alleged father appeared to gainsay the claim. Now this judgment was directly against one of the laws of the twelve tables, which Appius himself had framed; for therein it was provided that any person being at freedom should continue free till it was proved that such person was a slave. Icilius, therefore,

[1] Dionysius is the authority for this legend.

with Numitorius, the uncle of the maiden, boldly argued against the legality of the judgment, and at length Appius, fearing a tumult, agreed to leave the girl in their hands on condition of their giving bail to bring her before him next morning; and then, if Virginius did not appear, he would at once, he said, give her up to her pretended master. To this Icilius consented, but he delayed giving bail, pretending that he could not procure it readily; and in the mean time he sent off a secret message to the camp on Algidus, to inform Virginius of what had happened. As soon as the bail was given, Appius also sent a message to the decemvirs in command of that army, ordering them to refuse leave of absence to Virginius. But when this last message arrived, Virginius was already halfway on his road to Rome; for the distance was not more than twenty miles, and he had started at nightfall.

Next morning, early, Virginius entered the Forum, leading his daughter by the hand, both clad in mean attire. A great number of friends and matrons attended him, and he went about among the people entreating them to support him against the tyranny of Appius. So when Appius came to take his place on the judgment seat he found the Forum full of people, all friendly to Virginius and his cause. But he inherited the boldness as well as the vices of his sires, and though he saw Virginius standing there ready to prove that he was the maiden's father, he at once gave judgment, against his own law, that Virginia should be given up to M. Claudius till it should be proved that she was free. The wretch came up to seize her, and the lictors kept the people from him. Virginius, now despairing of deliverance, begged Appius to allow him to ask the maiden whether she were indeed his daughter or not. "If," said he, "I find I am not her father, I shall bear her loss the lighter." Under this pretence he drew her aside to a spot upon the northern side of the Forum, afterward called the "*Novæ Tabernæ*," and here, snatching up a knife from a butcher's stall, he cried: "In this way only can I keep thee free!"—and so saying, stabbed her to the heart. Then he turned to the tribunal and said, "On thee, Appius, and on thy head be this blood!" Appius cried out to seize "the murderer," but the crowd made way for Virginius, and he passed through them holding up the bloody knife, and went out at the gate and made straight for the army. There, when the soldiers had heard his tale, they at once abandoned their decemviral generals and marched to Rome. They were soon followed by the other army from the Sabine frontier; for to them Icilius had gone, and Numitorius; and they found willing ears among men who were already enraged by the murder of old Siccius Dentatus. So the two armies joined their banners, elected new generals, and encamped upon the Aventine hill, the quarter of the plebeians.

Meantime the people at home had risen against Appius, and after driving him from the Forum they joined their armed fellow-citizens upon the Aventine. There the whole body of the commons, armed and unarmed, hung like a dark cloud ready to burst upon the city.

Whatever may be the truth of the legends of Siccius and Virginia, there can be no doubt that the conduct of the decemvirs had brought matters to the verge of civil war. At this juncture the senate met, and the moderate party so far prevailed as to send their own leaders, M. Horatius Barbatus and L. Valerius Potitus, to negotiate with the insurgents. The plebeians were ready to listen to the voices of these men; for they remembered that the consuls of the first year of the Republic, when the patrician burgesses were friends to the plebeians, were named Valerius and Horatius; and so they appointed M. Duillius, a former tribune, to be their spokesman. But no good came of it; and Duillius persuaded the plebeians to leave the city, and once more to occupy the Sacred Mount.

Then remembrances of the great secession came back upon the minds of the patricians, and the senate, observing the calm and resolute bearing of the plebeian leaders, compelled the decemvirs to resign, and sent back Valerius and Horatius to negotiate anew.

The leaders of the plebeians demanded: First, that the tribuneship should be restored, and the *Comitia Tributa* recognized; secondly, that a right of appeal to the people against the power of the supreme magistrate should be secured; thirdly, that full indemnity should be granted to the movers and pro-

moters of the late secession; fourthly, that the decemvirs
should be burnt alive.

Of these demands the deputies of the senate agreed to the
three first; but the fourth, they said, was unworthy of a free
people; it was a piece of tyranny, as bad as any of the worst
acts of the late government; and it was needless, because anyone who had reason of complaint against the late decemvirs
might proceed against them according to law. The plebeians
listened to these words of wisdom, and withdrew their savage
demand. The other three were confirmed by the fathers, and
the plebeians returned to their quarters on the Aventine.
Here they held an assembly according to their tribes, in which
the pontifex Maximus presided; and they now, for the first
time, elected ten tribunes—first Virginius, Numitorius, and
Icilius, then Duillius and six others: so full were their minds
of the wrong done to the daughter of Virginius; so entirely
was it the blood of young Virginia that overthrew the decemvirs, even as that of Lucretia had driven out the Tarquins.

The plebeians had now returned to the city, headed by their
ten tribunes, a number which was never again altered so long
as the tribunate continued in existence. It remained for the
patricians to redeem the pledges given by their agents Valerius
and Horatius on the other demands of the plebeian leaders.

The first thing to settle was the election of the supreme
magistrates. The decemvirs had fallen, and the state was
without any executive government.

It has been supposed, as we have said above, that the government of the decemvirs was intended to be perpetual. The
patricians gave up their consuls, and the plebeians their tribunes, on condition that each order was to be admitted to an
equal share in the new decemviral college. But the tribunes
were now restored in augmented number, and it was but natural that the patricians should insist on again occupying all
places in the supreme magistracy. By common consent, as it
would seem, the Comitia of the Centuries met and elected to
the consulate the two patricians who had shown themselves
the friends of both orders: L. Valerius Potitus and M. Horatius
Barbatus. Thus ended the government of the decemvirate.

PERICLES RULES IN ATHENS

B.C. 444

PLUTARCH

Under the sway of Pericles many changes occurred in the civil affairs of Athens affecting the constitution of the state and the character and administration of its laws. Events of magnitude marked the struggles of the Athenians with other powers. The development of art and learning was carried to an unprecedented height, and the Age of Pericles is the most illustrious in ancient history.

Pericles began his career by opposing the aristocratic party of Athens, led by Cimon. In this policy he was aided by complications arising with Sparta and Argos. Directing his attack particularly against the Areopagus, he succeeded in greatly modifying the composition of that body and diminishing its powers. The exile of Cimon, the strengthening of Athens by new alliances, and the vigorous prosecution of wars against Persia and Corinth combined to establish his supremacy, which was still further confirmed by the building of the long walls connecting Athens with the sea, and by the acquisition of neighboring territory.

A favorable convention was concluded with Persia, Athens resumed a state of general peace, and Pericles found himself at the head of a powerful empire formed out of a confederacy previously existing. The strength of this empire was indeed soon impaired by ill-judged military movements, against the advice of Pericles himself, but during six years of peace which followed he succeeded in perfecting a state whose preeminence in intellectual, political, and artistic development has had no rival.

In the later wars of Athens the renown of Pericles was still further enhanced; but his chief glory arose from the architectural adornment of the city, and especially from the building of the Parthenon and the splendid decoration of the Acropolis; while his work of judicial reform remains an added monument to his fame, and among the masters of eloquence his orations preserve for him a foremost place.

PERICLES was of the tribe Acamantis, and of the township of Cholargos, and was descended from the noblest families in Athens, on both his father's and mother's side. His father, Xanthippus, defeated the Persian generals at Mycale, while his mother, Agariste, was a descendant of Clisthenes, who drove the sons of Pisistratus out of Athens, put an end to their despotic rule, and established a new constitution admirably calculated to reconcile all parties and save the country. She dreamed that she had brought forth a lion, and a few days afterward was delivered of Pericles. His body was symmetrical, but his head was long, out of all proportion; for which reason, in nearly all his statues he is represented wearing a helmet, as the sculptors did not wish, I suppose, to reproach him with this blemish. The Attic poets called him squill-head, and the comic poet Cratinus, in his play *Chirones*, says:

> " From Chronos old and faction
> Is sprung a tyrant dread,
> And all Olympus calls him
> The man-compelling head."

And again in the play of *Nemesis*:

> " Come, hospitable Zeus, with lofty head."

Teleclides, too, speaks of him as sitting

> " Bowed down
> With a dreadful frown,
> Because matters of state have gone wrong,
> Until at last,
> From his head so vast,
> His ideas burst forth in a throng.

And Eupolis, in his play of *Demoi*, asking questions about each of the great orators as they come up from the other world one after the other, when at last Pericles ascends, says:

> " The great headpiece of those below."

Most writers tell us that his tutor in music was Damon, whose name they say should be pronounced with the first syllable short. Aristotle, however, says that he studied under Pythoclides. This Damon, it seems, was a sophist of the highest order, who used the name of music to conceal this accomplishment from the world, but who really trained Pericles for his political contests just as a trainer prepares an athlete for the games. However, Damon's use of music as a pretext did not impose upon the Athenians, who banished him by ostracism, as a busybody and lover of despotism.

Pericles greatly admired Anaxagoras, and became deeply interested in grand speculations, which gave him a haughty spirit and a lofty style of oratory far removed from vulgarity and low buffoonery, and also an imperturbable gravity of countenance and a calmness of demeanor and appearance which no incident could disturb as he was speaking, while the tone of his voice never showed that he heeded any interruption. These advantages greatly impressed the people. The poet Ion, however, says that Pericles was overbearing and insolent in conversation, and that his pride had in it a great deal of contempt for others; while he praises Cimon's civil, sensible, and polished address. But we may disregard Ion as a mere dramatic poet who always sees in great men something upon which to exercise his satiric vein; whereas Zeno used to invite those who called the haughtiness of Pericles a mere courting of popularity and affectation of grandeur, to court popularity themselves in the same fashion, since the acting of such a part might insensibly mould their dispositions until they resembled that of their model.

Pericles when young greatly feared the people. He had a certain personal likeness to the despot Pisistratus; and as his own voice was sweet, and he was ready and fluent in speech, old men who had known Pisistratus were struck by his resemblance to him. He was also rich, of noble birth, and had powerful friends, so that he feared he might be banished by ostracism, and consequently held aloof from politics, but proved himself a brave and daring soldier in the wars. But when Aristides was dead, Themistocles banished, and Cimon generally absent on distant campaigns, Pericles engaged in public affairs, taking the popular side, that of the poor and many, against that of the rich and few; quite contrary to his own feelings, which were entirely aristocratic. He feared, it seems, that he might be suspected of a design to make himself despot, and seeing that Cimon took the side of the nobility, and was much beloved by them, he betook himself to the people, as a means of obtaining safety for himself, and a strong party to combat that of Cimon. He immediately altered his mode of life; was never seen in any street except that which led to the market-place and the national assembly, and declined all invitations to dinner and such like social gatherings. But Pericles feared to make himself too common even with the people, and only addressed them after long intervals; not speaking upon every subject, and not constantly addressing them, but, as Critolaus says, keeping himself like the Salaminian trireme for great crises, and allowing his friends and the other orators to manage matters of less moment.

Wishing to adopt a style of speaking consonant with his haughty manner and lofty spirit, Pericles made free use of the instrument which Anaxagoras, as it were, put into his hand, and often tinged his oratory with natural philosophy. He far surpassed all others by using this "lofty intelligence and power of universal consummation," as the divine Plato calls it; in addition to his natural advantages, adorning his oratory with apt illustrations drawn from physical science. For this reason some think that he was nicknamed the Olympian; though some refer this to his improvement of the city by new and beautiful buildings, and others from his power both as a politician and a general. It is not by any means unlikely that these causes all combined to produce the name.

Pericles was very cautious about his words, and, whenever he ascended the tribune to speak, used first to pray to the gods that nothing unfitted for the present occasion might fall from his lips. He left no writings, except the measures which he brought forward, and very few of his sayings are recorded.

Thucydides represents the constitution under Pericles as a democracy in name, but really an aristocracy, because the government was all in the hands of one leading citizen. But as many other writers tell us that, during his administration, the people received grants of land abroad, and were indulged with dramatic entertainments, and payments for their services, in consequence of which they fell into bad habits, and became extravagant and licentious, instead of sober hard-working people as they had been before, let us consider the history of this change, viewing it by the light of the facts themselves. First of all, Pericles had to measure himself with Cimon, and to transfer the affections of the people from Cimon to himself. As he was not so rich a man as Cimon, who used from his own ample means to give a dinner daily to any poor Athenian who required it, clothe aged persons, and take away the fences round his property, so that anyone might gather the fruit, Pericles, unable to vie with him in this, turned his attention to a distribution of the public funds among the people, at the suggestion, we are told by Aristotle, of Damonides of Oia. By the money paid for public spectacles, for citizens acting as jurymen, and other paid offices, and largesses, he soon won over the people to his side, so that he was able to use them in his attack upon the senate of the Areopagus, of which he himself was not a member, never having been chosen *archon*, or *thesmothete*, or *king archon*, or *polemarch*. These offices had from ancient times been obtained by lot, and it was only through them that those who had approved themselves in the discharge of them were advanced to the Areopagus. For this reason it was that Pericles, when he gained strength with the populace, destroyed this senate, making Ephialtes bring forward a bill which restricted its judicial powers, while he himself succeeded in getting Cimon banished by ostracism, as a friend of Sparta and a hater of the people, although he was second to no Athenian in birth or fortune, and won most brilliant victories over the Persians, and had filled Athens with plunder and spoils of war. So great was the power of Pericles with the common people.

One of the provisions of ostracism was that the person banished should remain in exile for ten years. But during this period the Lacedæmonians with a great force invaded the territory of Tanagra, and, as the Athenians at once marched out to attack them, Cimon came back from exile, took his place in full armor among the ranks of his own tribe, and hoped by distinguishing himself in the battle among his fellow-citizens to prove the falsehood of the Laconian sympathies with which he had been charged. However, the friends of Pericles drove him away, as an exile. On the other hand, Pericles fought more bravely in that battle than he had ever fought before, and surpassed everyone in reckless daring. The friends of Cimon also, whom Pericles had accused of Laconian leanings, fell, all together, in their ranks; and the Athenians felt great sorrow for their treatment of Cimon, and a great longing for his restoration, now that they had lost a great battle on the frontier, and expected to be hard pressed during the summer by the Lacedæmonians. Pericles, perceiving this, lost no time in gratifying the popular wish, but himself proposed the decree for his recall; and Cimon on his return reconciled the two states, for he was on familiar terms with the Spartans, who were hated by Pericles and the other leaders of the common people. Some say that, before Cimon's recall by Pericles, a secret compact was made with him by Elpinice, Cimon's sister, that Cimon was to proceed on foreign service against the Persians with a fleet of two hundred ships, while Pericles was to retain his power in the city. It is also said that, when Cimon was being tried for his life, Elpinice softened the resentment of Pericles, who was one of those appointed to impeach him. When Elpinice came to beg her brother's life of him, he answered with a smile, "Elpinice, you are too old to meddle in affairs of this sort." But, for all that, he spoke only once, for form's sake, and pressed Cimon less than any of his other prosecutors. How, then, can one put any faith in Idomeneus, when he accuses Pericles of procuring the assassination of his friend and colleague Ephialtes, because he was jealous of his reputation? This seems an ignoble calumny which Idomeneus has drawn from some obscure source to fling at a man who, no doubt, was not faultless, but of a generous spirit and noble mind, incapable of entertaining so savage and brutal a design. Ephialtes was disliked and feared by the nobles, and was inexorable in punishing those who wronged the people; wherefore his enemies had him assassinated by means of Aristodicus of Tanagra. This we are told by Aristotle. Cimon died in Cyprus while in command of the Athenian forces.

The nobles now perceived that Pericles was the most important man in the state, and far more powerful than any other citizen; wherefore, as they still hoped to check his authority, and not allow him to be omnipotent, they set up Thucydides, of the township of Alopecæ, as his rival, a man of good sense and a relative of Cimon, but less of a warrior and more of a politician, who, by watching his opportunities, and opposing Pericles in debate, soon brought about a balance of power. He did not allow the nobles to mix themselves up

with the people in the public assembly as they had been wont
to do, so that their dignity was lost among the masses; but he
collected them into a separate body, and by thus concentrating
their strength was able to use it to counterbalance that of the
other party. From the beginning these two factions had been
but imperfectly welded together, because their tendencies
were different; but now the struggle for power between Pericles and Thucydides drew a sharp line of demarcation between
them, and one was called the party of the Many, the other that
of the Few. Pericles now courted the people in every way,
constantly arranging public spectacles, festivals, and processions in the city, by which he educated the Athenians to take
pleasure in refined amusements; and also he sent out sixty
triremes to cruise every year, in which many of the people
served for hire for eight months, learning and practising seamanship. Besides this he sent a thousand settlers to the
Chersonese, five hundred to Naxos, half as many to Andros,
a thousand to dwell among the Thracian tribe of the Bisaltæ,
and others to the new colony in Italy founded by the city of
Sybaris, which was named Thurii. By this means he relieved
the state of numerous idle agitators, assisted the necessitous,
and overawed the allies of Athens by placing his colonists near
them to watch their behavior.

The building of the temples, by which Athens was adorned,
the people delighted, and the rest of the world astonished, and
which now alone prove that the tales of the ancient power and
glory of Greece are no fables, was what particularly excited
the spleen of the opposite faction, who inveighed against him
in the public assembly, declaring that the Athenians had disgraced themselves by transferring the common treasury of the
Greeks from the island of Delos to their own custody. "Pericles himself," they urged, "has taken away the only possible
excuse for such an act—the fear that it might be exposed to
the attacks of the Persians when at Delos, whereas it would be
safe at Athens. Greece has been outraged, and feels itself
openly tyrannized over, when it sees us using the funds—which
we extorted from it for the war against the Persians—for gilding and beautifying our city as if it were a vain woman, and
adorning it with precious marbles and statues and temples

worth a thousand talents." To this Pericles replied that the allies had no right to consider how their money was spent, so long as Athens defended them from the Persians; while they supplied neither horses, ships, nor men, but merely money, which the Athenians had a right to spend as they pleased, provided they afforded them that security which it purchased. It was right, he argued, that after the city had provided all that was necessary for war, it should devote its surplus money to the erection of buildings which would be a glory to it for all ages, while these works would create plenty by leaving no man unemployed, and encouraging all sorts of handicraft, so that nearly the whole city would earn wages, and thus derive both its beauty and its profit from itself. For those who were in the flower of their age, military service offered a means of earning money from the common stock; while, as he did not wish the mechanics and lower classes to be without their share, nor yet to see them receive it without doing work for it, he had laid the foundations of great edifices which would require industries of every kind to complete them; and he had done this in the interests of the lower classes, who thus, although they remained at home, would have just as good a claim to their share of the public funds as those who were serving at sea, in garrison, or in the field. The different materials used, such as stone, brass, ivory, gold, ebony, cypress-wood, and so forth, would require special artisans for each, such as carpenters, modellers, smiths, stone-masons, dyers, melters and moulders of gold, and ivory painters, embroiderers, workers in relief; and also men to bring them to the city, such as sailors and captains of ships and pilots for such as came by sea; and, for those who came by land, carriage builders, horse breeders, drivers, ropemakers, linen manufacturers, shoemakers, road menders, and miners. Each trade, moreover, employed a number of unskilled laborers, so that, in a word, there would be work for persons of every age and every class, and general prosperity would be the result.

These buildings were of immense size, and unequalled in beauty and grace, as the workmen endeavored to make the execution surpass the design in beauty; but what was most remarkable was the speed with which they were built. All these edifices, each of which one would have thought it would have taken many generations to complete, were all finished during the most brilliant period of one man's administration. In beauty each of them at once appeared venerable as soon as it was built; but even at the present day the work looks as fresh as ever, for they bloom with an eternal freshness which defies time, and seems to make the work instinct with an unfading spirit of youth.

The overseer and manager of the whole was Phidias, although there were other excellent architects and workmen, such as Callicrates and Ictinus, who built the Parthenon on the site of the old Hecatompedon, which had been destroyed by the Persians, and Coroebus, who began to build the Temple of Initiation at Eleusis, but who only lived to see the columns erected and the architraves placed upon them. On his death, Metagenes, of Xypete, added the frieze and the upper row of columns, and Xenocles, of Cholargos, crowned it with the domed roof over the shrine. As to the long wall, about which Socrates says that he heard Pericles bring forward a motion, Callicrates undertook to build it. The Odeum, which internally consisted of many rows of seats and many columns, and externally of a roof sloping on all sides from a central point, was said to have been built in imitation of the king of Persia's tent, and was built under Pericles' direction.

The Propylæa, before the Acropolis, were finished in five years by Mnesicles the architect; and a miraculous incident during the work seemed to show that the goddess did not disapprove, but rather encouraged and assisted the building. The most energetic and active of the workmen fell from a great height, and lay in a dangerous condition, given over by his doctors. Pericles grieved much for him; but the goddess appeared to him in a dream, and suggested a course of treatment by which Pericles quickly healed the workman. In consequence of this, he set up the brazen statue of Athene the Healer, near the old altar in the Acropolis. The golden statue of the goddess was made by Phidias, and his name appears upon the basement in the inscription. Almost everything was in his hands, and he gave his orders to all the workmen—as has been said before—because of his friendship with Pericles.

When the speakers of Thucydides' party complained that Pericles had wasted the public money, and destroyed the revenue, he asked the people in the assembly whether they thought he had spent much. When they answered, "Very much indeed," he said in reply: "Do not, then, put it down to the public account, but to mine; and I will inscribe my name upon all the public buildings." When Pericles said this, the people, either in admiration of his magnificence of manner, or being eager to bear their share in the glory of the new buildings, shouted to him with one accord to take what money he pleased from the treasury, and spend it as he pleased, without stint. And finally, he underwent the trial of ostracism with Thucydides, and not only succeeded in driving him into exile, but broke up his party.

As now there was no opposition to encounter in the city, and all parties had been blended into one, Pericles undertook the sole administration of the home and foreign affairs of Athens, dealing with the public revenue, the army, the navy, the islands and maritime affairs, and the great sources of strength which Athens derived from her alliances, as well with Greek as with foreign princes and states. Henceforth he became quite a different man: he no longer gave way to the people, and ceased to watch the breath of popular favor; but he changed the loose and licentious democracy which had hitherto existed, into a stricter aristocratic, or rather monarchical, form of government. This he used honorably and unswervingly for the public benefit, finding the people, as a rule, willing to second the measures which he explained to them to be necessary and to which he asked their consent, but occasionally having to use violence, and to force them, much against their will, to do what was expedient; like a physician dealing with some complicated disorder, who at one time allows his patient innocent recreation, and at another inflicts upon him sharp pains and bitter though salutary draughts. Every possible kind of disorder was to be found among a people possessing so great an empire as the Athenians, and he alone was able to bring them into harmony by playing alternately upon their hopes and fears, checking them when overconfident, and raising their spirits when they were cast down and disheartened. Thus, as Plato says, he was able to prove that oratory is the art of influencing men's minds, and to use it in its highest application, when it deals with men's passions and characters, which, like certain strings of a musical instrument, require a skilful and delicate touch. The secret of his power is to be found, however, as Thucydides says, not so much in his mere oratory as in his pure and blameless life, because he was so well known to be incorruptible, and indifferent to money; for though he made the city, which was a great one, into the greatest and richest city of Greece, and though he himself became more powerful than many independent sovereigns, who were able to leave their kingdoms to their sons, yet Pericles did not increase by one single drachma the estate which he received from his father. For forty years he held the first place among such men as Ephialtes, Leocrates, Myronides, Cimon, Tolmides, and Thucydides; and, after the fall and banishment of Thucydides by ostracism, he united in himself for five-and-twenty years all the various offices of state, which were supposed to last only for one year; and yet during the whole of that period proved himself incorruptible by bribes.

As the Lacedæmonians began to be jealous of the prosperity of the Athenians, Pericles, wishing to raise the spirit of the people and to make them feel capable of immense operations, passed a decree, inviting all the Greeks, whether inhabiting Europe or Asia, whether living in large cities or small ones, to send representatives to a meeting at Athens to deliberate about the restoration of the Greek temples which had been burned by the barbarians, about the sacrifices which were due in consequence of the vows which they had made to the gods on behalf of Greece before joining battle, and about the sea, that all men might be able to sail upon it in peace and without fear. To carry out this decree twenty men, selected from the citizens over fifty years of age, were sent out, five of whom invited the Ionian and Dorian Greeks in Asia and the islands as far as Lesbos and Rhodes, five went to the inhabitants of the Hellespont and Thrace as far as Byzantium, and five more proceeded to Bœotia, Phocis, and Peloponnesus, passing from thence through Locris to the neighboring continent as far as Acarnania and Ambracia; while the remainder journeyed through Eubœa to the Œtæans and the Malian Gulf, and to the Achæans of Phthia and the Thessalians, urging them to join the assembly and take part in the deliberations concerning the peace and well-being of Greece. However, nothing was effected, and the cities never assembled, in consequence it is said of the covert hostility of the Lacedæmonians, and because the attempt was first made in Peloponnesus and failed there: yet I have inserted an account of it in order to show the lofty spirit and the magnificent designs of Pericles.

In his campaigns he was chiefly remarkable for caution, for he would not, if he could help it, begin a battle of which the issue was doubtful; nor did he wish to emulate those generals who have won themselves a great reputation by running risks and trusting to good luck. But he ever used to say to his countrymen, that none of them should come by their deaths through any act of his. Observing that Tolmides, the son of Tolmæus, elated by previous successes and by the credit which he had gained as a general, was about to invade Bœotia in a reckless manner, and had persuaded a thousand young men to follow him without any support whatever, he endeavored to stop him, and made that memorable saying in the public assembly, that if Tolmides would not take the advice of Pericles, he would at any rate do well to consult that best of advisers, Time. This speech had but little success at the time; but when, a few days afterward, the news came that Tolmides had fallen in action at Coronea, and many noble citizens with him, Pericles was greatly respected and admired as a wise and patriotic man.

His most successful campaign was that in the Chersonesus, which proved the salvation of the Greeks residing there: for he not only settled a thousand colonists there, and thus increased the available force of the cities, but built a continuous line of fortifications reaching across the isthmus from one sea to the other, by which he shut off the Thracians, who had previously ravaged the peninsula, and put an end to a constant and harassing border warfare to which the settlers were exposed, as they had for neighbors tribes of wild plundering barbarians.

But that by which he obtained most glory and renown was

when he started from Pegæ, in the Megarian territory, and sailed round the Peloponnesus with a fleet of a hundred triremes; for he not only laid waste much of the country near the coast, as Tolmides had previously done, but he proceeded far inland, away from his ships, leading the troops who were on board, and terrified the inhabitants so much that they shut themselves up in their strongholds.   The men of Sicyon alone ventured to meet him at Nemea, and them he overthrew in a pitched battle, and erected a trophy.   Next he took on board troops from the friendly district of Achaia, and, crossing over to the opposite side of the Corinthian Gulf, coasted along past the mouth of the river Achelous, overran Acarnania, drove the people of Œneadæ to the shelter of their city walls, and after ravaging the country returned home, having made himself a terror to his enemies, and done good service to Athens; for not the least casualty, even by accident, befell the troops under his command.

When he sailed into the Black Sea with a great and splendidly equipped fleet, he assisted the Greek cities there, and treated them with consideration, and showed the neighboring savage tribes and their chiefs the greatness of his force, and his confidence in his power, by sailing where he pleased, and taking complete control over that sea.   He left at Sinope thirteen ships, and a land force under the command of Lamachus, to act against Timesileon, who had made himself despot of that city.   When he and his party were driven out, Pericles passed a decree that six hundred Athenian volunteers should sail to Sinope, and become citizens there, receiving the houses and lands which had formerly been in the possession of the despot and his party.   But in other cases he would not agree to the impulsive proposals of the Athenians, and he opposed them when, elated by their power and good fortune, they talked of recovering Egypt and attacking the seaboard of the Persian empire.   Many, too, were inflamed with that ill-starred notion of an attempt on Sicily, which was afterward blown into a flame by Alcibiades and other orators.   Some even dreamed of the conquest of Etruria and Carthage, in consequence of the greatness which the Athenian empire had already reached, and the full tide of success which seemed to attend it.

Pericles, however, restrained these outbursts, and would not allow the people to meddle with foreign states, but used the power of Athens chiefly to preserve and guard her already existing empire, thinking it to be of paramount importance to oppose the Lacedæmonians, a task to which he bent all his energies, as is proved by many of his acts, especially in connection with the Sacred War. In this war the Lacedæmonians sent a force to Delphi, and made the Phocians, who held it, give it up to the people of Delphi: but as soon as they were gone Pericles made an expedition into the country, and restored the temple to the Phocians; and as the Lacedæmonians had scratched the oracle which the Delphians had given them, on the forehead of the brazen wolf there, Pericles got a response from the oracle for the Athenians, and carved it on the right side of the same wolf.

Events proved that Pericles was right in confining the Athenian empire to Greece. First of all Eubœa revolted, and he was obliged to lead an army to subdue that island. Shortly after this, news came that the Megarians had become hostile, and that an army, under the command of Plistoanax, king of the Lacedæmonians, was menacing the frontier of Attica. Pericles now in all haste withdrew his troops from Eubœa, to meet the invader. He did not venture on an engagement with the numerous and warlike forces of the enemy, although repeatedly invited by them to fight: but, observing that Plistoanax was a very young man, and entirely under the influence of Cleandrides, whom the *ephors* had sent to act as his tutor and counsellor because of his tender years, he opened secret negotiations with the latter, who at once, for a bribe, agreed to withdraw the Peloponnesians from Attica. When their army returned and dispersed, the Lacedæmonians were so incensed that they imposed a fine on their king, and condemned Cleandrides, who fled the country, to be put to death. This Cleandrides was the father of Gylippus, who caused the ruin of the Athenian expedition in Sicily. Avarice seems to have been hereditary in the family, for Gylippus himself, after brilliant exploits in war, was convicted of taking bribes, and banished from Sparta in disgrace.

When Pericles submitted the accounts of the campaign to

the people, there was an item of ten talents, "for a necessary purpose," which the people passed without any questioning, or any curiosity to learn the secret. Some historians, among whom is Theophrastus the philosopher, say that Pericles sent ten talents annually to Sparta, by means of which he bribed the chief magistrates to defer the war, thus not buying peace, but time to make preparations for a better defence. He immediately turned his attention to the insurgents in Eubœa, and proceeding thither with a fleet of fifty sail, and five thousand heavy armed troops, he reduced their cities to submission. He banished from Chalcis the "equestrian order," as it was called, consisting of men of wealth and station; and he drove all the inhabitants of Hestiæa out of their country, replacing them by Athenian settlers. He treated these people with this pitiless severity, because they had captured an Athenian ship, and put its crew to the sword. After this, as the Athenians and Lacedæmonians made a truce for thirty years, Pericles decreed the expedition against Samos, on the pretext that they had disregarded the commands of the Athenians to cease from their war with the Milesians.

Pericles is accused of going to war with Samos to save the Milesians. These states were at war about the possession of the city of Priene, and the Samians, who were victorious, would not lay down their arms and allow the Athenians to settle the matter by arbitration, as they ordered them to do. For this reason Pericles proceeded to Samos, put an end to the oligarchical form of government there, and sent fifty hostages and as many children to Lemnos, to insure the good behavior of the leading men. It is said that each of these hostages offered him a talent for his own freedom, and that much more was offered by that party which was loath to see a democracy established in the city. Besides all this, Pissuthnes the Persian, who had a liking for the Samians, sent and offered him ten thousand pieces of gold if he would spare the city. Pericles, however, took none of these bribes, but dealt with Samos as he had previously determined, and returned to Athens. The Samians now at once revolted, as Pissuthnes managed to get them back their hostages, and furnished them with the means of carrying on the war. Pericles now made a second expedition against them, and found them in no mind to submit quietly, but determined to dispute the empire of the seas with the Athenians. Pericles gained a signal victory over them in a sea-fight off the Goats' Island, beating a fleet of seventy ships with only forty-four, twenty of which were transports.

Simultaneously with his victory and the flight of the enemy he obtained command of the harbor of Samos, and besieged the Samians in their city. They, in spite of their defeat, still possessed courage enough to sally out and fight a battle under the walls; but soon a larger force arrived from Athens, and the Samians were completely blockaded.

Pericles now with sixty ships sailed out of the Archipelago into the Mediterranean, according to the most current report intending to meet the Phœnician fleet which was coming to help the Samians, but, according to Stesimbrotus, with the intention of attacking Cyprus, which seems improbable. Whatever his intention may have been, his expedition was a failure, for Melissus, the son of Ithagenes, a man of culture, who was then in command of the Samian forces, conceiving a contempt for the small force of the Athenians and the want of experience of their leaders after Pericles' departure, persuaded his countrymen to attack them. In the battle the Samians proved victorious, taking many Athenians prisoners, and destroying many of their ships. By this victory they obtained command of the sea, and were able to supply themselves with more warlike stores than they had possessed before. Aristotle even says that Pericles himself was before this beaten by Melissus in a sea-fight. The Samians branded the figure of an owl on the foreheads of their Athenian prisoners, to revenge themselves for the branding of their own prisoners by the Athenians with the figure of a *samaina*. This is a ship having a beak turned up like a swine's snout, but with a roomy hull, so as both to carry a large cargo and sail fast. This class of vessel is called *samaina* because it was first built at Samos by Polycrates, the despot of that island.

When Pericles heard of the disaster which had befallen his army, he returned in all haste to assist them. He beat Melissus, who came out to meet him, and, after putting the enemy to rout, at once built a wall round their city, preferring to reduce it by blockade to risking the lives of his countrymen in an assault. In the ninth month of the siege the Samians surrendered. Pericles demolished their walls, confiscated their fleet, and imposed a heavy fine upon them, some part of which was paid at once by the Samians, who gave hostages for the payment of the remainder at fixed periods.

Pericles, after the reduction of Samos, returned to Athens, where he buried those who had fallen in the war in a magnificent manner, and was much admired for the funeral oration which, as is customary, was spoken by him over the graves of his countrymen. Ion says that his victory over the Samians wonderfully flattered his vanity. Agamemnon, he was wont to say, took ten years to take a barbarian city, but he in nine months had made himself master of the first and most powerful city in Ionia. And the comparison was not an unjust one, for truly the war was a very great undertaking, and its issue quite uncertain, since, as Thucydides tells us, the Samians came very near to wresting the empire of the sea from the Athenians.

After these events, as the clouds were gathering for the Peloponnesian war, Pericles persuaded the Athenians to send assistance to the people of Corcyra, who were at war with the Corinthians, and thus to attach to their own side an island with a powerful naval force, at a moment when the Peloponnesians had all but declared war against them.

When the people passed this decree, Pericles sent only ten ships under the command of Lacedæmonius, the son of Cimon, as if he designed a deliberate insult; for the house of Cimon was on peculiarly friendly terms with the Lacedæmonians. His design in sending Lacedæmonius out, against his will, and with so few ships, was that if he performed nothing brilliant he might be accused, even more than he was already, of leaning to the side of the Spartans. Indeed, by all means in his power, he always threw obstacles in the way of the advancement of Cimon's family, representing that by their very names they were aliens, one son being named Lacedæmonius, another Thessalus, another Elius. Moreover, the mother of all three was an Arcadian.

Now Pericles was much reproached for sending these ten

ships, which were of little value to the Corcyreans, and gave a
great handle to his enemies to use against him, and in consequence sent a larger force after them to Corcyra, which arrived
there after the battle. The Corinthians, enraged at this, complained in the congress of Sparta of the conduct of the Athenians, as did also the Megarians, who said that they were excluded from every market and every harbor which was in
Athenian hands, contrary to the ancient rights and common
privileges of the Hellenic race. The people of Ægina also
considered themselves to be oppressed and ill-treated, and secretly bemoaned their grievances in the ears of the Spartans,
for they dared not openly bring any charges against the Athenians. At this time, too, Potidæa, a city subject to Athens,
but a colony of Corinth, revolted, and its siege materially hastened the outbreak of the war. Archidamus, indeed, the king
of the Lacedæmonians, sent ambassadors to Athens, was willing to submit all disputed points to arbitration, and endeavored to moderate the excitement of his allies, so that war probably would not have broken out if the Athenians could have
been persuaded to rescind their decree of exclusion against the
Megarians, and to come to terms with them. And, for this
reason, Pericles, who was particularly opposed to this, and
urged the people not to give way to the Megarians, alone bore
the blame of having begun the war.

Pericles passed a decree for a herald to be sent to the
Megarians, and then to go on to the Lacedæmonians to complain of their conduct. This decree of Pericles is worded in a
candid and reasonable manner; but the herald, Anthemocritus,
was thought to have met his death at the hands of the Megarians, and Charinus passed a decree to the effect that Athens
should wage war against them to the death, without truce or
armistice; that any Megarian found in Attica should be punished with death, and that the generals, when taking the usual
oath for each year, should swear in addition that they would
invade the Megarian territory twice every year; and that Anthemocritus should be buried near the city gate leading into the
Thriasian plain, which is now called the Double Gate. How
the dispute originated it is hard to say, but all writers agree in
throwing on Pericles the blame of refusing to reverse the decree.

Now, as the Lacedæmonians knew that if he could be removed from power they would find the Athenians much more easy to deal with, they bade them "drive forth the accursed thing," alluding to Pericles' descent from the Alcmæonidæ by his mother's side, as we are told by Thucydides the historian. But this attempt had just the contrary effect to that which they intended; for, instead of suspicion and dislike, Pericles met with much greater honor and respect from his countrymen than before, because they saw that he was an object of especial dislike to the enemy. For this reason, before the Peloponnesians, under Archidamus, invaded Attica, he warned the Athenians that if Archidamus, when he laid waste everything else, spared his own private estate because of the friendly private relations existing between them, or in order to give his personal enemies a ground for impeaching him, he should give both the land and the farm buildings upon it to the state.

The Lacedæmonians invaded Attica with a great host of their own troops and those of their allies, led by Archidamus, their king. They proceeded, ravaging the country as they went, as far as Acharnæ (close to Athens), where they encamped, imagining that the Athenians would never endure to see them there, but would be driven by pride and shame to come out and fight them. However, Pericles thought that it would be a very serious matter to fight for the very existence of Athens against sixty thousand Peloponnesian and Bœotian heavy-armed troops, and so he pacified those who were dissatisfied at his inactivity by pointing out that trees when cut down quickly grow again, but that when the men of a state are lost, it is hard to raise up others to take their place. He would not call an assembly of the people, because he feared that they would force him to act against his better judgment, but, just as the captain of a ship, when a storm comes on at sea, places everything in the best trim to meet it, and trusting to his own skill and seamanship, disregarding the tears and entreaties of the seasick and terrified passengers, so did Pericles shut the gates of Athens, place sufficient forces to insure the safety of the city at all points, and calmly carry out his own policy, taking little heed of the noisy grumblings of the discontented. Many of his friends besought him to attack, many of his enemies threatened him and abused him, and many songs and offensive jests were written about him, speaking of him as a coward, and one who was betraying the city to its enemies. Cleon too attacked him, using the anger which the citizens felt against him to advance his own personal popularity.

Pericles was unmoved by any of these attacks, but quietly endured all this storm of obloquy. He sent a fleet of a hundred ships to attack Peloponnesus, but did not sail with it himself, remaining at home to keep a tight hand over Athens until the Peloponnesians drew off their forces. He regained his popularity with the common people, who suffered much from the war, by giving them allowances of money from the public revenue, and grants of land; for he drove out the entire population of the island of Ægina, and divided the land by lot among the Athenians. A certain amount of relief also was experienced by reflecting upon the injuries which they were inflicting on the enemy; for the fleet as it sailed round Peloponnesus destroyed many small villages and cities, and ravaged a great extent of country, while Pericles himself led an expedition into the territory of Megara and laid it all waste. By this it is clear that the allies, although they did much damage to the Athenians, yet suffered equally themselves, and never could have protracted the war for such a length of time as it really lasted, but, as Pericles foretold, must soon have desisted had not Providence interfered and confounded human counsels. For now the pestilence fell among the Athenians, and cut off the flower of their youth. Suffering both in body and mind they raved against Pericles, just as people when delirious with disease attack their fathers or their physicians. They endeavored to ruin him, urged on by his personal enemies, who assured them that he was the author of the plague, because he had brought all the country people into the city, where they were compelled to live during the heat of summer, crowded together in small rooms and stifling tents, living an idle life too, and breathing foul air instead of the pure country breeze to which they were accustomed. The cause of this, they said, was the man who, when the war began, admitted the masses of the country people into the city, and then made no use of them, but allowed them to be penned up together like cattle, and transmit the contagion from one to another, without devising any remedy or alleviation of their sufferings.

Hoping to relieve them somewhat, and also to annoy the enemy, Pericles manned a hundred and fifty ships, placed on board, besides the sailors, many brave infantry and cavalry soldiers, and was about to put to sea. The Athenians conceived great hopes, and the enemy no less terror from so large an armament. When all was ready, and Pericles himself had just embarked in his own trireme, an eclipse of the sun took place, producing total darkness, and all men were terrified at so great a portent. Pericles sailed with the fleet, but did nothing worthy of so great a force. He besieged the sacred city of Epidaurus, but, although he had great hopes of taking it, he failed on account of the plague, which destroyed not only his own men, but every one who came in contact with them. After this he again endeavored to encourage the Athenians, to whom he had become an object of dislike. However, he did not succeed in pacifying them, but they condemned him by a public vote to be general no more, and to pay a fine which is stated at the lowest estimate to have been fifteen talents, and at the highest fifty. This was carried, according to Idomeneus, by Cleon, but, according to Theophrastus, by Simmias; while Heraclides of Pontus says that it was effected by Lacratides.

He soon regained his public position, for the people's outburst of anger was quenched by the blow they had dealt him, just as a bee leaves its sting in the wound; but his private affairs were in great distress and disorder, as he had lost many of his relatives during the plague, while others were estranged from him on political grounds. Yet he would not yield, nor abate his firmness and constancy of spirit because of these afflictions, but was not observed to weep or mourn, or attend the funeral of any of his relations, until he lost Paralus, the last of his legitimate offspring. Crushed by this blow, he tried in vain to keep up his grand air of indifference, and when carrying a garland to lay upon the corpse he was overpowered by his feelings, so as to burst into a passion of tears and sobs, which he had never done before in his whole life.

Athens made trial of her other generals and public men to conduct her affairs, but none appeared to be of sufficient weight or reputation to have such a charge intrusted to him. The city longed for Pericles, and invited him again to lead its counsels and direct its armies; and he, although dejected in spirits and living in seclusion in his own house, was yet persuaded by Alcibiades and his other friends to resume the direction of affairs.

After this it appears that Pericles was attacked by the plague, not acutely or continuously, as in most cases, but in a slow wasting fashion, exhibiting many varieties of symptoms, and gradually undermining his strength. As he was now on his death-bed, the most distinguished of the citizens and his surviving friends collected round him and spoke admiringly of his nobleness and immense power, enumerating also the number of his exploits, and the trophies which he had set up for victories gained; for while in chief command he had won no less than nine victories for Athens.

Events soon made the loss of Pericles felt and regretted by the Athenians. Those who during his lifetime had complained that his power completely threw them into the shade, when after his death they had made trial of other orators and statesmen, were obliged to confess that with all his arrogance no man ever was really more moderate, and that his real mildness in dealing with men was as remarkable as his apparent pride and assumption. His power, which had been so grudged and envied, and called monarchy and despotism, now was proved to have been the saving of the State; such an amount of corrupt dealing and wickedness suddenly broke out in public affairs, which he before had crushed and forced to hide itself, and so prevented its becoming incurable through impunity and license.

GREAT PLAGUE AT ATHENS

B.C. 430

GEORGE GROTE

Almost at the beginning of the Peloponnesian war, when the prosperity of Athens had placed her at the height of her power and given her unquestioned supremacy among the Grecian states, her strength was greatly impaired by a visitation against which there was nothing in military prowess or patriotic pride and devotion that could prevail.

It is one of the tragic contrasts of history—the picture of Athens, in her full triumph and glory, smitten, at a moment when she needed to put forth her full strength, by a deadly foe against whose might mortal arms were vain. Her citizens were rejoicing in her social no less than her military preëminence, and they had already been trained in the hardships necessary to be endured in defence of an invaded country. Again they were prepared to undergo whatever service might be laid upon them in her behalf. They could foresee the arduous tasks and inevitable sufferings of a great war, but had no warning of an impending calamity far worse than those which even war, though always attended with horrors, usually entails. Pericles had lately delivered his great funeral oration at the public interment of soldiers who had fallen for Athens. "The bright colors and tone of cheerful confidence," says Grote, whose account of the plague follows, "which pervaded the discourse of Pericles, appear the more striking from being in immediate antecedence to the awful description of this distemper."

The death of Pericles himself, who directly or indirectly fell a victim to the prevailing pestilence, marked a grievous crisis for Athens in what was already become a measureless public woe. During the autumn of the year B.C. 427 the epidemic again broke out, after a considerable intermission, and for one year continued, "to the sad ruin both of the strength and the comfort of the city."

A T the close of one year after the attempted surprise of Platæa by the Thebans, the belligerent parties in Greece remained in an unaltered position as to relative strength. Nothing decisive had been accomplished on either side, either by the invasion of Attica or by the flying descents round the coast of Peloponnesus. In spite of mutual damage inflicted— doubtless in the greatest measure upon Attica — no progress was yet made toward the fulfilment of those objects which had induced the Peloponnesians to go to war. Especially the most pressing among all their wishes—the relief of Potidæa—was in no way advanced; for the Athenians had not found it necessary to relax the blockade of that city. The result of the first year's operations had thus been to disappoint the hopes of the Corinthians and the other ardent instigators of war, while it justified the anticipations both of Pericles and of Archidamus.

A second devastation of Attica was resolved upon for the commencement of spring; and measures were taken for carrying it all over that territory, since the settled policy of Athens, not to hazard a battle with the invaders, was now ascertained. About the end of March or beginning of April the entire Peloponnesian force—two-thirds from each confederate city as before—was assembled under the command of Archidamus and marched into Attica. This time they carried the work of systematic destruction not merely over the Thriasian plain and the plain immediately near to Athens, as before; but also to the more southerly portions of Attica, down even as far as the mines of Laurium. They traversed and ravaged both the eastern and the western coast, remaining not less than forty days in the country. They found the territory deserted as before, all the population having retired within the walls.

In regard to this second invasion, Pericles recommended the same defensive policy as he had applied to the first; and apparently the citizens had now come to acquiesce in it, if not willingly, at least with a full conviction of its necessity. But a new visitation had now occurred, diverting their attention from the invader, though enormously aggravating their sufferings. A few days after Archidamus entered Attica, a pestilence or epidemic sickness broke out unexpectedly at Athens.

It appears that this terrific disorder had been raging for some time throughout the regions round the Mediterranean; having begun, as was believed, in Ethiopia—thence passing into Egypt and Libya, and overrunning a considerable portion of Asia under the Persian government. About sixteen years before, there had been a similar calamity in Rome and in various parts of Italy. Recently it had been felt in Lemnos and some other islands of the Ægean, yet seemingly not with such intensity as to excite much notice generally in the Grecian world: at length it passed to Athens, and first showed itself in the Piræus. The progress of the disease was as rapid and destructive as its appearance had been sudden; while the extraordinary accumulation of people within the city and long walls, in consequence of the presence of the invaders in the country, was but too favorable to every form of contagion. Families crowded together in close cabins and places of temporary shelter—throughout a city constructed, like most of those in Greece, with little regard to the conditions of salubrity—and in a state of mental chagrin from the forced abandonment and sacrifice of their properties in the country, transmitted the disorder with fatal facility from one to the other. Beginning as it did about the middle of April, the increasing heat of summer further aided the disorder, the symptoms of which, alike violent and sudden, made themselves the more remarked because the year was particularly exempt from maladies of every other description.

Of this plague—or, more properly, eruptive typhoid fever, distinct from, yet analogous to, the smallpox—a description no less clear than impressive has been left by the historian Thucydides, himself not only a spectator but a sufferer. It is not one of the least of his merits, that his notice of the symptoms, given at so early a stage of medical science and observation, is such as to instruct the medical reader of the present age, and to enable the malady to be understood and identified. The observations with which that notice is ushered in deserve particular attention. "In respect to this distemper (he says), let every man, physician or not, say what he thinks respecting the source from whence it may probably have arisen, and respecting the causes which he deems sufficiently powerful to have produced so great a revolution. But I, having myself had the distemper, and having seen others suffering under it, will state *what it actually was*, and will indicate in addition such other matters as will furnish any man, who lays them to heart, with knowledge and the means of calculation beforehand, in case the same misfortune should ever occur again."

To record past facts, as a basis for rational prevision in regard to the future — the same sentiment which Thucydides

mentions in his preface, as having animated him to the composition of his history—was at that time a duty so little understood that we have reason to admire not less the manner in
which he performs it in practice than the distinctness with
which he conceives it in theory. We infer from his language
that speculation in his day was active respecting the causes of
this plague, according to the vague and fanciful physics, and
scanty stock of ascertained facts, which was all that could then
be consulted. By resisting the itch of theorizing from one of
those loose hypotheses which then appeared plausibly to explain everything, he probably renounced the point of view
from which most credit and interest would be derivable at the
time. But his simple and precise summary of observed facts
carries with it an imperishable value, and even affords grounds
for imagining that he was no stranger to the habits and training of his contemporary Hippocrates, and the other Asclepiads
of Cos.

It is hardly within the province of a historian of Greece to
repeat after Thucydides the painful enumeration of symptoms,
violent in the extreme and pervading every portion of the bodily system, which marked this fearful disorder. Beginning in
Piræus, it quickly passed into the city, and both the one and
the other was speedily filled with sickness and suffering, the
like of which had never before been known. The seizures
were sudden, and a large proportion of the sufferers perished
after deplorable agonies on the seventh or on the ninth day.
Others, whose strength of constitution carried them over this
period, found themselves the victims of exhausting and incurable diarrhœa afterward; with others again, after traversing
both these stages, the distemper fixed itself in some particular
member, the eyes, the genitals, the hands, or the feet, which
were rendered permanently useless, or in some cases ampu-
tated, even where the patient himself recovered.

There were also some whose recovery was attended with
a total loss of memory, so that they no more knew themselves
or recognized their friends. No treatment or remedy appearing, except in accidental cases, to produce any beneficial effect,
the physicians or surgeons whose aid was invoked became
completely at fault. While trying their accustomed means

without avail, they soon ended by catching the malady themselves and perishing.   The charms and incantations, to which the unhappy patient resorted, were not likely to be more efficacious.   While some asserted that the Peloponnesians had poisoned the cisterns of water, others referred the visitation to the wrath of the gods, and especially to Apollo, known by hearers of the *Iliad* as author of pestilence in the Greek host before Troy.   It was remembered that this Delphian god had promised the Lacedæmonians, in reply to their application immediately before the war, that he would assist them whether invoked or uninvoked; and the disorder now raging was ascribed to the intervention of their irresistible ally; while the elderly men further called to mind an oracular verse sung in the time of their youth: "The Dorian war will come, and pestilence along with it."   Under the distress which suggested, and was reciprocally aggravated by these gloomy ideas, prophets were consulted, and supplications with solemn procession were held at the temples, to appease the divine wrath.

When it was found that neither the priest nor the physician could retard the spread or mitigate the intensity of the disorder, the Athenians abandoned themselves to despair, and the space within the walls became a scene of desolating misery. Every man attacked with the malady at once lost his courage —a state of depression itself among the worst features of the case, which made him lie down and die, without any attempt to seek for preservatives.   And although at first friends and relatives lent their aid to tend the sick with the usual family sympathies, yet so terrible was the number of these attendants who perished, "like sheep," from such contact, that at length no man would thus expose himself; while the most generous spirits, who persisted longest in the discharge of their duty, were carried off in the greatest numbers.   The patient was thus left to die alone and unheeded.   Sometimes all the inmates of a house were swept away one after the other, no man being willing to go near it: desertion on the one hand, attendance on the other, both tended to aggravate the calamity.   There remained only those who, having had the disorder and recovered, were willing to tend the sufferers.

These men formed the single exception to the all-pervading misery of the time—for the disorder seldom attacked anyone twice, and when it did the second attack was never fatal. Elate with their own escape, they deemed themselves out of the reach of all disease, and were full of compassionate kindness for others whose sufferings were just beginning. It was from them too that the principal attention to the bodies of deceased victims proceeded: for such was the state of dismay and sorrow that even the nearest relatives neglected the sepulchral duties, sacred beyond all others in the eyes of a Greek. Nor is there any circumstance which conveys to us so vivid an idea of the prevalent agony and despair as when we read, in the words of an eyewitness, that the deaths took place among this close-packed crowd without the smallest decencies of attention—that the dead and the dying lay piled one upon another not merely in the public roads, but even in the temples, in spite of the understood defilement of the sacred building—that half-dead sufferers were seen lying round all the springs, from insupportable thirst—that the numerous corpses thus unburied and exposed were in such a condition that the dogs which meddled with them died in consequence, while no vultures or other birds of the like habits ever came near.

Those bodies which escaped entire neglect were burnt or buried without the customary mourning, and with unseemly carelessness. In some cases the bearers of a body, passing by a funeral pile on which another body was burning, would put their own there to be burnt also; or perhaps, if the pile was prepared ready for a body not yet arrived, would deposit their own upon it, set fire to the pile, and then depart. Such indecent confusion would have been intolerable to the feelings of the Athenians in any ordinary times.

To all these scenes of physical suffering, death, and reckless despair was superadded another evil, which affected those who were fortunate enough to escape the rest. The bonds both of law and morality became relaxed, amid such total uncertainty of every man both for his own life and that of others. Men cared not to abstain from wrong, under circumstances in which punishment was not likely to overtake them, nor to put a check upon their passions, and endure privations, in obedience even to their strongest conviction, when the chance was so small of their living to reap reward or enjoy any future esteem. An interval, short and sweet, before their doom was realized—before they became plunged in the widespread misery which they witnessed around, and which affected indiscriminately the virtuous and the profligate—was all that they looked to enjoy; embracing with avidity the immediate pleasures of sense, as well as such positive gains, however ill-gotten, as could be made the means of procuring them, and throwing aside all thought both of honor and of long-sighted advantage. Life and property being alike ephemeral, there was no hope left but to snatch a moment of enjoyment, before the outstretched hand of destiny should fall upon its victims.

The picture of society under the pressure of a murderous epidemic, with its train of physical torments, wretchedness, and demoralization, has been drawn by more than one eminent author, but by none with more impressive fidelity and conciseness than by Thucydides, who had no predecessor, nor anything but the reality, to copy from. We may remark that amid all the melancholy accompaniments of the time there are no human sacrifices, such as those offered up at Carthage during pestilence to appease the anger of the gods—there are no cruel persecutions against imaginary authors of the disease, such as those against the Untori (anointers of doors) in the plague of Milan in 1630.

Three years altogether did this calamity desolate Athens: continuously, during the entire second and third years of the war—after which followed a period of marked abatement for a year and a half; but it then revived again, and lasted for another year, with the same fury as at first. The public loss, over and above the private misery, which this unexpected enemy inflicted upon Athens, was incalculable. Out of twelve hundred horsemen, all among the rich men of the state, three hundred died of the epidemic; besides forty-four hundred *hoplites* out of the roll formally kept, and a number of the poorer population so great as to defy computation. No efforts of the Peloponnesians could have done so much to ruin Athens, or to bring the war to a termination such as they desired: and the distemper told the more in their favor, as it never spread at all into Peloponnesus, though it passed from Athens to some of the more populous islands. The Lacedæmonian army was withdrawn from Attica somewhat earlier than it would otherwise have been, for fear of taking the contagion.

But it was while the Lacedæmonians were yet in Attica, and during the first freshness of the terrible malady, that Pericles equipped and conducted from Piræus an armament of one hundred triremes and four thousand hoplites to attack the coasts of Peloponnesus; three hundred horsemen were also carried in some horse-transports, prepared for the occasion out of old triremes. To diminish the crowd accumulated in the city was doubtless of beneficial tendency, and perhaps those who went aboard might consider it as a chance of escape to quit an infected home. But unhappily they carried the infection along with them, which desolated the fleet not less than the city, and crippled all its efforts. Reënforced by fifty ships of war from Chios and Lesbos, the Athenians first landed near Epidaurus in Peloponnesus, ravaging the territory and making an unavailing attempt upon the city; next they made like incursions on the most southerly portions of the Argolic peninsula—Trœzen, Halieis, and Hermione—and lastly attacked and captured Prasiæ, on the eastern coast of Laconia. On returning to Athens, the same armament was immediately conducted under Agnon and Cleopompus, to press the siege of Potidæa, the blockade of which still continued without any visible progress. On arriving there an attack was made on the walls by battering engines and by the other aggressive methods then practised; but nothing whatever was achieved. In fact, the armament became incompetent for all serious effort, from the aggravated character which the distemper here assumed, communicated by the soldiers fresh from Athens even to those who had before been free from it at Potidæa. So frightful was the mortality that out of the four thousand hoplites under Agnon no fewer than one thousand and fifty died in the short space of forty days. The armament was brought back in this distressed condition to Athens, while the reduction of Potidæa was left as before, to the slow course of blockade.

On returning from the expedition against Peloponnesus, Pericles found his countrymen almost distracted with their manifold sufferings. Over and above the raging epidemic they had just gone over Attica and ascertained the devastations committed by the invaders throughout all the territory— except the Marathonian Tetrapolis and Deceleia, districts spared, as we are told, through indulgence founded on an ancient legendary sympathy—during their long stay of forty days. The rich had found their comfortable mansions and farms, the poor their modest cottages, in the various *demes*, torn down and ruined. Death, sickness, loss of property, and despair of the future now rendered the Athenians angry and intractable to the last degree. They vented their feelings against Pericles as the cause not merely of the war, but also of all that they were now enduring. Either with or without his consent, they sent envoys to Sparta to open negotiations for peace, but the Spartans turned a deaf ear to the proposition. This new disappointment rendered them still more furious against Pericles, whose long-standing political enemies now doubtless found strong sympathy in their denunciations of his character and policy. That unshaken and majestic firmness, which ranked first among his many eminent qualities, was never more imperiously required and never more effectively manifested.

In his capacity of *strategus*, or general, Pericles convoked a formal assembly of the people, for the purpose of vindicating himself publicly against the prevailing sentiment, and recommending perseverance in his line of policy. The speeches made by his opponents, assuredly very bitter, are not given by Thucydides; but that of Pericles himself is set down at considerable length, and a memorable discourse it is. It strikingly brings into relief both the character of the man and the impress of actual circumstances—an impregnable mind conscious not only of right purposes, but of just and reasonable anticipations, and bearing up with manliness, or even defiance, against the natural difficulty of the case, heightened by an extreme of incalculable misfortune. He had foreseen, while advising the war originally, the probable impatience of his countrymen under its first hardships, but he could not foresee

the epidemic by which that impatience had been exasperated
into madness: and he now addressed them not merely with
unabated adherence to his own deliberate convictions, but also
in a tone of reproachful remonstrance against their unmerited
change of sentiment· toward him—seeking at the same time
to combat that uncontrolled despair which for the moment
overlaid both their pride and their patriotism. Far from hum-
bling himself before the present sentiment, it is at this time
that he sets forth his titles to their esteem in the most direct
and unqualified manner, and claims the continuance of that
which they had so long accorded, as something belonging to
him by acquired right.

His main object, through this discourse, is to fill the minds
of his audience with patriotic sympathy for the weal of the
entire city, so as to counterbalance the absorbing sense of private woe. If the collective city flourishes, he argues, private
misfortunes may at least be borne; but no amount of private
prosperity will avail if the collective city falls—a proposition
literally true in ancient times and under the circumstances of
ancient warfare, though less true at present. "Distracted
by domestic calamity, ye are now angry both with me who
advised you to go to war, and with yourselves who followed
the advice. Ye listened to me, considering me superior to
others in judgment, in speech, in patriotism, and in incorruptible probity—nor ought I now to be treated as culpable for
giving such advice, when in point of fact the war was unavoidable and there would have been still greater danger in shrink-
ing from it. I am the same man, still unchanged—but ye in
your misfortunes cannot stand to the convictions which ye
adopted when yet unhurt. Extreme and unforeseen, indeed,
are the sorrows which have fallen upon you: yet inhabiting as
ye do a great city, and brought up in dispositions suitable to
it, ye must also resolve to bear up against the utmost pressure
of adversity, and never to surrender your dignity. I have
often explained to you that ye have no reason to doubt of
eventual success in the war, but I will now remind you, more
emphatically than before, and even with a degree of ostentation suitable as a stimulus to your present unnatural depression, that your naval force makes you masters not only of your

allies, but of the entire sea—one-half of the visible field for action and employment. Compared with so vast a power as this, the temporary use of your houses and territory is a mere trifle, an ornamental accessory not worth considering: and this too, if ye preserve your freedom, ye will quickly recover. It was your fathers who first gained this empire, without any of the advantages which ye now enjoy; ye must not disgrace yourselves by losing what they acquired.

"Delighting as ye all do in the honor and empire enjoyed by the city, ye must not shrink from the toils whereby alone that honor is sustained: moreover, ye now fight, not merely for freedom instead of slavery, but for empire against loss of empire, with all the perils arising out of imperial unpopularity. It is not safe for you now to abdicate, even if ye chose to do so; for ye hold your empire like a despotism—unjust perhaps in the original acquisition, but ruinous to part with when once acquired. Be not angry with me, whose advice ye followed in going to war, because the enemy have done such damage as might be expected from them: still less on account of this unforeseen distemper: I know that this makes me an object of your special present hatred, though very unjustly, unless ye will consent to give me credit also for any unexpected good-luck which may occur. Our city derives its particular glory from unshaken bearing up against misfortune: her power, her name, her empire of Greeks over Greeks, are such as have never before been seen; and if we choose to be great, we must take the consequence of that temporary envy and hatred which is the necessary price of permanent renown. Behave ye now in a manner worthy of that glory: display that courage which is essential to protect you against disgrace at present, as well as to guarantee your honor for the future. Send no further embassy to Sparta, and bear your misfortunes without showing symptoms of distress."

The irresistible reason, as well as the proud and resolute bearing of this discourse, set forth with an eloquence which it was not possible for Thucydides to reproduce—together with the age and character of Pericles—carried the assent of the assembled people; who when in the Pnyx, and engaged according to habit on public matters, would for a moment forget their private sufferings in considerations of the safety and grandeur of Athens. Possibly, indeed, those sufferings, though still continuing, might become somewhat alleviated when the invaders quitted Attica, and when it was no longer indispensable for all the population to confine itself within the walls. Accordingly, the assembly resolved that no further propositions should be made for peace, and that the war should be prosecuted with vigor.

But though the public resolution thus adopted showed the ancient habit of deference to the authority of Pericles, the sentiments of individuals taken separately were still those of anger against him as the author of that system which had brought them into so much distress. His political opponents— Cleon, Simmias, or Lacratidas, perhaps all three in conjunction—took care to provide an opportunity for this prevalent irritation to manifest itself in act, by bringing an accusation against him before the *dicastery*. The accusation is said to have been preferred on the ground of pecuniary malversation, and ended by his being sentenced to pay a considerable fine, the amount of which is differently reported—fifteen, fifty, or eighty talents, by different authors. The accusing party thus appeared to have carried their point, and to have disgraced, as well as excluded from reëlection, the veteran statesman. The event, however, disappointed their expectations. The imposition of the fine not only satiated all the irritation of the people against him, but even occasioned a serious reaction in his favor, and brought back as strongly as ever the ancient sentiment of esteem and admiration. It was quickly found that those who had succeeded Pericles as generals neither possessed nor deserved in an equal degree the public confidence. He was accordingly soon reëlected, with as much power and influence as he had ever in his life enjoyed.

But that life, long, honorable, and useful, had already been prolonged considerably beyond the sixtieth year, and there were but too many circumstances, besides the recent fine, which tended to hasten as well as to embitter its close. At the very moment when Pericles was preaching to his countrymen, in a tone almost reproachful, the necessity of manful and unabated devotion to the common country in the midst of

private suffering, he was himself among the greatest of sufferers, and most hardly pressed to set the example of observing
his own precepts. The epidemic carried off not merely his
two sons—the only two legitimate, Xanthippus and Paralus—
but also his sister, several other relatives, and his best and
most useful political friends. Amid this train of domestic
calamities, and in the funeral obsequies of so many of his
dearest friends, he remained master of his grief, and maintained his habitual self-command, until the last misfortune—
the death of his favorite son Paralus, which left his house
without any legitimate representative to maintain the family
and the hereditary sacred rites. On this final blow, though
he strove to command himself as before, yet at the obsequies
of the young man, when it became his duty to place a wreath
on the dead body, his grief became uncontrollable, and he
burst out, for the first time in his life, into profuse tears and
sobbing.

In the midst of these several personal trials he received
the intimation, through Alcibiades and some other friends, of
the restored confidence of the people toward him, and of his
reëlection to the office of strategus. But it was not without
difficulty that he was persuaded to present himself again at
the public assembly and resume the direction of affairs. The
regret of the people was formally expressed to him for the
recent sentence—perhaps, indeed, the fine may have been
repaid to him, or some evasion of it permitted, saving the
forms of law—in the present temper of the city; which was
further displayed toward him by the grant of a remarkable
exemption from a law of his own original proposition.

He had himself, some years before, been the author of that
law whereby the citizenship of Athens was restricted to persons born both of Athenian fathers and Athenian mothers,
under which restriction several thousand persons, illegitimate
on the mother's side, are said to have been deprived of the
citizenship, on occasion of a public distribution of corn. Invidious as it appeared to grant, to Pericles singly, an exemption from a law which had been strictly enforced against so
many others, the people were now moved not less by compassion than by anxiety to redress their own previous severity.

Without a legitimate heir, the house of Pericles, one branch of the great Alcmæonid gens by his mother's side, would be left deserted, and the continuity of the family sacred rites would be broken—a misfortune painfully felt by every Athenian family, as calculated to wrong all the deceased members, and provoke their posthumous displeasure toward the city. Accordingly, permission was granted to Pericles to legitimize, and to inscribe in his own gens and phratry, his natural son by Aspasia, who bore his own name.

It was thus that Pericles was reinstated in his post of strategus as well as in his ascendency over the public counsels—seemingly about August or September, B.C. 430. He lived about one year longer, and seems to have maintained his influence as long as his health permitted. Yet we hear nothing of him after this moment, and he fell a victim, not to the violent symptoms of the epidemic, but to a slow and wearing fever, which undermined his strength as well as his capacity. To a friend who came to ask after him when in this disease, Pericles replied by showing a charm or amulet which his female relations had hung about his neck—a proof how low he was reduced, and how completely he had become a passive subject in the hands of others.

And according to another anecdote which we read—yet more interesting and equally illustrative of his character—it was during his last moments, when he was lying apparently unconscious and insensible, that the friends around his bed were passing in review the acts of his life, and the nine trophies which he had erected at different times for so many victories. He heard what they said, though they fancied that he was past hearing, and interrupted them by remarking: "What you praise in my life belongs partly to good fortune —and is, at best, common to me with many other generals. But the peculiarity of which I am most proud, you have not noticed—no Athenian has ever put on mourning through any action of mine."

DEFEAT OF THE ATHENIANS AT SYRACUSE

B.C. 413

SIR EDWARD SHEPHERD CREASY

That great writer of the history of the Romans, Thomas Arnold, says of the defeat of the Athenian fleet at Syracuse: "The Romans knew not, and could not know, how deeply the greatness of their own posterity, and the fate of the whole western world, were involved in the destruction of the fleet of Athens in the harbor of Syracuse. Had that great expedition proved victorious, the energies of Greece during the next eventful century would have found their field in the West no less than in the East; Greece, and not Rome, might have conquered Carthage; Greek instead of Latin might have been at this day the principal element of the language of Spain, of France, and of Italy; and the laws of Athens, rather than of Rome, might be the foundation of the law of the civilized world."

The foregoing, the author's own selection, really sums up all that need be said as to the importance of the great event so finely treated by Creasy.

FEW cities have undergone more memorable sieges during ancient and mediæval times than has the city of Syracuse. Athenian, Carthaginian, Roman, Vandal, Byzantine, Saracen, and Norman have in turns beleaguered her walls; and the resistance which she successfully opposed to some of her early assailants was of the deepest importance, not only to the fortunes of the generations then in being, but to all the subsequent current of human events. To adopt the eloquent expressions of Arnold respecting the check which she gave to the Carthaginian arms, "Syracuse was a breakwater which God's providence raised up to protect the yet immature strength of Rome." And her triumphant repulse of the great Athenian expedition against her was of even more widespread and enduring importance. It forms a decisive epoch in the strife for universal empire, in which all the great states of antiquity successively engaged and failed.

The present city of Syracuse is a place of little or no military strength, as the fire of artillery from the neighboring heights would almost completely command it. But in ancient warfare its position, and the care bestowed on its walls, rendered it formidably strong against the means of offence which were then employed by besieging armies.

The ancient city, in its most prosperous times, was chiefly built on the knob of land which projects into the sea on the eastern coast of Sicily, between two bays; one of which, to the north, was called the Bay of Thapsus, while the southern one formed the great harbor of the city of Syracuse itself. A small island, or peninsula (for such it soon was rendered), lies at the southeastern extremity of this knob of land, stretching almost entirely across the mouth of the great harbor, and rendering it nearly land-locked. This island comprised the original settlement of the first Greek colonists from Corinth, who founded Syracuse two thousand five hundred years ago; and the modern city has shrunk again into these primary limits. But, in the fifth century before our era, the growing wealth and population of the Syracusans had led them to occupy and include within their city walls portion after portion of the mainland lying next to the little isle, so that at the time of the Athenian expedition the seaward part of the land between the two bays already spoken of was built over, and fortified from bay to bay, and constituted the larger part of Syracuse.

The landward wall, therefore, of this district of the city traversed this knob of land, which continues to slope upward from the sea, and which, to the west of the old fortifications, that is, toward the interior of Sicily, rises rapidly for a mile or two, but diminishes in width, and finally terminates in a long narrow ridge, between which and Mount Hybla a succession of chasms and uneven low ground extends. On each flank of this ridge the descent is steep and precipitous from its summits to the strips of level land that lie immediately below it, both to the southwest and northwest.

The usual mode of assailing fortified towns in the time of the Peloponnesian war was to build a double wall round them sufficiently strong to check any sally of the garrison from within or any attack of a relieving force from without. The interval within the two walls of the circumvallation was roofed over, and formed barracks, in which the besiegers posted themselves, and awaited the effects of want or treachery among the besieged in producing a surrender; and in every Greek city of those days, as in every Italian republic of the Middle Ages, the rage of domestic sedition between aristocrats and democrats ran high. Rancorous refugees swarmed in the camp of every invading enemy; and every blockaded city was sure to contain within its walls a body of intriguing malcontents, who were eager to purchase a party triumph at the expense of a national disaster. Famine and faction were the allies on whom besiegers relied. The generals of that time trusted to the operation of these sure confederates as soon as they could establish a complete blockade. They rarely ventured on the attempt to storm any fortified post, for the military engines of antiquity were feeble in breaching masonry before the improvements which the first Dionysius effected in the mechanics of destruction; and the lives of spearmen the boldest and most high-trained would, of course, have been idly spent in charges against unshattered walls.

A city built close to the sea, like Syracuse, was impregnable save by the combined operations of a superior hostile fleet and a superior hostile army; and Syracuse, from her size, her population, and her military and naval resources, not unnaturally thought herself secure from finding in another Greek city a foe capable of sending a sufficient armament to menace her with capture and subjection. But in the spring of B.C. 414 the Athenian navy was mistress of her harbor and the adjacent seas; an Athenian army had defeated her troops, and cooped them within the town; and from bay to bay a blockading wall was being rapidly carried across the strips of level ground and the high ridge outside the city (then termed Epipolæ), which, if completed, would have cut the Syracusans off from all succor from the interior of Sicily, and have left them at the mercy of the Athenian generals. The besiegers' works were, indeed, unfinished; but every day the unfortified interval in their lines grew narrower, and with it diminished all apparent hope of safety for the beleaguered town.

Athens was now staking the flower of her forces, and the accumulated fruits of seventy years of glory, on one bold throw for the dominion of the western world. As Napoleon from Mount Cœur de Lion pointed to St. Jean d'Acre, and told his staff that the capture of that town would decide his destiny and would change the face of the world, so the Athenian officers, from the heights of Epipolæ, must have looked on Syracuse, and felt that with its fall all the known powers of the earth would fall beneath them. They must have felt also that Athens, if repulsed there, must pause forever from her career of conquest, and sink from an imperial republic into a ruined and subservient community.

At Marathon, the first in date of the great battles of the world, we beheld Athens struggling for self-preservation against the invading armies of the East. At Syracuse she appears as the ambitious and oppressive invader of others. In her, as in other republics of old and of modern times, the same energy that had inspired the most heroic efforts in defence of the national independence soon learned to employ itself in daring and unscrupulous schemes of self-aggrandizement at the expense of neighboring nations. In the interval between the Persian and the Peloponnesian wars she had rapidly grown into a conquering and dominant state, the chief of a thousand tributary cities, and the mistress of the largest and best-manned navy that the Mediterranean had yet beheld. The occupations of her territory by Xerxes and Mardonius, in the second Persian war, had forced her whole population to become marines; and the glorious results of that struggle confirmed them in their zeal for their country's service at sea.

The voluntary suffrage of the Greek cities of the coasts and islands of the Ægean first placed Athens at the head of the confederation formed for the further prosecution of the war against Persia. But this titular ascendency was soon converted by her into practical and arbitrary dominion. She protected them from piracy and the Persian power, which soon fell into decrepitude and decay, but she exacted in return implicit obedience to herself. She claimed and enforced a prerogative of taxing them at her discretion, and proudly refused to be accountable for her mode of expending their supplies.

Remonstrance against her assessments was treated as factious disloyalty, and refusal to pay was promptly punished as revolt. Permitting and encouraging her subject allies to furnish all their contingents in money, instead of part consisting of ships and men, the sovereign republic gained the double object of training her own citizens by constant and well-paid service in her fleets, and of seeing her confederates lose their skill and discipline by inaction, and become more and more passive and powerless under her yoke. Their towns were generally dismantled, while the imperial city herself was fortified with the greatest care and sumptuousness; the accumulated revenues from her tributaries serving to strengthen and adorn to the utmost her havens, her docks, her arsenals, her theatres, and her shrines, and to array her in that plenitude of architectural magnificence the ruins of which still attest the intellectual grandeur of the age and people which produced a Pericles to plan and a Phidias to execute.

All republics that acquire supremacy over other nations rule them selfishly and oppressively. There is no exception to this in either ancient or modern times. Carthage, Rome, Venice, Genoa, Florence, Pisa, Holland, and republican France, all tyrannized over every province and subject state where they gained authority. But none of them openly avowed their system of doing so upon principle with the candor which the Athenian republicans displayed when any remonstrance was made against the severe exactions which they imposed upon their vassal allies. They avowed that their empire was a tyranny, and frankly stated that they solely trusted to force and terror to uphold it. They appealed to what they called "the eternal law of nature, that the weak should be coerced by the strong." Sometimes they stated, and not without some truth, that the unjust hatred of Sparta against themselves forced them to be unjust to others in self-defence. To be safe, they must be powerful; and to be powerful, they must plunder and coerce their neighbors. They never dreamed of communicating any franchise, or share in office, to their dependants, but jealously monopolized every post of command and all political and judicial power; exposing themselves to every risk with unflinching gallantry; embarking readily in

every ambitious scheme; and never suffering difficulty or
disaster to shake their tenacity of purpose: in the hope of
acquiring unbounded empire for their country, and the means
of maintaining each of the thirty thousand citizens who made
up the sovereign republic, in exclusive devotion to military occupations, and to those brilliant sciences and arts in which
Athens already had reached the meridian of intellectual splen
dor.

Her great political dramatist speaks of the Athenian empire as comprehending a thousand states. The language of
the stage must not be taken too literally; but the number of
the dependencies of Athens, at the time when the Peloponnesian confederacy attacked her, was undoubtedly very great.
With a few trifling exceptions, all the islands of the Ægean,
and all the Greek cities which in that age fringed the coasts
of Asia Minor, the Hellespont, and Thrace, paid tribute to
Athens, and implicitly obeyed her orders. The Ægean Sea
was an Attic lake. Westward of Greece, her influence, though
strong, was not equally predominant. She had colonies and
allies among the wealthy and populous Greek settlements in
Sicily and South Italy, but she had no organized system of confederates in those regions; and her galleys brought her no
tribute from the Western seas. The extension of her empire
over Sicily was the favorite project of her ambitious orators
and generals. While her great statesman, Pericles, lived, his
commanding genius kept his countrymen under control, and
forbade them to risk the fortunes of Athens in distant enterprises, while they had unsubdued and powerful enemies at their
own doors. He taught Athens this maxim; but he also taught
her to know and to use her own strength; and when Pericles
had departed, the bold spirit which he had fostered overleaped
the salutary limits which he had prescribed.

When her bitter enemies, the Corinthians, succeeded, B.C.
431, in inducing Sparta to attack her, and a confederacy was
formed of five-sixths of the continental Greeks, all animated
by anxious jealousy and bitter hatred of Athens; when armies
far superior in numbers and equipment to those which had
marched against the Persians were poured into the Athenian
territory, and laid it waste to the city walls, the general opin-

ion was that Athens would be reduced, in two or three years at the furthest, to submit to the requisitions of her invaders. But her strong fortifications, by which she was girt and linked to her principal haven, gave her, in those ages, almost all the advantages of an insular position. Pericles had made her trust to her empire of the seas. Every Athenian in those days was a practised seaman. A state, indeed, whose members, of an age fit for service, at no time exceeded thirty thousand, could only have acquired such a naval dominion as Athens once held by devoting and zealously training all its sons to service in its fleets. In order to man the numerous galleys which she sent out, she necessarily employed large numbers of hired mariners and slaves at the oar; but the staple of her crews was Athenian, and all posts of command were held by native citizens. It was by reminding them of this, of their long practice in seamanship, and the certain superiority which their discipline gave them over the enemy's marine, that their great minister mainly encouraged them to resist the combined power of Lacedæmon and her allies. He taught them that Athens might thus reap the fruit of her zealous devotion to maritime affairs ever since the invasion of the Medes; "she had not, indeed, perfected herself; but the reward of her superior training was the rule of the sea—a mighty dominion, for it gave her the rule of much fair land beyond its waves, safe from the idle ravages with which the Lacedæmonians might harass Attica, but never could subdue Athens."

Athens accepted the war with which her enemies threatened her rather than descend from her pride of place; and though the awful visitation of the plague came upon her, and swept away more of her citizens than the Dorian spear laid low, she held her own gallantly against her enemies. If the Peloponnesian armies in irresistible strength wasted every spring her corn-lands, her vineyards, and her olive groves with fire and sword, she retaliated on their coasts with her fleets; which, if resisted, were only resisted to display the preëminent skill and bravery of her seamen. Some of her subject allies revolted, but the revolts were in general sternly and promptly quelled. The genius of one enemy had indeed inflicted blows on her power in Thrace which she was unable to remedy; but he fell in battle in the tenth year of the war, and with the loss of Brasidas the Lacedæmonians seemed to have lost all energy and judgment. Both sides at length grew weary of the war, and in 421 a truce for fifty years was concluded, which, though ill kept, and though many of the confederates of Sparta refused to recognize it, and hostilities still continued in many parts of Greece, protected the Athenian territory from the ravages of enemies, and enabled Athens to accumulate large sums out of the proceeds of her annual revenues. So also, as a few years passed by, the havoc which the pestilence and the sword had made in her population was repaired; and in 415 Athens was full of bold and restless spirits, who longed for some field of distant enterprise wherein they might signalize themselves and aggrandize the state, and who looked on the alarm of Spartan hostility as a mere old-woman's tale. When Sparta had wasted their territory she had done her worst; and the fact of its always being in her power to do so seemed a strong reason for seeking to increase the transmarine dominion of Athens.

The West was now the quarter toward which the thoughts of every aspiring Athenian were directed. From the very beginning of the war Athens had kept up an interest in Sicily, and her squadron had, from time to time, appeared on its coasts and taken part in the dissensions in which the Sicilian Greeks were universally engaged one against the other. There were plausible grounds for a direct quarrel, and an open attack by the Athenians upon Syracuse.

With the capture of Syracuse, all Sicily, it was hoped, would be secured. Carthage and Italy were next to be attacked. With large levies of Iberian mercenaries she then meant to overwhelm her Peloponnesian enemies. The Persian monarchy lay in hopeless imbecility, inviting Greek invasion; nor did the known world contain the power that seemed capable of checking the growing might of Athens, if Syracuse once should be hers.

The national historian of Rome has left us an episode of his great work, a disquisition on the probable effects that would have followed if Alexander the Great had invaded Italy. Posterity has generally regarded that disquisition as proving

Livy's patriotism more strongly than his impartiality or acute-ness. Yet, right or wrong, the speculations of the Roman writer were directed to the consideration of a very remote possibility. To whatever age Alexander's life might have been prolonged, the East would have furnished full occupation for his martial ambition, as well as for those schemes of commercial grandeur and imperial amalgamation of nations in which the truly great qualities of his mind loved to display themselves. With his death the dismemberment of his empire among his generals was certain, even as the dismemberment of Napoleon's empire among his marshals would certainly have ensued if he had been cut off in the zenith of his power. Rome, also, was far weaker when the Athenians were in Sicily than she was a century afterward in Alexander's time. There can be little doubt but that Rome would have been blotted out from the independent powers of the West, had she been attacked at the end of the fifth century B.C. by an Athenian army, largely aided by Spanish mercenaries, and flushed with triumphs over Sicily and Africa, instead of the collision between her and Greece having been deferred until the latter had sunk into decrepitude, and the Roman Mars had grown into full vigor.

The armament which the Athenians equipped against Syracuse was in every way worthy of the state which formed such projects of universal empire, and it has been truly termed "the noblest that ever yet had been sent forth by a free and civilized commonwealth." The fleet consisted of one hundred and thirty-four war-galleys, with a multitude of storeships. A powerful force of the best heavy-armed infantry that Athens and her allies could furnish was sent on board it, together with a smaller number of slingers and bowmen. The quality of the forces was even more remarkable than the number. The zeal of individuals vied with that of the republic in giving every galley the best possible crew and every troop the most perfect accoutrements. And with private as well as public wealth eagerly lavished on all that could give splendor as well as efficiency to the expedition, the fated fleet began its voyage for the Sicilian shores in the summer of 415.

The Syracusans themselves, at the time of the Peloponnesian war, were a bold and turbulent democracy, tyrannizing over the weaker Greek cities in Sicily, and trying to gain in that island the same arbitrary supremacy which Athens maintained along the eastern coast of the Mediterranean. In numbers and in spirit they were fully equal to the Athenians, but far inferior to them in military and naval discipline. When the probability of an Athenian invasion was first publicly discussed at Syracuse, and efforts were made by some of the wiser citizens to improve the state of the national defences and prepare for the impending danger, the rumors of coming war and the proposal for preparation were received by the mass of the Syracusans with scornful incredulity. The speech of one of their popular orators is preserved to us in Thucydides.

The Syracusan orator told his countrymen to dismiss with scorn the visionary terrors which a set of designing men among themselves strove to excite, in order to get power and influence thrown into their own hands. He told them that Athens knew her own interest too well to think of wantonly provoking their hostility: "Even if the enemies were to come," said he, "so distant from their resources, and opposed to such a power as ours, their destruction would be easy and inevitable. Their ships will have enough to do to get to our island at all, and to carry such stores of all sorts as will be needed. They cannot therefore carry, besides, an army large enough to cope with such a population as ours. They will have no fortified place from which to commence their operations, but must rest them on no better base than a set of wretched tents, and such means as the necessities of the moment will allow them. But, in truth, I do not believe that they would even be able to effect a disembarkation. Let us, therefore, set at naught these reports as altogether of home manufacture; and be sure that if any enemy does come, the state will know how to defend itself in a manner worthy of the national honor."

Such assertions pleased the Syracusan assembly; but the invaders of Syracuse came, made good their landing in Sicily; and if they had promptly attacked the city itself, instead of wasting nearly a year in desultory operations in other parts of Sicily, the Syracusans must have paid the penalty of their self-sufficient carelessness in submission to the Athenian yoke. But, of the three generals who led the Athenian expedition, two only were men of ability, and one was most weak and incompetent. Fortunately for Syracuse, Alcibiades, the most skilful of the three, was soon deposed from his command by a factious and fanatic vote of his fellow-countrymen, and the other competent one, Lamachus, fell early in a skirmish; while, more fortunately still for her, the feeble and vacillating Nicias remained unrecalled and unhurt, to assume the undivided leadership of the Athenian army and fleet, and to mar, by alternate over-caution and over-carelessness, every chance of success which the early part of the operations offered. Still, even under him, the Athenians nearly won the town. They defeated the raw levies of the Syracusans, cooped them within the walls, and, as before mentioned, almost effected a continuous fortification from bay to bay over Epipolæ, the completion of which would certainly have been followed by a capitulation.

Alcibiades—the most complete example of genius without principle that history produces; the Bolingbroke of antiquity, but with high military talents superadded to diplomatic and oratorical powers—on being summoned home from his command in Sicily to take his trial before the Athenian tribunal, had escaped to Sparta, and had exerted himself there with all the selfish rancor of a renegade to renew the war with Athens and to send instant assistance to Syracuse.

When we read his words in the pages of Thucydides—who was himself an exile from Athens at this period, and may probably have been at Sparta, and heard Alcibiades speak—we are at a loss whether most to admire or abhor his subtle counsels. After an artful exordium, in which he tried to disarm the suspicions which he felt must be entertained of him, and to point out to the Spartans how completely his interests and theirs were identified, through hatred of the Athenian democracy, he thus proceeded:

"Hear me, at any rate, on the matters which require your grave attention, and which I, from the personal knowledge that I have of them, can and ought to bring before you. We Athenians sailed to Sicily with the design of subduing, first the Greek cities there, and next those in Italy. Then we intended to make an attempt on the dominions of Carthage, and on Carthage itself.[1] If all these projects succeeded—nor did we limit ourselves to them in these quarters—we intended to increase our fleet with the inexhaustible supplies of ship timber which Italy affords, to put in requisition the whole military force of the conquered Greek states, and also to hire large armies of the barbarians, of the Iberians,[2] and others in those regions, who are allowed to make the best possible soldiers. *Then*, when we had done all this, we intended to assail Peloponnesus with our collected force. Our fleets would blockade you by sea and desolate your coasts, our armies would be landed at different points and assail your cities. Some of these we expected to storm,[3] and others we meant to take by surrounding them with fortified lines. We thought that it would thus be an easy matter thoroughly to war you down; and then we should become the masters of the whole Greek race. As for expense, we reckoned that each conquered state would give us supplies of money and provisions sufficient to pay for its own conquest, and furnish the means for the conquest of its neighbors.

"Such are the designs of the present Athenian expedition to Sicily, and you have heard them from the lips of the man who, of all men living, is most accurately acquainted with them. The other Athenian generals, who remain with the expedition, will endeavor to carry out these plans. And be sure that without your speedy interference they will all be accomplished. The Sicilian Greeks are deficient in military

---

[1] Arnold, in his notes on this passage, well reminds the reader that Agathocles, with a Greek force far inferior to that of the Athenians at this period, did, some years afterward, very nearly conquer Carthage.

[2] It will be remembered that Spanish infantry were the staple of the Carthaginian armies. Doubtless Alcibiades and other leading Athenians had made themselves acquainted with the Carthaginian system of carrying on war, and meant to adopt it. With the marvellous powers which Alcibiades possessed of ingratiating himself with men of every class and every nation, and his high military genius, he would have been as formidable a chief of an army of *condottieri* as Hannibal afterward was.

[3] Alcibiades here alluded to Sparta itself, which was unfortified. His Spartan hearers must have glanced round them at these words with mixed alarm and indignation.

training; but still, if they could at once be brought to combine in an organized resistance to Athens, they might even now be saved. But as for the Syracusans resisting Athens by themselves, they have already, with the whole strength of their population, fought a battle and been beaten; they cannot face the Athenians at sea; and it is quite impossible for them to hold out against the force of their invaders. And if this city falls into the hands of the Athenians, all Sicily is theirs, and presently Italy also; and the danger, which I warned you of from that quarter, will soon fall upon yourselves. You must, therefore, in Sicily, fight for the safety of Peloponnesus. Send some galleys thither instantly. Put men on board who can work their own way over, and who, as soon as they land, can do duty as regular troops. But, above all, let one of yourselves, let a man of Sparta, go over to take the chief command, to bring into order and effective discipline the forces that are in Syracuse, and urge those who at present hang back to come forward and aid the Syracusans. The presence of a Spartan general at this crisis will do more to save the city than a whole army."

The renegade then proceeded to urge on them the necessity of encouraging their friends in Sicily, by showing that they themselves were in earnest in hostility to Athens. He exhorted them not only to march their armies into Attica again, but to take up a permanent fortified position in the country; and he gave them in detail information of all that the Athenians most dreaded, and how his country might receive the most distressing and enduring injury at their hands.

The Spartans resolved to act on his advice, and appointed Gylippus to the Sicilian command. Gylippus was a man who, to the national bravery and military skill of a Spartan united political sagacity that was worthy of his great fellow-countryman Brasidas; but his merits were debased by mean and sordid vices; and his is one of the cases in which history has been austerely just, and where little or no fame has been accorded to the successful but venal soldier. But for the purpose for which he was required in Sicily, an abler man could not have been found in Lacedæmon. His country gave him neither men nor money, but she gave him her authority; and the influence of her name and of his own talents was speedily seen in the zeal with which the Corinthians and other Peloponnesian Greeks began to equip a squadron to act under him for the rescue of Sicily. As soon as four galleys were ready, he hurried over with them to the southern coast of Italy, and there, though he received such evil tidings of the state of Syracuse that he abandoned all hope of saving that city, he determined to remain on the coast, and do what he could in preserving the Italian cities from the Athenians.

So nearly, indeed, had Nicias completed his beleaguering lines, and so utterly desperate had the state of Syracuse seemingly become, that an assembly of the Syracusans was actually convened, and they were discussing the terms on which they should offer to capitulate, when a galley was seen dashing into the great harbor, and making her way toward the town with all the speed which her rowers could supply. From her shunning the part of the harbor where the Athenian fleet lay, and making straight for the Syracusan side, it was clear that she was a friend; the enemy's cruisers, careless through confidence of success, made no attempt to cut her off; she touched the beach, and a Corinthian captain, springing on shore from her, was eagerly conducted to the assembly of the Syracusan people just in time to prevent the fatal vote being put for a surrender.

Providentially for Syracuse, Gongylus, the commander of the galley, had been prevented by an Athenian squadron from following Gylippus to South Italy, and he had been obliged to push direct for Syracuse from Greece.

The sight of actual succor, and the promise of more, revived the drooping spirits of the Syracusans. They felt that they were not left desolate to perish, and the tidings that a Spartan was coming to command them confirmed their resolution to continue their resistance. Gylippus was already near the city. He had learned at Locri that the first report which had reached him of the state of Syracuse was exaggerated, and that there was unfinished space in the besiegers' lines through which it was barely possible to introduce reënforcements into the town. Crossing the Straits of Messina, which the culpable negligence of Nicias had left unguarded, Gylippus landed on the northern coast of Sicily, and there began to collect from the Greek cities an army, of which the regular troops that he brought from Peloponnesus formed the nucleus. Such was the influence of the name of Sparta, and such were his own abilities and activity, that he succeeded in raising a force of about two thousand fully armed infantry, with a larger number of irregular troops. Nicias, as if infatuated, made no attempt to counteract his operation, nor, when Gylippus marched his little army toward Syracuse, did the Athenian commander endeavor to check him. The Syracusans marched out to meet him; and while the Athenians were solely intent on completing their fortifications on the southern side toward the harbor, Gylippus turned their position by occupying the high ground in the extreme rear of Epipolæ. He then marched through the unfortified interval of Nicias' lines into the besieged town, and joining his troops with the Syracusan forces, after some engagements with varying success, gained the mastery over Nicias, drove the Athenians from Epipolæ, and hemmed them into a disadvantageous position in the low grounds near the great harbor.

The attention of all Greece was now fixed on Syracuse, and every enemy of Athens felt the importance of the opportunity now offered of checking her ambition, and, perhaps, of striking a deadly blow at her power. Larger reënforcements from Corinth, Thebes, and other cities now reached the Syracusans, while the baffled and dispirited Athenian general earnestly besought his countrymen to recall him, and represented the further prosecution of the siege as hopeless.

But Athens had made it a maxim never to let difficulty or disaster drive her back from any enterprise once undertaken, so long as she possessed the means of making any effort, however desperate, for its accomplishment. With indomitable pertinacity, she now decreed, instead of recalling her first armament from before Syracuse, to send out a second, though her enemies near home had now renewed open warfare against her, and by occupying a permanent fortification in her territory had severely distressed her population, and were pressing her with almost all the hardships of an actual siege. She still was mistress of the sea, and she sent forth another fleet of seventy galleys, and another army, which seemed to drain almost the last reserves of her military population, to try if Syracuse could not yet be won, and the honor of the Athenian arms be preserved from the stigma of a retreat. Hers was, indeed, a spirit that might be broken, but never would bend. At the head of this second expedition she wisely placed her best general, Demosthenes, one of the most distinguished officers that the long Peloponnesian war had produced, and who, if he had originally held the Sicilian command, would soon have brought Syracuse to submission.

The fame of Demosthenes the general has been dimmed by the superior lustre of his great countryman, Demosthenes the orator. When the name of Demosthenes is mentioned, it is the latter alone that is thought of. The soldier has found no biographer. Yet out of the long list of great men whom the Athenian republic produced, there are few that deserve to stand higher than this brave, though finally unsuccessful leader of her fleets and armies in the first half of the Peloponnesian war. In his first campaign in Ætolia he had shown some of the rashness of youth, and had received a lesson of caution by which he profited throughout the rest of his career, but without losing any of his natural energy in enterprise or in execution. He had performed the distinguished service of rescuing Naupactus from a powerful hostile armament in the seventh year of the war; he had then, at the request of the Acarnanian republics, taken on himself the office of commander-in-chief of all their forces, and at their head he had gained some important advantages over the enemies of Athens in Western Greece. His most celebrated exploits had been the occupation of Pylos on the Messenian coast, the successful defence of that place against the fleet and armies of Lacedæmon, and the subsequent capture of the Spartan forces on the isle of Sphacteria, which was the severest blow dealt to Sparta throughout the war, and which had mainly caused her to humble herself to make the truce with Athens.

Demosthenes was as honorably unknown in the war of party politics at Athens as he was eminent in the war against the foreign enemy. We read of no intrigues of his on either the aristocratic or democratic side. He was neither in the interest of Nicias nor of Cleon. His private character was free from any of the stains which polluted that of Alcibiades On all these points the silence of the comic dramatist is decisive evidence in his favor. He had also the moral courage, not always combined with physical, of seeking to do his duty to his country, irrespective of any odium that he himself might incur, and unhampered by any petty jealousy of those who were associated with him in command. There are few men named in ancient history of whom posterity would gladly know more or whom we sympathize with more deeply in the calamities that befell them than Demosthenes, the son of Alcisthenes, who, in the spring of the year 413, left Piræus at the head of the second Athenian expedition against Sicily.

His arrival was critically timed; for Gylippus had encouraged the Syracusans to attack the Athenians under Nicias by sea as well as by land, and by one able stratagem of Ariston, one of the admirals of the Corinthian auxiliary squadron, the Syracusans and their confederates had inflicted on the fleet of Nicias the first defeat that the Athenian navy had ever sustained from a numerically inferior enemy. Gylippus was preparing to follow up his advantage by fresh attacks on the Athenians on both elements, when the arrival of Demosthenes completely changed the aspect of affairs and restored the superiority to the invaders. With seventy-three war-galleys in the highest state of efficiency, and brilliantly equipped, with a force of five thousand picked men of the regular infantry of Athens and her allies, and a still larger number of bowmen, javelin-men, and slingers on board, Demosthenes rowed round the great harbor with loud cheers and martial music, as if in defiance of the Syracusans and their confederates. His arrival had indeed changed their newly born hopes into the deepest consternation.

The resources of Athens seemed inexhaustible, and resistance to her hopeless. They had been told that she was reduced to the last extremities, and that her territory was occupied by an enemy; and yet here they saw her sending forth, as if in prodigality of power, a second armament, to make foreign conquests, not inferior to that with which Nicias had first landed on the Sicilian shores.

With the intuitive decision of a great commander, Demosthenes at once saw that the possession of Epipolæ was the key to the possession of Syracuse, and he resolved to make a prompt and vigorous attempt to recover that position while his force was unimpaired and the consternation which its arrival had produced among the besieged remained unabated. The Syracusans and their allies had run out an outwork along Epipolæ from the city walls, intersecting the fortified lines of circumvallation which Nicias had commenced, but from which he had been driven by Gylippus. Could Demosthenes succeed in storming this outwork, and in reëstablishing the Athenian troops on the high ground, he might fairly hope to be able to resume the circumvallation of the city and become the conqueror of Syracuse; for when once the besiegers' lines were completed, the number of the troops with which Gylippus had garrisoned the place would only tend to exhaust the stores of provisions and accelerate its downfall.

An easily repelled attack was first made on the outwork in the daytime, probably more with the view of blinding the besieged to the nature of the main operations than with any expectation of succeeding in an open assault, with every disadvantage of the ground to contend against. But, when the darkness had set in, Demosthenes formed his men in columns, each soldier taking with him five days' provisions, and the engineers and workmen of the camp following the troops with their tools and all portable implements of fortification, so as at once to secure any advantage of ground that the army might gain. Thus equipped and prepared, he led his men along by the foot of the southern flank of Epipolæ, in a direction toward the interior of the island, till he came immediately below the narrow ridge that forms the extremity of the high ground looking westward. He then wheeled his vanguard to the right, sent them rapidly up the paths that wind along the face of the cliff, and succeeded in completely surprising the Syracusan outposts, and in placing his troops fairly on the extreme summit of the all-important Epipolæ. Thence the Athenians marched eagerly down the slope toward the town, routing some Syracusan detachments that were quartered in their way, and vigorously assailing the unprotected side of the outwork.

All at first favored them. The outwork was abandoned by its garrison, and the Athenian engineers began to dismantle it. In vain Gylippus brought up fresh troops to check the assault; the Athenians broke and drove them back, and continued to press hotly forward, in the full confidence of victory. But, amid the general consternation of the Syracusans and their confederates, one body of infantry stood firm. This was a brigade of their Bœotian allies, which was posted low down the slope of Epipolæ, outside the city walls. Coolly and steadily the Bœotian infantry formed their line, and, undismayed by the current of flight around them, advanced against the advancing Athenians. This was the crisis of the battle. But the Athenian van was disorganized by its own previous successes; and, yielding to the unexpected charge thus made on it by troops in perfect order, and of the most obstinate courage, it was driven back in confusion upon the other divisions of the army that still continued to press forward. When once the tide was thus turned, the Syracusans passed rapidly from the extreme of panic to the extreme of vengeful daring, and with all their forces they now fiercely assailed the embarrassed and receding Athenians. In vain did the officers of the latter strive to reform their line. Amid the din and the shouting of the fight, and the confusion inseparable upon a night engagement, especially one where many thousand combatants were pent and whirled together in a narrow and uneven area, the necessary manœuvres were impracticable; and though many companies still fought on desperately, wherever the moonlight showed them the semblance of a foe, they fought without concert or subordination; and not infrequently, amid the deadly chaos, Athenian troops assailed each other. Keeping their ranks close, the Syracusans and their allies pressed on against the disorganized masses of the besiegers, and at length drove them, with heavy slaughter, over the cliffs, which an hour or two before they had scaled full of hope and apparently certain of success.

This defeat was decisive of the event of the siege. The Athenians afterward struggled only to protect themselves from the vengeance which the Syracusans sought to wreak in the complete destruction of their invaders. Never, however, was vengeance more complete and terrible. A series of sea-fights followed, in which the Athenian galleys were utterly destroyed or captured. The mariners and soldiers who escaped death in disastrous engagements, and a vain attempt to force a retreat into the interior of the island, became prisoners of war. Nicias and Demosthenes were put to death in cold blood, and their men either perished miserably in the Syracusan dungeons or were sold into slavery to the very persons whom, in their pride of power, they had crossed the seas to enslave.

All danger from Athens to the independent nations of the West was now forever at an end. She, indeed, continued to struggle against her combined enemies and revolted allies with unparalleled gallantry, and many more years of varying warfare passed away before she surrendered to their arms. But no success in subsequent contests could ever have restored her to the preëminence in enterprise, resources, and maritime skill which she had acquired before her fatal reverses in Sicily. Nor among the rival Greek republics, whom her own rashness aided to crush her, was there any capable of reorganizing her empire, or resuming her schemes of conquest. The dominion of Western Europe was left for Rome and Carthage to dispute two centuries later, in conflicts still more terrible, and with even higher displays of military daring and genius than Athens had witnessed either in her rise, her meridian, or her fall.

RETREAT OF THE TEN THOUSAND GREEKS

B.C. 401–399

XENOPHON

The expedition of the Greeks, generally known as the " Retreat of the Ten Thousand," was conducted by Xenophon, a Greek historian, essayist, and military commander. Xenophon was a pupil of Socrates, of whom he left a famous memoir. In B.C. 401 he accepted the invitation of his friend Proxenus of Bœotia, a general of Greek mercenaries, to take service under Cyrus the Younger, brother of Artaxerxes Mnemon, king of Persia.

Cyrus had considered himself as deeply wronged by his elder brother, who had thrown him into prison on the death of their father, Darius. Escaping from prison, he formed a design to wrest the throne from Artaxerxes. For this purpose he engaged the forces of Proxenus, and to this army Xenophon attached himself. The rendezvous was Sardis, from which the army marched east under the pretext of chastising the revolting mountaineers of Pisidia. Instead of attacking the Pisidians, the followers of Cyrus proceeded east through Asia and Babylonia till they met the forces of Artaxerxes at Cunaxa. A furious battle took place, and the rout of the king's army had begun when Cyrus, elated with the victory that seemed just within his grasp, challenged his brother to single combat. In the duel that ensued Cyrus was slain. Proxenus had already fallen, and the virtual command of the Greek army soon devolved upon Xenophon, who thereupon began the famous retreat.

A vivid account of battles, and of hardships endured from the cold, in the struggle through mountain snows, through almost impassable forests, and across bridgeless rivers, is given in Xenophon's *Anabasis*, the celebrated work, in seven books, which forms the classical narrative of the campaign and the retreat. Soon after the death of Cyrus, in September, B.C. 401, the seizure and murder of the leading Greek generals by the treacherous Persian satrap, Tissaphernes, placed the Greek army in great peril. Xenophon, who now took practical command, counselled and exhorted the surviving leaders, and on the next day the Greeks formed in a hollow square, the baggage in the centre, and began their retreat, which led them along the Tigris to the territory of the Carduchi (Kurds), through Armenia, and across Georgia, the enemy often harassing them.

At the point where the climax of the story, which is presented here, may be said to begin, the Greeks have entered Armenia, passed the sources of the Tigris, and reached the Teleboas. Having made a treaty with Tiribazus, governor of the province, and discovered his insincerity, and that he was ready to attack them in their passage over the mountains, they resolved upon a quick resumption of their march.

When, in the fifth month of the retreat the Greeks at last from a hilltop beheld the Euxine, they sent up a cry, "The sea ! the sea !" which has echoed through succeeding ages as one of the great historic jubilations of humanity. At the end of the retreat their numbers were reduced to about six thousand, and from the starting-point at Cunaxa to the middle of the southern coast of the Black Sea they had travelled as much as two thousand miles. From Ephesus to Cunaxa and thence to the Black Sea region they had marched in fifteen months (February, B.C. 401, to June, 400), and nine months more passed before they joined the Spartan army in Asia Minor, and their task was fully accomplished. Their great performance is regarded as having prepared the way for Alexander's triumphant advances in the East. The young conqueror, on the eve of the battle of Issus, declared that he owed inspiration to the feat of the Ten Thousand.

IT was thought necessary to march away as fast as possible, before the enemy's force should be reassembled, and get possession of the pass.

Collecting their baggage at once, therefore, they set forward through a deep snow, taking with them several guides, and, having the same day passed the height on which Tiribazus had intended to attack them, they encamped. Hence they proceeded three days' journey through a desert tract of country, a distance of fifteen *parasangs*, to the river Euphrates, and passed it without being wet higher than the middle. The sources of the river were said not to be far off. From hence they advanced three days' march, through much snow and a level plain, a distance of fifteen parasangs; the third day's march was extremely troublesome, as the north wind blew full in their faces, completely parching up everything and benumbing the men. One of the augurs, in consequence, advised that they should sacrifice to the wind, and a sacrifice was accordingly offered, when the vehemence of the wind appeared to everyone manifestly to abate. The depth of the snow was a fathom, so that many of the baggage cattle and slaves perished, with about thirty of the soldiers.

They continued to burn fires through the whole night, for there was plenty of wood at the place of encampment. But those who came up late could get no wood; those, therefore, who had arrived before and had kindled fires would not admit the late comers to the fire unless they gave them a share of the corn or other provisions that they had brought. Thus they shared with each other what they respectively had. In the places where the fires were made, as the snow melted, there were formed large pits that reached down to the ground, and here there was accordingly opportunity to measure the depth of the snow.

From hence they marched through snow the whole of the following day, and many of the men contracted the *bulimia.*[1] Xenophon, who commanded in the rear, finding in his way such of the men as had fallen down with it, knew not what disease it was. But as one of these acquainted with it told him that they were evidently affected with bulimia, and that they would get up if they had something to eat, he went round among the baggage and wherever he saw anything eatable he gave it out, and sent such as were able to run to distribute it among those diseased, who, as soon as they had eaten, rose up and continued their march. As they proceeded, Chirisophus came, just as it grew dark, to a village, and found, at a spring in front of the rampart, some women and girls belonging to the place fetching water. The women asked them who they were, and the interpreter answered, in the Persian language, that they were people going from the king to the satrap. They replied that he was not there, but about a parasang off.

However, as it was late, they went with the water-carriers within the rampart, to the head man of the village, and here Chirisophus and as many of the troops as could come up encamped; but of the rest, such as were unable to get to the end of the journey spent the night on the way without food or fire, and some of the soldiers lost their lives on that occasion. Some of the enemy too, who had collected themselves into a body, pursued our rear, and seized any of the baggage-cattle

[1] Spelman quotes a description of the bulimia from Galen, in which it is said to be " a disease in which the patient frequently craves for food, loses the use of his limbs, falls down, turns pale, feels his extremities become cold, his stomach oppressed, and his pulse feeble." Here, however, it seems to mean little more than a faintness from long fasting.

that were unable to proceed, fighting with one another for the possession of them. Such of the soldiers also as had lost their sight from the effects of the snow, or had their toes mortified by the cold, were left behind. It was found to be a relief to the eyes against the snow, if the soldiers kept something black before them on the march, and to the feet, if they kept constantly in motion, and allowed themselves no rest, and if they took off their shoes in the night. But as to such as slept with their shoes on, the straps worked into their feet, and the soles were frozen about them, for when their old shoes had failed them, shoes of raw hides had been made by the men themselves from the newly skinned oxen.

From such unavoidable sufferings some of the soldiers were left behind, who, seeing a piece of ground of a black appearance, from the snow having disappeared there, conjectured that it must have melted, and it had in fact melted in the spot from the effect of a fountain, which was sending up vapor in a wooded hollow close at hand. Turning aside thither, they sat down and refused to proceed farther. Xenophon, who was with the rear-guard, as soon as he heard this tried to prevail on them by every art and means not to be left behind, telling them, at the same time, that the enemy were collected and pursuing them in great numbers. At last he grew angry, and they told him to kill them, as they were quite unable to go forward. He then thought it the best course to strike a terror, if possible, into the enemy that were behind, lest they should fall upon the exhausted soldiers. It was now dark, and the enemy were advancing with a great noise, quarrelling about the booty that they had taken, when such of the rear-guard as were not disabled started up and rushed toward them, while the tired men, shouting as loud as they could, clashed their spears against their shields. The enemy, struck with alarm, threw themselves among the snow into the hollow, and no one of them afterward made himself heard from any quarter.

Xenophon and those with him, telling the sick men that a party should come to their relief next day, proceeded on their march, but before they had gone four *stadia* they found other soldiers resting by the way in the snow, and covered up with it, no guard being stationed over them. They roused them up, but they said that the head of the army was not moving forward. Xenophon, going past them and sending on some of the ablest of the *peltasts*, ordered them to ascertain what it was that hindered their progress. They brought word that the whole army was in that manner taking rest. Xenophon and his men, therefore, stationing such a guard as they could, took up their quarters there without fire or supper. When it was near day, he sent the youngest of his men to the sick, telling them to rouse them and oblige them to proceed. At this juncture Chirisophus sent some of his people from the village to see how the rear were faring. The young men were rejoiced to see them, and gave them the sick to conduct to the camp, while they themselves went forward, and, before they had gone twenty stadia, found themselves at the village in which Chirisophus was quartered. When they came together, it was thought safe enough to lodge the troops up and down in the village. Chirisophus accordingly remained where he was, and the other officers, appropriating by lot the several villages that they had in sight, went to their respective quarters with their men.

Here Polycrates, an Athenian captain, requested leave of absence, and taking with him the most active of his men, and hastening to the village to which Xenophon had been allotted, surprised all the villagers and their head man in their houses, together with seventeen colts that were bred as a tribute for the king, and the head man's daughter, who had been but nine days married; her husband was gone out to hunt hares, and was not found in any of the villages. Their houses were underground, the entrance like the mouth of a well, but spacious below; there were passages dug into them for the cattle, but the people descended by ladders. In the houses were goats, sheep, cows, and fowls, with their young; all the cattle were kept on fodder within the walls.[1] There were also wheat, barley, legu-

---

[1] This description of a village on the Armenian uplands applies itself to many that I visited in the present day. The descent by wells is now rare, but is still to be met with; but in exposed and elevated situations the houses are uniformly semi-subterraneous and entered by as small an aperture as possible, to prevent the cold getting in. Whatever the kind of cottage used, cows, sheep, goats, and fowls participate with the family in the warmth and protection thereof.

minous vegetables, and barley wine [1] in large bowls; the grains of barley floated in it even with the brim of the vessels, and reeds also lay in it, some larger and some smaller, without joints; and these, when any one was thirsty, he was to take in his mouth and suck.[2] The liquor was very strong, unless one mixed water with it, and a very pleasant drink to those accustomed to it.

Xenophon made the chief man of his village sup with him, and told him to be of good courage, assuring him that he should not be deprived of his children, and that they would not go away without filling his house with provisions in return for what they took, if he would but prove himself the author of some service to the army till they should reach another tribe. This he promised, and, to show his good-will, pointed out where some wine [3] was buried. This night, therefore, the soldiers rested in their several quarters in the midst of great abundance, setting a guard over the chief, and keeping his children at the same time under their eye. The following day Xenophon took the head man and went with him to Chirisophus, and wherever he passed by a village he turned aside to visit those who were quartered in it, and found them in all parts feasting and enjoying themselves; nor would they anywhere let them go till they had set refreshments before them; and they placed everywhere upon the same table lamb, kid, pork, veal, and fowl, with plenty of bread, both of wheat and barley. Whenever any person, to pay a compliment, wished to drink to another, he took him to the large bowl, where he had to stoop down and drink, sucking like an ox. The chief they allowed to take whatever he pleased, but he accepted nothing from them; where he found any of his relatives, however, he took them with him.

When they came to Chirisophus, they found his men also

[1] Something like our ale.

[2] The reeds were used, says Krueger, that none of the grains of barley might be taken into the mouth.

[3] Xenophon seems to mean *grape* wine, rather than to refer to the barley wine just before mentioned, of which the taste does not appear to have been much liked by the Greeks. Wine from grapes was not made, it is probable, in these parts, on account of the cold, but Strabo speaks of the fruit wine of Armenia Minor as not inferior to any of the Greek wines.—*Schneider.*

feasting in their quarters, crowned with wreaths made of hay, and Armenian boys, in their barbarian dress, waiting upon them, to whom they made signs what they were to do as if they had been deaf and dumb. When Chirisophus and Xenophon had saluted one another, they both asked the chief man, through the interpreter who spoke the Persian language, what country it was. He replied that it was Armenia. They then asked him for whom the horses were bred, and he said that they were a tribute for the king, and added that the neighboring country was that of Chalybes, and told them in what direction the road lay. Xenophon then went away, conducting the chief back to his family, giving him the horse that he had taken, which was rather old, to fatten and offer in sacrifice (for he had heard that it had been consecrated to the sun), being afraid, indeed, that it might die, as it had been injured by the journey. He then took some of the young horses, and gave one of them to each of the other generals and captains. The horses in this country were smaller than those of Persia, but far more spirited. The chief instructed the men to tie little bags round the feet of the horses and other cattle when they drove them through the snow, for without such bags they sunk up to their bellies.

When the eighth day was come, Xenophon committed the guide to Chirisophus. He left the chief [1] all the members of his family, except his son, a youth just coming to mature age; him he gave in charge to Episthenes of Amphipolis, in order that if the father should conduct them properly he might return home with him. At the same time they carried to his house as many provisions as they could, and then broke up their camp and resumed their march. The chief conducted them through the snow, walking at liberty. When he came to the end of the third day's march, Chirisophus was angry at him for not guiding them to some villages. He said that there was none in that part of the country. Chirisophus then struck him, but did not confine him, and in consequence he ran off in the night, leaving his son behind him. This affair, the ill-treatment and neglect of the guide, was the only cause

[1] This is rather oddly expressed, for the guide and the chief were the same person.

of dissension between Chirisophus and Xenophon during the march. Episthenes conceived an affection for the youth, and, taking him home, found him extremely attached to him.

After this occurrence they proceeded seven days' journey, five parasangs each day, till they came to the river Phasis, the breadth of which is a *plethrum*. Hence they advanced two days' journey, ten parasangs, when, on the pass that led over the mountains into the plain, the Chalybes, Taochi, and Phasians were drawn up to oppose their progress. Chirisophus, seeing these enemies in possession of the height, came to a halt, at the distance of about thirty stadia, that he might not approach them while leading the army in a column. He accordingly ordered the other officers to bring up their companies, that the whole force might be formed in line.

When the rear-guard was come up, he called together the generals and captains and spoke to them as follows: "The enemy, as you see, is in possession of the pass over the mountains, and it is proper for us to consider how we may encounter them to the best advantage. It is my opinion, therefore, that we should direct the troops to get their dinner and that we ourselves should hold a council, in the mean time, whether it is advisable to cross the mountain to-day or to-morrow."

"It seems best to me," exclaimed Cleanor, "to march at once, as soon as we have dined and resumed our arms, against the enemy; for if we waste the present day in inaction the enemy, who are now looking down upon us, will grow bolder, and it is likely that, as their confidence is increased, others will join them in greater numbers."

After him Xenophon said: "I am of opinion that if it be necessary to fight, we ought to make our arrangements so as to fight with the greatest advantage; but that if we propose to pass the mountains as easily as possible, we ought to consider how we may incur the fewest wounds and lose the fewest men. The range of hills, as far as we see, extends more than sixty stadia in length; but the people nowhere seem to be watching us except along the line of road; and it is, therefore, better, I think, to endeavor to try to seize unobserved some part of the unguarded range, and to get possession of it, if we can, beforehand, than to attack a strong post and men prepared to resist us, for it is far less difficult to march up a steep ascent without fighting than along a level road with enemies on each side; and in the night, if men are not obliged to fight, they can see better what is before them than by day if engaged with enemies; while a rough road is easier to the feet to those who are marching without molestation than a smooth one to those who are pelted on the head with missiles. Nor do I think it at all impracticable for us to steal a way for ourselves, as we can march by night, so as not to be seen, and can keep at such a distance from the enemy as to allow no possibility of being heard. We seem likely, too, in my opinion, if we make a pretended attack on this point, to find the rest of the range still less guarded, for the enemy will so much the more probably stay where they are. But why should I speak doubtfully about stealing? For I hear that you Lacedæmonians, O Chirisophus, such of you at least as are of the better class, practise stealing from your boyhood, and it is not a disgrace, but an honor, to steal whatever the law does not forbid; while, in order that you may steal with the utmost dexterity, and strive to escape discovery, it is appointed by law that, if you are caught stealing, you are scourged. It is now high time for you, therefore, to give proof of your education, and to take care that we may not receive many stripes."

"But I hear that you Athenians also," rejoined Chirisophus, "are very clever at stealing the public money, though great danger threatens him that steals it; and that your best men steal it most, if indeed your best men are thought worthy to be your magistrates; so that it is time for you likewise to give proof of your education."

"I am then ready," exclaimed Xenophon, "to march with the rear-guard, as soon as we have supped, to take possession of the hills. I have guides too, for our light-armed men captured some of the marauders following us, by lying in ambush, and from them I learn that the mountains are not impassable, but are grazed over by goats and oxen, so that if we once gain possession of any part of the range, there will be tracks also for our baggage cattle. I expect also that the enemy will no longer keep their ground, when they see us upon a level with them on the heights, for they will not now come down to be upon a level with us." Chirisophus then said: "But why should you go, and leave the charge of the rear? Rather send others, unless some volunteers present themselves." Upon this Aristonymus of Methydria came forward with his heavy-armed men, and Aristeas of Chios and Nichomachus of Œta with their light-armed; and they made an arrangement that as soon as they should reach the top they should light a number of fires. Having settled these points, they went to dinner; and after dinner Chirisophus led forward the whole army ten stadia toward the enemy, that he might appear to be fully resolved to march against them on that quarter.

When they had taken their supper, and night came on, those appointed for the service went forward and got possession of the hills; the other troops rested where they were. The enemy, when they saw the heights occupied, kept watch and burned a number of fires all night. As soon as it was day, Chirisophus, after having offered sacrifice, marched forward along the road; while those who had gained the heights advanced by the ridge. Most of the enemy, meanwhile, stayed at the pass, but a part went to meet the troops coming along the heights. But before the main bodies came together, those on the ridge closed with one another, and the Greeks had the advantage, and put the enemy to flight. At the same time the Grecian peltasts ran up from the plain to attack the enemy drawn up to receive them, and Chirisophus followed at a quick pace with the heavy-armed men. The enemy at the pass, however, when they saw those above defeated, took to flight. Not many of them were killed, but a great number of shields were taken, which the Greeks, by hacking them with their swords, rendered useless. As soon as they had gained the ascent, and had sacrificed and erected a trophy, they went down into the plain before them, and arrived at a number of villages stored with abundance of excellent provisions.

From hence they marched five days' journey, thirty parasangs, to the country of the Taochi, where provisions began to fail them; for the Taochi inhabited strong fastnesses, in which they had laid up all their supplies. Having at length, however, arrived at one place which had no city or houses attached to it, but in which men and women and a great number of cattle were assembled, Chirisophus, as soon as he came before it, made it the object of an attack; and when the first division that assailed it began to be tired, another succeeded, and then another, for it was not possible for them to surround it in a body, as there was a river about it. When Xenophon came up with his rear-guard, peltasts, and heavy-armed men, Chirisophus exclaimed: "You come seasonably, for we must take this place, as there are no provisions for the army unless we take it."

They then deliberated together, and Xenophon asking what hindered them from taking the place, Chirisophus replied: "The only approach to it is the one which you see; but when any of our men attempt to pass along it, the enemy roll down stones over yonder impending rock, and whoever is struck is treated as you behold"; and he pointed, at the same moment, to some of the men who had had their legs and ribs broken. "But if they expend all their stones," rejoined Xenophon, "is there anything else to prevent us from advancing? For we see, in front of us, only a few men, and but two or three of them armed. The space, too, through which we have to pass under exposure to the stones is, as you see, only about a hundred and fifty feet in length; and of this about a hundred feet is covered with large pine trees in groups, against which, if the men place themselves, what would they suffer either from the flying stones or the rolling ones? The remaining part of the space is not above fifty feet, over which, when the stones cease, we must pass at a running pace."

"But," said Chirisophus, "the instant we offer to go to the part covered with trees, the stones fly in great numbers."

"That," cried Xenophon, "would be the very thing we want, for thus they will exhaust their stones the sooner. Let us then advance, if we can, to the point whence we shall have but a short way to run, and from which we may, if we please, easily retreat."

Chirisophus and Xenophon, with Callimachus of Parrhasia, one of the captains, who had that day the lead of all the other captains of the rear-guard, then went forward, all the rest of the captains remaining out of danger. Next, about seventy of the men advanced under the trees, not in a body, but one by one, each sheltering himself as he could. Agasias of Stymphalus, and Aristonymus of Methydria, who were also captains of the rear-guard, with some others were at the same time standing behind, without the trees, for it was not safe for more than one company to stand under them. Callimachus then adopted the following stratagem: he ran forward two or three paces from the tree under which he was sheltered, and when the stones began to be hurled, hastily drew back; and at each of his sallies more than ten cartloads of stones were spent.

Agasias, observing what Callimachus was doing, and that the eyes of the whole army were upon him, and fearing that he himself might not be the first to enter the place, began to advance alone—neither calling to Aristonymus who was next him, nor to Eurylochus of Lusia, both of whom were his intimate friends, nor to any other person—and passed by all the rest. Callimachus, seeing him rushing by, caught hold of the rim of his shield, and at that moment Aristonymus of Methydria ran past them both, and after him Eurylochus of Lusia, for all these sought distinction for valor, and were rivals to one another; and thus, in mutual emulation, they got possession of the place, for when they had once rushed in, not a stone was hurled from above. But a dreadful spectacle was then to be seen; for the women, flinging their children over the precipice, threw themselves after them; and the men followed their example. Æneas of Stymphalus, a captain, seeing one of them, who had on a rich garment, running to throw himself over, caught hold of it with intent to stop him. But the man dragged him forward, and they both went rolling down the rocks together, and were killed. Thus very few prisoners were taken, but a great number of oxen, asses, and sheep.

Hence they advanced, seven days' journey, a distance of fifty parasangs, through the country of the Chalybes. These were the most warlike people of all that they passed through, and came to close combat with them. They had linen cuirasses, reaching down to the groin, and, instead of skirts, thick cords twisted. They had also greaves and helmets, and at their girdles a short falchion, as large as a Spartan crooked dagger, with which they cut the throats of all whom they could master, and then, cutting off their heads, carried them away with them. They sang and danced when the enemy were likely to see them. They carried also a spear of about fifteen cubits in length, having one spike.[1] They stayed in their villages till the Greeks had passed by, when they pursued and perpetually harassed them. They had their dwellings in strong places, in which they had also laid up their provisions, so that the Greeks could get nothing from that country, but lived upon the cattle which they had taken from the Taochi.

The Greeks next arrived at the river Harpasus, the breadth of which was four *plethra*. Hence they proceeded through the territory of the Scythini, four days' journey, making twenty parasangs, over a level tract, until they came to some villages, in which they halted three days and collected provisions. From this place they advanced four days' journey, twenty parasangs, to a large, rich and populous city, called Gymnias, from which the governor of the country sent the Greeks a guide to conduct them through a region at war with his own people. The guide, when he came, said that he would take them in five days to a place whence they should see the sea; if not, he would consent to be put to death. When, as he proceeded, he entered the country of their enemies, he exhorted them to burn and lay waste the lands; whence it was evident that he had come for this very purpose, and not from any good-will to the Greeks.

On the fifth day they came to the mountain; and the name of it was Theches. When the men who were in the front had mounted the height, and looked down upon the sea, a great shout proceeded from them; and Xenophon and the rear-guard, on hearing it, thought that some new enemies were assailing the front, for in the rear, too, the people from the country that they had burned were following them, and the rear-guard, by placing an ambuscade, had killed some, and taken others prisoners, and had captured about twenty shields made of raw ox-hides with the hair on. But as the noise still increased, and drew nearer, and as those who came up from

[1] Having one iron point at the upper end, and no point at the lower for fixing the spear in the ground.

time to time kept running at full speed to join those who were
continually shouting, the cries becoming louder as the men
became more numerous, it appeared to Xenophon that it must
be something of very great moment.   Mounting his horse,
therefore, and taking with him Lycius and the cavalry, he hastened forward to give aid, when presently they heard the
soldiers shouting, "The sea, the sea!" and cheering on one
another.   They then all began to run, the rear-guard as well
as the rest, and the baggage-cattle and horses were put to their
speed; and when they had all arrived at the top, the men embraced one another and their generals and captains, with tears
in their eyes.   Suddenly, whoever it was that suggested it, the
soldiers brought stones, and raised a large mound, on which
they laid a number of raw ox-hides, staves, and shields taken
from the enemy.   The shields the guide himself hacked in
pieces, and exhorted the rest to do the same.   Soon after, the
Greeks sent away the guide, giving him presents from the
common stock: a horse, a silver cup, a Persian robe, and ten
darics; but he showed most desire for the rings on their fin-
gers, and obtained many of them from the soldiers.   Having
then pointed out to them a village where they might take up
their quarters, and the road by which they were to proceed to
the Macrones, when the evening came on he departed, pursuing his way during the night.

Hence the Greeks advanced three days' journey, a distance
of ten parasangs, through the country of the Macrones.   On
the first day they came to a river which divides the territories
of the Macrones from those of the Scythini.   On their right
they had an eminence extremely difficult of access, and on
their left another river, into which the boundary river, which
they had to cross, empties itself.   This stream was thickly
edged with trees, not indeed large, but growing closely together.   These the Greeks, as soon as they came to the spot,
cut down,[1] being in haste to get out of the country as soon
as possible.   The Macrones, however, equipped with wicker
shields, and spears, and hair tunics, were drawn up on the
opposite side of the crossing-place; they were animating one

[1] The Greeks cut down the trees in order to throw them into the
stream, and form a kind of bridge on which they might cross.

another and throwing stones into the river.[1]   They did not hit
our men or cause them any inconvenience.

At this juncture one of the peltasts came up to Xenophon,
saying that he had been a slave at Athens, and adding that he
knew the language of these men.   " I think, indeed," said he,
"that this is my country, and, if there is nothing to prevent, I
should wish to speak to the people."

"There is nothing to prevent," replied Xenophon; "so
speak to them, and first ascertain what people they are."
When he asked them, they said that they were the Macrones.
"Inquire, then," said Xenophon, "why they are drawn up to
oppose us and wish to be our enemies."   They replied, "Because you come against our country."   The generals then told
him to acquaint them that we were not come with any wish to
do them injury, but that we were returning to Greece after
having been engaged in war with the king, and that we were
desirous to reach the sea.   They asked if the Greeks would
give pledges to this effect; and the Greeks replied that they
were willing both to give and receive them.   The Macrones
accordingly presented the Greeks with a barbarian lance, and the
Greeks gave them a Grecian one; for they said that such were
their usual pledges.   Both parties called the gods to witness.

After these mutual assurances, the Macrones immediately
assisted them in cutting away the trees and made a passage
for them as if to bring them over, mingling freely among the
Greeks; they also gave such facilities as they could for buying
provisions, and conducted them through their country for three
days, until they brought them to the confines of the Colchians.
Here was a range of hills, high, but accessible, and upon them
the Colchians were drawn up in array.   The Greeks, at first,
drew up against them in a line, with the intention of marching
up the hill in this disposition; but afterward the generals
thought proper to assemble and deliberate how they might engage with the best effect.

Xenophon then said it appeared to him that they ought to
relinquish the arrangement in line, and to dispose the troops

[1] They threw stones into the river that they might stand on them and
approach nearer to the Greeks, so as to use their weapons with more
effect.

in columns; "for a line," pursued he, "will be broken at once, as we shall find the hills in some parts impassable, though in others easy of access; and this disruption will immediately produce despondency in the men, when, after being ranged in a regular line, they find it dispersed. Again, if we advance drawn up very many deep, the enemy will stretch beyond us on both sides, and will employ the parts that outreach us in any way they may think proper; and if we advance only a few deep, it would not be at all surprising if our line be broken through by showers of missiles and men falling upon us in large bodies. If this happen in any part, it will be ill for the whole extent of the line. I think, then, that having formed our companies in columns, we should keep them so far apart from each other as that the last companies on each side may be beyond the enemy's wings. Thus our extreme companies will both outflank the line of the enemy, and, as we march in file, the bravest of our men will close with the enemy first, and wherever the ascent is easiest, there each division will direct its course. Nor will it be easy for the enemy to penetrate into the intervening spaces when there are companies on each side, nor will it be easy to break through a column as it advances; while, if any one of the companies be hard pressed, the neighboring one will support it; and if but one of the companies can by any path attain the summit, the enemy will no longer stand their ground."

This plan was approved, and they threw the companies into columns. Xenophon, riding along from the right wing to the left, said: "Soldiers, the enemy whom you see before you is now the only obstacle to hinder us from being where we have long been eager to be. These, if we can, we must eat up alive."

When the men were all in their places, and they had formed the companies into columns, there were about eighty companies of heavy-armed men, and each company consisted of about eighty men. The peltasts and archers they divided into three bodies, each about six hundred men, one of which they placed beyond the left wing, another beyond the right, and the third in the centre. The generals then desired the soldiers to make their vows to the gods; and having made them, and sung the pæan, they moved forward. Chirisophus and Xenophon, and the peltasts that they had with them, who were beyond the enemy's flanks, pushed on; and the enemy, observing their motions, and hurrying forward to receive them, was drawn off, some to the right and others to the left, and left a great void in the centre of the line; when the peltasts in the Arcadian division, whom Æschines the Acarnanian commanded, seeing the Colchians separate, ran forward in all haste, thinking that they were taking to flight; and these were the first that reached the summit. The Arcadian heavy-armed troop, of which Clearnor the Orchomenian was captain, followed them. But the enemy, when once the Greeks began to run, no longer stood its ground, but went off in flight, some one way and some another.

Having passed the summit, the Greeks encamped in a number of villages containing abundance of provisions. As to other things here, there was nothing at which they were surprised; but the number of bee-hives was extraordinary, and all the soldiers that ate of the combs lost their senses, vomited, and were affected with purging, and not any of them was able to stand upright; such as had eaten a little were like men greatly intoxicated, and such as had eaten much were like madmen, and some like persons at the point of death. They lay upon the ground, in consequence, in great numbers, as if there had been a defeat; and there was general dejection. The next day no one of them was found dead; and they recovered their senses about the same hour that they had lost them on the preceding day; and on the third and fourth days they got up as if after having taken physic.[1]

From hence they proceeded two days' march, seven parasangs, and arrived at Trebizond, a Greek city, of large popula-

[1] That there was honey in these parts, with intoxicating qualities, was well known to antiquity. Pliny mentions two sorts of it, one produced at Heraclea in Pontus, and the other among the Sanni or Macrones. The peculiarities of the honey arose from the herbs to which the bees resorted; the first came from the flower of a plant called *ægolethron*, or goatsbane; the other from a species of rhododendron. Tournefort, when he was in that country, saw honey of this description. Ainsworth found that the intoxicating honey had a bitter taste. This honey is also mentioned by Dioscorides.

tion, on the Euxine Sea; a colony of Sinope, but lying in the territory of the Colchians. Here they stayed about thirty days, encamping in the villages of the Colchians, whence they made excursions and plundered the country of Colchis. The people of Trebizond provided a market for the Greeks in the camp, and entertained them in the city; and made them presents of oxen, barley-meal, and wine. They negotiated with them also on behalf of the neighboring Colchians, those especially who dwelt in the plain, and from them too were brought presents of oxen.

Soon after, they prepared to perform the sacrifice which they had vowed. Oxen enough had been brought them to offer to Jupiter the Preserver, and to Hercules, for their safe conduct, and whatever they had vowed to the other gods. They also celebrated gymnastic games upon the hill where they were encamped, and chose Dracontius, a Spartan—who had become an exile from his country when quite a boy, for having involuntarily killed a child by striking him with a dagger—to prepare the course and preside at the contests. When the sacrifice was ended, they gave the hides [1] to Dracontius, and desired him to conduct them to the place where he had made the course. Dracontius, pointing to the place where they were standing, said, "This hill is an excellent place for running, in whatever direction the men may wish."

"But how will they be able," said they, "to wrestle on ground so rough and bushy?"

"He that falls," said he, "will suffer the more." Boys, most of them from among the prisoners, contended in the short course, and in the long course above sixty Cretans ran; while others were matched in wrestling, boxing, and the *pancratium*. It was a fine sight; for many entered the lists, and as their friends were spectators, there was great emulation. Horses also ran; and they had to gallop down the steep, and, turning

---

[1] Lion and Kuehner have a notion that these skins were to be given as prizes to the victors, referring to Herodotus, who says that the Egyptians, in certain games which they celebrate in honor of Perseus, offer as prizes cattle, cloaks, and hides. Krueger doubts whether they were intended for prizes, or were given as a present to Dracontius.

round in the sea, to come up again to the altar. In the descent, many rolled down; but in the ascent, against the exceedingly steep ground, the horses could scarcely get up at a walking pace. There was consequently great shouting and laughter and cheering from the people.

CONDEMNATION AND DEATH OF SOCRATES

B.C. 399

PLATO

The death of Socrates was brought about under the restored democracy by three of his enemies—Lycon, Meletus, and Anytus, the last a
man of high rank and reputation in the state. Socrates was accused by
them of despising the ancient gods of the state, introducing new divini-
ties and corrupting the youth of Athens. He was charged with having
taught his followers, young men of the first Athenian families, to despise
the established government, to be turbulent and seditious, and his ac-
cusors pointed to Alcibiades and Critias, notorious for their lawlessness,
as examples of the fruits of his teaching.

It is quite certain that Socrates disliked the Athenian government
and considered democracy as tyrannical as despotism. But there was
no law at Athens by which he could be put to death for his words and
actions, and the vague charge could never have been made unless the
whole trial of the philosopher had been a party movement, headed by
men like Lycon and Anytus, whose support of the unjust measure made
the condemnation of Socrates a foregone conclusion. Xenophon, the
pupil and admirer of the philosopher, expresses in his *Memorabilia of
Socrates* his surprise that the Athenians should have condemned to death
a man of such exalted character and transparent innocence. But the influence of the teacher with his pupils, most of them sons of the wealthiest
citizens, might well have been dreaded by those in office and engaged in
the conduct of public business. By them, the common politicians of the
day, Socrates, with his keen and witty criticism of political corruption
and demagogism, must have been considered a formidable adversary.

Accordingly, by the decision of the Athenian court, the philosopher
was sentenced to death by drinking a cup of hemlock. Although it was
usual for criminals to be executed the day following their condemnation,
he enjoyed a respite of thirty days, during which time his friends had
access to his prison cell. It was the time when the ceremonial galley
was crowned and sent on her pilgrimage to the holy Isle of Delos, and
no criminal could be executed until her return. Socrates exhibited
heroic constancy and cheerfulness during this interval, and repudiated
the offers of his friends to aid in his escape, though they had chartered a

87

ship to carry him to Thessaly. With calm composure he reasoned on the immortality of the soul, and cheered his visitors with words of hope.

The literary portraits of Socrates furnished by himself, and the writings of Plato, are among the most precious monuments of antiquity, and the life and death of such a man form a memorable era in the moral and intellectual history of mankind.

Plato, in his *Phædo, or the Immortality of the Soul*, gives the following dialogue between Echecrates and Phædo—two friends and disciples of the late philosopher—evidently with no other purpose in view than to lend to the account of the great teacher's last hours, and the last words his followers were to hear from his lips, the additional force and dramatic value of a personal narrative in the mouth of a loving pupil and an actual eyewitness of his death.

ECHECRATES. Were you personally present, Phædo, with Socrates on that day when he drank the poison in prison? or did you hear an account of it from someone else?

Phædo. I was there myself, Echecrates.

Ech. What then did he say before his death? and how did he die? for I should be glad to hear; for scarcely any citizen of Phlius[1] ever visits Athens now, nor has any stranger for a long time come from thence, who was able to give us a clear account of the particulars, except that he died from drinking poison; but he was unable to tell us anything more.

Phæd. And did you not hear about the trial how it went off?

Ech. Yes; some one told me this; and I wondered, that as it took place so long ago, he appears to have died long afterward. What was the reason of this, Phædo?

Phæd. An accidental circumstance happened in his favor, Echecrates: for the poop of the ship which the Athenians send to Delos, chanced to be crowned on the day before the trial.

Ech. But what is this ship?

Phæd. It is the ship, as the Athenians say, in which Theseus formerly conveyed the fourteen boys and girls to Crete and saved both them and himself. They, therefore, made a vow to Apollo on that occasion, as it is said, that if they were saved they would every year despatch a solemn embassy to Delos; which, from that time to the present, they send yearly

[1] Phlius, to which Echecrates belonged, was a town of Sicyonia in Peloponnesus.

to the god.   When they begin the preparations for this solemn embassy, they have a law that the city shall be purified during this period, and that no public execution shall take place until the ship has reached Delos, and returned to Athens: and this occasionally takes a long time, when the winds happen to impede their passage.   The commencement of the embassy is when the priest of Apollo has crowned the poop of the ship. And this was done, as I said, on the day before the trial: on this account Socrates had a long interval in prison between the trial and his death.

Ech. And what, Phædo, were the circumstances of his death? what was said and done? and who of his friends were with him? or would not the magistrates allow them to be present, but did he die destitute of friends?

Phæd. By no means; but some, indeed several, were present.

Ech. Take the trouble, then, to relate to me all the particulars as clearly as you can, unless you have any pressing business.

Phæd. I am at leisure, and will endeavor to give you a full account: for to call Socrates to mind, whether speaking myself or listening to some one else, is always most delightful to me.

Ech. And indeed, Phædo, you have others to listen to you who are of the same mind.   However, endeavor to relate everything as accurately as you can.

Phæd. I was indeed wonderfully affected by being present, for I was not impressed with a feeling of pity, like one present at the death of a friend; for the man appeared to me to be happy, Echecrates, both from his manner and discourse, so fearlessly and nobly did he meet his death: so much so that it occurred to me that in going to Hades he was not going without a divine destiny, but that when he arrived there he would be happy, if anyone ever was.   For this reason I was entirely uninfluenced by any feeling of pity, as would seem likely to be the case with one present on so mournful an occasion; nor was I affected by pleasure from being engaged in philosophical discussions, as was our custom; for our conversation was of that kind.   But an altogether unaccountable feeling possessed me, a kind of unusual mixture compounded of pleasure and pain together, when I considered that he was immediately about to die. And all of us who were present were affected in much the same manner, at one time laughing, at another weeping, one of us especially, Apollodorus, for you know the man and his manner.

Ech. How should I not?

Phæd. He, then, was entirely overcome by these emotions; and I too was troubled, as well as the others.

Ech. But who were present, Phædo?

Phæd. Of his fellow-countrymen, this Apollodorus was present, and Critobulus, and his father Crito, moreover Hermogenes, Epigenes, Æschines, and Antisthenes; Ctesippus the Pæanian, Menexenus, and some other of his countrymen were also there: Plato I think was sick.

Ech. Were any strangers present?

Phæd. Yes: Simmias the Theban, Cebes, and Phædondes: and from Megara, Euclides and Terpsion.

Ech. But what! were not Aristippus and Cleombrotus present?

Phæd. No: for they were said to be at Ægina.

Ech. Was anyone else there?

Phæd. I think that these were nearly all who were present.

Ech. Well, now, what do you say was the subject of conversation?

Phæd. I will endeavor to relate the whole to you from the beginning. On the preceding days I and the others were constantly in the habit of visiting Socrates, meeting early in the morning at the court-house where the trial took place, for it was near the prison. Here then we waited every day till the prison was opened, conversing with each other; for it was not opened very early, but, as soon as it was opened we went in to Socrates, and usually spent the day with him. On that occasion, however, we met earlier than usual; for on the preceding day, when we left the prison in the evening, we heard that the ship had arrived from Delos. We therefore urged each other to come as early as possible to the accustomed place; accordingly we came, and the porter, who used to admit us, coming out, told us to wait, and not enter until he called us. "For," he said, "the Eleven are now freeing Socrates from his bonds, and announcing to him that he must die to-day." But in no long time he returned, and bade us enter.

When we entered, we found Socrates just freed from his bonds, and Xantippe (you know her), holding his little boy and sitting by him. As soon as Xantippe saw us, she wept aloud and said such things as women usually do on such occasions, as, "Socrates, your friends will now converse with you for the last time, and you with them." But Socrates, looking toward Crito, said, "Crito, let some one take her home." Upon which some of Crito's attendants led her away, wailing and beating herself.

But Socrates, sitting up in bed, drew up his leg and rubbed it with his hand, and as he rubbed it said: "What an unaccountable thing, my friends, that seems to be which men call pleasure; and how wonderfully is it related toward that which appears to be its contrary, pain; in that they will not both be present to a man at the same time, yet, if anyone pursues and attains the one, he is almost always compelled to receive the other, as if they were both united together from one head.

"And it seems to me," he said, "that if Æsop had observed this he would have made a fable from it, how the Deity, wishing to reconcile these warring principles, when he could not do so, united their heads together, and from hence whomsoever the one visits the other attends immediately after; as appears to be the case with me, since I suffered pain in my leg before from the chain, but now pleasure seems to have succeeded."

Hereupon Cebes, interrupting him, said: "By Jupiter, Socrates, you have done well in reminding me. With respect to the poems which you made, by putting into metre those Fables of Æsop and the hymn to Apollo, several other persons asked me, and especially Evenus recently, with what design you made them after you came here, whereas before, you had never made any. If, therefore, you care at all that I should be able to answer Evenus when he asks me again—for I am sure he will do so—tell me what I must say to him."

"Tell him the truth then, Cebes," he replied, "that I did not make them from a wish to compete with him, or his poems, for I knew that this would be no easy matter; but that I might discover the meaning of certain dreams, and discharge my conscience, if this should happen to be the music which they have often ordered me to apply myself to. For they were to the following purport: often in my past life the same dream visited me, appearing at different times in different forms, yet always saying the same thing. 'Socrates,' it said, ' apply yourself to and practise music.' And I formerly supposed that it exhorted and encouraged me to continue the pursuit I was engaged in, as those who cheer on racers, so that the dream encouraged me to continue the pursuit I was engaged in, namely, to apply myself to music, since philosophy is the highest music, and I was devoted to it. But now since my trial took place, and the festival of the god retarded my death, it appeared to me that, if by chance the dream so frequently enjoined me to apply myself to popular music, I ought not to disobey it but do so, for that it would be safer for me not to depart hence before I had discharged my conscience by making some poems in obedience to the dream. Thus, then, I first of all composed a hymn to the god whose festival was present, and after the god, considering that a poet, if he means to be a poet, ought to make fables and not discourses, and knowing that I was not skilled in making fables, I therefore put into verse those fables of Æsop, which were at hand, and were known to me, and which first occurred to me.

"Tell this then to Evenus, Cebes, and bid him farewell, and, if he is wise, to follow me as soon as he can. But I depart, as it seems, to-day; for so the Athenians order."

To this Simmias said: "What is this, Socrates, which you exhort Evenus to do? for I often meet with him; and from what I know of him, I am pretty certain that he will not at all be willing to comply with your advice."

"What then," said he, "is not Evenus a philosopher?"

"To me he seems to be so," said Simmias.

"Then he will be willing," rejoined Socrates, "and so will everyone who worthily engages in this study; perhaps indeed he will not commit violence on himself, for that they say is not allowable." And as he said this he let down his leg from the bed on the ground, and in this posture continued during the remainder of the discussion.

Cebes then asked him: "What do you mean, Socrates, by

DEATH OF SOCRATES 93

saying that it is not lawful to commit violence on one's self, but that a philosopher should be willing to follow one who is dying?"

"What, Cebes, have not you and Simmias, who have conversed familiarly with Philolaus [1] on this subject, heard?"

"Nothing very clearly, Socrates."

"I however speak only from hearsay; what then I have heard I have no scruple in telling. And perhaps it is most becoming for one who is about to travel there, to inquire and speculate about the journey thither, what kind we think it is. What else can one do in the interval before sunset?"

"Why, then, Socrates, do they say that it is not allowable to kill one's self? for I, as you asked just now, have heard both Philolaus, when he lived with us, and several others say that it was not right to do this; but I never heard anything clear upon the subject from anyone."

"Then you should consider it attentively," said Socrates, "for perhaps you may hear: probably, however, it will appear wonderful to you, if this alone of all other things is an universal truth,[2] and it never happens to a man, as is the case in all other things, that at some times and to some persons only it is better to die than to live; yet that these men for whom it is better to die—this probably will appear wonderful to you— may not, without impiety, do this good to themselves, but must await another benefactor."

Then Cebes, gently smiling, said, speaking in his own dialect, "Jove be witness."

"And indeed," said Socrates, "it would appear to be unreasonable, yet still perhaps it has some reason on its side. The maxim indeed given on this subject in the mystical doctrines,[3] that we men are in a kind of prison, and that we ought not to free ourselves from it and escape, appears to me difficult to be understood, and not easy to penetrate. This however appears to me, Cebes, to be well said, that the gods take care of us, and that we men are one of their possessions. Does it not seem so to you?"

[1] A Pythagorean of Crotona.
[2] Namely, "that it is better to die than live."
[3] Of Pythagoras.

"It does," replied Cebes.

"Therefore," said he, "if one of your slaves were to kill himself, without your having intimated that you wished him to die, should you not be angry with him, and should you not punish him if you could?"

"Certainly," he replied.

"Perhaps then, in this point of view, it is not unreasonable to assert, that a man ought not to kill himself before the deity lays him under a necessity of doing so, such as that now laid on me."

"This, indeed," said Cebes, "appears to be probable. But what you said just now, Socrates, that philosophers should be very willing to die, appears to be an absurdity, if what we said just now is agreeable to reason, that it is God who takes care of us, and that we are his property. For that the wisest men should not be grieved at leaving that service in which they govern them who are the best of all masters, namely, the gods, is not consistent with reason. For surely he cannot think that he will take better care of himself when he has become free: but a foolish man might perhaps think thus, that he should fly from his master, and would not reflect that he ought not to fly from a good one, but should cling to him as much as possible, therefore he would fly against all reason; but a man of sense would desire to be constantly with one better than himself. Thus, Socrates, the contrary of what you just now said is likely to be the case; for it becomes the wise to be grieved at dying, but the foolish to rejoice."

Socrates, on hearing this, appeared to me to be pleased with the pertinacity of Cebes, and looking toward us said: "Cebes, you see, always searches out arguments, and is not at all willing to admit at once anything one has said."

Whereupon Simmias replied: "But indeed, Socrates, Cebes appears to me, now, to say something to the purpose; for with what design should men really wise fly from masters who are better than themselves, and so readily leave them? And Cebes appears to me to direct his argument against you, because you so easily endure to abandon both us and those good rulers—as you yourself confess—the gods."

"You speak justly," said Socrates, "for I think you mean

that I ought to make my defence to this charge, as if I were in a court of justice."

"Certainly," replied Simmias.

"Come then," said he, "I will endeavor to defend myself more successfully before you than before the judges. For," he proceeded, "Simmias and Cebes, if I did not think that I should go first of all among other deities who are both wise and good, and next among men who have departed this life better than any here, I should be wrong in not grieving at death: but now be assured, I hope to go among good men, though I would not positively assert it; that, however, I shall go among gods who are perfectly good masters, be assured I can positively assert this, if I can anything of the kind. So that, on this account, I am not so much troubled, but I entertain a good hope that something awaits those who die, and that, as was said long since, it will be far better for the good than the evil."

"What then, Socrates," said Simmias, "would you go away keeping this persuasion to yourself, or would you impart it to us? For this good appears to me to be also common to us; and at the same time it will be an apology for you, if you can persuade us to believe what you say."

"I will endeavor to do so," he said. "But first let us attend to Crito here, and see what it is he seems to have for some time wished to say."

"What else, Socrates," said Crito, "but what he who is to give you the poison told me some time ago, that I should tell you to speak as little as possible? For he says that men become too much heated by speaking, and that nothing of this kind ought to interfere with the poison, and that, otherwise, those who did so were sometimes compelled to drink two or three times."

To which Socrates replied: "Let him alone, and let him attend to his own business, and prepare to give it me twice, or, if occasion requires, even thrice."

"I was almost certain what you would say," answered Crito, "but he has been some time pestering me."

"Never mind him," he rejoined.

"But now I wish to render an account to you, my judges,

of the reason why a man who has really·devoted his life to philosophy, when he is about to die appears to me, on good grounds, to have confidence, and to entertain a firm hope that the greatest good will befall him in the other world, when he has departed this life. How then this comes to pass, Simmias and Cebes, I will endeavor to explain.

"For as many as rightly apply themselves to philosophy seem to have left all others in ignorance, that they aim at nothing else than to die and be dead. If this then is true, it would surely be absurd to be anxious about nothing else than this during their whole life, but when it arrives, to be grieved at what they have been long anxious about and aimed at."

Upon this, Simmias, smiling, said: "By Jupiter, Socrates, though I am not now at all inclined to smile, you have made me do so; for I think that the multitude, if they heard this, would think it was very well said in reference to philosophers, and that our countrymen particularly would agree with you, that true philosophers do desire death, and that they are by no means ignorant that they deserve to suffer it."

"And indeed, Simmias, they would speak the truth, except in asserting that they are not ignorant; for they are ignorant of the sense in which true philosophers desire to die, and in what sense they deserve death, and what kind of death. But," he said, "let us take leave of them, and speak to one another. Do we think that death is anything?"

"Certainly," replied Simmias.

"Is it anything else than the separation of the soul from the body? and is not this to die, for the body to be apart by itself separated from the soul, and for the soul to subsist apart by itself separated from the body? Is death anything else than this?"

"No, but this," he replied.

"Consider then, my good friend, whether you are of the same opinion as me; for thus I think we shall understand better the subject we are considering. Does it appear to you to be becoming in a philosopher to be anxious about pleasures, as they are called, such as meats and drinks?"

"By no means, Socrates," said Simmias.

"But what? about the pleasures of love?"

"Not at all."

"What then? does such a man appear to you to think other bodily indulgences of value? for instance, does he seem to you to value or despise the possession of magnificent garments and sandals, and other ornaments of the body, except so far as necessity compels him to use them?"

"The true philosopher," he answered, "appears to me to despise them."

"Does not, then," he continued, "the whole employment of such a man appear to you to be, not about the body, but to separate himself from it as much as possible, and be occupied about his soul?"

"It does."

"First of all, then, in such matters, does not the philosopher, above all other men, evidently free his soul as much as he can from communion with the body?"

"It appears so."

"And it appears, Simmias, to the generality of men, that he who takes no pleasure in such things, and who does not use them, does not deserve to live; but that he nearly approaches to death who cares nothing for the pleasures that subsist through the body."

"You speak very truly."

"But what with respect to the acquisition of wisdom, is the body an impediment or not, if anyone takes it with him as a partner in the search? What I mean is this: Do sight and hearing convey any truth to men, or are they such as the poets constantly sing, who say that we neither hear nor see anything with accuracy? If, however, these bodily senses are neither accurate nor clear, much less can the others be so: for they are all far inferior to these. Do they not seem so to you?"

"Certainly," he replied.

"When, then," said he, "does the soul light on the truth? for, when it attempts to consider anything in conjunction with the body, it is plain that it is then led astray by it."

"You say truly."

"Must it not then be by reasoning, if at all, that any of the things that really are become known to it?"

"Yes."

"And surely the soul then reasons best when none of these things disturbs it, neither hearing, nor sight, nor pain, nor pleasure of any kind, but it retires as much as possible within itself, taking leave of the body, and, as far as it can, not communicating or being in contact with it, it aims at the discovery of that which is."

"Such is the case."

"Does not then the soul of the philosopher, in these cases, despise the body, and flee from it, and seek to retire within itself?"

"It appears so."

"But what as to such things as these, Simmias? Do we say that justice itself is something or nothing?"

"We say it is something, by Jupiter."

"And that beauty and goodness are something?"

"How not?"

"Now, then, have you ever seen anything of this kind with your eyes?"

"By no means," he replied.

"Did you ever lay hold of them by any other bodily sense? but I speak generally, as of magnitude, health, strength, and, in a word, of the essence of everything, that is to say, what each is. Is then the exact truth of these perceived by means of the body, or is it thus, whoever among us habituates himself to reflect most deeply and accurately on each several thing about which he is considering, he will make the nearest approach to the knowledge of it?"

"Certainly."

"Would not he, then, do this with the utmost purity, who should in the highest degree approach each subject by means of the mere mental faculties, neither employing the sight in conjunction with the reflective faculty, nor introducing any other sense together with reasoning; but who, using pure reflection by itself, should attempt to search out each essence purely by itself, freed as much as possible from the eyes and ears, and, in a word, from the whole body, as disturbing the soul, and not suffering it to acquire truth and wisdom, when it is in communion with it. Is not he the person, Simmias, if any one can, who will arrive at the knowledge of that which is?"

"You speak with wonderful truth, Socrates," replied Simmias.

"Wherefore," he said, "it necessarily follows from all this, that some such opinion as this should be entertained by genuine philosophers, so that they should speak among themselves as follows: 'A by-path, as it were, seems to lead us on in our researches undertaken by reason,' because as long as we are encumbered with the body, and our soul is contaminated with such an evil, we can never fully attain to what we desire; and this, we say, is truth. For the body subjects us to innumerable hinderances on account of its necessary support, and moreover if any diseases befall us, they impede us in our search after that which is; and it fills us with longings, desires, fears, all kinds of fancies, and a multitude of absurdities, so that, as it is said in real truth, by reason of the body it is never possible for us to make any advances in wisdom.

"For nothing else but the body and its desires occasions wars, seditions, and contests; for all wars among us arise on account of our desire to acquire wealth; and we are compelled to acquire wealth on account of the body, being enslaved to its service; and consequently on all these accounts we are hindered in the pursuit of philosophy. But the worst of all is, that if it leaves us any leisure, and we apply ourselves to the consideration of any subject, it constantly obtrudes itself in the midst of our researches, and occasions trouble and disturbance, and confounds us so that we are not able by reason of it to discern the truth. It has then in reality been demonstrated to us, that if we are ever to know anything purely, we must be separated from the body, and contemplate the things themselves by the mere soul. And then, as it seems, we shall obtain that which we desire, and which we profess ourselves to be lovers of, wisdom, when we are dead, as reason shows, but not while we are alive. For if it is not possible to know anything purely in conjunction with the body, one of these two things must follow, either that we can never acquire knowledge, or only after we are dead; for then the soul will subsist apart by itself, separate from the body, but not before. And while we live, we shall thus, as it seems, approach nearest to knowledge, if we hold no intercourse or communion at all with the body, except what absolute necessity requires, nor suffer ourselves to be polluted by its nature, but purify ourselves from it, until God himself shall release us. And thus being pure, and freed from the folly of body, we shall in all likelihood be with others like ourselves, and shall of ourselves know the whole real essence, and that probably is truth; for it is not allowable for the impure to attain to the pure. Such things, I think, Simmias, all true lovers of wisdom must both think and say to one another. Does it not seem so to you?"

"Most assuredly, Socrates."

"If this, then," said Socrates, "is true, my friend, there is great hope for one who arrives where I am going, there, if anywhere, to acquire that perfection for the sake of which we have taken so much pains during our past life; so that the journey now appointed me is set out upon with good hope, and will be so by any other man who thinks that his mind has been as it were purified.

"This earth and the whole region here are decayed and corroded, as things in the sea by the saltness; for nothing of any value grows in the sea, nor, in a word, does it contain anything perfect, but there are caverns, and sand, and mud in abundance, and filth in whatever parts of the sea there is earth, nor are they at all worthy to be compared with the beautiful things with us. But, on the other hand, those things in the upper regions of the earth would appear far more to excel the things with us. For, if we may tell a beautiful fable, it is well worth hearing, Simmias, what kind the things are on the earth beneath the heavens."

"Indeed, Socrates," said Simmias, "we should be very glad to hear that fable."

"First of all, then, my friend," he continued, "this earth, if anyone should survey it from above, is said to have the appearance of balls covered with twelve different pieces of leather, variegated and distinguished with colors, of which the colors found here, and which painters use, are as it were copies. But there the whole earth is composed of such, and far more brilliant and pure than these; for one part of it is purple, and of wonderful beauty, part of a golden color, and part of white, more white than chalk or snow, and in like manner composed of other colors, and those more in number and more beautiful than any we have ever beheld. And those very hollow parts of the earth, though filled with water and air, exhibit a certain species of color, shining among the variety of other colors, so that one continually variegated aspect presents itself to the view. In this earth, being such, all things that grow grow in a manner proportioned to its nature—trees, flowers, and fruits; and again, in like manner, its mountains and stones possess, in the same proportion, smoothness and transparency and more beautiful colors; of which the well-known stones here that are so highly prized are but fragments, such as sardin-stones, jaspers, and emeralds, and all of that kind. But there, there is nothing subsists that is not of this character, and even more beautiful than these.

"But the reason of this is, because the stones there are pure, and not eaten up and decayed, like those here, by rottenness and saltness, which flow down hither together, and which produce deformity and disease in the stones and the earth, and in other things, even animals and plants. But that earth is adorned with all these, and moreover with gold and silver, and other things of the kind: for they are naturally conspicuous, being numerous and large, and in all parts of the earth; so that to behold it is a sight for the blessed. There are also many other animals and men upon it, some dwelling in mid-earth, others about the air, as we do about the sea, and others in islands which the air flows round, and which are near the continent: and in one word, what water and the sea are to us for our necessities, the air is to them; and what air is to us, that ether is to them.

"But their seasons are of such a temperament that they are free from disease, and live for a much longer time than those here, and surpass us in sight, hearing, and smelling, and everything of this kind, as much as air excels water, and ether air, in purity. Moreover, they have abodes and temples of the gods, in which gods really dwell, and voices and oracles, and sensible visions of the gods, and such-like intercourse with them; the sun, too, and moon, and stars, are seen by them such as they really are, and their felicity in other respects is correspondent with these things.

"And such, indeed, is the nature of the whole earth and the parts about the earth; but there are many places all round it throughout its cavities, some deeper and more open than that in which we dwell: but others that are deeper have less chasm than in our region, and other are shallower in depth than they are here, and broader.

"But all these are in many places perforated one into another under the earth, some with narrower and some with wider channels, and have passages through, by which a great quantity of water flows from one into another, as into basins, and there are immense bulks of ever-flowing rivers under the earth, both of hot and cold water, and a great quantity of fire, and mighty rivers of fire, and many of liquid mire, some purer and some more miry, as in Sicily there are rivers of mud that flow before the lava, and the lava itself, and from these the several places are filled, according as the overflow from time to time happens to come to each of them. But all these move up and down as it were by a certain oscillation existing in the earth. And this oscillation proceeds from such natural cause as this: one of the chasms of the earth is exceedingly large, and perforated through the entire earth, and is that which Homer [1] speaks of, ' very far off, where is the most profound abyss beneath the earth,' which elsewhere both he and many other poets have called Tartarus. For into this chasm all rivers flow together, and from it flow out again, but they severally derive their character from the earth through which they flow.

"And the reason why all streams flow out from thence and flow into it is because this liquid has neither bottom nor base. Therefore it oscillates and fluctuates up and down, and the air and the wind around it do the same; for they accompany it, both when it rushes to those parts of the earth, and when to these. And as in respiration the flowing breath is continually breathed out and drawn in, so there the wind, oscillating with the liquid, causes certain vehement and irresistible winds both as it enters and goes out. When, therefore, the water rushing in descends to the place which we call the lower region, it flows through the earth into the streams there and

[1] *Iliad*, lib. viii., v. 14.

fills them, just as men pump up water. But when again it leaves those regions and rushes hither, it again fills the rivers here, and these, when filled, flow through channels and through the earth, and having severally reached the several places to which they are journeying, they make seas, lakes, rivers, and fountains.

"Then sinking again from thence beneath the earth, some of them having gone round longer and more numerous places, and others round fewer and shorter, they again discharge themselves into Tartarus, some much lower than they were drawn up, others only a little so, but all of them flow in again beneath the point at which they flowed out. And some issue out directly opposite the place by which they flow in, others on the same side: there are also some which having gone round altogether in a circle, folding themselves once or several times round the earth, like serpents, when they had descended as low as possible, discharge themselves again; and it is possible for them to descend on either side as far as the middle, but not beyond; for in each direction there is an acclivity to the streams both ways.

"Now there are many other large and various streams, and among this great number there are four certain streams, of which the largest, and that which flows most outwardly round the earth, is called Ocean, but directly opposite this, and flowing in a contrary direction, is Acheron, which flows through other desert places, and moreover passing under the earth, reaches the Acherusian lake, where the souls of most who die arrive, and having remained there for certain destined periods, some longer and some shorter, are again sent forth into the generations of animals. A third river issues midway between these, and near its source falls into a vast region, burning with abundance of fire, and forms a lake larger than our sea, boiling with water and mud; from hence it proceeds in a circle, turbulent and muddy, and folding itself round it reaches both other places and the extremity of the Acherusian lake, but does not mingle with its water; but folding itself oftentimes beneath the earth, it discharges itself into the lower parts of Tartarus. And this is the river which they call Pyriphlegethon, whose burning streams emit dissevered fragments in whatever part of the earth they happen to be. Opposite to this again the fourth river first falls into a place dreadful and savage, as it is said, having its whole color like *cyanus*: this they call Stygian, and the lake which the river forms by its discharge, Styx. This river having fallen in here, and received awful power in the water, sinking beneath the earth, proceeds, folding itself round, in an opposite course to Pyriphlegethon, and meets it in the Acherusian lake from a contrary direction. Neither does the water of this river mingle with any other, but it, too, having gone round in a circle, discharges itself into Tartarus opposite to Pyriphlegethon. Its name, as the poets say, is Cocytus.

" These things being thus constituted, when the dead arrive at the place to which their demon leads them severally, first of all they are judged, as well those who have lived well and piously as those who have not. And those who appear to have passed a middle kind of life, proceeding to Acheron, and embarking in the vessels they have, on these arrive at the lake, and there dwell, and when they are purified, and have suffered punishment for the iniquities they may have committed, they are set free, and each receives the reward of his good deeds, according to his deserts: but those who appear to be incurable, through the magnitude of their offences, either from having committed many and great sacrileges, or many unjust and law-less murders, or other similar crimes, these a suitable destiny hurls into Tartarus, whence they never come forth.

" But those who appear to have been guilty of curable yet great offences, such as those who through anger have com-mitted any violence against father or mother, and have lived the remainder of their life in a state of penitence, or they who have become homicides in a similar manner, these must of necessity fall into Tartarus, but after they have fallen, and have been there for a year, the wave casts them forth, the homicides into Cocytus, but the parricides and matricides into Pyriphlege-thon: but when, being borne along, they arrive at the Ache-rusian lake, there they cry out to and invoke, some those whom they slew, others those whom they injured, and invoking them they entreat and implore them to suffer them to go out into the lake, and to receive them, and if they persuade them they go out and are freed from their sufferings; but if not, they are borne back to Tartarus, and thence again to the rivers, and they do not cease from suffering this until they have persuaded those whom they have injured, for this sentence was imposed on them by the judges.

"But those who are found to have lived an eminently holy life, these are they who, being freed and set at large from these regions in the earth, as from a prison, arrive at the pure abode above, and dwell on the upper parts of the earth. And among these, they who have sufficiently purified themselves by philosophy shall live without bodies, throughout all future time, and shall arrive at habitations yet more beautiful than these, which it is neither easy to describe nor at present is there sufficient time for the purpose.

"But for the sake of these things which we have described, we should use every endeavor, Simmias, so as to acquire virtue and wisdom in this life; for the reward is noble, and the hope great.

"To affirm positively, indeed, that these things are exactly as I have described them does not become a man of sense; that however either this or something of the kind takes place with respect to our souls and their habitations—since our soul is certainly immortal—this appears to me most fitting to be believed, and worthy the hazard for one who trusts in its reality; for the hazard is noble, and it is right to allure ourselves with such things, as with enchantments; for which reason I have prolonged my story to such a length.

"On account of these things, then, a man ought to be confident about his soul who during this life has disregarded all the pleasures and ornaments of the body as foreign from his nature, and who, having thought that they do more harm than good, has zealously applied himself to the acquirement of knowledge, and who having adorned his soul not with a foreign but its own proper ornament—temperance, justice, fortitude, freedom, and truth—thus waits for his passage to Hades, as one who is ready to depart whenever destiny shall summon him. You, then," he continued, "Simmias and Cebes, and the rest, will each of you depart at some future time; but now 'destiny summons me,' as a tragic writer would say, and it is nearly time for me to betake myself to the bath; for it appears to me to be better to drink the poison after I have bathed myself, and not to trouble the women with washing my dead body."

When he had thus spoken, Crito said: "So be it, Socrates, but what commands have you to give to these or to me, either respecting your children or any other matter, in attending to which we can most oblige you?"

"What I always say, Crito," he replied, "nothing new; that by taking care of yourselves you will oblige both me and mine and yourselves, whatever you do, though you should not now promise it; but if you neglect yourselves, and will not live as it were in the footsteps of what has been now and formerly said, even though you should promise much at present, and that earnestly, you will do no good at all."

"We will endeavor then so to do," he said; "but how shall we bury you?"

"Just as you please," he said, "if only you can catch me, and I do not escape from you." And at the same time smiling gently, and looking round on us, he said: "I cannot persuade Crito, my friends, that I am that Socrates who is now conversing with you, and who methodizes each part of the discourse; but he thinks that I am he whom he will shortly behold dead, and asks how he should bury me. But that which I some time since argued at length, that when I have drunk the poison I shall no longer remain with you, but shall depart to some happy state of the blessed, this I seem to have urged to him in vain, though I meant at the same time to console both you and myself. Be ye then my sureties to Crito," he said, "in an obligation contrary to that which he made to the judges; for he undertook that I should remain; but do you be sureties that, when I die, I shall not remain, but shall depart, that Crito may more easily bear it, and when he sees my body either burnt or buried, may not be afflicted for me, as if I suffered some dreadful thing, nor say at my interment that Socrates is laid out, or is carried out, or is buried.

"For be well assured," he said, "most excellent Crito, that to speak improperly is not only culpable as to the thing itself, but likewise occasions some injury to our souls. You must have a good courage, then, and say that you bury my body, and bury it in such a manner as is pleasing to you, and as you think is most agreeable to our laws."

When he had said thus he rose and went into a chamber to bathe, and Crito followed him, but he directed us to wait for him. We waited, therefore, conversing among ourselves about what had been said, and considering it again, and sometimes speaking about our calamity, how severe it would be to us, sincerely thinking that, like those who are deprived of a father, we should pass the rest of our life as orphans. When he had bathed, and his children were brought to him, for he had two little sons, and one grown up; and the women belonging to his family were come, having conversed with them in the presence of Crito and given them such injunctions as he wished, he directed the women and children to go away, and then returned to us. And it was now near sunset; for he spent a considerable time within.

But when he came from bathing he sat down, and did not speak much afterward; then the officer of the Eleven came in, and standing near him, said: "Socrates, I shall not have to find that fault with you that I do with others, that they are angry with me and curse me, when, by order of the archons, I bid them drink the poison. But you, on all other occasions during the time you have been here, I have found to be the most noble, meek, and excellent man of all that ever came into this place; and therefore I am now well convinced that you will not be angry with me (for you know who are to blame) but with them. Now, then, for you know what I came to announce to you, farewell; and endeavor to bear what is inevitable as easily as possible." And at the same time, bursting into tears, he turned away and withdrew.

And Socrates, looking after him, said: "And thou too, farewell; we will do as you direct." At the same time turning to us, he said: "How courteous the man is; during the whole time I have been here he has visited me, and conversed with me sometimes, and proved the worthiest of men; and now how generously he weeps for me. But come, Crito, let us obey him, and let some one bring the poison, if it is ready pounded, but if not, let the man pound it."

Then Crito said: "But I think, Socrates, that the sun is

still on the mountains and has not yet set. Besides, I know
that others have drunk the poison very late, after it had been
announced to them, and have supped and drunk freely, and
some even have enjoyed the objects of their love. Do not
hasten, then, for there is yet time."

Upon this Socrates replied: "These men whom you mention, Crito, do these things with good reason, for they think
they shall gain by so doing, and I too with good reason shall
not do so; for I think I shall gain nothing by drinking a little
later, except to become ridiculous to myself, in being so fond
of life, and sparing of it when none any longer remains. Go,
then," he said, "obey, and do not resist."

Crito having heard this, nodded to the boy that stood near.
And the boy having gone out, and stayed for some time, came,
bringing with him the man that was to administer the poison,
who brought it ready pounded in a cup. And Socrates, on seeing the man, said: "Well, my good friend, as you are skilled
in these matters, what must I do?"

"Nothing else," he replied, "than when you have drunk it
walk about until there is a heaviness in your legs, then lie
down; thus it will do its purpose." And at the same time he
held out the cup to Socrates. And he having received it very
cheerfully, Echecrates, neither trembling nor changing at all
in color or countenance, but, as he was wont, looking stead-
fastly at the man, said: "What say you of this potion, with
respect to making a libation to anyone, is it lawful or not?"

"We only pound so much, Socrates," he said, "as we
think sufficient to drink."

"I understand you," he said; "but it is certainly both lawful and right to pray to the gods, that my departure hence
thither may be happy; which therefore I pray, and so may it
be." And as he said this he drank it off readily and calmly.
Thus far, most of us were with difficulty able to restrain ourselves from weeping, but when we saw him drinking, and having finished the draught, we could do so no longer; but in spite
of myself the tears came in full torrent, so that, covering my
face, I wept for myself, for I did not weep for him, but for my
own fortune, in being deprived of such a friend. But Crito, even
before me when he could not restrain his tears, had risen up.

But Apollodorus, even before this, had not ceased weeping, and then bursting into an agony of grief, weeping and lamenting, he pierced the heart of everyone present except Socrates himself. But he said: "What are you doing, my admirable friends? I indeed, for this reason chiefly, sent away the women that they might not commit any folly of this kind. For I have heard that it is right to die with good omens. Be quiet, therefore, and bear up."

When we heard this we were ashamed and restrained our tears. But he, having walked about, when he said that his legs were growing heavy, laid down on his back; for the man so directed him. And at the same time he who gave him the poison, taking hold of him, after a short interval examined his feet and legs; and then having pressed his foot hard, he asked if he felt it.

He said that he did not.

And after this he pressed his thighs; and thus going higher, he showed us that he was growing cold and stiff.

Then Socrates touched himself, and said that when the poison reached his heart he should then depart.

But now the parts around the lower belly were almost cold; when, uncovering himself (for he had been covered over), he said, and they were his last words: "Crito, we owe a cock to Æsculapius; pay it, therefore, and do not neglect it!"

"It shall be done," said Crito; "but consider whether you have anything else to say?"

To this question he gave no reply; but shortly after he gave a convulsive movement, and the man covered him, and his eyes were fixed; and Crito, perceiving it, closed his mouth and eyes.

This, Echecrates, was the end of our friend, a man, as we may say, the best of all of his time that we have known, and, moreover, the most wise and just.

BRENNUS BURNS ROME

B.C. 388

BARTHOLD GEORG NIEBUHR

Julius Cæsar is the first writer who gives us an authentic and en-
lightening account of the Gauls, whom he divided into three groups.
The Gauls were the chief branch of the great original stock of Celts.
They were a nomadic people, and from their home in Western Europe
they spread to Britain, invaded Spain, and swarmed over the Alps into
Italy, and it is from the latter event that this tall, fair, and fighting nation
first came into the region of history.

Before the Gauls had come within the borders of Italy, Camillus, the
Dictator, had dealt the death-blow to the Etruscan League through his
capture and destruction of its stronghold, Veii. But at the very summit
of his triumph he lost the grace of his countrymen by demanding a tenth
of their spoil taken at Veii, and which he claimed to have vowed to
Apollo. It was popularly considered a ruse to increase his private
fortune. Furthermore, a counter-claim was brought against him for appropriating bronze gates, which in Rome at that time were nothing less
than actual money—bronze being the medium of currency. Camillus
went into exile in consequence of the accusation. His parting prayer
was that his country might feel his need and call him back. His desire
was fulfilled, for soon after " the Gaul was at the gates " under the leadership of the haughty Brennus, who had come upon the Romans at a most
opportune moment. This event of the overthrow of the Romans on the
Alia has been the occasion for the well-known tale of the cackling of the
geese in the temple of Juno, which alarmed the garrison. The episode
also gave rise to the saying of the conqueror, Brennus, who, when reproached by his antagonists with using false weights, cast his sword into
the scale, crying, " Woe to the conquered ! "

AT that time no Roman foresaw the calamity which was
threatening the empire. Rome had become great, because
the country which she had conquered was weak through its oligarchical institutions; the subjects of the other states gladly
joined the Romans, because under them their lot was more
favorable, and probably because they were kindred nations.
But matters went with the Romans as they did with Basilius,
who subdued the Armenians when they were threatened by

the Turks, and who soon after attacked the whole Greek empire and took away far more than had been gained before.

The expedition of the Gauls into Italy must be regarded as a migration, and not as an invasion for the purpose of conquest: as for the historical account of it, we must adhere to Polybius and Diodorus, who place it shortly before the taking of Rome by the Gauls. We can attach no importance to the statement of Livy that they had come into Italy as early as the time of Tarquinius Priscus, having been driven from their country by a famine. It undoubtedly arose from the fact that some Greek writer, perhaps Timæus, connected this migration with the settlement of the Phocians at Massilia. It is possible that Livy even here made use of Dionysius; and that the latter followed Timæus; for as Livy made use of Dionysius in the eighth book, why not also in the fifth? He himself knew very little of Greek history;[1] but Justin's account is here evidently opposed to Livy.

Trogus Pompeius was born in the neighborhood of Massilia, and in writing his forty-third book he obviously made use of native chronicles, for from no other source could he derive the account of the *decreta honorifica* of the Romans to the Massilians for the friendship which the latter had shown to the Romans during the Gallic war; and from the same source must he have obtained his information about the maritime wars of Massilia against Carthage. Trogus knows nothing of the story that the Gauls assisted the Phocians on their arrival; but according to him, they met with a kind reception among the Ligurians, who continued to inhabit those parts for a long time after. Even the story of the *lucumo* who is said to have invited the Gauls is opposed to him, and if it were referred to Clusium alone it would be absurd. Polybius places the passage of the Gauls across the Alps about ten or twenty years before the taking of Rome; and Diodorus describes them as advancing toward Rome by an uninterrupted march. It is further stated that Melpum in the country of the Insubrians was destroyed on the same day as Veii: without admitting this coincidence, we have no reason to doubt that the statement is substantially true; and it is made by Cornelius Nepos, who, as

[1] Comp. *Hist. of Rome*, vol. iii. n. 485.

a native of Gallia Transpadana, might possess accurate information, and whose chronological accounts were highly esteemed
by the Romans.

There was no other passage for the Gauls except either
across the Little St. Bernard or across the Simplon; it is not
probable that they took the former road, because their country
extended only as far as the Ticinus, and if they had come
across the Little St. Bernard, they would naturally have occupied also all the country between that mountain and the
Ticinus.   The Salassi may indeed have been a Gallic people,
but it is by no means certain; moreover, between them and
the Gauls who had come across the Alps the Lævi also lived;
and there can be no doubt that at that time Ligurians still
continued to dwell on the Ticinus.

Melpum must have been situated in the district of Milan.
The latter place has an uncommonly happy situation: often as
it has been destroyed, it has always been restored, so that it is
not impossible that Melpum may have been situated on the
very spot afterward occupied by Milan.   The Gallic migration
undoubtedly passed by like a torrent with irresistible rapidity:
how then is it possible to suppose that Melpum resisted them
for two centuries, or that they conquered it and yet did not
disturb the Etruscans for two hundred years?   It would be
absurd to believe it, merely to save an uncritical expression of
Livy.   According to the common chronology, the Triballi,
who in the time of Herodotus inhabited the plains, and were
afterward expelled by the Gauls, appeared in Thrace twelve
years after the taking of Rome—according to a more correct
chronology it was only nine years after that event.   It was the
same movement assuredly which led the Gauls to the countries
through which the middle course of the Danube extends, and
to the Po; and could the people who came in a few days from
Clusium to Rome, and afterward appeared in Apulia, have
been sitting quiet in a corner of Italy for two hundred years?
If they had remained there because they had not the power to
advance, they would have been cut to pieces by the Etruscans.
We must therefore look upon it as an established fact, that
the migration took place at the late period mentioned by Polybius and Diodorus.

These Gauls were partly Celts, and partly (indeed principally) Belgæ or Cymri, as may be perceived from the circumstance that their king, as well as the one who appeared before Delphi, is called Brennus. *Brenin*, according to Adelung, in his *Mithridates*, signifies in the language of Wales and Lower Brittany a *king*. But what caused this whole emigration? The statement of Livy, that the Gauls were compelled by famine to leave their country, is quite in keeping with the nature of all traditions about migrations, such as we find them in Saxo Grammaticus, in Paul Warnefried from the sagas of the Swedes, in the Tyrrhenian traditions of Lydia, and others. However, in the case of a people like the Celts, every specific statement of this kind, in which even the names of their leaders are mentioned, is of no more value than the traditions of other barbarous nations which were unacquainted with the art of writing. It is indeed well known that the Celts in writing used the Greek alphabet, but they probably employed it only in the transactions of daily life; for we know that they were not allowed to commit their ancient songs to writing.

During the Gallic migration we are again made aware how little we know of the history of Italy generally: our knowledge is limited to Rome, so that we are in the same predicament there, as if of all the historical authorities of the whole German empire we had nothing but the annals of a single imperial city. According to Livy's account, it would seem as if the only object of the Gauls had been to march to Rome; and yet this immigration changed the whole aspect of Italy. After the Gauls had once crossed the Apennines, there was no further obstacle to prevent their marching to the south of Italy by any road they pleased; and it is in fact mentioned that they did proceed farther south. The Umbrians still inhabited the country on the lower Po, in the modern Romagna and Urbino, parts of which were occupied by Liburnians. Polybius says that many people there became tributary to the Gauls, and that this was the case with the Umbrians is quite certain.

The first historical appearance of the Gauls is at Clusium, whither a noble Clusine is said to have invited them for the purpose of taking vengeance on his native city. Whether this account is true, however, must remain undecided, and if there

is any truth in it, it is more probable that the offended Clusine
went across the Apennines and fetched his avengers.   Clusium
has not been mentioned since the time of Porsena; the fact of
the Clusines soliciting the aid of Rome is a proof how little
that northern city of Etruria was concerned about the fate of
the southern towns, and makes us even suspect that it was
allied with Rome; however, the danger was so great that all
jealousy must have been suppressed.   The natural road for the
Gauls would have been along the Adriatic, then through the
country of Umbrians who were tributary to them and already
quite broken down, and thence through the Romagna across
the Apennines.

But the Apennines which separate Tuscany from the Romagna are very difficult to cross, especially for sumpter-horses;
as therefore the Gauls could not enter Etruria on that
side—which the Etruscans had intentionally allowed to grow
wild—and as they had been convinced of this in an unsuccessful attempt, they crossed the Apennines in the neighborhood
of Clusium, and appeared before that city.   Clusium was the
great bulwark of the valley of the Tiber; and if it were taken,
the roads along the Tiber and the Arno would be open, and
the Gauls might reach Arezzo from the rear: the Romans
therefore looked upon the fate of Clusium as decisive of their
own.   The Clusines sued for a treaty with the mighty city of
Rome, and the Romans were wise enough readily to accept
the offer: they sent ambassadors to the Gauls, ordering them
to withdraw.   According to a very probable account, the Gauls
had demanded of the Clusines a division of their territory as
the condition of peace, and not, as was customary with the
Romans, as a tax upon a people already subdued: if this is
correct, the Romans sent the embassy confiding in their own
strength.   But the Gauls scorned the ambassadors, and the
latter, allowing themselves to be carried away by their warlike
disposition, joined the Etruscans in a fight against the Gauls.
This was probably only an insignificant and isolated engagement.   Such is the account of Livy, who goes on to say that
the Gauls, as soon as they perceived this violation in the law
of nations, gave the signal for a retreat, and, having called upon
the gods to avenge the wrong, marched against Rome.

This is evidently a mere fiction, for a barbarous nation like the Gauls cannot possibly have had such ideas, nor was there in reality any violation of the law of nations, as the Romans stood in no kind of connection with the Gauls. But it was a natural feeling with the Romans to look upon the fall of their city as the consequence of a *nefas,* which no human power could resist. Roman vanity also is at work here, inasmuch as the Roman ambassadors are said to have so distinguished themselves that they were recognized by the barbarians among the hosts of Etruscans. Now, according to another tradition directly opposed to these statements, the Gauls sent to Rome to demand the surrender of those ambassadors: as the senate was hesitating and left the decision to the people, the latter not only rejected the demand, but appointed the same ambassadors to the office of military tribunes, whereupon the Gauls with all their forces at once marched toward Rome.

Livy here again speaks of the *populus* as the people to whom the senate left the decision: this must have been the patricians only, for they alone had the right to decide upon the fate of the members of their own order. It is not fair to accuse the Romans on that occasion of dishonesty; but this account assuredly originated with later writers, who transferred to barbarians the right belonging to a nation standing in a legal relation to another. The statement that the three ambassadors, all of whom were Fabii, were appointed military tribunes, is not even the usual one, for there is another in Diodorus, who must here have used Roman authorities written in Greek, that is, Fabius; since he calls the Cærites Καίριοι and not 'Αγυλλαῖοι. He speaks of a single ambassador, who being a son of a military tribune fought against the Gauls. This is at least a sign how uncertain history yet is. The battle on the Alia was fought on the 16th of July; the military tribunes entered upon their office on the first of that month; and the distance between Clusium and Rome is only three good days' marches. It is impossible to restore the true history, but we can discern what is fabulous from what is really historical.

An innumerable host of Gauls now marched from Clusium toward Rome. For a long time the Gauls were most formidable to the Romans, as well as to all other nations with whom they came in contact, even as far east as the Ukraine; as to Rome, we see this as late as the Cisalpine war of the year A.U. 527. Polybius and Diodorus are our best guides in seeking for information about the manners of the Gauls, for in the time of Cæsar they had already become changed. In the description of their persons we partly recognize the modern Gael, or the inhabitants of the Highlands of Scotland: huge bodies, blue eyes, bristly hair; even their dress and armor are those of the Highlanders, for they wore the checked and variegated tartans; their arms consisted of the broad, unpointed battle-sword, the same weapon as the claymore among the Highlanders. They had a vast number of horns, which were used in the Highlands for many centuries after, and threw themselves upon the enemy in immense irregular masses with terrible fury, those standing behind impelling those stationed in front, whereby they became irresistible by the tactics of those times.

The Romans ought to have used against them their phalanx and doubled it, until they were accustomed to this enemy and were enabled by their greater skill to repel them. If the Romans had been able to withstand their first shock, the Gauls would have easily been thrown into disorder, and put to flight. The Gauls who were subsequently conquered by the Romans were the descendants of such as were born in Italy, and had lost much of their courage and strength. The Goths under Vitiges, not fifty years after the immigration of Theodoric into Italy, were cowards, and unable to resist the twenty thousand men of Belisarius: showing how easily barbarians degenerate in such climates.

The Gauls, moreover, were terrible on account of their inhuman cruelty, for, wherever they settled, the original towns and their inhabitants completely disappeared from the face of the earth. In their own country they had the feudal system and a priestly government: the Druids were their only rulers, who avenged the oppressed people on the lords, but in their turn became tyrants: all the people were in the condition of serfs, a proof that the Gauls, in their own country too, were the conquerors who had subdued an earlier population. We always find mention of the wealth of the Gauls in gold, and yet France has no rivers that carry gold-sand, and the Pyrenees were then no longer in their possession: the gold must therefore have been obtained by barter. Much may be exaggeration; and the fact of some noble individuals wearing gold chains was probably transferred by ancient poets to the whole nation, since popular poetry takes great liberty, especially in such embellishments.

Pliny states that previous to the Gallic calamity the census amounted to one hundred and fifty thousand persons, which probably refers only to men entitled to vote in the assemblies, and does not comprise women, children, slaves, and strangers. If this be correct, the number of citizens was enormous; but it must not be supposed to include the inhabitants of the city only, the population of which was doubtless much smaller. The statement of Diodorus that all men were called to arms to resist the Gauls, and that the number amounted to forty thousand, is by no means improbable: according to the testimony of Polybius, Latins and Hernicans also were enlisted. Another account makes the Romans take the field against the Gauls with twenty-four thousand men, that is, with four field legions and four civic legions: the field legions were formed only of plebeians, and served, according to the order of the classes, probably in *maniples;* the civic legions contained all those who belonged neither to the patricians nor to the plebeians, that is, all the *aerarii, proletarii,* freedmen, and artisans who had never before faced an enemy. They were certainly not armed with the *pilum,* nor drawn up in *maniples;* but used pikes and were employed in phalanxes.

Now as for the field legions, each consisted half of Latins and half of Romans, there being in each *maniple* one century of Roman and one of Latins. There were at that time four legions, and as a legion, including the reserve troops, contained three thousand men, the total is twelve thousand; now the account which mentions twenty-four thousand men must have presumed that there were four field legions and four irregular civic ones. There would accordingly have been no more than six thousand plebeians, and, even if the legions were all made up of Romans, only twelve thousand; if in addition to these we take twelve thousand irregular troops and sixteen thousand allies, the number of forty thousand would be completed. In this case, the population of Rome would not have been as large as that of Athens in the Peloponnesian war, and this is indeed very probable. The cavalry is not included in this calculation: but forty thousand must be taken as the maximum of the whole army. There seems to be no exaggeration in this statement, and the battle on the Alia, speaking generally, is an historical event.

It is surprising that the Romans did not appoint a dictator to command in the battle; it cannot be said indeed that they regarded this war as an ordinary one, for in that case they would not have raised so great a force, but they cannot have comprehended the danger in all its greatness. New swarms continued to come across the Alps; the Senones also now appeared to seek habitations for themselves; they, like the Germans in after-times, demanded land, as they found the In- subrians, Boians, and others already settled; the latter had taken up their abode in Umbria, but only until they should find a more extensive and suitable territory.

The Romans committed the great mistake of fighting with their hurriedly collected troops a battle against an enemy who had hitherto been invincible. The hills along which the right wing is said to have been drawn up are no longer discernible, and they were probably nothing but little mounds of earth: at any rate it was senseless to draw up a long line against the immense mass of enemies. The Gauls, on the other hand, were enabled without any difficulty to turn off to the left. They proceeded to a higher part of the river, where it was more easily fordable, and with great prudence threw them- selves with all their force upon the right wing, consisting of the civic legions. The latter at first resisted, but not long; and when they fled, the whole remaining line, which until then seems to have been useless and inactive, was seized with a panic.

Terror preceded the Gauls as they laid waste everything on their way, and this paralyzed the courage of the Romans, instead of rousing them to a desperate resistance. The Romans therefore were defeated on the Alia in the most inglorious manner. The Gauls had taken them in their rear, and cut off their return to Rome. A portion fled toward the Tiber, where some effected a retreat across the river, and others were drowned; another part escaped into a forest. The loss of life must have been prodigious, and it is inconceivable how Livy could have attached so much importance to the mere disgrace. If the Roman army had not been almost annihilated, it would not have been necessary to give up the defence of the city, as was done, for the city was left undefended and deserted by all. Many fled to Veii instead of returning to Rome: only a few, who had escaped along the high road, entered the city by the Colline gate.

Rome was exhausted, her power shattered, her legions defenceless, and her warlike allies had partly been beaten in the same battle, and were partly awaiting the fearful enemy in their own countries. At Rome it was believed that the whole army was destroyed, for nothing was known of those who had reached Veii. In the city itself there were only old men, women, and children, so that there was no possibility of defending it. It is, however, inconceivable that the gates should have been left open, and that the Gauls, from fear of a stratagem, should have encamped for several days outside the gates. A more probable account is that the gates were shut and barricaded. We may form a vivid conception of the condition of Rome after this battle, by comparing it with that of Moscow before the conflagration: the people were convinced that a long defence was impossible, since there was probably a want of provisions.

Livy gives a false notion of the evacuation of the city, as if the defenceless citizens had remained immovable in their consternation, and only a few had been received into the Capitol. The determination, in fact, was to defend the Capitol, and the tribune Sulpicius had taken refuge there, with about one thousand men. There was on the Capitol an ancient well which still exists, and without which the garrison would soon have perished. This well remained unknown to all antiquaries, till I discovered it by means of information gathered from the people who live there. Its depth in the rock descends to the level of the Tiber, but the water is now not fit to drink. The

Capitol was a rock which had been hewn steep, and thereby
made inaccessible, but a *clivus,* closed by gates both below
and above, led up from the Forum and the Sacred Way. The
rock, indeed, was not so steep as in later times, as is clear
from the account of the attempt to storm it; but the Capitol
was nevertheless very strong. Whether some few remained
in the city, as at Moscow, who in their stupefaction did not
consider what kind of enemy they had before them, cannot be
decided. The narrative is very beautiful, and reminds us of
the taking of the Acropolis of Athens by the Persians, where,
likewise, the old men allowed themselves to be cut down by
the Persians.

Notwithstanding the improbability of the matter, I am
inclined to believe that a number of aged patricians—their
number may not be exactly historical—sat down in the Forum,
in their official robes, on their curule chairs, and that the chief
pontiff devoted them to death. Such devotions are a well-
known Roman custom. It is certainly not improbable that
the Gauls were amazed when they found the city deserted, and
only these old men sitting immovable, that they took them for
statues or supernatural visions, and did nothing to them, until
one of them struck a Gaul who touched him, whereupon all
were slaughtered. To commit suicide was repugnant to the
customs of the Romans, who were guided in many things by
feelings more correct and more resembling our own, than
many other ancient nations. The old men, indeed, had given
up the hope of their country being saved; but the Capitol
might be maintained, and the survivors preferred dying in the
attempt of self-defence to taking refuge at Veii, where after
all they could not have maintained themselves in the end.

The sacred treasures were removed to Cære, and the hope
of the Romans now was that the barbarians would be tired of
the long siege. Provisions for a time had been conveyed to
the Capitol, where a couple of thousand men may have been
assembled, and where all buildings, temples, as well as public
and private houses, were used as habitations. The Gauls made
fearful havoc at Rome, even more fearful than the Spaniards
and Germans did in the year 1527. Soldiers plunder, and
when they find no human beings they engage in the work of

destruction; and fires break out, as at Moscow, without the existence of any intention to cause a conflagration. The whole city was changed into a heap of ashes, with the exception of a few houses on the Palatine, which were occupied by the leaders of the Gauls. It is astonishing to find, nevertheless, that a few monuments of the preceding period, such as statues, situated at some distance from the Capitol, are mentioned as having been preserved; but we must remember that *travertino* is tolerably fireproof. That Rome was burned down is certain; and when it was rebuilt, not even the ancient streets were restored.

The Gauls were now encamped in the city. At first they attempted to storm the *clivus*, but were repelled with great loss, which is surprising, since we know that at an earlier time the Romans succeeded in storming it against Appius Herdonius. Afterward they discovered the footsteps of a messenger who had been sent from Veii, in order that the State might be taken care of in due form; for the Romans in the Capitol were patricians, and represented the *curies* and the Government, whereas those assembled at Veii represented the tribes, but had no leaders. The latter had resolved to recall Camillus, and raise him to the dictatorship. For this reason Pontius Cominius had been sent to Rome to obtain the sanction of the senate and the curies. This was quite in the spirit of the ancient times. If the curies had interdicted him *aqua et igni*, they alone could recall him, if they previously obtained a resolution of the senate authorizing them to do so; but if he had gone into voluntary exile, and had given up his Roman franchise by becoming a citizen of Ardea before a sentence had been passed upon him by the centuries, it was again in the power of the curies alone, he being a patrician, to recall him as a citizen; and otherwise he could not have become dictator, nor could he have regarded himself as such.

It was the time of the dog-days when the Gauls came to Rome, and as the summer at Rome is always pestilential, especially during the two months and a half before the first of September, the unavoidable consequence must have been, as Livy relates, that the barbarians, bivouacking on the ruins of the city in the open air, were attacked by disease and carried

off, like the army of Frederick Barbarossa when encamped
before the castle of St. Angelo. The whole army of the Gauls,
however, was not in the city, but only as many as were necessary to blockade the garrison of the Capitol; the rest were
scattered far and wide over the face of the country, and were
ravaging all the unprotected places and isolated farms in
Latium; many an ancient town, which is no longer mentioned
after this time, may have been destroyed by the Gauls. None
but fortified places like Ostia, which could obtain supplies by
sea, made a successful resistance, for the Gauls were unacquainted with the art of besieging.

The Ardeatans, whose territory was likewise invaded by
the Gauls, opposed them, under the command of Camillus; the
Etruscans would seem to have endeavored to avail themselves
of the opportunity of recovering Veii, for we are told that the
Romans at Veii, commanded by Cædicius, gained a battle
against them, and that, encouraged by this success, they began
to entertain a hope of regaining Rome, since by this victory
they got possession of arms.

A Roman of the name of Fabius Dorso is said to have
offered up, in broad daylight, a *gentilician* sacrifice on the
Quirinal; and the astonished Gauls are said to have done him
no harm—a tradition which is not improbable.

The provisions in the Capitol were exhausted, but the
Gauls themselves being seized with epidemic diseases became
tired of their conquests, and were not inclined to settle in a
country so far away from their own home. They once more
attempted to take the Capitol by storm, having observed that
the messenger from Veii had ascended the rock, and come
down again near the Porta Carmentalis, below Araceli. The
ancient rock is now covered with rubbish, and no longer discernible. The besieged did not think of a storm on that side;
it may be that formerly there had in that part been a wall,
which had become decayed; and in southern countries an
abundant vegetation always springs up between the stones,
and if this had actually been neglected it cannot have been
very difficult to climb up. The Gauls had already gained a
firm footing, as there was no wall at the top—the rock which
they stormed was not the Tarpeian, but the Arx—when Manlius,

who lived there, was roused by the screaming of the geese: he came to the spot and thrust down those who were climbing up.

This rendered the Gauls still more inclined to commence negotiations; they were, moreover, called back by an inroad of some Alpine tribes into Lombardy, where they had left their wives and children: they offered to depart if the Romans would pay them a ransom of a thousand pounds of gold, to be taken no doubt from the Capitoline treasury. Considering the value of money at that time, the sum was enormous: in the time of Theodosius, indeed, there were people at Rome who possessed several hundredweight of gold, nay, one is said to have had an annual revenue of two hundredweight. There can be no doubt that the Gauls received the sum they demanded, and quitted Rome; that in weighing it they scornfully imposed upon the Romans is very possible, and the *vae victis* too may be true: we ourselves have seen similar things before the year 1813.

But there can be no truth in the story told by Livy, that while they were disputing Camillus appeared with an army and stopped the proceedings, because the military tribunes had had no right to conclude the treaty. He is there said to have driven the Gauls from the city, and afterward in a twofold battle to have so completely defeated them that not even a messenger escaped. Beaufort, inspired by Gallic patriotism, has most excellently shown what a complete fable this story is. To attempt to disguise the misfortunes of our forefathers by substituting fables in their place is mere childishness. This charge does not affect Livy, indeed, for he copied only what others had written before him; but he did not allow his own conviction to appear as he generally does, for he treats the whole of the early history with a sort of irony, half believing, half disbelieving it.

According to another account in Diodorus, the Gauls besieged a town allied with Rome—its name seems to be miswritten, but is probably intended for Vulsinii—and the Romans relieved it and took back from the Gauls the gold which they had paid them; but this siege of Vulsinii is quite unknown to Livy. A third account in Strabo and also mentioned by Diodorus does not allow this honor to the Romans, but states that

the Cærites pursued the Gauls, attacked them in the country
of the Sabines, and completely annihilated them.   In like manner the Greeks endeavored to disguise the fact that the Gauls
took the money from the Delphic treasury, and that in a quite
historical period (Olymp. 120).   The true explanation is undoubtedly the one found in Polybius, that the Gauls were
induced to quit Rome by an insurrection of the Alpine tribes,
after it had experienced the extremity of humiliation.

Whatever the enemy had taken as booty was consumed;
they had not made any conquests, but only indulged in plunder
and devastation; they had been staying at Rome for seven or
eight months, and could have gained nothing further than the
Capitol and the very money which they received without taking that fortress.   The account of Polybius throws light upon
many discrepant statements, and all of them, not even except-
ing Livy's fairy-tale-like embellishment, may be explained by
means of it.   The Romans attempted to prove that the Gauls
had actually been defeated, by relating that the gold afterward
taken from the Gauls and buried in the Capitol was double
the sum paid to them as a ransom; but it is much more probable that the Romans paid their ransom out of the treasury of
the temple of the Capitoline Jupiter and of other temples, and
that afterward double this sum was made up by a tax; which
agrees with a statement in the history of Manlius, that a tax
was imposed for the purpose of raising the Gallic ransom:
surely this could not have been done at the time of the siege,
when the Romans were scattered in all parts of the country,
but must have taken place afterward for the purpose of restoring the money that had been taken.   Now if at a later time
there actually existed in the Capitol such a quantity of gold, it
is clear that it was believed to be a proof that the Gauls had
not kept the gold which was paid to them.

Even as late as the time of Cicero and Cæsar, the spot was
shown at Rome in the Carinæ, where the Gauls had heaped up
and burned their dead; it was called *busta Gallica*, which was
corrupted in the Middle Ages into Protogallo, whence the
church which was built there was in reality called *S. Andreas
in bustis Gallicis*, or, according to the later Latinity, *in busta
Gallica—busta Gallica* not being declined.

The Gauls departed with their gold, which the Romans had been compelled to pay on account of the famine that prevailed in the Capitol, which was so great that they pulled the leather from their shields and cooked it, just as was done during the siege of Jerusalem. The Gauls were certainly not destroyed. Justin has preserved the remarkable statement that the same Gauls who sacked Rome went to Apulia, and there offered for money their assistance to the elder Dionysius of Syracuse. From this important statement it is at any rate clear that they traversed all Italy, and then probably returned along the shore of the Adriatic: their devastations extended over many parts of Italy, and there is no doubt that the Æquians received their death-blow at that time, for henceforth we hear no more of the hostilities of the Æquians against Rome. Præneste, on the other hand, which must formerly have been subject to the Æquians, now appears as an independent town. The Æquians, who inhabited small and easily destructible towns, must have been annihilated during the progress of the Gauls.

There is nothing so strange in the history of Livy as his view of the consequences of the Gallic calamity; he must have conceived it as a transitory storm by which Rome was humbled but not broken. The army, according to him, was only scattered, and the Romans appear afterward just as they had been before, as if the preceding period had only been an evil dream, and as if there had been nothing to do but to rebuild the city. But assuredly the devastation must have been tremendous throughout the Roman territory: for eight months the barbarians had been ravaging the country, every trace of cultivation, every farmer's house, all the temples and public buildings were destroyed; the walls of the city had been purposely pulled down, a large number of its inhabitants were led into slavery, the rest were living in great misery at Veii; and what they had saved scarcely sufficed to buy their bread. In this condition they returned to Rome. Camillus as dictator is called a second Romulus, and to him is due the glory of not having despaired in those distressing circumstances.

TARTAR INVASION OF CHINA BY MEHA

B.C. 341

DEMETRIUS CHARLES BOULGER

The first Chinese are supposed to have been a nomad tribe in the provinces of Shensi, which lies in the northwest of China, and among them at last appeared a ruler, Fohi, whose name at least has been preserved. His deeds and his person are mythical, but he is credited with having given his country its first regular institutions.

The annalists of the Chinese chronicles placed the date of the Creation at a point of time two millions of years before Confucius; this interval they filled up with lines of dynasties. Preceding the Chow dynasty the chronicles give ten epochs—prior to the eighth of these there is no authentic history. Yew-chow She (the "Nest-having") taught the people to build huts of the boughs of trees. Fire was discovered by Say-jin She (the "Fire producer"). Fuh-he (B.C. 2862) was the discoverer of iron. With Yaou (B.C. 2356) is the period whence Confucius begins his story. He says of that epoch: "The house door could safely be left open." Yaou greatly extended and strengthened the empire and established fairs and marts over the land.

One of China's most notable rulers was Tsin Chi Hwangti, who was studious in providing for the security of his empire, and with this object began the construction of a fortified wall across the northern frontier to serve as a defence against the troublesome Hiongnou tribes, who are identified with the Huns of Attila. This wall, which he began in the first years of his reign—about the close of the third century B.C.—was finished before his death. It still exists, known as the Great Wall of China, and has long been considered one of the wonders of the world. Every third man of the whole empire was employed on this work. It is said that five hundred thousand of them died of starvation. The contents of the Great Wall would be enough to build two walls six feet high and two feet thick around the equator. It is the largest artificial structure in the world; carried for fourteen hundred miles over height and hollow, reaching in one place the level of five thousand feet—nearly one mile—above the sea. Earth, gravel, brick, and stone were used in its construction.

The weak successors of Hwangti finally gave way to the usurper, Kaotsou, who had been originally the ruler of a small town, and had borne the name of Lieou Pang.

The reign of Kaotsou was distinguished by the consolidation of the empire; the connection of Western with Eastern China by high walls and bridges, some of which are still in perfect condition, and the institution of an elaborate code of court etiquette. His attention to these things was, however, rudely interrupted by an irruption of the Hiongnou Tartars.

THE death of Tsin Chi Hwangti proved the signal for the outbreak of disturbances throughout the realm. Within a few months five princes had founded as many kingdoms, each hoping, if not to become supreme, at least to remain independent. Moungtien, beloved by the army, and at the head, as he tells us in his own words, of three hundred thousand soldiers, might have been the arbiter of the empire; but a weak feeling of respect for the imperial authority induced him to obey an order, sent by Eulchi, Hwangti's son and successor, commanding him "to drink the waters of eternal life." Eulchi's brief reign of three years was a succession of misfortunes. The reins of office were held by the eunuch Chow-kow, who first murdered the minister Lissep and then Eulchi himself.

Ing Wang, a grandson of Hwangti, was the next and last of the Tsin emperors. On coming to power, he at once caused Chow-kow, whose crimes had been discovered, to be arrested and executed. This vigorous commencement proved very transitory, for when he had enjoyed nominal authority during six weeks, Ing Wang's troops, after a reverse in the field, went over in a body to Lieou Pang, the leader of a rebel force. Ing Wang put an end to his existence, thus terminating, in a manner not less ignominious than any of its predecessors, the dynasty of the Tsins, which Hwangti had hoped to place permanently on the throne of China, and to which his genius gave a lustre far surpassing that of many other families who had enjoyed the same privilege during a much longer period.

The crisis in the history of the country had afforded one of those great men who rise periodically from the ranks of the people to give law to nations the opportunity for advancing his personal interests at the same time that he made them appear to be identical with the public weal. Of such geniuses, if the test applied be the work accomplished, there have been few with higher claims to respectful and admiring consideration than Lieou Pang, who after the fall of the Tsins became the founder of the Han dynasty under the style of Kaotsou. Originally the governor of a small town, he had, soon after the death of Hwangti, gathered round him the nucleus of a formidable army, and while nominally serving under one of the greater princes, he scarcely affected to conceal that he was fighting for his own interest. On the other hand, he was no mere soldier of fortune, and the moderation which he showed after victory enhanced his reputation as a general. The path to the throne being thus cleared, the successful general became emperor.

His first act was to proclaim an amnesty to all those who had borne arms against him. In a public proclamation he expressed his regret at the suffering of the people "from the evils which follow in the train of war." During the earlier years of his reign he chose the city of Loyang as his capital— now the flourishing and populous town of Honan—but at a later period he removed it to Singanfoo, in the western province of Shensi. His dynasty became known by the name of the small state where he was born, and which had fallen early in his career into his hands.

Kaotsou sanctioned or personally undertook various important public works, which in many places still exist to testify to the greatness of his character. Prominent among those must be placed the bridges constructed along the great roads of Western China. Some of them are still believed to be in perfect condition. No act of Kaotsou's reign places him higher in the scale of sovereigns than the improvement of the roads and the construction of those remarkable bridges. Kaotsou loved splendor and sought to make his receptions and banquets imposing by their brilliance. He drew up a special ceremonial which must have proved a trying ordeal for his courtiers, and dire was the offence if it were infringed in the smallest particular. He kept up festivities at Singanfoo for several weeks, and on one of these occasions he exclaimed: "To-day I feel I am emperor and perceive all the difference between a subject and his master."

Kaotsou's attention was rudely summoned away from these trivialities by the outbreak of revolts against his authority and by inroads on the part of the Tartars. The latter were the more serious. The disturbances that followed Hwangti's death were a fresh inducement to these clans to again gather round a common head and prey upon the weakness of China, for Kaotsou's authority was not yet recognized in many of the tributary states which had been fain to admit the supremacy of the great Tsin emperor. About this time the Hiongnou[1] Tartars were governed by two chiefs in particular, one named Tonghou, the other Meha or Mehe. Of these the former appears to have been instigated by a reckless ambition or an overweening arrogance, and at first it seemed that the forbearance of Meha would allow his pretensions[2] to pass unchallenged.

Meha's successes followed rapidly upon each other. Issuing from the desert, and marching in the direction of China, he wrested many fertile districts from the feeble hands of those who held them; and while establishing his personal authority on the banks of the Hoangho, his lieutenants returned laden with plunder from expeditions into the rich provinces of Shensi and Szchuen. He won back all the territory lost by his ancestors to Hwangti and Moungtien, and he paved the way to greater success by the siege and capture of the city of Maye, thus obtaining possession of the key of the road to Tsinyang. Several of the border chiefs and of the Emperor's lieutenants, dreading the punishment allotted in China to want of success, went over to the Tartars, and took service under Meha.

The Emperor, fully aroused to the gravity of the danger, assembled his army, and placing himself at its head marched against the Tartars. Encouraged by the result of several preliminary encounters, the Emperor was eager to engage Meha's main army, and after some weeks' searching and manœuvring,

[1] Probably the same race as the Huns.

[2] Meha had become chief of his clan by murdering his father, Teouman, who was on the point of ordering his son's assassination when thus forestalled in his intention. Tonghou sent to demand from him a favorite horse, which Meha sent him. His kinsmen advised him to refuse compliance; but he replied: "What! Would you quarrel with your neighbors for a horse?" Shortly afterward Tonghou sent to ask for one of the wives of the former chief. This also Meha granted, saying: "Why should we undertake a war for the sake of a woman?" It was only when Tonghou menaced his possessions that Meha took up arms.

the two forces halted in front of each other. Kaotsou, imagining that victory was within his grasp, and believing the stories
brought to him by spies of the weakness of the Tartar army,
resolved on an immediate attack. He turned a deaf ear to the
cautious advice of one of his generals, who warned him that
"in war we should never despise an enemy," and marched in
person at the head of his advance guard to find the Tartars.
Meha, who had been at all these pains to throw dust in the
Emperor's eyes and to conceal his true strength, no sooner saw
how well his stratagem had succeeded, and that Kaotsou was
rushing into the trap so elaborately laid for him, than by a skilful movement he cut off his communications with the main body
of his army, and, surrounding him with an overwhelming force,
compelled him to take refuge in the city of Pingching in Shensi.

With a very short supply of provisions, and hopelessly outnumbered, it looked as if the Chinese Emperor could not possibly escape the grasp of the desert chief. In this strait one
of his officers suggested as a last chance that the most beautiful virgin in the town should be discovered, and sent as a
present to mollify the conqueror. Kaotsou seized at this suggestion, as the drowning man will catch at a straw, and the
story is preserved, though her name has passed into oblivion,
of how the young Chinese girl entered into the plan and
devoted all her wits to charming the Tartar conqueror. She
succeeded as much as their fondest hopes could have led them
to believe; and Meha permitted Kaotsou, after signing an ignominious treaty, to leave his place of confinement and rejoin
his army, glad to welcome the return of the Emperor, yet without him helpless to stir a hand to effect his release. Meha
retired to his own territory, well satisfied with the material
results of the war and the rich booty which had been obtained in
the sack of Chinese cities, while Kaotsou, like the ordinary type
of an oriental ruler, vented his discomfiture on his subordinates.

The closing acts of the war were the lavishing of rewards
on the head of the general to whose warnings he had paid no
heed, and the execution of the scouts who had been misled by
the wiles of Meha.

The success which had attended this incursion and the spoil
of war were potent inducements to the Tartars to repeat the

invasion. While Kaotsou was meditating over the possibility
of revenge, and considering schemes for the better protection
of his frontier, the Tartars, disregarding the truce that had
been concluded, retraced their steps, and pillaged the border
districts with impunity. In this year (B.C. 199) they were
carrying everything before them, and the Emperor, either un-
nerved by recent disaster or appalled at the apparently irresistible energy of the followers of Meha, remained apathetic
in his palace. The representations of his ministers and generals failed to rouse him from his stupor, and the weapon to
which he resorted was the abuse of his opponent, and not his
prompt chastisement. Meha was "a wicked and faithless man,
who had risen to power by the murder of his father, and one
with whom oaths and treaties carried no weight." In the
mean while the Tartars were continuing their victorious career.
The capital itself could not be pronounced safe from their
assaults, or from the insult of their presence.

In this crisis counsels of craft and dissimulation alone found
favor in the Emperor's cabinet. No voice was raised in support of the bold and only true course of going forth to meet
the national enemy. The capitulation of Pingching had for
the time destroyed the manhood of the race, and Kaotsou held
in esteem the advice of men widely different to those who had
placed him on the throne. Kaotsou opened fresh negotiations
with Meha, who concluded a treaty on condition of the Emperor's daughter being given to him in marriage, and on the
assumption that he was an independent ruler. With these
terms Kaotsou felt obliged to comply, and thus for the first
time this never-ceasing collision between the tribes of the
desert and the agriculturists of the plains of China closed with
the admitted triumph of the former. The contest was soon
to be renewed with different results, but the triumph of Meha
was beyond question.[1]

The weakness thus shown against a foreign foe brought its
own punishment in domestic troubles. The palace became
the scene of broils, plots, and counterplots, and so badly did

---

[1] One historian had the courage to declare that " Never was so great
a shame inflicted on the Middle Kingdom, which then lost its dignity and
honor."

Kaotsou manage his affairs at this epoch that one of his favor-ite generals raised the standard of revolt against him through apparently a mere misunderstanding. In this instance Kaot-sou easily put down the rising, but others followed which, if not pregnant with danger, were at the least extremely trouble-some. The murder of Hansin, to whose aid Kaotsou owed his elevation to the throne as much as to any other, by order of the empress, during a reception at the palace, shook confidence still more in the ruler, and many of his followers were forced into open rebellion through dread of personal danger. What wonder that, as he has said, "the very name of revolt inspired Kaotsou with apprehension."

In B.C. 195 we find Kaotsou going out of his way to visit the tomb of Confucius. Shortly after this event it became evident that he was approaching his end. His eldest son Hiaohoei was proclaimed heir apparent. Kaotsou died in the fifty-third year of his age, having reigned as emperor during eight years. The close of his reign did not bear out all the promise of its commencement; and the extent of his authority was greatly curtailed by the disastrous effects of the war with the Tartars and the subsequent revolts among his generals.

Despite these reverses there remains much in favor of his character. He had performed his part in the consolidation of the Hans; it remained for those who came after him to com-plete what he left half finished.

Under Hoeiti, the Tartar King Meha sent an envoy to the capital, but either the form or the substance of his message enraged the empress-mother, who ordered his execution. The two peoples were thus again brought to the brink of war, but eventually the difference was sunk for the time, and the Chi-nese chroniclers have represented that the satisfactory turn in the question was due to Meha seeing the error of his ways.[1] Not long afterward the Tartar King died, and was succeeded by his son Lao Chang.

---

[1] Meha's letter of excuse is thus given: "In the barbarous country which I govern both virtue and the decencies of life are unknown. I have been unable to free myself from them, and, therefore, I blush. China has her wise men; that is a happiness which I envy. They would have prevented my being wanting in the respect due to your rank."

ALEXANDER REDUCES TYRE: LATER FOUNDS ALEXANDRIA

B.C. 332

OLIVER GOLDSMITH

The master spirit who could sigh for more worlds to conquer was at this time high in his dazzling flight. Alexander has always been considered one of the most striking and picturesque characters of history. His personality was pleasing, his endurance remarkable, and courage dauntless. Educated by Aristotle, his keen mind was well trained. He was skilled in horsemanship, and his control over the fiery Bucephalus, untamable by others, has become a household tale in all lands. There never was a more kingly prince.

A king at twenty, his career has been an object of wonder to succeeding generations. He shot like a meteor across the sky of ancient civilization. His military achievements were remarkable for quickness of conception and rapidity of execution; his life was a progress from conquest to conquest. Alexander's army, with its solid phalanx, its darting cavalry, and light troops, had become irresistible. He possessed Napoleon's ability to select good generals and to make the most of his talents. In battle Alexander was entirely devoid of fear. After a victory his chief thoughts were for the wounded. Like Napoleon, he also possessed that personal equation of absolute popularity with his soldiers. Their devotion to him was simply complete.

After Thebes came the invasion of Asia. The invincible Macedonian had fought and won the battle of the Granicus. In this battle nearly all of the Persian leaders were slain, and its result spread terror throughout Persia. Halicarnassus was next reduced. The march of Alexander was ever onward. In the citadel of Gordium he cut the "Gordian knot," and prophecy marked him for the lord of Asia.

And now Darius marched to meet him, making a fatally bad choice of battle-ground. Darius was totally defeated at the celebrated battle of Issus, although he had anticipated a victory. After the Persian rout and the flight of Darius, whose numbers counted for nothing before the Macedonian's skill, Lindon welcomed the invaders, and Alexander determined to take Tyre. This was accomplished after a siege, which was attended with much cruelty.

The siege of Gaza followed, in which nearly all of the citizens perished.

In B.C. 332 Alexander began his expedition to Egypt. He conciliated the natives by paying honors to their gods. In his progress he was struck by the advantages of a certain site for a city, and founded there the town which is now called Alexandria.

ALL Phœnicia was subdued except Tyre, the capital city. This city was justly entitled the " Queen of the Sea," that element bringing to it the tribute of all nations. She boasted of having first invented navigation and taught mankind the art of braving the winds and waves by the assistance of a frail bark. The happy situation of Tyre, at the upper end of the Mediterranean; the conveniency of its ports, which were both safe and capacious; and the character of its inhabitants, who were industrious, laborious, patient, and extremely courteous to strangers, invited thither merchants from all parts of the globe; so that it might be considered, not so much a city belonging to any particular nation, as the common city of all nations and the centre of their commerce.

Alexander thought it necessary, both for his glory and his interest, to take this city. The spring was now coming on. Tyre was at that time seated on an island of the sea, about a quarter of a league from the continent. It was surrounded by a strong wall, a hundred and fifty feet high, which the waves of the sea washed; and the Carthaginians, a colony from Tyre, a mighty people, and sovereigns of the ocean, promised to come to the assistance of their parent State. Encouraged, therefore, by these favorable circumstances, the Tyrians determined not to surrender, but to hold out the place to the last extremity. This resolution, however imprudent, was certainly magnanimous, but it was soon after followed by an act which was as blamable as the other was praiseworthy.

Alexander was desirous of gaining the place rather by treaty than by force of arms, and with this in view sent heralds into the town with offers of peace; but the inhabitants were so far from listening to his proposals, or endeavoring to avert his resentment by any kind of concession, that they actually killed his ambassadors and threw their bodies from the top of the walls into the sea. It is easy to imagine what effect so shocking an outrage must produce in a mind like Alexander's. He instantly resolved to besiege the place, and not to desist until he had made himself master of it and razed it to the ground.

As Tyre was divided from the continent by an arm of the sea, there was necessity for filling up the intermediate space with a bank or pier, before the place could be closely invested. This work, accordingly, was immediately undertaken and in a great measure completed; when all the wood, of which it was principally composed, was unexpectedly burned by means of a fire-ship sent in by the enemy. The damage, however, was very soon repaired, and the mole rendered more perfect than formerly, and carried nearer to the town, when all of a sudden a furious tempest arose, which, undermining the stonework that supported the wood, laid the whole at once in the bottom of the sea.

Two such disasters, following so closely on the heels of each other, would have cooled the ardor of any man except Alexander, but nothing could daunt his invincible spirit, or make him relinquish an enterprise he had once undertaken. He, therefore, resolved to prosecute the siege; and in order to encourage his men to second his views, he took care to inspire them with the belief that heaven was on their side and would soon crown their labors with the wished-for success. At one time he gave out that Apollo was about to abandon the Tyrians to their doom, and that, to prevent his flight, they had bound him to his pedestal with a golden chain; at another, he pretended that Hercules, the tutelar deity of Macedon, had appeared to him, and, having opened prospects of the most glorious kind, had invited him to proceed to take possession of Tyre.

These favorable circumstances were announced by the augurs as intimations from above; and every heart was in consequence cheered. The soldiers, as if that moment arrived before the city, forgetting all the toils they had undergone and the disappointments they had suffered, began to raise a new mole, at which they worked incessantly.

To protect them from being annoyed by the ships of the enemy, Alexander fitted out a fleet, with which he not only secured his own men, but offered the Tyrians battle, which, however, they thought proper to decline, and withdrew all their galleys into the harbor.

The besiegers, now allowed to proceed unmolested, went on with the work with the utmost vigor, and in a little time completed it and brought it close to the walls. A general attack was therefore resolved on, both by sea and land, and with this in view the King, having manned his galleys and joined them together with strong cables, ordered them to approach the walls about midnight and attack the city with resolution. But just as the assault was going to begin, a dreadful storm arose, which not only shook the ships asunder, but even shattered them in a terrible manner, so that they were all obliged to be towed toward the shore, without having made the least impression on the city.

The Tyrians were elated with this gleam of good fortune; but that joy was of short duration, for in a little time they received intelligence from Carthage that they must expect no assistance from that quarter, as the Carthaginians themselves were then overawed by a powerful army of Syracusans, who had invaded their country. Reduced, therefore, to the hard necessity of depending entirely upon their own strength and their own resources, the Tyrians sent all their women and children to Carthage, and prepared to encounter the very last extremities. For now the enemy was attacking the place with greater spirit and activity than ever. And, to do the Tyrians justice, it must be acknowledged that they employed a number of methods of defence which, considering the rude state of the art of war at that early period, were really astonishing. They warded off the darts discharged from the ballisters against them, by the assistance of turning wheels, which either broke them to pieces or carried them another way. They deadened the violence of the stones that were hurled at them, by setting up sails and curtains made of a soft substance which easily gave way.

To annoy the ships which advanced against their walls, they fixed grappling irons and scythes to joists or beams; then, straining their catapultas—an enormous kind of crossbow—they laid those great pieces of timber upon them instead of arrows, and shot them off on a sudden at the enemy.

These crushed some of their ships by their great weight, and, by means of the hooks or hanging scythes, tore others to pieces. They also had brazen shields, which they drew red-hot out of the fire; and filling these with burning sand, hurled them in an instant from the top of the wall upon the enemy.

There was nothing the Macedonians dreaded so much as this fatal instrument; for the moment the burning sand got to the flesh through the crevices of the armor, it penetrated to the very bone, and stuck so close that there was no pulling it off; so that the soldiers, throwing down their arms, and tearing their clothes to pieces, were in this manner exposed, naked and defenceless, to the shot of the enemy.

Alexander, finding the resources and even the courage of the Tyrians increased in proportion as the siege continued, resolved to make a last effort, and attack them at once both by sea and land, in order, if possible, to overwhelm them with the multiplicity of dangers to which they would be thus exposed. With this view, having manned his galleys with some of the bravest of his troops, he commanded them to advance against the enemy's fleet, while he himself took his post at the head of his men on the mole.

And now the attack began on all sides with irresistible and unremitting fury. Wherever the battering-rams had beat down any part of the wall, and the bridges were thrown out, instantly the argyraspides mounted the breach with the utmost valor, being led on by Admetus, one of the bravest officers in the army, who was killed by the thrust of a spear as he was encouraging his soldiers.

The presence of the King, and the example he set, fired his troops with unusual bravery. He himself ascended one of the towers on the mole, which was of a prodigious height, and there was exposed to the greatest dangers he had ever yet encountered; for being immediately known by his insignia and the richness of his armor, he served as a mark for all the arrows of the enemy. On this occasion he performed wonders, killing with javelins several of those who defended the wall; then, advancing nearer to them, he forced some with his sword, and others with his shield, either into the city or the sea, the tower on which he fought almost touching the wall.

He soon ascended the wall, followed by his principal officers, and possessed himself of two towers and the space
between them.   The battering-rams had already made several
breaches; the fleet had forced its way into the harbor; and
some of the Macedonians had possessed themselves of the
towers which were abandoned.   The Tyrians, seeing the enemy
masters of their rampart, retired toward an open place, called
Agenor, and there stood their ground; but Alexander, marching up with his regiment of bodyguards, killed part of them
and obliged the rest to fly.

At the same time, Tyre being taken on that side which
lay toward the harbor, a general carnage of the citizens ensued, and none was spared, except the few that fell into the
hands of the Sidonians in Alexander's army, who—considering
the Tyrians as countrymen—granted them protection and carried them privately on board their ships.

The number that was slaughtered on this occasion is almost
incredible; even after conquest, the victor's resentment did
not subside.   He ordered no less than five thousand men, who
were taken in the storming, to be nailed to crosses along the
shore.   The number of prisoners amounted to thirty thousand
and were all sold as slaves in different parts of the world.
Thus fell Tyre, that had been for many ages the most flourishing city in the world, and had spread the arts and commerce
into the remotest regions.

While Alexander was employed in the siege of Tyre he
received a second letter from Darius, in which that monarch
treated him with greater respect than before.   He now gave
him the title of king; he offered him ten thousand talents as a
ransom for his captive mother and queen; and he promised
him his daughter Statira in marriage, with all the country he
had conquered, as far as the river Euphrates, provided he
would agree to a peace.   These terms were so advantageous
that, when the King debated upon them in council, Parmenio,
one of his generals, could not help observing that he would
certainly accept of them were he Alexander.   "And so would
I," replied the King, "were I Parmenio!"   But deeming it
inconsistent with his dignity to listen to any proposals from
a man whom he had so lately overcome, he haughtily rejected

them, and scorned to accept of that as a favor which he already considered his own by conquest.

From Tyre, Alexander marched to Jerusalem, fully determined to punish that city for having refused to supply his army with provisions during the siege; but his resentment was mollified by a deputation of the citizens coming out to meet him, with their high priest, Taddua, before them, dressed in white, and having a mitre on his head, on the front of which the name of God was written. The moment the King perceived the high priest, he advanced toward him with an air of the most profound respect, bowed his body, adored the august name upon his front, and saluted him who wore it with religious veneration.

And when some of his courtiers expressed their surprise that he, who was adored by everyone, should adore the high priest of the Jews: "I do not," said he, "adore the high priest, but the God whose minister he is; for while I was at Dium in Macedonia, my mind wholly fixed on the great design of the Persian war, as I was revolving the methods how to conquer Asia, this very man, dressed in the same robes, appeared to me in a dream, exhorted me to banish my fear, bade me cross the Hellespont boldly, and assured me that God would march at the head of my army and give me the victory over the Persians." This speech, delivered with an air of sincerity, no doubt had its effect in encouraging the army and establishing an opinion that his mission was from heaven.

From Jerusalem he went to Gaza, where, having met with a more obstinate resistance than he expected, he cut to pieces the whole garrison, consisting of ten thousand men. Not satisfied with this act of cruelty, he caused holes to be bored through the heels of Bœtis, the governor, and tying him with cords to the back of his chariot dragged him in this manner around the walls of the city. This he did in imitation of Achilles, whom Homer describes as having dragged Hector around the walls of Troy in the same manner. It was reading the past to very little, or rather, indeed, to very bad purpose, to imitate this hero in the most unworthy part of his character.

Alexander, having left a garrison in Gaza, turned his arms toward Egypt; of which he made himself master without oppo-

sition. Here he formed the design of visiting the temple of
Jupiter, which was situated in the sandy deserts of Lybia at
the distance of twelve days' journey from Memphis, the capital
of Egypt. His chief object in going thither was to get himself
acknowledged the son of Jupiter, an honor he had long aspired
to. In this journey he founded the city of Alexandria, which
soon became one of the greatest towns in the world for commerce.

Nothing could be more dreary than the desert through
which he passed, nor anything more charming—according to
the fabulous accounts of the poets—than the particular spot
where the temple was situated.

It was a perfect paradise in the midst of an immeasurable
wilderness. At last, having reached the place, and appeared
before the altar of the deity, the priest, who was no stranger
to Alexander's wishes, declared him to be the son of Jupiter.

The conqueror, elated with this high compliment, asked
whether he should have success in his expedition. The priest
answered that he should be monarch of the world. The conqueror inquired if his father's murderers were punished. The
priest replied that his father Jupiter was immortal, but that
the murderers of Philip had all been extirpated.

THE BATTLE OF ARBELA

B.C. 331

SIR EDWARD SHEPHERD CREASY

When Alexander, having returned from his campaign against the barbarians of the North, had suppressed a revolt which meanwhile had
broken out in Greece, he found himself free for undertaking those great
foreign conquests which he had planned. When he left Greece to conquer the world, he said farewell to his own country forever. Crossing
the Hellespont into Asia Minor with a small but well equipped and disci-
plined army, he advanced unopposed until he reached the river Granicus,
where he found himself confronted with a Persian host. Upon this army
he inflicted a defeat so signal as to bring at once to submission nearly
the whole of Asia Minor. He next advanced into Syria and met the
Persian king, Darius III, who in person commanded an immense body
of soldiers, against which the young conqueror fought at Issus, winning
a decisive victory. He not only captured the Persian camp, but also
secured the King's treasures and took his family prisoners. From this
time Alexander held complete mastery of the western dominions of
Darius, whom the conqueror afterward dethroned.

After he had next invaded and subjugated Egypt and there founded
the city of Alexandria, he pursued King Darius, who had taken flight,
into the very heart of his empire, where the Persian monarch, on the
plains of Gaugamela, near the village of Arbela, made his last stand
against his invincible foe. Of the battle to which Arbela gave its name,
and which proved the death-blow of the Persian empire, Creasy's narrative furnishes a realistic description.

A LONG and not uninstructive list might be made out of
illustrious men whose characters have been vindicated
during recent times from aspersions which for centuries had
been thrown on them. The spirit of modern inquiry, and the
tendency of modern scholarship, both of which are often said to
be solely negative and destructive, have, in truth, restored to
splendor, and almost created anew, far more than they have
assailed with censure or dismissed from consideration as un-
real.

The truth of many a brilliant narrative of brilliant exploits

141

has of late years been triumphantly demonstrated, and the shallowness of the sceptical scoffs with which little minds have carped at the great minds of antiquity has been in many instances decisively exposed. The laws, the politics, and the lines of action adopted or recommended by eminent men and powerful nations have been examined with keener investigation and considered with more comprehensive judgment than formerly were brought to bear on these subjects. The result has been at least as often favorable as unfavorable to the persons and the states so scrutinized, and many an oft-repeated slander against both measures and men has thus been silenced, we may hope forever.

The veracity of Herodotus, the pure patriotism of Pericles, of Demosthenes, and of the Gracchi, the wisdom of Clisthenes and of Licinius as constitutional reformers, may be mentioned as facts which recent writers have cleared from unjust suspicion and censure. And it might be easily shown that the defensive tendency which distinguishes the present and recent great writers of Germany, France, and England has been equally manifested in the spirit in which they have treated the heroes of thought and heroes of action who lived during what we term the Middle Ages, and whom it was so long the fashion to sneer at or neglect.

The name of the victor of Arbela has led to these reflections; for, although the rapidity and extent of Alexander's conquests have through all ages challenged admiration and amazement, the grandeur of genius which he displayed in his schemes of commerce, civilization, and of comprehensive union and unity among nations, has, until lately, been comparatively unhonored. This long-continued depreciation was of early date. The ancient rhetoricians—a class of babblers, a school for lies and scandal, as Niebuhr justly termed them—chose, among the stock themes for their commonplaces, the character and exploits of Alexander.

They had their followers in every age; and, until a very recent period, all who wished to "point a moral or adorn a tale," about unreasoning ambition, extravagant pride, and the formidable frenzies of free will when leagued with free power, have never failed to blazon forth the so-called madman of

Macedonia as one of the most glaring examples. Without doubt, many of these writers adopted with implicit credence traditional ideas, and supposed, with uninquiring philanthropy, that in blackening Alexander they were doing humanity good service. But also, without doubt, many of his assailants, like those of other great men, have been mainly instigated by "that strongest of all antipathies, the antipathy of a second-rate mind to a first-rate one," and by the envy which talent too often bears to genius.

Arrian, who wrote his history of Alexander when Hadrian was emperor of the Roman world, and when the spirit of declamation and dogmatism was at its full height, but who was himself, unlike the dreaming pedants of the schools, a statesman and a soldier of practical and proved ability, well rebuked the malevolent aspersions which he heard continually thrown upon the memory of the great conqueror of the East.

He truly says: "Let the man who speaks evil of Alexander not merely bring forward those passages of Alexander's life which were really evil, but let him collect and review *all* the actions of Alexander, and then let him thoroughly consider first who and what manner of man he himself is, and what has been his own career; and then let him consider who and what manner of man Alexander was, and to what an eminence of human grandeur *he* arrived. Let him consider that Alexander was a king, and the undisputed lord of the two continents, and that his name is renowned throughout the whole earth.

"Let the evil-speaker against Alexander bear all this in mind, and then let him reflect on his own insignificance, the pettiness of his own circumstances and affairs, and the blunders that he makes about these, paltry and trifling as they are. Let him then ask himself whether he is a fit person to censure and revile such a man as Alexander. I believe that there was in his time no nation of men, no city, nay, no single individual with whom Alexander's name had not become a familiar word. I therefore hold that such a man, who was like no ordinary mortal, was not born into the world without some special providence."

And one of the most distinguished soldiers and writers, Sir Walter Raleigh, though he failed to estimate justly the full merits of Alexander, has expressed his sense of the grandeur of the part played in the world by "the great Emathian conqueror" in language that well deserves quotation:

"So much hath the spirit of some one man excelled as it hath undertaken and effected the alteration of the greatest states and commonweals, the erection of monarchies, the conquest of kingdoms and empires, guided handfuls of men against multitudes of equal bodily strength, contrived victories beyond all hope and discourse of reason, converted the fearful passions of his own followers into magnanimity, and the valor of his enemies into cowardice; such spirits have been stirred up in sundry ages of the world, and in divers parts thereof, to erect and cast down again, to establish and to destroy, and to bring all things, persons, and states to the same certain ends which the infinite spirit of the *Universal*, piercing, moving, and governing all things, hath ordained. Certainly, the things that this King did were marvellous and would hardly have been undertaken by anyone else; and though his father had determined to have invaded the Lesser Asia, it is like enough that he would have contented himself with some part thereof, and not have discovered the river of Indus, as this man did."

A higher authority than either Arrian or Raleigh may now be referred to by those who wish to know the real merit of Alexander as a general, and how far the commonplace assertions are true that his successes were the mere results of fortunate rashness and unreasoning pugnacity. Napoleon selected Alexander as one of the seven greatest generals whose noble deeds history has handed down to us, and from the study of whose campaigns the principles of war are to be learned. The critique of the greatest conqueror of modern times on the military career of the great conqueror of the Old World is no less graphic than true:

"Alexander crossed the Dardanelles B.C. 334, with an army of about forty thousand men, of which one-eighth was cavalry; he forced the passage of the Granicus in opposition to an army under Memnon, the Greek, who commanded for Darius on the coast of Asia, and he spent the whole of the year 333 in establishing his power in Asia Minor. He was seconded by the Greek colonies, who dwelt on the borders of the Black Sea and on the Mediterranean, and in Sardis, Ephesus, Tarsus, Miletus, etc. The kings of Persia left their provinces and towns to be governed according to their own particular laws. Their empire was a union of confederated states, and did not form one nation; this facilitated its conquest. As Alexander only wished for the throne of the monarch, he easily effected the change by respecting the customs, manners, and laws of the people, who experienced no change in their condition.

"In the year 332 he met with Darius at the head of sixty thousand men, who had taken up a position near Tarsus, on the banks of the Issus, in the province of Cilicia. He defeated him, entered Syria, took Damascus, which contained all the riches of the Great King, and laid siege to Tyre. This superb metropolis of the commerce of the world detained him nine months.

"He took Gaza after a siege of two months; crossed the desert in seven days; entered Pelusium and Memphis, and founded Alexandria. In less than two years, after two battles and four or five sieges, the coasts of the Black Sea, from Phasis to Byzantium, those of the Mediterranean as far as Alexandria, all Asia Minor, Syria, and Egypt, had submitted to his arms.

"In 331 he repassed the desert, encamped in Tyre, recrossed Syria, entered Damascus, passed the Euphrates and Tigris, and defeated Darius on the field of Arbela when he was at the head of a still stronger army than that which he commanded on the Issus, and Babylon opened her gates to him. In 330 he overran Susa and took that city, Persepolis, and Pasargada, which contained the tomb of Cyrus. In 329 he directed his course northward, entered Ecbatana, and extended his conquests to the coasts of the Caspian, punished Bessus, the cowardly assassin of Darius, penetrated into Scythia, and subdued the Scythians.

"In 328 he forced the passage of the Oxus, received sixteen thousand recruits from Macedonia, and reduced the neighboring people to subjection. In 327 he crossed the Indus, vanquished Porus in a pitched battle, took him prisoner, and treated him as a king. He contemplated passing the Ganges, but his army refused. He sailed down the Indus, in the year

326, with eight hundred vessels; having arrived at the ocean, he sent Nearchus with a fleet to run along the coasts of the Indian Ocean and the Persian Gulf as far as the mouth of the Euphrates. In 325 he took sixty days in crossing from Gedrosia, entered Keramania, returned to Pasargada, Persepolis, and Susa, and married Statira, the daughter of Darius. In 324 he marched once more to the north, passed Ecbatana, and terminated his career at Babylon."

The enduring importance of Alexander's conquests is to be estimated, not by the duration of his own life and empire, or even by the duration of the kingdoms which his generals after his death formed out of the fragments of that mighty dominion. In every region of the world that he traversed, Alexander planted Greek settlements and founded cities, in the populations of which the Greek element at once asserted its predominance. Among his successors, the Seleucidæ and the Ptolemies imitated their great captain in blending schemes of civilization, of commercial intercourse, and of literary and scientific research with all their enterprises of military aggrandizement and with all their systems of civil administration.

Such was the ascendency of the Greek genius, so wonderfully comprehensive and assimilating was the cultivation which it introduced, that, within thirty years after Alexander crossed the Hellespont, the Greek language was spoken in every country from the shores of the Ægean to the Indus, and also throughout Egypt—not, indeed, wholly to the extirpation of the native dialects, but it became the language of every court, of all literature, of every judicial and political function, and formed a medium of communication among the many myriads of mankind inhabiting these large portions of the Old World.

Throughout Asia Minor, Syria, and Egypt the Hellenic character that was thus imparted remained in full vigor down to the time of the Mahometan conquests. The infinite value of this to humanity in the highest and holiest point of view has often been pointed out, and the workings of the finger of Providence have been gratefully recognized by those who have observed how the early growth and progress of Christianity were aided by that diffusion of the Greek language and civilization throughout Asia Minor, Syria, and Egypt which had been caused by the Macedonian conquest of the East.

In Upper Asia, beyond the Euphrates, the direct and material influence of Greek ascendency was more short-lived. Yet, during the existence of the Hellenic kingdoms in these regions, especially of the Greek kingdom of Bactria, the modern Bokhara, very important effects were produced on the intellectual tendencies and tastes of the inhabitants of those countries, and of the adjacent ones, by the animating contact of the Grecian spirit. Much of Hindu science and philosophy, much of the literature of the later Persian kingdom of the Arsacidæ, either originated from or was largely modified by Grecian influences. So, also, the learning and science of the Arabians were in a far less degree the result of original invention and genius than the reproduction, in an altered form, of the Greek philosophy and the Greek lore acquired by the Saracenic conquerors, together with their acquisition of the provinces which Alexander had subjugated, nearly a thousand years before the armed disciples of Mahomet commenced their career in the East.

It is well known that Western Europe in the Middle Ages drew its philosophy, its arts, and its science principally from Arabian teachers. And thus we see how the intellectual influence of ancient Greece, poured on the Eastern world by Alexander's victories, and then brought back to bear on mediæval Europe by the spread of the Saracenic powers, has exerted its action on the elements of modern civilization by this powerful though indirect channel, as well as by the more obvious effects of the remnants of classic civilization which survived in Italy, Gaul, Britain, and Spain, after the irruption of the Germanic nations.

These considerations invest the Macedonian triumphs in the East with never-dying interest, such as the most showy and sanguinary successes of mere "low ambition and the pride of kings," however they may dazzle for a moment, can never retain with posterity. Whether the old Persian empire which Cyrus founded could have survived much longer than it did, even if Darius had been victorious at Arbela, may safely be disputed. That ancient dominion, like the Turkish at the present time, labored under every cause of decay and dissolution. The satraps, like the modern pachas, continually rebelled against the central power, and Egypt in particular was almost always in a state of insurrection against its nominal sovereign. There was no longer any effective central control, or any internal principle of unity fused through the huge mass of the empire, and binding it together.

Persia was evidently about to fall; but, had it not been for Alexander's invasion of Asia, she would most probably have fallen beneath some other oriental power, as Media and Babylon had formerly fallen before herself, and as, in after-times, the Parthian supremacy gave way to the revived ascendency of Persia in the East, under the sceptres of the Arsacidæ. A revolution that merely substituted one Eastern power for another would have been utterly barren and unprofitable to mankind.

Alexander's victory at Arbela not only overthrew an oriental dynasty, but established European rulers in its stead. It broke the monotony of the eastern world by the impression of western energy and superior civilization, even as England's present mission is to break up the mental and moral stagnation of India and Cathay by pouring upon and through them the impulsive current of Anglo-Saxon commerce and conquest.

Arbela, the city which has furnished its name to the decisive battle which gave Asia to Alexander, lies more than twenty miles from the actual scene of conflict. The little village, then named Gaugamela, is close to the spot where the armies met, but has ceded the honor of naming the battle to its more euphonious neighbor. Gaugamela is situated in one of the wide plains that lie between the Tigris and the mountains of Kurdistan. A few undulating hillocks diversify the surface of this sandy tract; but the ground is generally level and admirably qualified for the evolutions of cavalry, and also calculated to give the larger of two armies the full advantage of numerical superiority.

The Persian King—who, before he came to the throne, had proved his personal valor as a soldier and his skill as a general —had wisely selected this region for the third and decisive encounter between his forces and the invader. The previous defeats of his troops, however severe they had been, were not looked on as irreparable. The Granicus had been fought by his generals rashly and without mutual concert; and, though Darius himself had commanded and been beaten at Issus, that defeat might be attributed to the disadvantageous nature of the ground, where, cooped up between the mountains, the river, and the sea, the numbers of the Persians confused and clogged alike the general's skill and the soldiers' prowess, and their very strength had been made their weakness. Here, on the broad plains of Kurdistan, there was scope for Asia's largest host to array its lines, to wheel, to skirmish, to condense or expand its squadrons, to manœuvre, and to charge at will. Should Alexander and his scanty band dare to plunge into that living sea of war, their destruction seemed inevitable.

Darius felt, however, the critical nature to himself as well as to his adversary of the coming encounter. He could not hope to retrieve the consequences of a third overthrow. The great cities of Mesopotamia and Upper Asia, the central provinces of the Persian empire, were certain to be at the mercy of the victor. Darius knew also the Asiatic character well enough to be aware how it yields to the *prestige* of success and the apparent career of destiny. He felt that the diadem was now either to be firmly replaced on his own brow or to be irrevocably transferred to the head of his European conqueror. He, therefore, during the long interval left him after the battle of Issus, while Alexander was subjugating Syria and Egypt, assiduously busied himself in selecting the best troops which his vast empire supplied, and in training his varied forces to act together with some uniformity of discipline and system.

The hardy mountaineers of Afghanistan, Bokhara, Khiva, and Tibet were then, as at present, far different from the generality of Asiatics in warlike spirit and endurance. From these districts Darius collected large bodies of admirable infantry; and the countries of the modern Kurds and Turkomans supplied, as they do now, squadrons of horsemen, hardy, skilful, bold, and trained to a life of constant activity and warfare. It is not uninteresting to notice that the ancestors of our own late enemies, the Sikhs, served as allies of Darius against the Macedonians. They are spoken of in Arrian as Indians who dwelt near Bactria. They were attached to the troops of that satrapy, and their cavalry was one of the most formidable forces in the whole Persian army.

Besides these picked troops, contingents also came in from the numerous other provinces that yet obeyed the Great King. Altogether, the horse are said to have been forty thousand, the scythe-bearing chariots two hundred, and the armed elephants fifteen in number. The amount of the infantry is uncertain; but the knowledge which both ancient and modern times supply of the usual character of oriental armies, and of their populations of camp-followers, may warrant us in believing that many myriads were prepared to fight or to encumber those who fought for the last Darius.

The position of the Persian King near Mesopotamia was chosen with great military skill. It was certain that Alexander, on his return from Egypt, must march northward along the Syrian coast before he attacked the central provinces of the Persian empire. A direct eastward march from the lower part of Palestine across the great Syrian Desert was then, as ever, utterly impracticable. Marching eastward from Syria, Alexander would, on crossing the Euphrates, arrive at the vast Mesopotamian plains. The wealthy capitals of the empire, Babylon, Susa, and Persepolis, would then lie to the south; and if he marched down through Mesopotamia to attack them, Darius might reasonably hope to follow the Macedonians with his immense force of cavalry, and, without even risking a pitched battle, to harass and finally overwhelm them.

We may remember that three centuries afterward a Roman army under Crassus was thus actually destroyed by the oriental archers and horsemen in these very plains, and that the ancestors of the Parthians who thus vanquished the Roman legions served by thousands under King Darius. If, on the contrary, Alexander should defer his march against Babylon, and first seek an encounter with the Persian army, the country on each side of the Tigris in this latitude was highly advantageous for such an army as Darius commanded, and he had close in his rear the mountainous districts of Northern Media, where he himself had in early life been satrap, where he had acquired reputation as a soldier and a general, and where he justly expected to find loyalty to his person, and a safe refuge in case of defeat.[1]

His great antagonist came on across the Euphrates against him, at the head of an army which Arrian, copying from the journals of Macedonian officers, states to have consisted of forty thousand foot and seven thousand horse. In studying the campaigns of Alexander, we possess the peculiar advantage of deriving our information from two of Alexander's generals of division, who bore an important part in all his enterprises. Aristobulus and Ptolemy — who afterward became king of Egypt — kept regular journals of the military events which they witnessed, and these journals were in the possession of Arrian when he drew up his history of Alexander's expedition.

The high character of Arrian for integrity makes us confident that he used them fairly, and his comments on the occasional discrepancies between the two Macedonian narratives prove that he used them sensibly. He frequently quotes the very words of his authorities; and his history thus acquires a charm such as very few ancient or modern military narratives possess. The anecdotes and expressions which he records we fairly believe to be genuine, and not to be the coinage of a rhetorician, like those in Curtius. In fact, in reading Arrian, we read General Aristobulus and General Ptolemy on the campaigns of the Macedonians, and it is like reading General Jomini or General Foy on the campaigns of the French.

The estimate which we find in Arrian of the strength of Alexander's army seems reasonable enough, when we take into account both the losses which he had sustained and the reënforcements which he had received since he left Europe. Indeed, to Englishmen, who know with what mere handfuls of men our own generals have, at Plassy, at Assaye, at Meeanee,

---

[1] Mitford's remarks on the strategy of Darius in his last campaign are very just. After having been unduly admired as a historian, Mitford is now unduly neglected. His partiality and his deficiency in scholarship have been exposed sufficiently to make him no longer a dangerous guide as to Greek politics, while the clearness and brilliance of his narrative, and the strong common sense of his remarks (where his party prejudices do not interfere), must always make his volumes valuable as well as entertaining.

and other Indian battles, routed large hosts of Asiatics, the disparity of numbers that we read of in the victories won by the Macedonians over the Persians presents nothing incredible. The army which Alexander now led was wholly composed of veteran troops in the highest possible state of equipment and discipline, enthusiastically devoted to their leader, and full of confidence in his military genius and his victorious destiny.

The celebrated Macedonian phalanx formed the main strength of his infantry. This force had been raised and organized by his father, Philip, who, on his accession to the Macedonian throne, needed a numerous and quickly formed army, and who, by lengthening the spear of the ordinary Greek phalanx, and increasing the depth of the files, brought the tactics of armed masses to the highest extent of which it was capable with such materials as he possessed. He formed his men sixteen deep, and placed in their grasp the *sarissa*, as the Macedonian pike was called, which was four-and-twenty feet in length, and, when couched for action, reached eighteen feet in front of the soldier; so that, as a space of about two feet was allowed between the ranks, the spears of the five files behind him projected in front of each front-rank man.

The phalangite soldier was fully equipped in the defensive armor of the regular Greek infantry. And thus the phalanx presented a ponderous and bristling mass, which, as long as its order was kept compact, was sure to bear down all opposition. The defects of such an organization are obvious, and were proved in after-years, when the Macedonians were opposed to the Roman legions. But it is clear that under Alexander the phalanx was not the cumbrous, unwieldy body which it was at Cynoscephalæ and Pydna. His men were veterans; and he could obtain from them an accuracy of movement and steadiness of evolution such as probably the recruits of his father would only have floundered in attempting, and such as certainly were impracticable in the phalanx when handled by his successors, especially as under them it ceased to be a standing force, and became only a militia.

Under Alexander the phalanx consisted of an aggregate of eighteen thousand men, who were divided into six brigades of three thousand each. These were again subdivided into regiments and companies; and the men were carefully trained to wheel, to face about, to take more ground, or to close up, as the emergencies of the battle required. Alexander also arrayed troops armed in a different manner in the intervals of the regiments of his phalangites, who could prevent their line from being pierced and their companies taken in flank, when the nature of the ground prevented a close formation, and who could be withdrawn when a favorable opportunity arrived for closing up the phalanx or any of its brigades for a charge, or when it was necessary to prepare to receive cavalry.

Besides the phalanx, Alexander had a considerable force of infantry who were called shield-bearers: they were not so heavily armed as the phalangites, or as was the case with the Greek regular infantry in general, but they were equipped for close fight as well as for skirmishing, and were far superior to the ordinary irregular troops of Greek warfare. They were about six thousand strong. Besides these, he had several bodies of Greek regular infantry; and he had archers, slingers, and javelin-men, who fought also with broadsword and target, and who were principally supplied him by the highlanders of Illyria and Thracia.

The main strength of his cavalry consisted in two chosen regiments of cuirassiers, one Macedonian and one Thessalian, each of which was about fifteen hundred strong. They were provided with long lances and heavy swords, and horse as well as man was fully equipped with defensive armor. Other regiments of regular cavalry were less heavily armed, and there were several bodies of light-horsemen, whom Alexander's conquests in Egypt and Syria had enabled him to mount superbly.

A little before the end of August, Alexander crossed the Euphrates at Thapsacus, a small corps of Persian cavalry under Mazæus retiring before him. Alexander was too prudent to march down through the Mesopotamian deserts, and continued to advance eastward with the intention of passing the Tigris, and then, if he was unable to find Darius and bring him to action, of marching southward on the left side of that river along the skirts of a mountainous district where his men would suffer less from heat and thirst, and where provisions would be more abundant.

Darius, finding that his adversary was not to be enticed into the march through Mesopotamia against his capital, determined to remain on the battle-ground, which he had chosen on the left of the Tigris; where, if his enemy met a defeat or a check, the destruction of the invaders would be certain with two such rivers as the Euphrates and the Tigris in their rear.

The Persian King availed himself to the utmost of every advantage in his power. He caused a large space of ground to be carefully levelled for the operation of his scythe-armed chariots; and he deposited his military stores in the strong town of Arbela, about twenty miles in his rear. The rhetoricians of after-ages have loved to describe Darius Codomanus as a second Xerxes in ostentation and imbecility; but a fair examination of his generalship in this his last campaign shows that he was worthy of bearing the same name as his great predecessor, the royal son of Hystaspes.

On learning that Darius was with a large army on the left of the Tigris, Alexander hurried forward and crossed that river without opposition. He was at first unable to procure any certain intelligence of the precise position of the enemy, and after giving his army a short interval of rest he marched for four days down the left bank of the river.

A moralist may pause upon the fact that Alexander must in this march have passed within a few miles of the ruins of Nineveh, the great city of the primæval conquerors of the human race. Neither the Macedonian King nor any of his followers knew what those vast mounds had once been. They had already sunk into utter destruction; and it is only within the last few years that the intellectual energy of one of our own countrymen has rescued Nineveh from its long centuries of oblivion.

On the fourth day of Alexander's southward march, his advance guard reported that a body of the enemy's cavalry was in sight. He instantly formed his army in order for battle, and directing them to advance steadily he rode forward at the head of some squadrons of cavalry and charged the Persian horse, whom he found before him. This was a mere reconnoitring party, and they broke and fled immediately; but the Macedonians made some prisoners, and from them

Alexander found that Darius was posted only a few miles off, and learned the strength of the army that he had with him. On receiving this news Alexander halted, and gave his men repose for four days, so that they should go into action fresh and vigorous. He also fortified his camp and deposited in it all his military stores and all his sick and disabled soldiers, intending to advance upon the enemy with the serviceable part of his army perfectly unencumbered.

After this halt, he moved forward, while it was yet dark, with the intention of reaching the enemy, and attacking them at break of day. About half way between the camps there were some undulations of the ground, which concealed the two armies from each other's view; but, on Alexander arriving at their summit, he saw, by the early light, the Persian host arrayed before him, and he probably also observed traces of some engineering operation having been carried on along part of the ground in front of them.

Not knowing that these marks had been caused by the Persians having levelled the ground for the free use of their war chariots, Alexander suspected that hidden pitfalls had been prepared with a view of disordering the approach of his cavalry. He summoned a council of war forthwith. Some of the officers were for attacking instantly, at all hazards; but the more prudent opinion of Parmenio prevailed, and it was determined not to advance farther till the battle-ground had been carefully surveyed.

Alexander halted his army on the heights, and, taking with him some light-armed infantry and some cavalry, he passed part of the day in reconnoitring the enemy and observing the nature of the ground which he had to fight on. Darius wisely refrained from moving from his position to attack the Macedonians on the eminences which they occupied, and the two armies remained until night without molesting each other.

On Alexander's return to his headquarters, he summoned his generals and superior officers together, and telling them that he knew well that *their* zeal wanted no exhortation, he besought them to do their utmost in encouraging and instructing those whom each commanded, to do their best in the next day's battle. They were to remind them that they were now not going to fight for a province as they had hitherto fought, but they were about to decide by their swords the dominion of all Asia. Each officer ought to impress this upon his subalterns, and they should urge it on their men. Their natural courage required no long words to excite its ardor; but they should be reminded of the paramount importance of steadiness in action. The silence in the ranks must be unbroken as long as silence was proper; but when the time came for the charge, the shout and the cheer must be full of terror for the foe. The officers were to be alert in receiving and communicating orders; and everyone was to act as if he felt that the whole result of the battle depended on his own single good conduct.

Having thus briefly instructed his generals, Alexander ordered that the army should sup and take their rest for the night.

Darkness had closed over the tents of the Macedonians when Alexander's veteran general, Parmenio, came to him and proposed that they should make a night attack on the Persians. The King is said to have answered that he scorned to filch a victory, and that Alexander must conquer openly and fairly. Arrian justly remarks that Alexander's resolution was as wise as it was spirited. Besides the confusion and uncertainty which are inseparable from night engagements, the value of Alexander's victory would have been impaired if gained under circumstances which might supply the enemy with any excuse for his defeat, and encourage him to renew the contest. It was necessary for Alexander not only to beat Darius, but to gain such a victory as should leave his rival without apology and without hope of recovery.

The Persians, in fact, expected and were prepared to meet a night attack. Such was the apprehension that Darius entertained of it that he formed his troops at evening in order of battle, and kept them under arms all night. The effect of this was that the morning found them jaded and dispirited, while it brought their adversaries all fresh and vigorous against them.

The written order of battle which Darius himself caused to be drawn up fell into the hands of the Macedonians after the engagement, and Aristobulus copied it into his journal. We thus possess, through Arrian, unusually authentic information as to the composition and arrangement of the Persian army. On the extreme left were the Bactrian, Daan, and Arachosian cavalry. Next to these Darius placed the troops from Persia proper, both horse and foot. Then came the Susians, and next to these the Cadusians. These forces made up the left wing.

Darius' own station was in the centre. This was composed of the Indians, the Carians, the Mardian archers, and the division of Persians who were distinguished by the golden apples that formed the knobs of their spears. Here also were stationed the bodyguard of the Persian nobility. Besides these, there were, in the centre, formed in deep order, the Uxian and Babylonian troops and the soldiers from the Red Sea. The brigade of Greek mercenaries whom Darius had in his service, and who alone were considered fit to stand the charge of the Macedonian phalanx, was drawn up on either side of the royal chariot.

The right wing was composed of the Cœlosyrians and Mesopotamians, the Medes, the Parthians, the Sacians, the Tapurians, Hyrcanians, Albanians, and Sacesinæ. In advance of the line on the left wing were placed the Scythian cavalry, with a thousand of the Bactrian horse and a hundred scythe-armed chariots. The elephants and fifty scythe-armed chariots were ranged in front of the centre; and fifty more chariots, with the Armenian and Cappadocian cavalry, were drawn up in advance of the right wing.

Thus arrayed, the great host of King Darius passed the night that to many thousands of them was the last of their existence. The morning of the first of October[1] dawned slowly to their wearied watching, and they could hear the note of the Macedonian trumpet sounding to arms, and could see King Alexander's forces descend from their tents on the heights and form in order of battle on the plain.

There was deep need of skill, as well as of valor, on Alexander's side; and few battle-fields have witnessed more con-

[1] The battle was fought eleven days after an eclipse of the moon, which gives the means of fixing the precise date.

summate generalship than was now displayed by the Macedonian King.   There were no natural barriers by which he could protect his flanks; and not only was he certain to be overlapped on either wing by the vast lines of the Persian army, but there was imminent risk of their circling round him, and charging him in the rear, while he advanced against their centre.   He formed, therefore, a second, or reserve line, which was to wheel round, if required, or to detach troops to either flank, as the enemy's movements might necessitate; and thus, with their whole army ready at any moment to be thrown into one vast hollow square, the Macedonians advanced in two lines against the enemy, Alexander himself leading on the right wing, and the renowned phalanx forming the centre, while Parmenio commanded on the left.

Such was the general nature of the disposition which Alexander made of his army.   But we have in Arrian the details of the position of each brigade and regiment; and as we know that these details were taken from the journals of Macedonian generals, it is interesting to examine them, and to read the names and stations of King Alexander's generals and colonels in this the greatest of his battles.

The eight regiments of the royal horse-guards formed the right of Alexander's line.   Their colonels were Clitus—whose regiment was on the extreme right, the post of peculiar danger —Glaucias, Ariston, Sopolis, Heraclides, Demetrias, Meleager, and Hegelochus.   Philotas was general of the whole division. Then came the shield-bearing infantry: Nicanor was their general.   Then came the phalanx in six brigades.   Cœnus' brigade was on the right, and nearest to the shield-bearers; next to this stood the brigade of Perdiccas, then Meleager's, then Polysperchon's; and then the brigade of Amynias, but which was now commanded by Simmias, as Amynias had been sent to Macedonia to levy recruits.   Then came the infantry of the left wing, under the command of Craterus.

Next to Craterus' infantry were placed the cavalry regiments of the allies, with Eriguius for their general.   The Thessalian cavalry, commanded by Philippus, were next, and held the extreme left of the whole army.   The whole left wing was intrusted to the command of Parmenio, who had round his person the Pharsalian regiment of cavalry, which was the strongest and best of all the Thessalian horse regiments.

The centre of the second line was occupied by a body of phalangite infantry, formed of companies which were drafted for this purpose from each of the brigades of their phalanx. The officers in command of this corps were ordered to be ready to face about if the enemy should succeed in gaining the rear of the army. On the right of this reserve of infantry, in the second line, and behind the royal horse-guards, Alexander placed half the Agrian light-armed infantry under Attalus, and with them Brison's body of Macedonian archers and Cleander's regiment of foot. He also placed in this part of his army Menidas' squadron of cavalry and Aretes' and Ariston's light horse. Menidas was ordered to watch if the enemy's cavalry tried to turn their flank, and, if they did so, to charge them before they wheeled completely round, and so take them in flank themselves.

A similar force was arranged on the left of the second line for the same purpose. The Thracian infantry of Sitalces were placed there, and Cœranus' regiment of the cavalry of the Greek allies, and Agathon's troops of the Odrysian irregular horse. The extreme left of the second line in this quarter was held by Andromachus' cavalry. A division of Thracian infantry was left in guard of the camp. In advance of the right wing and centre was scattered a number of light-armed troops, of javelin-men and bowmen, with the intention of warding off the charge of the armed chariots.[1]

Conspicuous by the brilliancy of his armor, and by the chosen band of officers who were round his person, Alexander took his own station, as his custom was, in the right wing, at the head of his cavalry; and when all the arrangements for the battle were complete, and his generals were fully instructed how to act in each probable emergency, he began to lead his men toward the enemy.

It was ever his custom to expose his life freely in battle,

[1] Kleber's arrangement of his troops at the battle of Heliopolis, where, with ten thousand Europeans, he had to encounter eighty thousand Asiatics in an open plain, is worth comparing with Alexander's tactics at Arbela. See Thiers' *Histoire du Consulat.*

and to emulate the personal prowess of his great ancestor, Achilles. Perhaps, in the bold enterprise of conquering Persia, it was politic for Alexander to raise his army's daring to the utmost by the example of his own heroic valor; and, in his subsequent campaigns, the love of the excitement, of "the raptures of the strife," may have made him, like Murat, continue from choice a custom which he commenced from duty But he never suffered the ardor of the soldier to make him lose the coolness of the general.

Great reliance had been placed by the Persian King on the effects of the scythe-bearing chariots. It was designed to launch these against the Macedonian phalanx, and to follow them up by a heavy charge of cavalry, which, it was hoped, would find the ranks of the spearmen disordered by the rush of the chariots, and easily destroy this most formidable part of Alexander's force. In front, therefore, of the Persian centre, where Darius took his station, and which it was supposed that the phalanx would attack, the ground had been carefully levelled and smoothed, so as to allow the chariots to charge over it with their full sweep and speed.

As the Macedonian army approached the Persian, Alexander found that the front of his whole line barely equalled the front of the Persian centre, so that he was outflanked on his right by the entire left wing of the enemy, and by their entire right wing on his left. His tactics were to assail some one point of the hostile army, and gain a decisive advantage, while he refused, as far as possible, the encounter along the rest of the line. He therefore inclined his order of march to the right, so as to enable his right wing and centre to come into collision with the enemy on as favorable terms as possible, although the manoeuvre might in some respect compromise his left.

The effect of this oblique movement was to bring the phalanx and his own wing nearly beyond the limits of the ground which the Persians had prepared for the operations of the chariots; and Darius, fearing to lose the benefit of this arm against the most important parts of the Macedonian force, ordered the Scythian and Bactrian cavalry, who were drawn up in advance on his extreme left, to charge round upon Alexander's right wing, and check its farther lateral progress. Against these assailants Alexander sent from his second line Menidas' cavalry. As these proved too few to make head against the enemy, he ordered Ariston also from the second line with his right horse, and Cleander with his foot, in support of Menidas.

The Bactrians and Scythians now began to give way; but Darius reënforced them by the mass of Bactrian cavalry from his main line, and an obstinate cavalry fight now took place. The Bactrians and Scythians were numerous, and were better armed than the horsemen under Menidas and Ariston; and the loss at first was heaviest on the Macedonian side. But still the European cavalry stood the charge of the Asiatics, and at last, by their superior discipline, and by acting in squadrons that supported each other,[1] instead of fighting in a confused mass like the barbarians, the Macedonians broke their adversaries and drove them off the field.

Darius now directed the scythe-armed chariots to be driven against Alexander's horse-guards and the phalanx, and these formidable vehicles were accordingly sent rattling across the plain, against the Macedonian line. When we remember the alarm which the war chariots of the Britons created among Cæsar's legions, we shall not be prone to deride this arm of ancient warfare as always useless. The object of the chariots was to create unsteadiness in the ranks against which they were driven, and squadrons of cavalry followed close upon

[1] The best explanation of this may be found in Napoleon's account of the cavalry fights between the French and the mamelukes: " Two mamelukes were able to make head against three Frenchmen, because they were better armed, better mounted, and better trained; they had two pair of pistols, a blunderbuss, a carbine, a helmet with a visor, and a coat of mail; they had several horses, and several attendants on foot. One hundred cuirassiers, however, were not afraid of one hundred mamelukes; three hundred could beat an equal number, and one thousand could easily put to the rout fifteen hundred, so great is the influence of tactics, order, and evolutions! Leclerc and Lasalle presented their men to the mamelukes in several lines. When the Arabs were on the point of overwhelming the first, the second came to its assistance on the right and left; the mamelukes then halted and wheeled, in order to turn the wings of this new line; this moment was always seized upon to charge them, and they were uniformly broken."

them to profit by such disorder. But the Asiatic chariots were rendered ineffective at Arbela by the light-armed troops, whom Alexander had specially appointed for the service, and who, wounding the horses and drivers with their missile weapons, and running alongside so as to cut the traces or seize the reins, marred the intended charge; and the few chariots that reached the phalanx passed harmlessly through the intervals which the spearmen opened for them, and were easily captured in the rear.

A mass of the Asiatic cavalry was now, for the second time, collected against Alexander's extreme right, and moved round it, with the view of gaining the flank of his army. At the critical moment, when their own flanks were exposed by this evolution, Aretes dashed on the Persian squadrons with his horsemen from Alexander's second line. While Alexander thus met and baffled all the flanking attacks of the enemy with troops brought up from his second line, he kept his own horse-guards and the rest of the front line of his wing fresh, and ready to take advantage of the first opportunity for striking a decisive blow.

This soon came. A large body of horse, who were posted on the Persian left wing nearest to the centre, quitted their station, and rode off to help their comrades in the cavalry fight that still was going on at the extreme right of Alexander's wing against the detachments from his second line. This made a huge gap in the Persian array, and into this space Alexander instantly charged with his guard and all the cavalry of his wing; and then, pressing toward his left, he soon began to make havoc in the left flank of the Persian centre. The shield-bearing infantry now charged also among the reeling masses of the Asiatics; and five of the brigades of the phalanx, with the irresistible might of their sarissas, bore down the Greek mercenaries of Darius, and dug their way through the Persian centre.

In the early part of the battle Darius had showed skill and energy; and he now, for some time, encouraged his men, by voice and example, to keep firm. But the lances of Alexander's cavalry and the pikes of the phalanx now pressed nearer and nearer to him. His charioteer was struck down by a javelin at his side; and at last Darius' nerve failed him, and, descending from his chariot, he mounted on a fleet horse and galloped from the plain, regardless of the state of the battle in other parts of the field, where matters were going on much more favorably for his cause, and where his presence might have done much toward gaining a victory.

Alexander's operations with his right and centre had exposed his left to an immensely preponderating force of the enemy. Parmenio kept out of action as long as possible; but Mazæus, who commanded the Persian right wing, advanced against him, completely outflanked him, and pressed him severely with reiterated charges by superior numbers.

Seeing the distress of Parmenio's wing, Simmias, who commanded the sixth brigade of the phalanx, which was next to the left wing, did not advance with the other brigades in the great charge upon the Persian centre, but kept back to cover Parmenio's troops on *their* right flank, as otherwise they would have been completely surrounded and cut off from the rest of the Macedonian army. By so doing, Simmias had unavoidably opened a gap in the Macedonian left centre; and a large column of Indian and Persian horse, from the Persian right centre, had galloped forward through this interval, and right through the troops of the Macedonian second line. Instead of then wheeling round upon Parmenio, or upon the rear of Alexander's conquering wing, the Indian and Persian cavalry rode straight on to the Macedonian camp, overpowered the Thracians who were left in charge of it, and began to plunder. This was stopped by the phalangite troops of the second line, who, after the enemy's horsemen had rushed by them, faced about, countermarched upon the camp, killed many of the Indians and Persians in the act of plundering, and forced the rest to ride off again.

Just at this crisis, Alexander had been recalled from his pursuit of Darius by tidings of the distress of Parmenio and of his inability to bear up any longer against the hot attacks of Mazæus. Taking his horse-guards with him, Alexander rode toward the part of the field where his left wing was fighting; but on his way thither he encountered the Persian and Indian cavalry on their return from his camp.

These men now saw that their only chance of safety was to cut their way through, and in one huge column they charged desperately upon the Macedonian regiments. There was here a close hand-to-hand fight, which lasted some time, and sixty of the royal horse-guards fell, and three generals, who fought close to Alexander's side, were wounded. At length the Macedonian discipline and valor again prevailed, and a large number of the Persian and Indian horsemen were cut down, some few only succeeding in breaking through and riding away.

Relieved of these obstinate enemies, Alexander again formed his regiments of horse-guards, and led them toward Parmenio; but by this time that general also was victorious. Probably the news of Darius' flight had reached Mazæus, and had damped the ardor of the Persian right wing, while the tidings of their comrades' success must have proportionally encouraged the Macedonian forces under Parmenio. His Thessalian cavalry particularly distinguished themselves by their gallantry and persevering good conduct; and by the time that Alexander had ridden up to Parmenio, the whole Persian army was in full flight from the field.

It was of the deepest importance to Alexander to secure the person of Darius, and he now urged on the pursuit. The river Lycus was between the field of battle and the city of Arbela, whither the fugitives directed their course, and the passage of this river was even more destructive to the Persians than the swords and spears of the Macedonians had been in the engagement.[1]

The narrow bridge was soon choked up by the flying thousands who rushed toward it, and vast numbers of the Persians threw themselves, or were hurried by others, into the rapid stream, and perished in its waters. Darius had crossed it, and had ridden on through Arbela without halting. Alexander reached the city on the next day, and made himself master of all Darius' treasure and stores; but the Persian King, unfortunately for himself, had fled too fast for his conqueror, but

[1] I purposely omit any statement of the loss in the battle. There is a palpable error of the transcribers in the numbers which we find in our present manuscripts of Arrian, and Curtius is of no authority.

Death of Alexander the Great, after a prolonged debauch. Painting by Carl von Piloty.

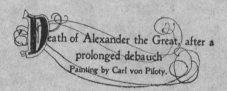

Death of Alexander the Great, after a prolonged debauch

Painting by Carl von Piloty.

had only escaped to perish by the treachery of his Bactrian satrap, Bessus.

A few days after the battle Alexander entered Babylon, "the oldest seat of earthly empire" then in existence, as its acknowledged lord and master. There were yet some campaigns of his brief and bright career to be accomplished. Central Asia was yet to witness the march of his phalanx. He was yet to effect that conquest of Afghanistan in which England since has failed. His generalship, as well as his valor, was yet to be signalized on the banks of the Hydaspes and the field of Chillianwallah; and he was yet to precede the queen of England in annexing the Punjab to the dominions of a European sovereign. But the crisis of his career was reached; the great object of his mission was accomplished; and the ancient Persian empire, which once menaced all the nations of the earth with subjection, was irreparably crushed when Alexander had won his crowning victory at Arbela.

FIRST BATTLE BETWEEN GREEKS AND ROMANS

B.C. 280–279

PLUTARCH

The Romans, in B.C. 290, had conquered the Samnites and this extended the Roman power to the very gates of the Grecian cities on the Gulf of Tarentine. Tarentum, the chief city among them, was almost totally controlled by a party which advised a peaceful submission to the Roman conquerors. The opposing party of patriots, against such cowardly measures, looked abroad for aid and found a ready ally in Pyrrhus, the Molossian king of Epirus. He was warlike and adventurous, and a member of the royal family of Macedonia, through Olympias, who was the mother of Alexander the Great.

Pyrrhus had established a reputation for fighting. Not alone had he fought at the memorable battle of Ipsus, in Phrygia, but he had proven a formidable opponent to Demetinus, king of Macedonia, having forced the latter powerful monarch to conclude a truce with him, though afterward he had been conquered and driven back to his little kingdom of Epirus. At the time the Tarentines sent to him to help them against Rome he was eager for a field in which he might do something to prove his mettle. This was the greatest opportunity of his life, and he seized upon it. The campaign is memorable for having brought the Romans and Greeks into conflict on the battle-field for the first time.

PYRRHUS, now that he had lost Macedonia, might have spent his days peacefully ruling his own subjects in Epirus; but he could not endure repose, thinking that not to trouble others and be troubled by them was a life of unbearable ennui, and, like Achilles in the *Iliad*,

> "he could not rest in indolence at home,
> He longed for battle, and the joys of war."

As he desired some new adventures he embraced the following opportunity. The Romans were at war with the Tarentines; and as that people were not sufficiently powerful to carry on the war, and yet were not allowed by the audacious folly of their mob orators to make peace, they proposed to make Pyrrhus their leader and to invite him to be their ally in the war, because he was more at leisure than any of the other kings, and also was the best general of them all.   Of the older and more sensible citizens some endeavored to oppose this fatal decision, but were overwhelmed by the clamor of the war party, while the rest, observing this, ceased to attend the public assembly.

There was one citizen of good repute, named Meton, who, on the day when the final decision was to be made, when the people were all assembled, took a withered garland and a torch, and like a drunkard, reeled into the assembly with a girl playing the flute before him.   At this, as one may expect in a disorderly popular meeting, some applauded and some laughed, but no one stopped him.   They next bade the girl play, and Meton come forward and dance to the music; and he made as though he would do so.   When he had obtained silence he said: "Men of Tarentum, you do well in encouraging those who wish to be merry and amuse themselves while they may. If you are wise you will all enjoy your freedom now, for when Pyrrhus is come to our city you will have very different things to think of and will live very differently."   By these words he made an impression on the mass of the Tarentine people, and a murmur ran through the crowd that he had spoken well. But those politicians who feared that if peace were made they should be delivered up to the Romans, reproached the people for allowing anyone to insult them by such a disgraceful exhibition, and prevailed on them to turn Meton out of the assembly.

Thus the vote for war was passed, and ambassadors were sent to Epirus, not from Tarentum alone, but from the other Greek cities in Italy, carrying with them presents for Pyrrhus, with instructions to tell him that they required a leader of skill and renown, and that they possessed a force of Lucanians, Messapians, Samnites, and Tarentines, which amounted to twenty thousand cavalry and three hundred and fifty thousand infantry.   This not only excited Pyrrhus, but also made all the Epirotes eager to take part in the campaign.

There was one Cineas, a Thessalian, who was thought to

be a man of good sense, and who, having heard Demosthenes the orator speak, was better able than any of the speakers of his age to delight his hearers with an imitation of the eloquence of that great master of rhetoric. He was now in the service of Pyrrhus, and being sent about to various cities, proved the truth of the Euripidean saw, that

> " All can be done by words
> Which foemen wish to do with conquering swords."

Pyrrhus at any rate used to say that more cities were won for him by Cineas with words than he himself won by force of arms. This man, observing that Pyrrhus was eagerly preparing for his Italian expedition, once when he was at leisure conversed with him in the following manner. "Pyrrhus," said he, "the Romans are said to be good soldiers, and to rule over many warlike nations. Now, if heaven grants us the victory over them, what use shall we make of it?"

"You ask what is self-evident," answered Pyrrhus. "If we can conquer the Romans, there is no city, Greek or barbarian, that can resist us, and we shall gain possession of the whole of Italy, a country whose size, richness, and power no one knows better than yourself." Cineas then, after waiting for a short time, said: "O King, when we have taken Italy, what shall we do then?"

Pyrrhus, not yet seeing his drift, answered: "Close to it Sicily invites us, a noble and populous island, and one which is very easy to conquer; for, my Cineas, now that Agathocles is dead, there is nothing there but revolution and faction and the violence of party spirit."

"What you say," answered Cineas, "is very probably true. But is this conquest of Sicily to be the extreme limit of our campaign?"

"Heaven," answered Pyrrhus, "alone can give us victory and success; but these conquests would merely prove to us the stepping-stones to greater things. Who could refrain from making an attempt upon Carthage and Libya when he was so close to them, countries which were all but conquered by Agathocles when he ran away from Syracuse with only a few ships? and if we were masters of these countries, none of the enemies who now give themselves such airs at our expense will dare to resist us."

"Certainly not," answered Cineas; "with such a force at our disposal we clearly could recover Macedonia, and have the whole of Greece at our feet. And after we have made all these conquests, what shall we do then?"

Pyrrhus laughing answered: "We will take our ease and carouse every day, and enjoy pleasant conversation with one another."

Having brought Pyrrhus to say this, Cineas asked in reply: "But what prevents our carousing and taking our ease now, since we have already at hand all those things which we propose to obtain with much bloodshed, and great toils and perils, and after suffering much ourselves and causing much suffering to others?"

By talking in this manner Cineas vexed Pyrrhus, because he made him reflect on the pleasant home which he was leaving, but his reasoning had no effect in turning him from his purpose.

He first despatched Cineas to Tarentum with three thousand men; next he collected from Tarentum many horse-transports, decked vessels, and boats of all sorts, and embarked upon them twenty elephants, twenty-three thousand cavalry, twenty-two thousand infantry, and five hundred slingers. When all was ready he put to sea; and when half way across a storm burst upon him from the north, which was unusual at that season of the year. He himself, though his ship was carried away by the tempest, yet, by the great pains and skill of the sailors and pilots, resisted it and reached the land, with great toil to the rowers, and beyond everyone's expectation; for the rest of the fleet was overpowered by the gale and scattered. Some ships were driven off the Italian coast altogether, and forced into the Libyan and Sicilian seas, and some which could not weather the Iapygian Cape were overtaken by night, and being dashed by a violent and boisterous sea against that harborless coast were utterly lost, except only the King's ship. She was so large and strongly built as to resist the waves as long as they broke upon her from the seaward; but when the wind changed and blew directly off the shore, the ship, which

now met the waves directly with her head, was in great danger of going to pieces, while to let her drive out to sea again
now that it was so rough, and the wind changed so frequently,
seemed more terrible than to remain where they were.

Pyrrhus rose and leaped into the water, and at once was
eagerly followed by his friends and his bodyguard. The darkness of night and the violent recoil of the roaring waves made
it hard for them to help him, and it was not until daybreak,
when the wind abated, that he reached the land, faint and helpless in body, but with his spirit invincible in misfortune. The
Messapians, upon whose coast he had been thrown, now assembled from the neighboring villages and offered their help,
while some of the ships which had outlived the storm appeared,
bringing a few horsemen, about two thousand foot, and two
elephants.

With these Pyrrhus marched to Tarentum; Cineas, as soon
as he heard of his arrival, bringing out the Tarentine army to
meet him. When he reached the city he did nothing to dis-
please the Tarentines until his fleet returned to the coast and
he had assembled the greater part of his army. But then, as
he saw that the populace, unless ruled by a strong hand, could
neither help him nor help themselves, but intended to stay
idling about their baths and entertainments at home, while he
fought their battles in the field, he closed the gymnasia and
public walks, in which the people were wont to waste their
time in empty talk about the war. He forbade all drinking,
feasting, and unseasonable revels, and forced the people to
take up arms, proving himself inexorable to everyone who
was on the muster-roll of able-bodied citizens. This conduct
made him much disliked, and many of the Tarentines left the
city in disgust; for they were so unused to discipline that they
considered that not to be able to pass their lives as they chose
was no better than slavery.

When news came that Lævinus, the Roman consul, was
marching to attack him with a large force, and was plundering
the country of Lucania as he advanced, while Pyrrhus' allies
had not yet arrived, he thought it a shameful thing to allow
the enemy to proceed any farther, and marched out with his
army. He sent before him a herald to the Roman general,

informing him that he was willing to act as arbitrator in the
dispute between the Romans and the Greek cities of Italy, if
they chose to terminate it peacefully.   On receiving for an
answer that the Romans neither wished for Pyrrhus as an
arbitrator, nor feared him as an enemy, he marched forward,
and encamped in the plain between the city of Pandosia and
Heraclea.

Learning that the Romans were close by, and were encamping on the farther side of the river Siris,[1] he rode up to the
river to view them; and when he observed their even ranks,
their orderly movements, and their well-arranged camp, he
was surprised, and said to the nearest of his friends: "These
barbarians, Megacles, have nothing barbarous in their military
discipline; but we shall soon learn what they can do." He
began indeed already to feel some uncertainty as to the issue
of the campaign, and determined to wait until his allies came
up, and till then to observe the movements of the Romans, and
prevent their crossing the river.   They, however, perceiving
his object, at once crossed the river, the infantry at a ford, the
cavalry at many points at once, so that the Greeks feared they
might be surrounded, and drew back.   Pyrrhus, perceiving
this, ordered his officers instantly to form the troops in order
of battle and wait under arms while he himself charged with
the cavalry, three thousand strong, hoping to catch the Romans
in the act of crossing the river and consequently in disorder.

When he saw many shields of the Roman infantry appearing over the river bank, and their horsemen all ranged in
order, he closed up his own ranks and charged them first himself, a conspicuous figure in his beautiful glittering armor, and
proving by his exploits that he deserved his high reputation;
especially as although he fought personally, and engaged in
combat with the enemy, yet he continually watched the whole
battle, and handled his troops with as much facility as though
he were not in the thick of the fight, appearing always wherever his presence was required, and reënforcing those who
seemed likely to give way.   In this battle Leonnatus the Macedonian, observing one of the Italians watching Pyrrhus and
constantly following him about the field, said to him: "My

[1] The river Aciris, now called Agri.

King, do you see that barbarian on the black horse with white feet? He seems to be meditating some desperate deed. He is a man of spirit and courage, and he never takes his eyes off you, and takes no notice of anyone else. Beware of that man."

Pyrrhus answered: "Leonnatus, no man can avoid his fate; but neither that Italian nor anyone else who attacks me will do so with impunity." While they were yet talking the Italian levelled his lance and urged his horse in full career against Pyrrhus. He struck the King's horse with his spear, and at the same instant his own horse was struck a sidelong blow by Leonnatus. Both horses fell; Pyrrhus was saved by his friends, and the Italian perished fighting. He was of the nation of the Frentani, Hoplacus by name, and was the captain of a troop of horse.

This incident taught Pyrrhus to be more cautious. He observed that his cavalry were inclined to give way, and therefore sent for his phalanx, and arrayed it against the enemy. Then he gave his cloak and armor to one of his companions, Megacles, and after partially disguising himself in those of his friend, led his main body to attack the Roman army. The Romans stoutly resisted him, and an obstinate battle took place, for it is said that the combatants alternately yielded and again pressed forward no less than seven distinct times. The King's exchange of armor, too, though it saved his life, yet very nearly lost him the victory: for many attacked Megacles, and the man who first struck him down, who was named Decius, snatched up his cloak and helmet, and rode with them to Lævinus, displaying them and shouting aloud that he had slain Pyrrhus.

The Romans, when they saw these spoils carried in triumph along their ranks, raised a joyful cry, while the Greeks were correspondingly disheartened, until Pyrrhus, learning what had taken place, rode along the line with his head bare, stretching out his hands to his soldiers and telling them that he was safe. At length he was victorious, chiefly by means of a sudden charge of his Thessalian horse on the Romans after they had been thrown into disorder by the advance of the elephants. The Roman horses were terrified at these animals, and, long before they came near, ran away with their riders

in panic. The slaughter was very great: Dionysius says that
of the Romans there fell but little short of fifteen thousand,
but Hieronymus reduces this to seven thousand, while on
Pyrrhus' side there fell, according to Dionysius, thirteen thousand, but according to Hieronymus less than four thousand.

These, however, were the very flower of Pyrrhus' army;
for he lost all his most trusty officers and his most intimate
personal friends. Still, he captured the Roman camp, which
was abandoned by the enemy, induced several of their allied
cities to join him, plundered a vast extent of country, and
advanced within three hundred stades—less than forty English miles — of Rome itself. After the battle many of the
Lucanians and Samnites came up; these allies he reproached
for their dilatory movements, but was evidently well pleased
at having conquered the great Roman army with no other
forces but his own Epirotes and the Tarentines.

The Romans did not remove Lævinus from his office of
consul, although Caius Fabricius is reported to have said that
it was not the Epirotes who had conquered the Romans,
but Pyrrhus who had conquered Lævinus; meaning that he
thought that the defeat was owing not to the greater force
but the superior generalship of the enemy. They astonished
Pyrrhus by quickly filling up their ranks with fresh levies, and
talking about the war in a spirit of fearless confidence. He
decided to try whether they were disposed to make terms with
him, as he perceived that to capture Rome and utterly subdue
the Roman people would be a work of no small difficulty, and
that it would be vain to attempt it with the force at his disposal, while after his victory he could make peace on terms
which would reflect great lustre on himself. Cineas was sent
as ambassador to conduct this negotiation.

He conversed with the leading men of Rome, and offered
their wives and children presents from the King. No one,
however, would accept them, but they all, men and women
alike, replied that if peace were publicly concluded with the
King, they would then have no objection to regard him as a
friend. And when Cineas spoke before the senate in a winning and persuasive manner he could not make any impression
upon his audience, although he announced to them that Pyr-

rhus would restore the prisoners he had taken without any ransom, and would assist them in subduing all Italy, while all that he asked in return was that he should be regarded as a friend, and that the people of Tarentum should not be molested. The common people, however, were evidently eager for peace, in consequence of their having been defeated in one great battle, and expecting that they would have to fight another against a larger force, because the Italian states would join Pyrrhus.

At this crisis Appius Claudius, an illustrious man, but who had long since been prevented by old age and blindness from taking any active part in politics, when he heard of the proposals of Pyrrhus, and that the question of peace or war was about to be voted upon by the senate, could no longer endure to remain at home, but caused his slaves to carry him through the Forum to the senate house in a litter. When he reached the doors of the senate house his sons and sons-in-law supported him and guided him into the house, while all the assembly observed a respectful silence.

Speaking from where he stood, he addressed them as follows: "My countrymen, I used to grieve at the loss of my sight, but now I am sorry not to be deaf also, when I hear the disgraceful propositions with which you are tarnishing the glory of Rome. What has become of that boast which we were so fond of making before all mankind, that if Alexander the Great had invaded Italy, and had met us when we were young, and our fathers when they were in the prime of life, he would not have been reputed invincible, but would either have fled or perhaps even have fallen, and added to the glory of Rome?

"You now prove that this was mere empty vaporing, by your terror of these Chaonians and Molossians, nations who have always been a prey and a spoil to the Macedonians, and by your fear of this Pyrrhus, who used formerly to dance attendance on one of Alexander's bodyguards,[1] and who has now wandered hither not so much in order to assist the Greeks in Italy as to escape from his enemies at home, and promises to be our friend and protector, forsooth, when the army he commands did not suffice to keep for him the least portion of that Macedonia which he once acquired. Do not imagine that you

[1] Demetrius.

will get rid of this man by making a treaty with him. Rather you will encourage other Greek princes to invade you, for they will despise you and think you an easy prey to all men if you let Pyrrhus go home again without paying the penalty of his outrages upon you, nay, with the power to boast that he has made Rome a laughing-stock for Tarentines and Samnites."

By these words Appius roused a warlike spirit in the Romans, and they dismissed Cineas with the answer that if Pyrrhus would leave Italy they would, if he wished, discuss the question of an alliance with him, but that while he remained in arms in their country the Romans would fight him to the death, however many Lævinuses he might defeat. It is related that Cineas, during his mission to Rome, took great interest in observing the national life of the Romans, and fully appreciated the excellence of their political constitution, which he learned by conversing with many of the leading men of the State. On his return he told Pyrrhus that the senate seemed to him like an assembly of kings, and that as to the populace he feared that the Greeks might find in them a new Lernæan hydra; for twice as many troops had been enrolled in the consul's army as he had before, and yet there remained many more Romans capable of bearing arms.

After this Caius Fabricius came to arrange terms for the exchange of prisoners; a man whom Cineas said the Romans especially valued for his virtue and bravery, but who was excessively poor. Pyrrhus, in consequence of this, entertained Fabricius privately, and made him an offer of money, not as a bribe for any act of baseness, but speaking of it as a pledge of friendship and sincerity. As Fabricius refused this, Pyrrhus waited till the next day, when, desirous of making an impression on him, as he had never seen an elephant, he had his largest elephant placed behind Fabricius during their conference, concealed by a curtain. At a given signal, the curtain was withdrawn, and the creature reached out his trunk over the head of Fabricius with a harsh and terrible cry. Fabricius, however, quietly turned round, and then said to Pyrrhus with a smile, "You could not move me by your gold yesterday, nor can you with your beast to-day."

At table that day they conversed upon all subjects, but

chiefly about Greece and Greek philosophy. Cineas repeated the opinion of Epicurus and his school, about the gods, and the practice of political life, and the objects at which we should aim, how they considered pleasure to be the highest good, and held aloof from taking any active part in politics, because it spoiled and destroyed perfect happiness; and about how they thought that the gods lived far removed from hopes and fears, and interest in human affairs, in a placid state of eternal fruition.[1] While he was speaking in this strain Fabricius burst out: "Hercules!" cried he, "may Pyrrhus and the Samnites continue to waste their time on these speculations as long as they remain at war with us!" Pyrrhus, at this, was struck by the spirit and noble disposition of Fabricius, and longed more than ever to make Rome his friend instead of his enemy. He begged him to arrange terms of peace, and after they were concluded to come and live with him as the first of his friends and officers.

Fabricius is said to have quietly answered: "That, O King, will not be to your advantage; for those who now obey you, and look up to you, if they had any experience of me, would prefer me to you for their king." Pyrrhus was not angry at this speech, but spoke to all his friends about the magnanimous conduct of Fabricius, and intrusted the prisoners to him alone, on the condition that, if the senate refused to make peace, they should be allowed to embrace their friends, and spend the festival of the Saturnalia with them, and then be sent back to him. And they were sent back after the Saturnalia, for the senate decreed that any of them who remained behind should be put to death.

After this, when C. Fabricius was consul, a man came into his camp bringing a letter from King Pyrrhus' physician, in which he offered to poison the King if he could be assured of a suitable reward for his services in thus bringing the war to

[1] I have translated the above passages almost literally from the Greek. Yet I am inclined to think that Arnold has penetrated the true meaning, and shows us the reason for Fabricius' exclamation when he states the Epicurean philosophy, as expounded by Cineas, to be "that war and state affairs were but toil and trouble, and that the wise man should imitate the blissful rest of the gods, who, dwelling in their own divinity, regarded not the vain turmoil of this lower world."

an end without a blow. Fabricius, disgusted at the man's treachery, brought his colleague to share his views, and in haste sent off a letter to Pyrrhus, bidding him be on his guard. The letter ran as follows: " Caius Fabricius and Quintus Æmilius, the Roman consuls, greet King Pyrrhus. You appear to be a bad judge both of your friends and of your enemies. You will perceive, by reading the enclosed letter which has been sent to us, that you are fighting against good and virtuous men, and trusting to wicked and treacherous ones. We do not give you this information out of any love we bear you, but for fear that we might be charged with having assassinated you and be thought to have brought the war to a close by treachery because we could not do so by manhood."

Pyrrhus on receiving this letter, and discovering the plot against his life, punished his physician, and, in return for the kindness of Fabricius and the Romans, delivered up their prisoners without ransom, and sent Cineas a second time to arrange terms of peace. However, the Romans refused to receive their prisoners back without ransom, being unwilling either to receive a favor from their enemy or to be rewarded for having abstained from treachery toward him, but set free an equal number of Tarentines and Samnites, and sent them to him. As to terms of peace, they refused to entertain the question unless Pyrrhus first placed his entire armament on board the ships in which it came, and sailed back to Epirus with it.

As it was now necessary that Pyrrhus should fight another battle, he advanced with his army to the city of Asculum, and attacked the Romans. Here he was forced to fight on rough ground, near the swampy banks of a river, where his elephants and cavalry were of no service, and he was forced to attack with his phalanx. After a drawn battle, in which many fell, night parted the combatants. Next day Pyrrhus manœuvred so as to bring the Romans fairly into the plain, where his elephants could act upon the enemy's line. He occupied the rough ground on either side, placed many archers and slingers among his elephants, and advanced with his phalanx in close order and irresistible strength.

The Romans, who were unable on the level ground to practise the bush-fighting and skirmishing of the previous day,

were compelled to attack the phalanx in front. They endeavored to force their way through that hedge of spears before the
elephants could come up, and showed marvellous courage in
hacking at the spears with their swords, exposing themselves
recklessly, careless of wounds or death. After a long struggle,
it is said that they first gave way at the point where Pyrrhus
was urging on his soldiers in person, though the defeat was
chiefly due to the weight and crushing charge of the elephants.
The Romans could not find any opportunity in this sort of
battle for the display of their courage, but thought it their
duty to stand aside and save themselves from a useless death,
just as they would have done in the case of a wave of the sea
or an earthquake coming upon them. In the flight to their
camp, which was not far off, Hieronymus says that six thousand Romans perished, and that in Pyrrhus' commentaries
his loss is stated at three thousand five hundred and five.

Dionysius, on the other hand, does not admit that there
were two battles at Asculum, or that the Romans suffered a
defeat, but tells us that they fought the whole of one day until
sunset, and then separated, Pyrrhus being wounded in the arm
by a javelin, and the Samnites having plundered his baggage.
He also states the total loss on both sides to be above fifteen
thousand.

The armies separated after the battle, and it is said that
Pyrrhus, when congratulated on his victory by his friends, said
in reply: "If we win one more such victory over the Romans,
we shall be utterly ruined." For a large part of the force which
he had brought with him had perished, and very nearly all his
friends and officers, and there were no more to send for at
home.

THE PUNIC WARS

B.C. 264-219-149

FLORUS

The three Punic wars stand out in history as a mighty "duel *à l'ou-trance*" (a fight to the death), as Victor Hugo says, in the final scene of which Rome, having herself been brought near to defeat, "rises again, uses the limits of her strength in a last blow, throws herself on Carthage, and effaces her from the world."

Jealousy and antagonism had long existed between Rome and Carthage, but it was the preëminence of the African city which held Roman ambition in check and for generations deferred the final struggle. But when at last Rome had acquired the strength she needed in order to assert her rivalry, it was only a question of actual preparation, and the first cause of quarrel was sure to be seized upon by either party, especially by the growing and haughty Italian Power.

The immediate object of contention was the island of Sicily, lying between the territory of Rome and that of Carthage. In Sicily the First Punic War, lasting about twenty-three years, was mainly carried on by the Romans with success, while on the sea Carthage for a long time maintained superiority.

During the intervals between the Punic wars two things appear with striking force in the history of these events—the passive strength and recuperative power of Carthage, which enabled her to return again and again to the struggle from almost crushing defeat, and the marvellous development of resources and aggressive vigor on the part of Rome, in whose case the rise of powerful individual leaders more than offset the weight of long-accumulated energies, supplemented as these were by the genius and achievement of great Carthaginian warriors.

The wars progressed in a spirit of deadly hatred, constantly intensified on both sides, and the Roman determination, of which Cato was the mouthpiece, that Carthage must be destroyed, met its stubborn answer in the endeavors of the Carthaginians to turn this vengeance against Rome herself.

Carthage had been mistress of the world, the richest and most powerful of cities. Her naval supremacy alone had sufficed to secure her safety and superiority over all rivals or possible combinations of force. But the strength of her government lay not so much in her people, or even in her statesmen and soldiers, as in her men of wealth. A political establishment founded upon such supports was peculiarly liable to all the dan-

179

gers of corruption and of public ignorance and apathy in the conduct of affairs. These causes appear conspicuously in the history of the Punic wars, as contributing largely to the overthrow and final extinguishment of Carthage, which left to her successful rival the open way to universal dominion.

The account of Florus presents in a style at once comprehensive and succinct a splendid narrative of these wars, with their decisive and world-changing events.

THE FIRST PUNIC WAR

THE victor-people of Italy, having now spread over the land as far as the sea, checked its course for a little, like a fire, which, having consumed the woods lying in its track, is stopped by some intervening river. But soon after, seeing at no great distance a rich prey, which seemed in a manner detached and torn away from their own Italy, they were so inflamed with a desire to possess it that, since it could neither be joined to their country by a mole or bridge, they resolved that it should be secured by arms and war, and reunited, as it were, to their continent. And behold! as if the Fates themselves opened a way for them, an opportunity was not wanting, for Messana, a city of Sicily in alliance with them, happened then to make a complaint concerning the tyranny of the Carthaginians.

As the Romans coveted Sicily, so likewise did the people of Carthage; and both at the same time, with equal desires and equal forces, contemplated the attainment of the empire of the world. Under the pretext, therefore, of assisting their allies, but in reality being allured by the prey, that rude people, that people sprung from shepherds, and merely accustomed to the land, made it appear, though the strangeness of the attempt startled them (yet such confidence is there in true courage), that to the brave it is indifferent whether a battle be fought on horseback or in ships, by land or by sea.

It was in the consulship of Appius Claudius that they first ventured upon that strait which has so ill a name from the strange things related of it, and so impetuous a current. But they were so far from being affrighted, that they regarded the violence of the rushing tide as something in their favor, and, sailing forward immediately and without delay, they defeated

Hiero, king of Syracuse, with so much rapidity that he owned he was conquered before he saw the enemy. In the consulship of Duilius and Cornelius, they likewise had courage to engage at sea, and then the expedition used in equipping the fleet was a presage of victory; for within sixty days after the timber was felled, a navy of a hundred and sixty ships lay at anchor; so that the vessels did not seem to have been made by art, but the trees themselves appeared to have been turned into ships by the aid of the gods. The aspect of the battle, too, was wonderful; as the heavy and slow ships of the Romans closed with the swift and nimble barks of the enemy. Little availed their naval arts, such as breaking off the oars of a ship, and eluding the beaks of the enemy by turning aside; for the grappling-irons and other instruments, which, before the engagement, had been greatly derided by the enemy, were fastened upon their ships, and they were compelled to fight as on solid ground. Being victorious, therefore, at Liparæ, by sinking and scattering the enemy's fleet, they celebrated their first naval triumph. And how great was the exultation at it! Duilius, the commander, not content with one day's triumph, ordered, during all the rest of his life, when he returned from supper, lighted torches to be carried, and flutes to play, before him, as if he would triumph every day. The loss in this battle was trifling, in comparison with the greatness of the victory; though the other consul, Cornelius Asina, was cut off, being invited by the enemy to a pretended conference, and put to death; an instance of Carthaginian perfidy.

Under the dictatorship of Calatinus, the Romans expelled almost all the garrisons of the Carthaginians from Agrigentum, Drepanum, Panormus, Eryx, and Lilybæum. Some alarm was experienced at the forest of Camarina, but we were rescued by the extraordinary valor of Calpurnius Flamma, a tribune of the soldiers, who, with a choice troop of three hundred men, seized upon an eminence occupied by the enemy, to our annoyance, and so kept them in play till the whole army escaped; thus, by eminent success, equalling the fame of Thermopylæ and Leonidas, though our hero was indeed more illustrious, inasmuch as he escaped and outlived so great an effort, notwithstanding he wrote nothing with his blood.

In the consulship of Lucius Cornelius Scipio, when Sicily was become as a suburban province of the Roman people, and the war was spreading farther, they crossed over into Sardinia, and into Corsica, which lies near it. In the latter they terrified the natives by the destruction of the city of Olbia, in the former by that of Aleria; and so effectually humbled the Carthaginians, both by land and sea, that nothing remained to be conquered but Africa itself. Accordingly, under the leadership of Marcus Atilius Regulus, the war passed over into Africa. Nor were there wanting some on the occasion who mutinied at the mere name and dread of the Punic sea, a tribune named Mannius increasing their alarm; but the general, threatening him with the axe if he did not obey, produced courage for the voyage by the terror of death. They then hastened their course by the aid of winds and oars, and such was the terror of the Africans at the approach of the enemy that Carthage was almost surprised with its gates opened.

The first prize taken in the war was the city of Clypea, which juts out from the Carthaginian shore as a fortress or watch-tower. Both this and more than three hundred fortresses besides were destroyed. Nor had the Romans to contend only with men, but with monsters also; for a serpent of vast size, born, as it were, to avenge Africa, harassed their camp on the Bagrada. But Regulus, who overcame all obstacles, having spread the terror of his name far and wide, having killed or taken prisoners a great number of the enemy's force, and their captains themselves, and having despatched his fleet, laden with much spoil and stored with materials for a triumph, to Rome, proceeded to besiege Carthage itself, the origin of the war, and took his position close to the gates of it. Here fortune was a little changed; but it was only that more proofs of Roman fortitude might be given, the greatness of which was generally best shown in calamities. For the enemy applying for foreign assistance, and Lacedæmon having sent them Xanthippus as a general, we were defeated by a captain so eminently skilled in military affairs. It was then that by an ignominious defeat, such as the Romans had never before experienced, their most valiant commander fell alive into the

enemy's hands. But he was a man able to endure so great a
calamity; as he was neither humbled by his imprisonment at
Carthage nor by the deputation which he headed to Rome;
for he advised what was contrary to the injunctions of the
enemy, and recommended that no peace should be made, and
no exchange of prisoners admitted. Even by his voluntary
return to his enemies, and by his last sufferings, whether in
prison or on the cross, the dignity of the man was not at all
obscured. But being rendered, by all these occurrences, even
more worthy of admiration, what can be said of him but that,
when conquered, he was superior to his conquerors, and that,
though Carthage had not submitted, he triumphed over Fortune herself?

The Roman people were now much keener and more ardent to revenge the fate of Regulus than to obtain victory.
Under the consul Metellus, therefore, when the Carthaginians
were growing insolent, and when the war had returned into
Sicily, they gave the enemy such a defeat at Panormus that
they thought no more of that island. A proof of the greatness
of this victory was the capture of about a hundred elephants,
a vast prey, even if they had taken that number, not in war,
but in hunting.[1] Under the consulship of Appius Claudius,
they were overcome, not by the enemy, but by the gods themselves, whose auspices they had despised, their fleet being sunk
in that very place where the consul had ordered the chickens
to be thrown overboard, because he was warned by them not
to fight. Under the consulship of Marcus Fabius Buteo, they
overthrew, near Ægimurus, in the African sea, a fleet of the
enemy which was just sailing for Italy. But, oh! how great
materials for a triumph were then lost by a storm, when the
Roman fleet, richly laden with spoil, and driven by contrary
winds, covered with its wreck the coasts of Africa and the
Syrtes, and of all the islands lying amid those seas! A great
calamity! But not without some honor to this eminent people, from the circumstance that their victory was intercepted
only by a storm, and that the matter for their triumph was lost

[1] "A vast prey—not in war, but in hunting." The sense is, it would
have been a considerable capture if he had taken these hundred elephants, not in battle, but in hunting, in which more are often taken.

only by a shipwreck. Yet, though the Punic spoils were scattered abroad, and thrown up by the waves on every promontory and island, the Romans still celebrated a triumph. In the consulship of Lutatius Catulus, an end was at last put to the war near the islands named Ægates. Nor was there any greater fight during this war; for the fleet of the enemy was laden with provisions, troops, towers, and arms; indeed, all Carthage, as it were, was in it; a state of things which proved its destruction, as the Roman fleet, on the contrary, being active, light, free from encumbrance, and in some degree resembling a land-camp, was wheeled about by its oars like cavalry in a battle by their reins; and the beaks of the vessels, directed now against one part of the enemy and now against another, presented the appearance of living creatures. In a very short time, accordingly, the ships of the enemy were shattered to pieces, and filled the whole sea between Sicily and Sardinia with their wrecks. So great, indeed, was the victory that there was no thought of demolishing the enemy's city; since it seemed superfluous to pour their fury on towers and walls, when Carthage had already been destroyed at sea.

THE SECOND PUNIC WAR

After the first Carthaginian war there was scarcely a rest of four years, when there was another war, inferior, indeed, in length of time, for it occupied but eighteen years, but so much more terrible, from the direfulness of its havoc, that if anyone compares the losses on both sides, the people that conquered was more like one defeated. What provoked this noble people was that the command of the sea was forced from them, that their islands were taken, and that they were obliged to pay tribute which they had before been accustomed to impose. Hannibal, when but a boy, swore to his father, before an altar, to take revenge on the Romans; nor was he backward to execute his oath. Saguntum, accordingly, was made the occasion of a war; an old and wealthy city of Spain, and a great but sad example of fidelity to the Romans. This city, though granted, by the common treaty, the special privilege of enjoying its liberty, Hannibal, seeking pretences for new disturbances, destroyed with his own hands and those of its inhabitants, in order that, by an infraction of the compact, he might open a passage for himself into Italy.

Among the Romans there is the highest regard to treaties, and consequently, on hearing of the siege of an allied city, and remembering, too, the compact made with the Carthaginians, they did not at once have recourse to arms, but chose rather to expostulate on legal grounds. In the mean time the Saguntines, exhausted with famine, the assaults of machines, and the sword, and their fidelity being at last carried to desperation, raised a vast pile in the market-place, on which they destroyed, with fire and sword, themselves, their wives and children, and all that they possessed. Hannibal, the cause of this great destruction, was required to be given up. The Carthaginians hesitating to comply, Fabius, who was at the head of the embassy, exclaimed: "What is the meaning of this delay? In the fold of this garment I carry war and peace; which of the two do you choose?" As they cried out "War," "Take war, then," he rejoined, and, shaking out the fore-part of his toga in the middle of the senate house, as if he really carried war in its folds, he spread it abroad, not without awe on the part of the spectators.

The sequel of the war was in conformity with its commencement; for, as if the last imprecations of the Saguntines, at their public self-immolation and burning of the city, had required such obsequies to be performed to them, atonement was made to their *manes* by the devastation of Italy, the reduction of Africa, and the destruction of the leaders and kings who engaged in that contest. When once, therefore, that sad and dismal force and storm of the Punic War had arisen in Spain, and had forged, in the fire of Saguntum, the thunderbolt long before intended for the Romans, it immediately burst, as if hurried along by resistless violence, through the middle of the Alps, and descended, from those snows of incredible altitude, on the plains of Italy, as if it had been hurled from the skies. The violence of its first assault burst, with a mighty sound, between the Po and the Ticinus. There the army under Scipio was routed; and the general himself, being wounded, would have fallen into the hands of the enemy, had not his son, then quite a boy, covered his father with his shield, and rescued him from death. This was the Scipio who grew up for the conquest of Africa, and who was to receive a name from its ill-fortune.

To Ticinus succeeded Trebia, where, in the consulship of Sempronius, the second outburst of the Punic War was spent. On that occasion, the crafty enemy, having chosen a cold and snowy day, and having first warmed themselves at their fires, and anointed their bodies with oil, conquered us, though they were men that came from the south and a warm sun, by the aid (strange to say!) of our own winter.

The third thunderbolt of Hannibal fell at the Trasimene lake, when Flaminius was commander. There also was employed a new stratagem of Carthaginian subtlety; for a body of cavalry, being concealed by a mist rising from the lake, and by the osiers growing in the fens, fell upon the rear of the Romans as they were fighting. Nor can we complain of the gods; for swarms of bees settling upon the standards, the reluctance of the eagles to move forward, and a great earthquake that happened at the commencement of the battle—unless, indeed, it was the tramping of horse and foot, and the violent concussion of arms, that produced this trembling of the ground—had forewarned the rash leader of approaching defeat.

The fourth and almost mortal wound of the Roman Empire was at Cannæ, an obscure village of Apulia; which, however, became famous by the greatness of the defeat, its celebrity being acquired by the slaughter of forty thousand men. Here the general, the ground, the face of heaven, the day, indeed, all nature conspired together for the destruction of the unfortunate army. For Hannibal, the most artful of generals, not content with sending pretended deserters among the Romans, who fell upon their rear as they were fighting, but having also noted the nature of the ground in those open plains, where the heat of the sun is extremely violent, the dust very great, and the wind blows constantly, and as it were stately, from the east, drew up his army in such a position that, while the Romans were exposed to all these inconveniences, he himself, having heaven, as it were, on his side, fought with wind, dust, and sun in his favor. Two vast armies, in consequence, were slaughtered till the enemy were satiated,

and till Hannibal said to his soldiers, "Put up your swords."
Of the two commanders, one escaped, the other was slain;
which of them showed the greater spirit is doubtful. Paulus
was ashamed to survive; Varro did not despair. Of the greatness of the slaughter the following proofs may be noticed:
that the Aufidus was for some time red with blood; that a
bridge was made of dead bodies, by order of Hannibal, over
the torrent of Vergellus, and that two *modii* of rings were
sent to Carthage, and the equestrian dignity estimated by
measure.

It was afterward not doubted but that Rome might have
seen its last day, and that Hannibal, within five days, might
have feasted in the Capitol, if—as they say that Adherbal, the
Carthaginian, the son of Bomilcar, observed—"he had known
as well how to use his victory as how to gain it." But at that
crisis, as is generally said, either the fate of the city that was
to be empress of the world, or his own want of judgment, and
the influence of deities unfavorable to Carthage, carried him
in a different direction. When he might have taken advantage of his victory, he chose rather to seek enjoyment from it,
and, leaving Rome, to march into Campania and to Tarentum,
where both he and his army soon lost their vigor, so that it
was justly remarked that "Capua proved a Cannæ to Hannibal"; since the sunshine of Campania and the warm springs
of Baiæ subdued—who could have believed it?—him who had
been unconquered by the Alps and unshaken in the field. In
the mean time the Romans began to recover and to rise, as it
were, from the dead. They had no arms, but they took them
down from the temples; men were wanting, but slaves were
freed to take the oath of service; the treasury was exhausted,
but the senate willingly offered their wealth for the public service, leaving themselves no gold but what was contained in
their children's *bullæ* [1] and in their own belts and rings. The
knights followed their example, and the common people that
of the knights; so that when the wealth of private persons was
brought to the public treasury—in the consulship of Lævinus

[1] A sort of ornament suspended from the necks of children, which,
among the wealthy, was made of gold. It was in the shape of a bubble
on water, or, as Pliny says, of a heart.

and Marcellus—the registers scarcely sufficed to contain the account of it, or the hands of the clerks to record it.

But how can I sufficiently praise the wisdom of the centuries in the choice of magistrates, when the younger sought advice from the elder as to what consuls should be created? They saw that against an enemy so often victorious, and so full of subtlety, it was necessary to contend, not only with courage, but with his own wiles. The first hope of the empire now recovering, and, if I may use the expression, coming to life again, was Fabius, who found a new mode of conquering Hannibal, which was, *not to fight.* Hence he received that new name, so salutary to the commonwealth, of *Cunctator,* or Delayer. Hence too it happened that he was called by the people *the shield of the empire.* Through the whole of Samnium, and through the Falerian and Gauran forests, he so harassed Hannibal that he who could not be reduced by valor was weakened by delay. The Romans then ventured, under the command of Claudius Marcellus, to engage him; they came to close quarters with him, drove him out of his dear Campania, and forced him to raise the siege of Nola. They ventured likewise, under the leadership of Sempronius Gracchus, to pursue him through Lucania, and to press hard upon his rear as he retired; though they then fought him (sad dishonor!) with a body of slaves, for to this extremity had so many disasters reduced them, but they were rewarded with liberty, and from slaves they made them Romans.

O amazing confidence in the midst of so much adversity! O extraordinary courage and spirit of the Roman people in such oppressive and distressing circumstances! At a time when they were uncertain of preserving their own Italy, they yet ventured to look to other countries; and when the enemy were at their throat, flying through Campania and Apulia, and making an Africa in the middle of Italy, they at the same time both withstood that enemy and dispersed their arms over the earth into Sicily, Sardinia, and Spain.

Sicily was assigned to Marcellus, and did not long resist his efforts; for the whole island was conquered in the conquest of one city. Syracuse, its great and, till that period, unconquered capital, though defended by the genius of Archimedes, was at last obliged to yield. Its triple wall and three citadels, its marble harbor and the celebrated fountain of Arethusa, were no defence to it, except so far as to procure consideration for its beauty when it was conquered.

Sardinia Gracchus reduced; the savageness of the inhabitants, and the vastness of its Mad Mountains—for so they are called—availed it nothing. Great severity was exercised upon its cities, and upon Caralis, the city of its cities, that a nation, obstinate and regardless of death, might at least be humbled by concern for the soil of its country.

Into Spain were sent the two Scipios, Cnæus, and Publius, who wrested almost the whole of it from the Carthaginians; but, being surprised by the artifices of Punic subtlety, they again lost it, even after they had slaughtered the enemy's forces in great battles. The wiles of the Carthaginians cut off one of them by the sword as he was pitching his camp, and the other by surrounding him with lighted fagots after he had made his escape into a tower. But the other Scipio, to whom the Fates had decreed so great a name from Africa, being sent with an army to revenge the death of his father and uncle, recovered all that warlike country of Spain, so famous for its men and arms, that seminary of the enemy's force, that instructress of Hannibal, from the Pyrenean mountains—the account is scarcely credible—to the Pillars of Hercules and the ocean, whether with greater speed or good fortune is difficult to decide; how great was his speed, four years bear witness; how remarkable his good fortune, even one city proves, for it was taken on the same day in which siege was laid to it, and it was an omen of the conquest of Africa that Carthage in Spain was so easily reduced. It is certain, however, that what most contributed to make the province submit was the eminent virtue of the general, who restored to the barbarians certain captive youths and maidens of extraordinary beauty, not allowing them even to be brought into his sight, that he might not seem, even by a single glance, to have detracted from their virgin purity.

These actions the Romans performed in different parts of the world, yet were they unable, notwithstanding, to remove Hannibal, who was lodged in the heart of Italy. Most of the towns had revolted to the enemy, whose vigorous commander used even the strength of Italy against the Romans. However, we had now forced him out of many towns and districts. Tarentum had returned to our side; and Capua, the seat, home, and second country of Hannibal, was again in our hands; the loss of which caused the Punic leader so much affliction that he then directed all his force against Rome.

O people worthy of the empire of the world, worthy of the favor and admiration of all, not only men, but gods! Though they were brought into the greatest alarm, they desisted not from their original design; though they were concerned for their own city, they did not abandon their attempts on Capua; but, part of their army being left there with the consul Appius, and part having followed Flaccus to Rome, they fought both at home and abroad at the same time. Why then should we wonder that the gods themselves, the gods, I say—nor shall I be ashamed [1] to admit it—again opposed Hannibal as he was preparing to march forward when at three miles' distance from Rome. For, at every movement of his force, so copious a flood of rain descended, and such a violent storm of wind arose, that it was evident the enemy was repulsed by divine influence, and the tempest proceeded, not from heaven, but from the walls of the city and the Capitol. He therefore fled and departed, and withdrew to the farthest corner of Italy, leaving the city in a manner adored. It is but a small matter to mention, yet sufficiently indicative of the magnanimity of the Roman people, that during those very days in which the city was besieged, the ground which Hannibal occupied with his camp was offered for sale at Rome, and, being put up to auction, actually found a purchaser. Hannibal, on the other side, wished to imitate such confidence, and put up for sale the bankers' houses in the city; but no buyer was found; so that it was evident that the Fates had their presages.

[1] Why should he be ashamed to admit that Rome was saved by the aid of the gods? To receive assistance from the gods was a proof of merit. The gods help those who help themselves, says the proverb. When he says that the gods "*again* opposed Hannibal," he seems to refer to what he said above in speaking of the battle of Cannæ, that the deities, averse to Carthage, prevented Hannibal from marching at that time to Rome.

But as yet nothing had been effectually accomplished by so much valor, or even through such eminent favor from the gods; for Hasdrubal, the brother of Hannibal, was approaching with a new army, new strength, and every fresh requisite for war. There had doubtless been an end of Rome, if that general had united himself with his brother; but Claudius Nero, in conjunction with Livius Salinator, overthrew him as he was pitching his camp. Nero was at that time keeping Hannibal at bay in the farthest corner of Italy; while Livius had marched to the very opposite quarter, that is, to the very entrance and confines of Italy; and of the ability and expedition with which the consuls joined their forces—though so vast a space, that is, the whole of Italy where it is longest, lay between them—and defeated the enemy with their combined strength, when they expected no attack, and without the knowledge of Hannibal, it is difficult to give a notion. When Hannibal, however, had knowledge of the matter, and saw his brother's head thrown down before his camp, he exclaimed, "I perceive the evil destiny of Carthage." This was his first confession of that kind, not without a sure presage of his approaching fate; and it was now certain, even from his own acknowledgment, that Hannibal might be conquered. But the Roman people, full of confidence from so many successes, thought it would be a noble enterprise to subdue such a desperate enemy in his own Africa. Directing their whole force, therefore, under the leadership of Scipio, upon Africa itself, they began to imitate Hannibal, and to avenge upon Africa the sufferings of their own Italy. What forces of Hasdrubal (good gods!), what armies of Syphax, did that commander put to flight! How great were the camps of both that he destroyed in one night by casting firebrands into them! At last, not at three miles distance, but by a close siege, he shook the very gates of Carthage itself. And thus he succeeded in drawing off Hannibal when he was still clinging to and brooding over Italy. There was no more remarkable day, during the whole course of the Roman Empire, than that on which those two generals, the greatest of all that ever lived, whether before or after them, the one the conqueror of Italy, and the other of Spain, drew up their forces for a close engagement. But previously a conference was held between them concerning conditions of peace. They stood motionless awhile in admiration of each other. When they could not agree on a peace, they gave the signal for battle. It is certain, from the confession of both, that no troops could have been better drawn up, and no fight more obstinately maintained. This Hannibal acknowledged concerning the army of Scipio, and Scipio concerning that of Hannibal. But Hannibal was forced to yield, and Africa became the prize of the victory; and the whole earth soon followed the fate of Africa.

THE THIRD PUNIC WAR

The third war with Africa was both short in its duration— for it was finished in four years—and, compared with those that preceded it, of much less difficulty; as we had to fight not so much against troops in the field as against the city itself; but it was far the greatest of the three in its consequences, for in it Carthage was at last destroyed. And if anyone contemplates the events of the three periods, he will understand that the war was begun in the first, greatly advanced in the second, and entirely finished in the third.

The cause of this war was that Carthage, in violation of an article in the treaty, had once fitted out a fleet and army against the Numidians, and had frequently threatened the frontiers of Masinissa. But the Romans were partial to this good king, who was also their ally.

When the war had been determined upon, they had to consider about the end of it. Cato, even when his opinion was asked on any other subject, pronounced, with implacable enmity, that Carthage should be destroyed. Scipio Nasica gave his voice for its preservation, lest, if the fear of the rival city were removed, the exultation of Rome should grow extravagant. The senate decided on a middle course, resolving that the city should only be removed from its place; for nothing appeared to them more glorious than that there should be a Carthage which should not be feared. In the consulship of Manlius and Censorinus, therefore, the Roman people having attacked Carthage, but giving them some hopes of peace, burned their fleet, which they voluntarily delivered up, in sight of the city. Having next summoned the chief men, they commanded them to quit the place if they wished to preserve their lives. This requisition, from its cruelty, so incensed them that they chose rather to submit to the utmost extremities. They accordingly bewailed their necessities publicly, and shouted with one voice *to arms;* and a resolution was made to resist the enemy by every means in their power; not because any hope of success was left, but because they had rather their birthplace should be destroyed by the hands of the enemy than by their own. With what spirit they resumed the war may be understood from the facts that they pulled down their roofs and houses for the equipment of a new fleet; that gold and silver, instead of brass and iron, were melted in their forges for the construction of arms; and that the women parted with their hair to make cordage for the engines of war.

Under the command of the consul Mancinus, the siege was warmly conducted both by land and sea. The harbor was dismantled of its works, and a first, second, and even third wall taken, while nevertheless the Byrsa, which was the name of the citadel, held out like another city. But though the destruction of the place was thus very far advanced, it was the name of the Scipios only that seemed fatal to Africa. The Government, accordingly, applying to another Scipio, desired from him a termination of the war. This Scipio, the son of Paulus Macedonicus, the son of the great Africanus had adopted as an honor to his family, and, as it appeared, with this destiny, that the grandson should overthrow the city which the grandfather had shaken. But as the bites of dying beasts are wont to be most fatal, so there was more trouble with Carthage half-ruined than when it was in its full strength. The Romans having shut the enemy up in their single fortress, had also blockaded the harbor; but upon this they dug another harbor on the other side of the city, not with a design to escape, but because no one supposed that they could even force an outlet there. Here a new fleet, as if just born, started forth; and, in the mean while, sometimes by day and sometimes by night, some new mole, some new machine, some new band of desperate men perpetually started up, like a sudden flame from a fire sunk in ashes. At last, their affairs becoming desperate, forty thousand men, and (what is hardly credible) with Has-drubal at their head, surrendered themselves. How much more nobly did a woman behave, the wife of the general, who, taking hold of her two children, threw herself from the top of her house into the midst of the flames, imitating the queen that built Carthage. How great a city was then destroyed is shown, to say nothing of other things, by the duration of the fire, for the flames could scarcely be extinguished at the end of seventeen days; flames which the enemy themselves had raised in their houses and temples, that, since the city could not be rescued from the Romans, all matter for triumph might at least be burned.

BATTLE OF THE METAURUS

B.C. 207

SIR EDWARD SHEPHERD CREASY

During the closing years of the Second Punic War the resources of the Romans were drained to such an extent as to bring great disheartenment to their rulers and generals.   Under the stress of financial difficulties, the cost of living greatly increased, and the State was compelled to resort to loans of various kinds, and to levy upon citizens of means for the pay of seamen.   This scheme for raising Roman " ship money " was one of the most significent indications of the extreme weight resting upon the republic in the prosecution of this arduous war.   A war with Sicily was fortunately terminated, releasing some additional force for employment against the Carthaginians; but for some time little headway was made by the Roman commanders, and when, in B.C. 207, the people were called upon to elect consuls, their affairs were still in a condition which caused serious anxiety.   The consuls chosen in that year were Marcus Livius and Caius Claudius Nero, and without delay they went to take command in southern Italy, which the Carthaginians under Hannibal, though not in much strength, had invaded.

But when, later in the season, Hasdrubal crossed the Alps from the north to join his brother, Hannibal, the aspect of the war became still more grave in the eyes of the Romans.   Hasdrubal solicited the support of the Gauls, but to little purpose.   Meanwhile Hannibal made skilful use of his small forces in eluding the consul Nero; but the capture by the Romans of despatches from Hasdrubal disclosed his plans, and Nero at once formed his own for intercepting him.   The result was that Nero and Livius joined their forces in Hasdrubal's front, and to the Carthaginian they offered immediate battle.   Hasdrubal attempted a retreat, but was compelled to give battle on the banks of the Metaurus.   Of this, one of the " decisive battles of the world," Creasy has left an authoritative and graphic account, which here follows.   The part of the consul Nero in the campaign is thus remarked upon by Lord Byron:

" The consul Nero, who made the unequalled march which deceived Hannibal and deceived Hasdrubal, thereby accomplished an achievement almost unrivalled in military annals.   The first intelligence of his return, to Hannibal, was the sight of Hasdrubal's head thrown into his camp.   When Hannibal saw this, he exclaimed, with a sigh, that 'Rome would now be the mistress of the world.'   To this victory of Nero's it might be owing that his imperial namesake reigned at all. But the infamy of the one has eclipsed the glory of the other. When the name of Nero is heard, who thinks of the consul? But such are human things."

ABOUT midway between Rimini and Ancona a little river falls into the Adriatic, after traversing one of those districts of Italy in which a vain attempt has lately been made to revive, after long centuries of servitude and shame, the spirit of Italian nationality and the energy of free institutions. That stream is still called the Metauro, and wakens by its name the recollections of the resolute daring of ancient Rome, and of the slaughter that stained its current two thousand and sixty-three years ago, when the combined consular armies of Livius and Nero encountered and crushed near its banks the varied hosts which Hannibal's brother was leading from the Pyrenees, the Rhone, the Alps, and the Po, to aid the great Carthaginian in his stern struggle to annihilate the growing might of the Roman republic, and make the Punic power supreme over all the nations of the world.

The Roman historian,[1] who termed that struggle the most memorable of all wars that ever were carried on, wrote in no spirit of exaggeration ; for it is not in ancient, but in modern history that parallels for its incidents and its heroes are to be found. The similitude between the contest which Rome maintained against Hannibal, and that which England was for many years engaged in against Napoleon, has not passed unobserved by recent historians. "Twice," says Arnold, "has there been witnessed the struggle of the highest individual genius against the resources and institutions of a great nation, and in both cases the nation has been victorious. For seventeen years Hannibal strove against Rome; for sixteen years Napoleon Bonaparte strove against England: the efforts of the first ended in Zama; those of the second in Waterloo."

One point, however, of the similitude between the two wars has scarcely been adequately dwelt on; that is, the remarkable parallel between the Roman general who finally defeated the great Carthaginian, and the English general who gave the last deadly overthrow to the French Emperor. Scipio and Well-

[1] Livy.

ington both held for many years commands of high importance, but distant from the main theatres of warfare. The same country was the scene of the principal military career of each. It was in Spain that Scipio, like Wellington, successively encountered and overthrew nearly all the subordinate generals of the enemy before being opposed to the chief champion and conqueror himself. Both Scipio and Wellington restored their countrymen's confidence in arms when shaken by a series of reverses, and each of them closed a long and perilous war by a complete and overwhelming defeat of the chosen leader and the chosen veterans of the foe.

Nor is the parallel between them limited to their military characters and exploits. Scipio, like Wellington, became an important leader of the aristocratic party among his countrymen, and was exposed to the unmeasured invectives of the violent section of his political antagonists. When, early in the last reign, an infuriated mob assaulted the Duke of Wellington in the streets of the English capital on the anniversary of Waterloo, England was even more disgraced by that outrage than Rome was by the factious accusations which demagogues brought against Scipio, but which he proudly repelled on the day of trial by reminding the assembled people that it was the anniversary of the battle of Zama. Happily, a wiser and a better spirit has now for years pervaded all classes of our community, and we shall be spared the ignominy of having worked out to the end the parallel of national ingratitude. Scipio died a voluntary exile from the malevolent turbulence of Rome. Englishmen of all ranks and politics have now long united in affectionate admiration of our modern Scipio; and even those who have most widely differed from the duke on legislative or administrative questions, forget what they deem the political errors of that time-honored head, while they gratefully call to mind the laurels that have wreathed it.

Scipio at Zama trampled in the dust the power of Carthage, but that power had been already irreparably shattered in another field, where neither Scipio nor Hannibal commanded. When the Metaurus witnessed the defeat and death of Hasdrubal, it witnessed the ruin of the scheme by which alone Carthage could hope to organize decisive success—the scheme

of enveloping Rome at once from the north and the south of
Italy by two chosen armies, led by two sons of Hamilcar.
That battle was the determining crisis of the contest, not
merely between Rome and Carthage, but between the two
great families of the world, which then made Italy the arena of
their oft-renewed contest for preëminence.

The French historian, Michelet, whose *Histoire Romaine*
would have been invaluable if the general industry and accuracy of the writer had in any degree equalled his originality
and brilliancy, eloquently remarks: "It is not without reason
that so universal and vivid a remembrance of the Punic wars
has dwelt in the memories of men. They formed no mere
struggle to determine the lot of two cities or two empires; but
it was a strife on the event of which depended the fate of two
races of mankind, whether the dominion of the world should
belong to the Indo-Germanic or to the Semitic family of nations. Bear in mind that the first of these comprises, besides
the Indians and the Persians, the Greeks, the Romans, and the
Germans. In the other are ranked the Jews and the Arabs,
the Phœnicians and the Carthaginians. On the one side is
the genius of heroism, of art, and legislation; on the other is
the spirit of industry, of commerce, of navigation.

"The two opposite races have everywhere come into contact,
everywhere into hostility. In the primitive history of Persia
and Chaldæa, the heroes are perpetually engaged in combat
with their industrious and perfidious neighbors. The struggle
is renewed between the Phœnicians and the Greeks on every
coast of the Mediterranean. The Greek supplants the Phœnician in all his factories, all his colonies in the East: soon will
the Roman come, and do likewise in the West. Alexander
did far more against Tyre than Shalmaneser or Nebuchadnezzar
had done. Not content with crushing her, he took care that
she never should revive; for he founded Alexandria as her
substitute, and changed forever the track of the commerce of
the world. There remained Carthage—the great Carthage,
and her mighty empire—mighty in a far different degree than
Phœnicia's had been. Rome annihilated it. Then occurred
that which has no parallel in history—an entire civilization
perished at one blow—banished, like a falling star. The *Peri-*

plus of Hanno, a few coins, a score of lines in Plautus, and, lo, all that remains of the Carthaginian world!

"Many generations must needs pass away before the struggle between the two races could be renewed; and the Arabs, that formidable rear-guard of the Semitic world, dashed forth from their deserts. The conflict between the two races then became the conflict of two religions. Fortunate was it that those daring Saracenic cavaliers encountered in the East the impregnable walls of Constantinople, in the West the chivalrous valor of Charles Martel and the sword of the Cid. The crusades were the natural reprisals for the Arab invasions, and form the last epoch of that great struggle between the two principal families of the human race."

It is difficult, amid the glimmering light supplied by the allusions of the classical writers, to gain a full idea of the character and institutions of Rome's great rival. But we can perceive how inferior Carthage was to her competitor in military resources, and how far less fitted than Rome she was to become the founder of centralized and centralizing dominion that should endure for centuries, and fuse into imperial unity the narrow nationalities of the ancient races that dwelt around and near the shores of the Mediterranean Sea.

Carthage was originally neither the most ancient nor the most powerful of the numerous colonies which the Phœnicians planted on the coast of Northern Africa. But her advantageous position, the excellence of her constitution—of which, though ill-informed as to its details, we know that it commanded the admiration of Aristotle—and the commercial and political energy of her citizens gave her the ascendency over Hippo, Utica, Leptis, and her other sister Phœnician cities in those regions; and she finally reduced them to a condition of dependency similar to that which the subject allies of Athens occupied relatively to that once imperial city. When Tyre and Sidon and the other cities of Phœnicia itself sank from independent republics into mere vassal states of the great Asiatic monarchies, and obeyed by turns a Babylonian, a Persian, and a Macedonian master, their power and their traffic rapidly declined, and Carthage succeeded to the important maritime and commercial character which they had previously maintained.

The Carthaginians did not seek to compete with the Greeks on the northeastern shores of the Mediterranean, or in the three inland seas which are connected with it; but they maintained an active intercourse with the Phœnicians, and through them with Lower and Central Asia; and they, and they alone, after the decline and fall of Tyre, navigated the waters of the Atlantic. They had the monopoly of all the commerce of the world that was carried on beyond the Straits of Gibraltar. We have yet extant (in a Greek translation) the narrative of the voyage of Hanno, one of their admirals, along the western coast of Africa as far as Sierra Leone; and in the Latin poem of Festus Avienus frequent references are made to the records of the voyages of another celebrated Carthaginian admiral, Himilco, who had explored the northwestern coast of Europe. Our own islands are mentioned by Himilco as the lands of the Hiberni and Albioni. It is indeed certain that the Carthaginians frequented the Cornish coast—as the Phœnicians had done before them—for the purpose of procuring tin; and there is every reason to believe that they sailed as far as the coasts of the Baltic for amber. When it is remembered that the mariner's compass was unknown in those ages, the boldness and skill of the seamen of Carthage, and the enterprise of her merchants, may be paralleled with any achievements that the history of modern navigation and commerce can produce.

In their Atlantic voyages along the African shores the Carthaginians followed the double object of traffic and colonization. The numerous settlements that were planted by them along the coast from Morocco to Senegal provided for the needy members of the constantly increasing population of a great commercial capital, and also strengthened the influence which Carthage exercised among the tribes of the African coast. Besides her fleets, her caravans gave her a large and lucrative trade with the native Africans; nor must we limit our belief of the extent of the Carthaginian trade with the tribes of Central and Western Africa by the narrowness of the commercial intercourse which civilized nations of modern times have been able to create in those regions.

Although essentially a mercantile and seafaring people, the Carthaginians by no means neglected agriculture. On the contrary, the whole of their territory was cultivated like a garden. The fertility of the soil repaid the skill and toil bestowed on it; and every invader, from Agathocles to Scipio Æmilianus, was struck with admiration at the rich pasture lands carefully irrigated, the abundant harvests, the luxuriant vineyards, the plantations of fig and olive trees, the thriving villages, the populous towns, and the splendid villas of the wealthy Carthaginians, through which his march lay, as long as he was on Carthaginian ground.

Although the Carthaginians abandoned the Ægean and the Pontus to the Greek, they were by no means disposed to relinquish to those rivals the commerce and the dominion of the coasts of the Mediterranean westward of Italy. For centuries the Carthaginians strove to make themselves masters of the islands that lie between Italy and Spain. They acquired the Balearic Islands, where the principal harbor, Port Mahon, still bears the name of a Carthaginian admiral. They succeeded in reducing the greater part of Sardinia; but Sicily could never be brought into their power. They repeatedly invaded that island, and nearly overran it; but the resistance which was opposed to them by the Syracusans under Gelon, Dionysius, Timoleon, and Agathocles preserved the island from becoming Punic, though many of its cities remained under the Carthaginian rule until Rome finally settled the question to whom Sicily was to belong by conquering it for herself.

With so many elements of success, with almost unbounded wealth, with commercial and maritime activity, with a fertile territory, with a capital city of almost impregnable strength, with a constitution that insured for centuries the blessing of social order, with an aristocracy singularly fertile in men of the highest genius, Carthage yet failed signally and calamitously in her contest for power with Rome. One of the immediate causes of this may seem to have been the want of firmness among her citizens, which made them terminate the First Punic War by begging peace, sooner than endure any longer the hardships and burdens caused by a state of warfare, although their antagonists had suffered far more severely than themselves. Another cause was the spirit of faction among their leading men, which prevented Hannibal in the second war from being properly reënforced and supported.   But there were also more general causes why Carthage proved inferior to Rome. These were her position relatively to the mass of the inhabitants of the country which she ruled, and her habit of trusting to mercenary armies in her wars.

Our clearest information as to the different races of men in and about Carthage is derived from Diodorus Siculus.   That historian enumerates four different races: first, he mentions the Phœnicians who dwelt in Carthage; next, he speaks of the Liby-Phœnicians: these, he tells us, dwelt in many of the maritime cities, and were connected by intermarriage with the Phœnicians, which was the cause of their compound name; thirdly, he mentions the Libyans, the bulk and the most ancient part of the population, hating the Carthaginians intensely on account of the oppressiveness of their domination; lastly, he names the Numidians, the nomad tribes of the frontier.

It is evident, from this description, that the native Libyans were a subject class, without franchise or political rights; and, accordingly, we find no instance specified in history of a Libyan holding political office or military command.   The half-castes, the Liby-Phœnicians, seem to have been sometimes sent out as colonists; but it may be inferred, from what Diodorus says of their residence, that they had not the right of the citizenship of Carthage; and only a single solitary case occurs of one of this race being intrusted with authority, and that, too, not emanating from the home government.   This is the instance of the officer sent by Hannibal to Sicily after the fall of Syracuse, whom Polybius calls Myttinus the Libyan, but whom, from the fuller account in Livy, we find to have been a Liby-Phœnician; and it is expressly mentioned what indignation was felt by the Carthaginian commanders in the island that this half-caste should control their operations.

With respect to the composition of their armies, it is observable that, though thirsting for extended empire, and though some of her leading men became generals of the highest order, the Carthaginians, as a people, were anything but personally warlike.   As long as they could hire mercenaries to fight for them, they had little appetite for the irksome training and the loss of valuable time which military service would have entailed on themselves.

As Michelet remarks: "The life of an industrious merchant, of a Carthaginian, was too precious to be risked, as long as it was possible to substitute advantageously for it that of a barbarian from Spain or Gaul. Carthage knew, and could tell to a drachma, what the life of a man of each nation came to. A Greek was worth more than a Campanian, a Campanian worth more than a Gaul or a Spaniard. When once this tariff of blood was correctly made out, Carthage began a war as a mercantile speculation. She tried to make conquests in the hope of getting new mines to work or to open fresh markets for her exports. In one venture she could afford to spend fifty thousand mercenaries, in another rather more. If the returns were good, there was no regret felt for the capital that had been sunk in the investment; more money got more men, and all went on well."

Armies composed of foreign mercenaries have in all ages been as formidable to their employers as to the enemy against whom they were directed. We know of one occasion—between the First and Second Punic wars—when Carthage was brought to the very brink of destruction by a revolt of her foreign troops. Other mutinies of the same kind must from time to time have occurred. Probably one of these was the cause of the comparative weakness of Carthage at the time of the Athenian expedition against Syracuse, so different from the energy with which she attacked Gelon half a century earlier and Dionysius half a century later. And even when we consider her armies with reference only to their efficiency in warfare, we perceive at once the inferiority of such bands of *condottieri*, brought together without any common bond of origin, tactics, or cause, to the legions of Rome, which, at the time of the Punic wars, were raised from the very flower of a hardy agricultural population, trained in the strictest discipline, habituated to victory, and animated by the most resolute patriotism.

And this shows, also, the transcendency of the genius of Hannibal, which could form such discordant materials into a compact organized force, and inspire them with the spirit of patient discipline and loyalty to their chief, so that they were true to him in his adverse as well as in his prosperous fortunes; and throughout the checkered series of his campaigns no panic rout ever disgraced a division under his command, no mutiny, or even attempt at mutiny, was ever known in his camp; and finally, after fifteen years of Italian warfare, his men followed their old leader to Zama, "with no fear and little hope,"[1] and there, on that disastrous field, stood firm around him, his Old Guard, till Scipio's Numidian allies came up on their flank, when at last, surrounded and overpowered, the veteran battalions sealed their devotion to their general by their blood!

"But if Hannibal's genius may be likened to the Homeric god, who, in his hatred to the Trojans, rises from the deep to rally the fainting Greeks and to lead them against the enemy, so the calm courage with which Hector met his more than human adversary in his country's cause is no unworthy image of the unyielding magnanimity displayed by the aristocracy of Rome. As Hannibal utterly eclipses Carthage, so, on the contrary, Fabius, Marcellus, Claudius Nero, even Scipio himself, are as nothing when compared to the spirit and wisdom and power of Rome. The senate, which voted its thanks to its political enemy, Varro, after his disastrous defeat, ' because he had not despaired of the commonwealth,' and which disdained either to solicit or to reprove or to threaten or in any way to notice the twelve colonies which had refused their accustomed supplies of men for the army, is far more to be honored than the conqueror of Zama. This we should the more carefully bear in mind because our tendency is to admire individual greatness far more than national; and, as no single Roman will bear comparison to Hannibal, we are apt to murmur at the event of the contest, and to think that the victory was awarded to the least worthy of the combatants. On the contrary, never was the wisdom of God's providence more manifest than in the issue of the struggle between Rome and Carthage.

"It was clearly for the good of mankind that Hannibal should be conquered; his triumph would have stopped the progress of the world; for great men can only act permanently

[1] "We advanced to Waterloo as the Greeks did to Thermopylæ: all of us without fear, and most of us without hope."—*Speech of General Foy.*

by forming great nations; and no one man, even though it were Hannibal himself, can in one generation effect such a work. But where the nation has been merely enkindled for a while by a great man's spirit, the light passes away with him who communicated it; and the nation, when he is gone, is like a dead body to which magic power had for a moment given unnatural life: when the charm has ceased, the body is cold and stiff as before. He who grieves over the battle of Zama should carry on his thoughts to a period thirty years later, when Hannibal must in the course of nature have been dead, and consider how the isolated Phœnician city of Carthage was fitted to receive and to consolidate the civilization of Greece, or by its laws and institutions to bind together barbarians of every race and language into an organized empire, and prepare them for becoming, when that empire was dissolved, the free members of the commonwealth of Christian Europe." [1]

It was in the spring of 207 B.C. that Hasdrubal, after skilfully disentangling himself from the Roman forces in Spain, and after a march conducted with great judgment and little loss through the interior of Gaul and the passes of the Alps, appeared in the country that now is the north of Lombardy, at the head of troops which he had partly brought out of Spain and partly levied among the Gauls and Ligurians on his way. At this time Hannibal, with his unconquered and seemingly unconquerable army, had been eight years in Italy, executing with strenuous ferocity the vow of hatred to Rome which had been sworn by him while yet a child at the bidding of his father, Hamilcar, who, as he boasted, had trained up his three sons, Hannibal, Hasdrubal, and Mago, like three lion's whelps, to prey upon the Romans. But Hannibal's latter campaigns had not been signalized by any such great victories as marked the first years of his invasion of Italy. The stern spirit of Roman resolution, ever highest in disaster and danger, had neither bent nor despaired beneath the merciless blows which "the dire African" dealt her in rapid succession at Trebia, at Thrasymene, and at Cannæ. Her population was thinned by repeated slaughter in the field; poverty and actual scarcity ground down the survivors, through the fearful ravages which

[1] Arnold.

Hannibal's cavalry spread through their cornfields, their pasture lands, and their vineyards; many of her allies went over to the invader's side, and new clouds of foreign war threatened her from Macedonia and Gaul. But Rome receded not. Rich and poor among her citizens vied with each other in devotion to their country. The wealthy placed their stores, and all placed their lives, at the State's disposal. And though Hannibal could not be driven out of Italy, though every year brought its sufferings and sacrifices, Rome felt that her constancy had not been exerted in vain. If she was weakened by the continued strife, so was Hannibal also; and it was clear that the unaided resources of his army were unequal to the task of her destruction. The single deerhound could not pull down the quarry which he had so furiously assailed. Rome not only stood fiercely at bay, but had pressed back and gored her antagonist, that still, however, watched her in act to spring. She was weary, and bleeding at every pore; and there seemed to be little hope of her escape if the other hound of old Hamilcar's race should come up in time to aid his brother in the death grapple.

Hasdrubal had commanded the Carthaginian armies in Spain for some time with varying but generally unfavorable fortune. He had not the full authority over the Punic forces in that country which his brother and his father had previously exercised. The faction at Carthage, which was at feud with his family, succeeded in fettering and interfering with his power; and other generals were from time to time sent into Spain, whose errors and misconduct caused the reverses that Hasdrubal met with. This is expressly attested by the Greek historian Polybius, who was the intimate friend of the younger Africanus, and drew his information respecting the Second Punic War from the best possible authorities. Livy gives a long narrative of campaigns between the Roman commanders in Spain and Hasdrubal, which is so palpably deformed by fictions and exaggerations as to be hardly deserving of attention.

It is clear that in the year B.C. 208, at least, Hasdrubal outmanœuvred Publius Scipio, who held the command of the Roman forces in Spain, and whose object was to prevent him from passing the Pyrenees and marching upon Italy. Scipio expected that Hasdrubal would attempt the nearest route along the coast of the Mediterranean, and he therefore carefully fortified and guarded the passes of the eastern Pyrenees. But Hasdrubal passed these mountains near their western extremity; and then, with a considerable force of Spanish infantry, with a small number of African troops, with some elephants and much treasure, he marched, not directly toward the coast of the Mediterranean, but in a northeastern line toward the centre of Gaul. He halted for the winter in the territory of the Arverni, the modern Auvergne, and conciliated or purchased the good-will of the Gauls in that region so far that he not only found friendly winter quarters among them, but great numbers of them enlisted under him, and, on the approach of spring, marched with him to invade Italy.

By thus entering Gaul at the southwest, and avoiding its southern maritime districts, Hasdrubal kept the Romans in complete ignorance of his precise operations and movements in that country; all that they knew was that Hasdrubal had baffled Scipio's attempts to detain him in Spain; that he had crossed the Pyrenees with soldiers, elephants, and money, and that he was raising fresh forces among the Gauls. The spring was sure to bring him into Italy, and then would come the real tempest of the war, when from the north and from the south the two Carthaginian armies, each under a son of the Thunderbolt,[1] were to gather together around the seven hills of Rome.

In this emergency the Romans looked among themselves earnestly and anxiously for leaders fit to meet the perils of the coming campaign.

The senate recommended the people to elect, as one of their consuls, Caius Claudius Nero, a patrician of one of the families of the great Claudian house. Nero had served during the preceding years of the war both against Hannibal in Italy and against Hasdrubal in Spain; but it is remarkable that the histories which we possess record no successes as having been achieved by him either before or after his great campaign of the Metaurus. It proves much for the sagacity of the leading

---

[1] Hamilcar was surnamed Barca, which means the Thunderbolt. Sultan Bajazet had the similar surname of Yilderim.

men of the senate that they recognized in Nero the energy and spirit which were required at this crisis, and it is equally creditable to the patriotism of the people that they followed the advice of the senate by electing a general who had no showy exploits to recommend him to their choice.

It was a matter of greater difficulty to find a second consul; the laws required that one consul should be a plebeian; and the plebeian nobility had been fearfully thinned by the events of the war. While the senators anxiously deliberated among themselves what fit colleague for Nero could be nominated at the coming comitia, and sorrowfully recalled the names of Marcellus, Gracchus, and other plebeian generals who were no more, one taciturn and moody old man sat in sullen apathy among the conscript fathers. This was Marcus Livius, who had been consul in the year before the beginning of this war, and had then gained a victory over the Illyrians. After his consulship he had been impeached before the people on a charge of peculation and unfair division of the spoils among his soldiers; the verdict was unjustly given against him, and the sense of this wrong, and of the indignity thus put upon him, had rankled unceasingly in the bosom of Livius, so that for eight years after his trial he had lived in seclusion in his country seat, taking no part in any affairs of State. Latterly the censors had compelled him to come to Rome and resume his place in the senate, where he used to sit gloomily apart, giving only a silent vote. At last an unjust accusation against one of his near kinsmen made him break silence, and he harangued the house in words of weight and sense, which drew attention to him and taught the senators that a strong spirit dwelt beneath that unimposing exterior.

Now, while they were debating on what noble of a plebeian house was fit to assume the perilous honors of the consulate, some of the elder of them looked on Marcus Livius, and remembered that in the very last triumph which had been celebrated in the streets of Rome, this grim old man had sat in the car of victory, and that he had offered the last thanksgiving sacrifice for the success of the Roman arms which had bled before Capitoline Jove. There had been no triumphs since Hannibal came into Italy. The Illyrian campaign of Livius was the last that had been so honored; perhaps it might be destined for him now to renew the long-interrupted series. The senators resolved that Livius should be put in nomination as consul with Nero; the people were willing to elect him: the only opposition came from himself. He taunted them with their inconsistency in honoring the man whom they had convicted of a base crime. "If I am innocent," said he, "why did you place such a stain on me? If I am guilty, why am I more fit for a second consulship than I was for my first one?" The other senators remonstrated with him, urging the example of the great Camillus, who, after an unjust condemnation on a similar charge, both served and saved his country. At last Livius ceased to object; and Caius Claudius Nero and Marcus Livius were chosen consuls of Rome.

A quarrel had long existed between the two consuls, and the senators strove to effect a reconciliation between them before the campaign. Here again Livius for a long time obstinately resisted the wish of his fellow-senators. He said it was best for the State that he and Nero should continue to hate one another. Each would do his duty better when he knew that he was watched by an enemy in the person of his own colleague. At last the entreaties of the senate prevailed, and Livius consented to forego the feud, and to coöperate with Nero in preparing for the coming struggle.

As soon as the winter snows were thawed, Hasdrubal commenced his march from Auvergne to the Alps. He experienced none of the difficulties which his brother had met with from the mountain tribes. Hannibal's army had been the first body of regular troops that had ever traversed their regions; and, as wild animals assail a traveller, the natives rose against it instinctively, in imagined defence of their own habitations, which they supposed to be the objects of Carthaginian ambition. But the fame of the war, with which Italy had now been convulsed for twelve years, had penetrated into the Alpine passes, and the mountaineers now understood that a mighty city southward of the Alps was to be attacked by the troops whom they saw marching among them. They now not only opposed no resistance to the passage of Hasdrubal, but many of them, out of love of enterprise and plunder, or allured by the high pay that he offered, took service with him; and thus he advanced upon Italy with an army that gathered strength at every league. It is said, also, that some of the most important engineering works which Hannibal had constructed were found by Hasdrubal still in existence, and materially favored the speed of his advance. He thus emerged into Italy from the Alpine valleys much sooner than had been anticipated. Many warriors of the Ligurian tribes joined him; and, crossing the River Po, he marched down its southern bank to the city of Placentia, which he wished to secure as a base for his future operations. Placentia resisted him as bravely as it had resisted Hannibal twelve years before, and for some time Hasdrubal was occupied with a fruitless siege before its walls.

Six armies were levied for the defence of Italy when the long-dreaded approach of Hasdrubal was announced. Seventy thousand Romans served in the fifteen legions of which, with an equal number of Italian allies, those armies and the garrisons were composed. Upward of thirty thousand more Romans were serving in Sicily, Sardinia, and Spain. The whole number of Roman citizens of an age fit for military duty scarcely exceeded a hundred and thirty thousand. The census taken before the commencement of the war had shown a total of two hundred and seventy thousand, which had been diminished by more than half during twelve years. These numbers are fearfully emphatic of the extremity to which Rome was reduced, and of her gigantic efforts in that great agony of her fate. Not merely men, but money and military stores, were drained to the utmost, and if the armies of that year should be swept off by a repetition of the slaughters of Thrasymene and Cannæ all felt that Rome would cease to exist.

Even if the campaign were to be marked by no decisive success on either side her ruin seemed certain. In South Italy, Hannibal had either detached Rome's allies from her or had impoverished them by the ravages of his army. If Hasdrubal could have done the same in Upper Italy; if Etruria, Umbria, and Northern Latium had either revolted or been laid waste, Rome must have sunk beneath sheer starvation, for the hostile or desolated territory would have yielded no supplies of corn for her population, and money to purchase it from abroad there was none. Instant victory was a matter of life or death. Three of her six armies were ordered to the North, but the first of these was required to overawe the disaffected Etruscan. The second army of the North was pushed forward, under Porcius, the prætor, to meet and keep in check the advanced troops of Hasdrubal; while the third, the grand army of the North, which was to be under the immediate command of the consul Livius, who had the chief command in all North Italy, advanced more slowly in its support. There were similarly three armies in the South, under the orders of the other consul, Claudius Nero.

The lot had decided that Livius was to be opposed to Hasdrubal, and that Nero should face Hannibal. And "when all was ordered as themselves thought best, the two consuls went forth from the city, each his several way. The people of Rome were now quite otherwise affected than they had been when L. Æmilius Paulus and C. Terentius Varro were sent against Hannibal. They did no longer take upon them to direct their generals, or bid them despatch and win the victory betimes, but rather they stood in fear lest all diligence, wisdom, and valor should prove too little; for since few years had passed wherein some one of their generals had not been slain, and since it was manifest that, if either of these present consuls were defeated or put to the worst, the two Carthaginians would forthwith join, and make short work with the other, it seemed a greater happiness than could be expected that each of them should return home victor, and come off with honor from such mighty opposition as he was like to find. With extreme difficulty had Rome held up her head ever since the battle of Cannæ; though it were so, that Hannibal alone, with little help from Carthage, had continued the war in Italy. But there was now arrived another son of Hamilcar, and one that in his present expedition had seemed a man of more sufficiency than Hannibal himself; for whereas, in that long and dangerous march through barbarous nations, over great rivers and mountains that were thought unpassable, Hannibal had lost a great part of his army, this Hasdrubal, in the same places, had multiplied his numbers, and gathering the people that he found in the way, descended from the Alps like a rolling snowball, far greater than he came over the Pyrenees at his first setting out of Spain. These considerations and the like, of which fear presented many unto them, caused the people of Rome to wait upon their consuls out of the town, like a pensive train of mourners, thinking upon Marcellus and Crispinus, upon whom, in the like sort, they had given attendance the last year, but saw neither of them return alive from a less dangerous war. Particularly old Q. Fabius gave his accustomed advice to M. Livius, that he should abstain from giving or taking battle until he well understood the enemy's condition. But the consul made him a froward answer, and said that he would fight the very first day, for that he thought it long till he should either recover his honor by victory, or, by seeing the overthrow of his own unjust citizens, satisfy himself with the joy of a great though not an honest revenge. But his meaning was better than his words."

Hannibal at this period occupied with his veteran but much-reduced forces the extreme south of Italy. It had not been expected either by friend or foe that Hasdrubal would effect his passage of the Alps so early in the year as actually occurred. And even when Hannibal learned that his brother was in Italy, and had advanced as far as Placentia, he was obliged to pause for further intelligence before he himself commenced active operations, as he could not tell whether his brother might not be invited into Etruria, to aid the party there that was disaffected to Rome, or whether he would march down by the Adriatic Sea. Hannibal led his troops out of their winter quarters in Bruttium, and marched northward as far as Canusium. Nero had his head-quarters near Venusia, with an army which he had increased to forty thousand foot and two thousand five hundred horse, by incorporating under his own command some of the legions which had been intended to act under other generals in the South. There was another Roman army, twenty thousand strong, south of Hannibal at Tarentum. The strength of that city secured this Roman force from any attack by Hannibal, and it was a serious matter to march northward and leave it in his rear, free to act against all his depots and allies in the friendly part of Italy, which for the two or three last campaigns had served him for a base of his operations. Moreover, Nero's army was so strong that Hannibal could not concentrate troops enough to assume the offensive against it without weakening his garrisons and relinquishing, at least for a time, his grasp upon the southern provinces. To do this before he was certainly informed of his brother's operations would have been a useless sacrifice, as Nero could retreat before him upon the other Roman armies near the capital, and Hannibal knew by experience that a mere advance of his army upon the walls of Rome would have no effect on the fortunes of the war. In the hope, probably, of inducing Nero to follow him and of gaining an opportunity of outmanœuvring the Roman consul and attacking him on his march, Hannibal moved into Lucania, and then back into Apulia; he again marched down into Bruttium, and strengthened his army by a levy of recruits in that district. Nero followed him, but gave him no chance of assailing him at a disadvantage. Some partial encounters seem to have taken place; but the consul could not prevent Hannibal's junction with his Bruttian levies, nor could Hannibal gain an opportunity of surprising and crushing the consul.' Hannibal returned to his former headquarters at Canusium, and halted there in expectation of further tidings of his brother's movements. Nero also resumed his former position in observation of the Carthaginian army.

¹ The annalists whom Livy copied spoke of Nero's gaining repeated victories over Hannibal, and killing and taking his men by tens of thousands. The falsehood of all this is self-evident. If Nero could thus always beat Hannibal, the Romans would not have been in such an agony of dread about Hasdrubal as all writers describe. Indeed, we have the express testimony of Polybius that the statements which we read in Livy of Marcellus, Nero, and others gaining victories over Hannibal in Italy must be all fabrications of Roman vanity. Polybius states that Hannibal was never defeated before the battle of Zama; and in another passage he mentions that after the defeats which Hannibal inflicted on the Romans in the early years of the war, they no longer dared face his army in a pitched battle on a fair field, and yet they resolutely maintained the war. He rightly explains this by referring to the superiority of Hannibal's cavalry, the arm which gained him all his victories. By keeping within fortified lines, or close to the sides of the mountains when Hannibal approached them, the Romans rendered his cavalry ineffective; and a glance at the geography of Italy will show how an army can traverse the greater part of that country without venturing far from the high grounds.

Meanwhile, Hasdrubal had raised the siege of Placentia, and was advancing toward Ariminum on the Adriatic, and driving before him the Roman army under Porcius. Nor when the consul Livius had come up, and united the second and third armies of the North, could he make head against the invaders. The Romans still fell back before Hasdrubal beyond Ariminum, beyond the Metaurus, and as far as the little town of Sena, to the southeast of that river. Hasdrubal was not unmindful of the necessity of acting in concert with his brother. He sent messengers to Hannibal to announce his own line of march, and to propose that they should unite their armies in South Umbria and then wheel round against Rome. Those messengers traversed the greater part of Italy in safety, but, when close to the object of their mission, were captured by a Roman detachment; and Hasdrubal's letter, detailing his whole plan of the campaign, was laid, not in his brother's hands, but in those of the commander of the Roman armies of the South. Nero saw at once the full importance of the crisis. The two sons of Hamilcar were now within two hundred miles of each other, and if Rome were to be saved the brothers must never meet alive. Nero instantly ordered seven thousand picked men, a thousand being cavalry, to hold themselves in readiness for a secret expedition against one of Hannibal's garrisons, and as soon as night had set in he hurried forward on his bold enterprise; but he quickly left the southern road toward Lucania, and, wheeling round, pressed northward with the utmost rapidity toward Picenum. He had, during the preceding afternoon, sent messengers to Rome, who were to lay Hasdrubal's letters before the senate. There was a law forbidding a consul to make war or march his army beyond the limits of the province assigned to him; but in such an emergency, Nero did not wait for the permission of the senate to execute his project, but informed them that he was already on his march to join Livius against Hasdrubal. He advised them to send the two legions which formed the home garrison on to Narnia, so as to defend that pass of the Flaminian road against Hasdrubal, in case he should march upon Rome before the consular armies could attack him. They were to supply the place of these two legions at Rome by a levy *en masse* in the city, and by ordering up the reserve legion from Capua. These were his communications to the senate. He also sent horse-men forward along his line of march, with orders to the local authorities to bring stores of provisions and refreshment of every kind to the roadside, and to have relays of carriages ready for the conveyance of the wearied soldiers. Such were the precautions which he took for accelerating his march; and when he had advanced some little distance from his camp, he briefly informed his soldiers of the real object of their expedi-tion. He told them that never was there a design more seem-ingly audacious and more really safe. He said he was leading them to a certain victory, for his colleague had an army large enough to balance the enemy already, so that *their* swords would decisively turn the scale. The very rumor that a fresh consul and a fresh army had come up, when heard on the bat-tle-field—and he would take care that they should not be heard of before they were seen and felt—would settle the business. They would have all the credit of the victory and of having dealt the final decisive blow. He appealed to the enthusiastic reception which they already met with on their line of march as a proof and an omen of their good fortune. And, indeed, their whole path was amid the vows and prayers and praises of their countrymen. The entire population of the districts through which they passed flocked to the roadside to see and bless the deliverers of their country. Food, drink, and refresh-ments of every kind were eagerly pressed on their acceptance. Each peasant thought a favor was conferred on him if one of Nero's chosen band would accept aught at his hands. The soldiers caught the full spirit of their leader. Night and day they marched forward, taking their hurried meals in the ranks, and resting by relay in the wagons which the zeal of the country people provided, and which followed in the rear of the column.

Meanwhile, at Rome, the news of Nero's expedition had caused the greatest excitement and alarm. All men felt the full audacity of the enterprise, but hesitated what epithet to apply to it. It was evident that Nero's conduct would be judged of by the event, that most unfair criterion, as the Roman historian truly terms it. People reasoned on the perilous state in which Nero had left the rest of his army, without a general, and deprived of the core of its strength, in the vicinity of the terrible Hannibal. They speculated on how long it would take Hannibal to pursue and overtake Nero himself, and his expeditionary force. They talked over the former disasters of the war, and the fall of both the consuls of the last year. All these calamities had come on them while they had only one Carthaginian general and army to deal with in Italy. Now they had two Punic wars at a time. They had two Carthaginian armies, they had almost two Hannibals, in Italy. Hasdrubal was sprung from the same father; trained up in the same hostility to Rome; equally practised in battle against their legions; and, if the comparative speed and success with which he had crossed the Alps were a fair test, he was even a better general than his brother. With fear for their interpreter of every rumor, they exaggerated the strength of their enemy's forces in every quarter, and criticised and distrusted their own.

Fortunately for Rome, while she was thus a prey to terror and anxiety, her consul's nerves were stout and strong, and he resolutely urged on his march toward Sena, where his colleague Livius and the prætor Porcius were encamped, Hasdrubal's army being in position about half a mile to their north. Nero had sent couriers forward to apprise his colleague of his project and of his approach; and by the advice of Livius, Nero so timed his final march as to reach the camp at Sena by night. According to a previous arrangement, Nero's men were received silently into the tents of their comrades, each according to his rank. By these means there was no enlargement of the camp that could betray to Hasdrubal the accession of force which the Romans had received. This was considerable, as Nero's numbers had been increased on the march by the volunteers, who offered themselves in crowds, and from whom he selected the most promising men, and especially the veterans of former campaigns. A council of war was held on the morning after his arrival, in which some advised that time should be given for Nero's men to refresh themselves after the fatigue of such a march. But Nero vehemently opposed all delay. "The officer," said he, "who is for giving time to my men here to rest themselves is for giving time to Hannibal to attack my men, whom I have left in the camp in Apulia. He is for giving time to Hannibal and Hasdrubal to discover my march, and to manœuvre for a junction with each other in Cisalpine Gaul at their leisure. We must fight instantly, while both the foe here and the foe in the South are ignorant of our movements. We must destroy this Hasdrubal, and I must be back in Apulia before Hannibal awakes from his torpor." Nero's advice prevailed. It was resolved to fight directly; and before the consuls and prætor left the tent of Livius, the red ensign, which was the signal to prepare for immediate action, was hoisted, and the Romans forthwith drew up in battle array outside the camp.

Hasdrubal had been anxious to bring Livius and Porcius to battle, though he had not judged it expedient to attack them in their lines. And now, on hearing that the Romans offered battle, he also drew up his men and advanced toward them. No spy or deserter had informed him of Nero's arrival, nor had he received any direct information that he had more than his old enemies to deal with. But as he rode forward to reconnoitre the Roman line, he thought that their numbers seemed to have increased, and that the armor of some of them was unusually dull and stained. He noticed, also, that the horses of some of the cavalry appeared to be rough and out of condition, as if they had just come from a succession of forced marches. So also, though, owing to the precaution of Livius, the Roman camp showed no change of size, it had not escaped the quick ear of the Carthaginian general that the trumpet which gave the signal to the Roman legions sounded that morning once oftener than usual, as if directing the troops of some additional superior officer. Hasdrubal, from his Spanish campaigns, was well acquainted with all the sounds and signals of Roman war, and from all that he heard and saw he felt convinced that both the Roman consuls were before him. In doubt and difficulty as to what might have taken place between the armies of the South, and probably hoping that Hannibal also was approaching, Hasdrubal determined to avoid an encounter with the combined Roman forces, and to endeavor to retreat upon Insubrian Gaul, where he would be in a friendly country, and could endeavor to reopen his communication with his brother. He therefore led his troops back into their camp; and as the Romans did not venture on an assault upon his intrenchments, and Hasdrubal did not choose to commence his retreat in their sight, the day passed away in inaction. At the first watch of the night Hasdrubal led his men silently out of their camp, and moved northward toward the Metaurus, in the hope of placing that river between himself and the Romans before his retreat was discovered. His guides betrayed him; and having purposely led him away from the part of the river that was fordable, they made their escape in the dark, and left Hasdrubal and his army wandering in confusion along the steep bank, and seeking in vain for a spot where the stream could be safely crossed. At last they halted; and when day dawned on them, Hasdrubal found that great numbers of his men, in their fatigue and impatience, had lost all discipline and subordination, and that many of his Gallic auxiliaries had got drunk, and were lying helpless in their quarters. The Roman cavalry was soon seen coming up in pursuit, followed at no great distance by the legions, which marched in readiness for an instant engagement. It was hopeless for Hasdrubal to think of continuing his retreat before them. The prospect of immediate battle might recall the disordered part of his troops to a sense of duty, and revive the instinct of discipline. He therefore ordered his men to prepare for action instantly, and made the best arrangement of them that the nature of the ground would permit.

Heeren has well described the general appearance of a Carthaginian army. He says: "It was an assemblage of the most opposite races of the human species from the farthest parts of the globe. Hordes of half-naked Gauls were ranged next to companies of white-clothed Iberians, and savage Ligurians next to the far-travelled Nasamones and Lotophagi. Carthaginians and Phœnici-Africans formed the centre, while innumerable troops of Numidian horsemen, taken from all the tribes of the Desert, swarmed about on unsaddled horses, and formed the wings; the van was composed of Balearic slingers; and a line of colossal elephants, with their Ethiopian guides, formed, as it were, a chain of moving fortresses before the whole army."

Such were the usual materials and arrangements of the hosts that fought for Carthage; but the troops under Hasdrubal were not in all respects thus constituted or thus stationed. He seems to have been especially deficient in cavalry, and he had few African troops, though some Carthaginians of high rank were with him. His veteran Spanish infantry, armed with helmets and shields, and short cut-and-thrust swords, were the best part of his army. These and his few Africans he drew up on his right wing, under his own personal command. In the centre he placed his Ligurian infantry, and on the left wing he placed or retained the Gauls, who were armed with long javelins and with huge broadswords and targets. The rugged nature of the ground in front and on the flank of this part of his line made him hope that the Roman right wing would be unable to come to close quarters with these unserviceable barbarians before he could make some impression with his Spanish veterans on the Roman left. This was the only chance that he had of victory or safety, and he seems to have done everything that good generalship could do to secure it. He placed his elephants in advance of his centre and right wing. He had caused the driver of each of them to be provided with a sharp iron spike and a mallet, and had given orders that every beast that became unmanageable, and ran back upon his own ranks, should be instantly killed by driving the spike into the vertebra at the junction of the head and the spine. Hasdrubal's elephants were ten in number. We have no trustworthy information as to the amount of his infantry, but it is quite clear that he was greatly outnumbered by the combined Roman forces.

The tactics of the Roman legions had not yet acquired that perfection which they received from the military genius of Marius,[1] and which we read of in the first chapter of Gibbon. We possess, in that great work, an account of the Roman legions at the end of the commonwealth, and during the early ages of the empire, which those alone can adequately admire who have attempted a similar description. We have also, in the sixth

[1] Most probably during the period of his prolonged consulship, from B.C. 104 to B.C. 101, while he was training his army against the Cimbri and the Teutons.

and seventeenth books of Polybius, an elaborate discussion on the military system of the Romans in his time, which was not far distant from the time of the battle of the Metaurus. But the subject is beset with difficulties; and instead of entering into minute but inconclusive details, I would refer to Gibbon's first chapter as serving for a general description of the Roman army in its period of perfection, and remark that the training and armor which the whole legion received in the time of Augustus were, two centuries earlier, only partially introduced. Two divisions of troops, called *hastati* and *principes*, formed the bulk of each Roman legion in the Second Punic War. Each of these divisions was twelve hundred strong. The hastatus and the princeps legionary bore a breastplate or coat of mail, brazen greaves, and a brazen helmet with a lofty upright crest of scarlet or black feathers. He had a large oblong shield; and, as weapons of offence, two javelins, one of which was light and slender, but the other was a strong and massive weapon, with a shaft about four feet long and an iron head of equal length. The sword was carried on the right thigh, and was a short cut-and-thrust weapon, like that which was used by the Spaniards. Thus armed, the hastati formed the front division of the legion, and the principes the second. Each division was drawn up about ten deep, a space of three feet being allowed between the files as well as the ranks, so as to give each legionary ample room for the use of his javelins and of his sword and shield. The men in the second rank did not stand immediately behind those in the first rank, but the files were alternate, like the position of the men on a draught-board. This was termed the *quincunx* order.

Niebuhr considers that this arrangement enabled the legion to keep up a shower of javelins on the enemy for some considerable time. He says: "When the first line had hurled its *pila*, it probably stepped back between those who stood behind it, and two steps forward restored the front nearly to its first position; a movement which, on account of the arrangement of the quincunx, could be executed without losing a moment. Thus one line succeeded the other in the front till it was time to draw the swords; nay, when it was found expedient, the lines which had already been in the front might repeat this change.

since the stores of pila were surely not confined to the two which each soldier took with him into battle.

"The same charge must have taken place in fighting with the sword, which, when the same tactics were adopted on both sides, was anything but a confused *mêlée;* on the contrary, it was a series of single combats." He adds that a military man of experience had been consulted by him on the subject and had given it as his opinion "that the change of the lines as described above was by no means impracticable; but, in the absence of the deafening noise of gunpowder, it cannot have had even any difficulty with well-trained troops."

The third division of the legion was six hundred strong and acted as a reserve. It was always composed of veteran soldiers, who were called the *triarii*. Their arms were the same as these of the principes and hastati, except that each *triarian* carried a spear instead of javelins. The rest of the legion consisted of light-armed troops, who acted as skirmishers. The cavalry of each legion was at this period about three hundred strong. The Italian allies who were attached to the legion seem to have been similarly armed and equipped, but their numerical proportion of cavalry was much larger.

Such was the nature of the forces that advanced on the Roman side to the battle of the Metaurus. Nero commanded the right wing, Livius the left, and the prætor Porcius had the command of the centre. "Both Romans and Carthaginians well understood how much depended upon the fortune of this day, and how little hope of safety there was for the vanquished. Only the Romans herein seemed to have had the better in conceit and opinion that they were to fight with men desirous to have fled from them; and according to this presumption came Livius the consul, with a proud bravery, to give charge on the Spaniards and Africans, by whom he was so sharply entertained that the victory seemed very doubtful. The Africans and Spaniards were stout soldiers, and well acquainted with the manner of the Roman fight. The Ligurians also were a hardy nation, and not accustomed to give ground, which they needed the less, or were able now to do, being placed in the midst. Livius, therefore, and Porcius found great opposition; and with great slaughter on both sides prevailed little or nothing.   Besides other difficulties, they were exceedingly troubled by the elephants, that brake their first ranks and put them in such disorder as the Roman ensigns were driven to fall back; all this while Claudius Nero, laboring in vain against a steep hill, was unable to come to blows with the Gauls that stood opposite him, but out of danger.   This made Hasdrubal the more confident, who, seeing his own left wing safe, did the more boldly and fiercely make impression on the other side upon the left wing of the Romans." [1]

But at last Nero, who found that Hasdrubal refused his left wing, and who could not overcome the difficulties of the ground in the quarter assigned to him, decided the battle by another stroke of that military genius which had inspired his march.   Wheeling a brigade of his best men round the rear of the rest of the Roman army, Nero fiercely charged the flank of the Spaniards and Africans.   The charge was as successful as it was sudden.   Rolled back in disorder upon each other, and overwhelmed by numbers, the Spaniards and Ligurians died, fighting gallantly to the last.   The Gauls, who had taken little or no part in the strife of the day, were then surrounded, and butchered almost without resistance.   Hasdrubal, after having, by the confession of his enemies, done all that a general could do, when he saw that the victory was irreparably lost, scorning to survive the gallant host which he had led, and to gratify, as a captive, Roman cruelty and pride, spurred his horse into the midst of a Roman cohort, and sword in hand, met the death that was worthy of the son of Hamilcar and the brother of Hannibal.

Success the most complete had crowned Nero's enterprise. Returning as rapidly as he had advanced, he was again facing the inactive enemies in the South before they even knew of his march.   But he brought with him a ghastly trophy of what he had done.   In the true spirit of that savage brutality which deformed the Roman national character, Nero ordered Hasdrubal's head to be flung into his brother's camp.   Ten years had passed since Hannibal had last gazed on those features. The sons of Hamilcar had then planned their system of warfare against Rome which they had so nearly brought to suc-

[1] Sir Walter Raleigh: *Historie of the World.*

cessful accomplishment. Year after year had Hannibal been struggling in Italy, in the hope of one day hailing the arrival of him whom he had left in Spain, and of seeing his brother's eye flash with affection and pride at the junction of their irresistible hosts. He now saw that eye glazed in death, and in the agony of his heart the great Carthaginian groaned aloud that he recognized his country's destiny.

Meanwhile, at the tidings of the great battle, Rome at once rose from the thrill of anxiety and terror to the full confidence of triumph. Hannibal might retain his hold on Southern Italy for a few years longer, but the imperial city and her allies were no longer in danger from his arms; and, after Hannibal's downfall, the great military republic of the ancient world met in her career of conquest no other worthy competitor. Byron has termed Nero's march "unequalled," and, in the magnitude of its consequences, it is so. Viewed only as a military exploit, it remains unparalleled save by Marlborough's bold march from Flanders to the Danube in the campaign of Blenheim, and perhaps also by the Archduke Charles' lateral march in 1796, by which he overwhelmed the French under Jourdan, and then, driving Moreau through the Black Forest and across the Rhine, for a while freed Germany from her invaders.

SCIPIO AFRICANUS CRUSHES HANNIBAL AT ZAMA AND SUBJUGATES CARTHAGE

B.C. 202

LIVY

Sprung from a colony of Tyre, Carthage, .ounded about B.C. 800, rapidly developed, through a wonderful system of colonization, into a dominating power, her rule extending through Northwestern Africa and Western Europe. In B.C. 509 Carthage made her first treaty with Rome. But the rivalry which grew up between the two Powers developed into a stubborn contest for the empire of the world, culminating in the three Punic wars. The first of these lasted from B.C. 264 to 241; the second, from B.C. 218 to 201. In the interval between these two wars Rome acquired the northern part of Italy, whence she sent victorious armies against the barbarians in Gaul. Meanwhile, under Hamilcar Barcar, the Carthaginians had effected the conquest of Southern Spain, which they reduced to the condition of a dependency.

Hamilcar's greater son, Hannibal, was compelled by his father to swear eternal enmity to Rome. Having established the Carthaginian empire in Spain, at the age of twenty-six he took the Spanish city of Saguntum, an ally of Rome, and this was the immediate cause of the Second Punic War, which the Romans declared. The passage of the Alps by Hannibal is regarded as one of the greatest military performances in history. He was welcomed by the Gauls as a deliverer, and was soon operating in Northern Italy, his appearance there being a complete surprise to the Romans. He won victories over them at the rivers Ticinus and Trebia, B.C. 218; another in 217 at Lake Trasimenus; a great triumph at Cannæ in 216; took Capua in the same year, and wintered there; in 212 captured Tarentum; marched against Rome in 211; and in 203 was recalled to Africa.

In the mean time the Romans had decided to carry the war into Africa, although in 215 they had beaten Hannibal, and in 211 had retaken Capua. Publius Cornelius Scipio (Scipio Africanus Major) in B.C. 210–206 drove the Carthaginians out of Spain. In 205 he was made consul, and the next year invaded Africa. Landing on the coast, he was met by the forces of the Numidian King, who became his allies against Carthage. In 203 he defeated Syphax and Hasdrubal. Hannibal now having returned to Carthage, he took command of the forces which she opposed to the Roman invaders, but in B.C. 202 suffered final overthrow at Zama,

224

in the battle that ended the Second Punic War. Livy's account of the closing scenes of that war, which here follows, gives the reader a clear understanding of the sequence and conclusion of the events related.

MARCUS SERVILIUS and Tiberius Claudius, having assembled the senate, consulted them respecting the provinces. As both were desirous of having Africa, they wished Italy and Africa to be disposed of by lots; but, principally in consequence of the exertions of Quintus Metellus, Africa was neither assigned to anyone nor withheld. The consuls were ordered to make application to the tribunes of the people, to the effect that, if they thought proper, they should put it to the people to decide whom they wished to conduct the war in Africa. All the tribes nominated Publius Scipio. Nevertheless, the consuls put the province of Africa to the lot, for so the senate had decreed. Africa fell to the lot of Tiberius Claudius, who was to cross over into Africa with a fleet of fifty ships, all quinqueremes, and have an equal command with Scipio. Marcus Servilius obtained Etruria. Caius Servilius was continued in command in the same province, in case the senate resolved that the consul should remain at the city. Of the prætors, Marcus Sextus obtained Gaul, which province, together with two legions, Publius Quinctilius Varus was to deliver to him; Caius Livius obtained Bruttium, with the two legions which Publius Sempronius, the proconsul, had commanded the former year; Cneius Tremellius had Sicily, and was to receive the province and two legions from Publius Villius Tappulus, a prætor of the former year; Villius, as proprætor, was to protect the coast of Sicily with twenty men-of-war and a thousand soldiers; and Marcus Pomponius was to convey thence to Rome one thousand five hundred soldiers, with the remaining twenty ships. The city jurisdiction fell to Caius Aurelius Cotta; and the rest of the prætors were continued in command of the respective provinces and armies which they then had. Not more than sixteen legions were employed this year in the defence of the empire. And, that they might have the gods favorably disposed toward them in all their undertakings and proceedings, it was ordered that the consuls, before they set out to the war, should celebrate those games and sacrifice those victims of the larger sort which, in the consulate of Marcus Claudius Marcellus and Titus Quinctius, Titus Manlius the dictator had vowed, provided the commonwealth should continue in the same state for the next five years. The games were exhibited in the circus during four days, and the victims sacrificed to those deities to whom they had been vowed.

Meanwhile, hope and anxiety daily and simultaneously increased; nor could the minds of men be brought to any fixed conclusion, whether it was a fit subject for rejoicing that Hannibal had now at length, after the sixteenth year, departed from Italy and left the Romans in the unmolested possession of it or whether they had not greater cause to fear from his having transported his army in safety into Africa. They said that the scene of action certainly was changed, but not the danger. That Quintus Fabius, lately deceased, who had foretold how arduous the contest would be, was used to predict, not without good reason, that Hannibal would prove a more formidable enemy in his own country than he had been in a foreign one; and that Scipio would have to encounter, not Syphax, a king of undisciplined barbarians whose armies Statorius, a man little better than a soldier's drudge, was used to lead, nor his father-in-law Hasdrubal, that most fugacious general, nor tumultuary armies hastily collected out of a crowd of half-armed rustics, but Hannibal, born in a manner in the pavilion of his father, that bravest of generals, nurtured and educated in the midst of arms, who served as a soldier formerly, when a boy, and became a general when he had scarcely attained the age of manhood; who, having grown old in victory, had filled Spain, Gaul, and Italy, from the Alps to the strait, with monuments of his vast achievements; who commanded troops who had served as long as he had himself; troops hardened by the endurance of every species of suffering, such as it is scarcely credible that men could have supported; stained a thousand times with Roman blood, and bearing with them the spoils not only of soldiers, but of generals. That many would meet the eyes of Scipio in battle who had with their own hands slain Roman prætors, generals, and consuls; many decorated with crowns in reward for having scaled walls and crossed ramparts; many who had traversed the captured camps and cities of the Romans. That the magistrates of the Roman people had not then so many fasces as Hannibal could have carried before him, having taken them from generals whom he had slain. While their minds were harassed by these apprehensions, their anxiety and fears were further increased from the circumstance that, whereas they had been accustomed to carry on war for several years in different parts of Italy, and within their view, with languid hopes and without the prospect of bringing it to a speedy termination, Scipio and Hannibal had stimulated the minds of all, as generals prepared for a final contest. Even those persons whose confidence in Scipio and hopes of victory were great, were affected with anxiety, increasing in proportion as they saw their completion approaching. The state of feeling among the Carthaginians was much the same; for when they turned their eyes on Hannibal, and the greatness of his achievements, they repented having solicited peace; but when again they reflected that they had been twice defeated in a pitched battle, that Syphax had been made prisoner, that they had been driven out of Spain and Italy, and that all this had been effected by the valor and conduct of Scipio alone, they regarded him with horror, as a general marked out by destiny, and born for their destruction.

Hannibal had by this time arrived at Adrumetum, from which place, after employing a few days there in refreshing his soldiers, who had suffered from the motion by sea, he proceeded by forced marches to Zama, roused by the alarming statements of messengers who brought word that all the country around Carthage was filled with armed troops. Zama is distant from Carthage a five days' journey. Some spies whom he sent out from this place, being intercepted by the Roman guard and brought before Scipio, he directed that they should be handed over to the military tribunes, and after having been desired fearlessly to survey everything, to be conducted through the camp wherever they chose; then, asking them whether they had examined everything to their satisfaction, he assigned them an escort and sent them back to Hannibal.

Hannibal received none of the circumstances which were reported to him with feelings of joy, for they brought word that, as it happened, Masinissa had joined the enemy that very day with six thousand infantry and four thousand horse; but he was principally dispirited by the confidence of his enemy, which, doubtless, was not conceived without some ground. Accordingly, though he himself was the originator of the war, and by his coming had upset the truce which had been entered into, and cut off all hopes of a treaty, yet concluding that more favorable terms might be obtained if he solicited peace while his strength was unimpaired than when vanquished, he sent a message to Scipio requesting permission to confer with him.

Scipio took up his position not far from the city of Nara-gara, in a situation convenient not only for other purposes, but also because there was a watering-place within a dart's throw. Hannibal took possession of an eminence four miles thence, safe and convenient in every respect, except that he had a long way to go for water. Here in the intermediate space a place was chosen open to view from all sides, that there might be no opportunity for treachery.

Their armed attendants having retired to an equal distance, they met, each attended by one interpreter, being the greatest generals not only of their own times, but of any to be found in the records of the times preceding them, and equal to any of the kings or generals of any nation whatever. When they came within sight of each other they remained silent for a short time, thunderstruck, as it were, with mutual admiration. At length Hannibal thus began: "Since fate hath so ordained it that I, who was the first to wage war upon the Romans, and who have so often had victory almost within my reach, should voluntarily come to sue for peace, I rejoice that it is you, above all others, from whom it is my lot to solicit it. To you, also, amid the many distinguished events of your life, it will not be esteemed one of the least glorious that Hannibal, to whom the gods had so often granted victory over the Roman generals, should have yielded to you; and that you should have put an end to this war, which has been rendered remarkable by your calamities before it was by ours.

"Peace is proposed at a time when you have the advantage. We who negotiate it are the persons whom it most concerns to obtain it, and we are persons whose arrangements, be they what they will, our states will ratify. You have recovered Spain, which had been lost, after driving thence four Carthaginian armies. When elected consul, though all others wanted courage to defend Italy, you crossed over into Africa, where having cut to pieces two armies, having at once captured and burnt two camps in the same hour, having made prisoner Syphax, a most powerful king, and seized so many towns of his dominions and so many of ours, you have dragged me from Italy, the possession of which I had firmly held for now sixteen years. While your affairs are in a favorable and ours in a dubious state, you would derive honor and splendor from granting peace; while to us, who solicit it, it would be considered as necessary rather than honorable.

"It is indeed the right of him who grants, and not of him who solicits it, to dictate the terms of peace, but perhaps we may not be unworthy to impose upon ourselves the fine. We do not refuse that all those possessions on account of which the war was begun should be yours; Sicily, Sardinia, Spain, with all the islands lying in any part of the sea, between Africa and Italy. Let us Carthaginians, confined within the shores of Africa, behold you, since such is the pleasure of the gods, extending your empire over foreign nations both by sea and land. I cannot deny that you have reason to suspect the Carthaginian faith, in consequence of their insincerity lately in soliciting a peace and while awaiting the decision. The sincerity with which a peace will be observed depends much, Scipio, on the person by whom it is sought. Your senate, as I hear, refused to grant a peace in some measure because the deputies were deficient in respectability. It is I, Hannibal, who now solicit peace; who would neither ask for it unless I believed it expedient, nor will I fail to observe it for the same reason of expedience on account of which I have solicited it. And in the same manner as I, because the war was commenced by me, brought it to pass that no one regretted it till the gods began to regard me with displeasure; so will I also exert myself that no one may regret the peace procured by my means."

In answer to these things the Roman general spoke nearly to the following effect: "I was aware that it was in consequence of the expectation of your arrival that the Carthaginians violated the existing faith of the truce and broke off all hope of a peace. Nor, indeed, do you conceal the fact, inasmuch as you artfully withdraw from the former conditions of peace every concession except what relates to those things which have for a long time been in our own power. But as it is your object that your countrymen should be sensible how great a burden they are relieved from by your means, so it is incumbent upon me to endeavor that they may not receive, as the reward of their perfidy, the concessions which they formerly stipulated, by expunging them now from the conditions of the peace. Though you do not deserve to be allowed the same conditions as before, you now request even to be benefited by your treachery.

"Neither did our fathers first make war respecting Sicily, nor did we respecting Spain. In the former case the danger which threatened our allies the Mamertines, and in the present the destruction of Saguntum, girded us with just and pious arms. That you were the aggressors, both you yourselves confess and the gods are witnesses, who determined the issue of the former war, and who are now determining and will determine the issue of the present according to right and justice. As to myself, I am not forgetful of the instability of human affairs, but consider the influence of fortune, and am well aware that all our measures are liable to a thousand casualties. But as I should acknowledge that my conduct would savor of insolence and oppression if I rejected you on your coming in person to solicit peace before I crossed over into Africa, you voluntarily retiring from Italy, and after you had embarked your troops, so now, when I have dragged you into Africa almost by manual force, notwithstanding your resistance and evasions, I am not bound to treat you with any respect. Wherefore, if in addition to those stipulations on which it was considered that a peace would at that time have been agreed upon, and what they are you are informed, a compensation is proposed for having seized our ships together with their stores during a truce, and for the violence offered to our ambassadors, I shall then have matter to lay before my council. But if these things also appear oppressive, prepare for war, since you could not brook the conditions of peace."

Thus, without effecting an accommodation, when they had returned from the conference to their armies, they informed them that words had been bandied to no purpose, that the question must be decided by arms, and that they must accept that fortune which the gods assigned them.

When they had arrived at their camps, they both issued orders that their soldiers should get their arms in readiness and prepare their minds for the final contest; in which, if fortune should favor them, they would continue victorious, not for a single day, but forever. "Before to-morrow night," they said, "they would know whether Rome or Carthage should give laws to the world, and that neither Africa nor Italy, but the whole world, would be the prize of victory. That the dangers which threatened those who had the misfortune to be defeated were proportioned to the rewards of the victors." For the Romans had not any place of refuge in an unknown and foreign land, and immediate destruction seemed to await Carthage if the troops which formed her last reliance were defeated. To this important contest, the day following, two generals, by far the most renowned of any, and belonging to two of the most powerful nations in the world, advanced either to crown or overthrow on that day the many honors they had previously acquired.

Scipio drew up his troops, posting the hastati in front, the principes behind them, and closing his rear line with the triarii. He did not draw up his cohorts in close order, but each before their respective standards; placing the companies at some distance from each other, so as to leave a space through which the elephants of the enemy passing might not at all break their ranks. Lælius, whom he had employed before as lieutenant-general, but this year as quæstor, by special appointment, according to a decree of the senate, he posted with the Italian cavalry in the left wing, Masinissa and the Numidians in the right. The open spaces between the companies of those in the van he filled with velites, which then formed the Roman light-armed troops, with an injunction that on the charge of the elephants they should either retire behind the files, which extended in a right line, or, running to the right and left and placing themselves by the side of those in the van, afford a passage by which the elephants might rush in between weapons on both sides.

Hannibal, in order to terrify the enemy, drew up his elephants in front, and he had eighty of them, being more than he had ever had in any battle; behind these his Ligurian and Gallic auxiliaries, with Balearians and Moors intermixed. In the second line he placed the Carthaginians, Africans, and a legion of Macedonians; then, leaving a moderate interval, he formed a reserve of Italian troops, consisting principally of Bruttians, more of whom had followed him on his departure from Italy by compulsion and necessity than by choice. His cavalry also he placed in the wings, the Carthaginian occupying the right, the Numidian the left. Various were the means of exhortation employed in an army consisting of a mixture of so many different kinds of men; men differing in language, customs, laws, arms, dress, and appearance, and in the motives for serving. To the auxiliaries, the prospect both of their present pay and many times more from the spoils was held out. The Gauls were stimulated by their peculiar and inherent animosity against the Romans. To the Ligurians the hope was held out of enjoying the fertile plains of Italy, and quitting their rugged mountains, if victorious. The Moors and Numidians were terrified with subjection to the government of Masinissa, which he would exercise with despotic severity.

Different grounds of hope and fear were represented to different persons. The view of the Carthaginians was directed to the walls of their city, their household gods, the sepulchres of their ancestors, their children and parents, and their trembling wives; they were told that either the destruction of their city and slavery or the empire of the world awaited them; that there was nothing intermediate which they could hope for or fear.

While the general was thus busily employed among the Carthaginians, and the captains of the respective nations among their countrymen, most of them employing interpreters among troops intermixed with those of different nations, the trumpets and cornets of the Romans sounded; and such a clamor arose that the elephants, especially those in the left wing, turned round upon their own party, the Moors and Numidians. Masinissa had no difficulty in increasing the alarm of the terrified enemy, and deprived them of the aid of their cavalry in that wing. A few, however, of the beasts which were driven against the enemy, and were not turned back through fear, made great havoc among the ranks of the velites, though not without receiving many wounds themselves; for when the velites, retiring to the companies, had made way for the elephants, that they might not be trampled down, they discharged their darts at them; exposed as they were to wounds on both sides, those in the van also keeping up a continual discharge of javelins, until driven out of the Roman line by the weapons which fell upon them from all quarters, these elephants also put to flight even the cavalry of the Carthaginians posted in their right wing. Lælius, when he saw the enemy in disorder, struck additional terror into them in their confusion.

The Carthaginian line was deprived of the cavalry on both sides, when the infantry, who were now not a match for the Romans in confidence or strength, engaged. In addition to this there was one circumstance, trifling in itself, but at the same time producing important consequences in the action. On the part of the Romans the shout was uniform, and on that account louder and more terrific, while the voices of the enemy, consisting as they did of many nations of different languages, were dissonant. The Romans used the stationary kind of fight, pressing upon the enemy with their own weight and that of their arms; but on the other side there was more of skirmishing and rapid movement than force. Accordingly, on the first charge, the Romans immediately drove back the line of their opponents; then pushing them with their elbows and the bosses of their shields, and pressing forward into the places from which they had pushed them, they advanced a considerable space, as though there had been no one to resist them, those who formed the rear urging forward those in front when they perceived the line of the enemy giving way, which circumstance itself gave great additional force in repelling them.

On the side of the enemy, the second line, consisting of the Africans and Carthaginians, were so far from supporting the first line when giving ground, that on the contrary they even retired, lest their enemy, by slaying those who made a firm resistance, should penetrate to themselves also. Accordingly the auxiliaries suddenly turned their backs, and facing about upon their own party, fled, some of them into the second line, while others slew those who did not receive them into their ranks, since before they did not support them, and now refused to receive them. And now there were, in a manner, two contests going on together, the Carthaginians being compelled to fight at once with the enemy and with their own party. Not even then, however, did they receive into their line the terrified and exasperated troops, but, closing their ranks, drove them out of the scene of action to the wings and the surrounding plain, lest they should mingle these soldiers, terrified with defeat and wounds, with that part of their line which was firm and fresh.

But such a heap of men and arms had filled the space in which the auxiliaries a little while ago had stood that it was almost more difficult to pass through it than through a close line of troops. The spearmen, therefore, who formed the front line, pursuing the enemy as each could find a way through the heap of arms and men and streams of blood, threw into complete disorder the battalions and companies. The standards also of the principes had begun to waver when they saw the line before them driven from their ground. Scipio, perceiving this, promptly ordered the signal to be given for the spearmen to retreat, and having taken his wounded into the rear, brought the principes and triarii to the wings in order that the line of spearmen in the centre might be more strong and secure. Thus a fresh and renewed battle commenced, inasmuch as they had penetrated to their real antagonists, men equal to them in the nature of their arms, in their experience in war, in the fame of their achievements, and the greatness of their hopes and fears. But the Romans were superior both in numbers and courage, for they had now routed both the cavalry and the elephants, and, having already defeated the front line, were fighting against the second.

Lælius and Masinissa, who had pursued the routed cavalry through a considerable space, returning very opportunely, charged the rear of the enemy's line. This attack of the cavalry at length routed them. Many of them, being surrounded, were slain in the field; and many, dispersed in flight through the open plain around, were slain on all hands, as the cavalry were in possession of every part.   Of the Carthaginians and their allies, above twenty thousand were slain on that day; about an equal number were captured, with a hundred and thirty-three military standards and eleven elephants.   Of the victors as many as two thousand fell.

Hannibal, slipping off during the confusion, with a few horsemen, came to Adrumetum, not quitting the field till he had tried every expedient both in the battle and before the engagement; having, according to the admission of Scipio and everyone skilled in military science, acquired the fame of having marshalled his troops on that day with singular judgment. He placed his elephants in the front, in order that their desultory attack and insupportable violence might prevent the Romans from following their standards and preserving their ranks, on which they placed their principal dependence.   Then he posted his auxiliaries before the line of Carthaginians, in order that men who were made up of the refuse of all nations, and who were not bound by honor but by gain, might not have any retreat open to them in case they fled; at the same time that the first ardor and impetuosity might be exhausted upon them, and, if they could render no other service, that the weapons of the enemy might be blunted in wounding them. Next he placed the Carthaginian and African soldiers, on whom he placed all his hopes, in order that, being equal to the enemy in every other respect, they might have the advantage of them inasmuch as, being fresh and unimpaired in strength themselves, they would fight with those who were fatigued and wounded.   The Italians he removed into the rear, separating them also by an intervening space, as he knew not with certainty whether they were friends or enemies.   Hannibal, after performing this as it were his last work of valor, fled to Adrumetum, whence, having been summoned to Carthage, he returned thither in the sixth and thirtieth year after he had left it when a boy, and confessed in the senate house that he was defeated, not only in the battle, but in the war, and that there was no hope of safety in anything but in obtaining peace.

Immediately after the battle, Scipio, having taken and plundered the enemy's camp, returned to the sea and his ships with an immense booty, news having reached him that Publius Lentulus had arrived at Utica with fifty men-of-war, and a hundred transports laden with every kind of stores. Concluding that he ought to bring before Carthage everything which could increase the consternation already existing there, after sending Lælius to Rome to report his victory, he ordered Cneius Octavius to conduct the legions thither by land, and setting out himself from Utica with the fresh fleet of Lentulus added to his former one, made for the harbor of Carthage. When he had arrived within a short distance he was met by a Carthaginian ship decked with fillets and branches of olive. There were ten deputies, the leading men in the State, sent at the instance of Hannibal to solicit peace, to whom, when they had come up to the stern of the general's ship, holding out the badges of suppliants, entreating and imploring the protection and compassion of Scipio, the only answer given was that they must come to Tunis, to which place he would move his camp. After taking a view of the site of Carthage, not so much for the sake of acquainting himself with it for any present object as to dispirit the enemy, he returned to Utica, having recalled Octavius to the same place.

As they were proceeding thence to Tunis, they received intelligence that Vermina, the son of Syphax, with a greater number of horse than foot, was coming to the assistance of the Carthaginians. A part of his infantry with all the cavalry having attacked them on their march on the first day of the Saturnalia, routed the Numidians with little opposition, and as every way by which they could escape in flight was blocked up, for the cavalry surrounded them on all sides, fifteen thousand men were slain, twelve hundred were taken alive, with fifteen hundred Numidian horses and seventy-two military standards. The prince himself fled from the field with a few attendants during the confusion. The camp was then pitched near Tunis in the same place as before, and thirty ambassadors came to Scipio from Carthage. These behaved in a manner even more calculated to excite compassion than the former, in proportion as their situation was more pressing; but from the recollection of their recent perfidy, they were heard with considerably less pity. In the council, though all were impelled by just resentment to demolish Carthage, yet, when they reflected upon the magnitude of the undertaking and the length of time which would be consumed in the siege of so well fortified and strong a city, while Scipio himself was uneasy in consequence of the expectation of a successor, who would come in for the glory of having terminated the war, though it was accomplished already by the exertions and danger of another, the minds of all were inclined to peace.

The next day the ambassadors being called in again, and with many rebukes of their perfidy, warned that instructed by so many disasters they would at length believe in the existence of the gods and the obligation of an oath, these conditions of the peace were stated to them: "That they should enjoy their liberty and live under their own laws; that they should possess such cities and territories as they had enjoyed before the war, and with the same boundaries, and that the Romans should on that day desist from devastation. That they should restore to the Romans all deserters and fugitives, giving up all their ships-of-war except ten triremes, with such tamed elephants as they had, and that they should not tame any more. That they should not carry on war in or out of Africa without the permission of the Roman people. That they should make restitution to Masinissa, and form a league with him. That they should furnish corn, and pay for the auxiliaries until the ambassadors had returned from Rome. That they should pay ten thousand talents of silver in equal annual instalments distributed over fifty years. That they should give a hundred hostages, according to the pleasure of Scipio, not younger than fourteen nor older than thirty. That he would grant them a truce on condition that the transports, together with their cargoes, which had been seized during the former truce, were restored. Otherwise they would have no truce, nor any hope of a peace." When the ambassadors who were ordered to bear these conditions home reported them in an assembly, and Gisgo had stood forth to dissuade them from the terms, and was being listened to by the multitude, who were at once indisposed for peace and unfit for war, Hannibal, indignant that such language should be held and listened to at such a juncture, laid hold of Gisgo with his own hand and dragged him from his elevated position.

This unusual sight in a free State having raised a murmur among the people, the soldier, disconcerted at the liberties which the citizens took, thus addressed them: "Having left you when nine years old, I have returned after a lapse of thirty-six years. I flatter myself I am well acquainted with the qualifications of a soldier, having been instructed in them from my childhood, sometimes by my own situation and sometimes by that of my country. The privileges, the laws, and customs of the city and the forum you ought to teach me." Having thus apologized for his indiscretion, he discoursed largely concerning the peace, showing how inoppressive the terms were, and how necessary it was. The greatest difficulty was that of the ships which had been seized during the truce nothing was to be found except the ships themselves, nor was it easy to collect the property, because those who were charged with having it were opposed to the peace. It was resolved that the ships should be restored and that the men at least should be looked up; and as to whatever else was missing, that it should be left to Scipio to put a value upon it, and that the Carthaginians should make compensation accordingly in money. There are those who say that Hannibal went from the field of battle to the sea-coast; whence he immediately sailed in a ship, which he had ready for the purpose, to king Antiochus; and that when Scipio demanded above everything that Hannibal should be given up to him, answer was made that Hannibal was not in Africa.

After the ambassadors returned to Scipio, the quæstors were ordered to give in an account, made out from the public registers, of the public property which had been in the ships; and the owners to make a return of the private property. For the amount of the value twenty-five thousand pounds of silver were required to be paid down; and a truce for three months was granted to the Carthaginians. It was added that during the time of the truce they should not send ambassadors anywhere else than to Rome; and that whatever ambassadors came to Carthage, they should not dismiss them before informing the Roman general who they were and what they sought. With the Carthaginian ambassadors, Lucius Veturius Philo, Marcus Marcius Ralla, and Lucius Scipio, brother of the general, were sent to Rome.

The Roman, together with the Carthaginian, ambassadors having arrived at Rome from Africa, the senate was assembled at the temple of Bellona; when Lucius Veturius Philo stated, to the great joy of the senate, that a battle had been fought with Hannibal which was decisive of the fate of the Carthaginians, and that a period was at length put to that calamitous war. He added what formed a small accession to their successes, that Vermina, the son of Syphax, had been vanquished. He was then ordered to go forth to the public assembly and impart the joyful tidings to the people. Then, a thanksgiving having been appointed, all the temples in the city were thrown open and supplications for three days were decreed. Publius Scipio was continued in command in the province of Africa with the armies which he then had. The Carthaginian ambassadors were called before the senate. On observing their ages and dignified appearance, for they were by far the first men of the State, all promptly declared their conviction that now they were sincere in their desire to effect a peace. Hasdrubal, however, surnamed by his countrymen Hædus, who had invariably recommended peace and was opposed to the Barcine faction, was regarded with greater interest than the rest.

On these accounts the greater weight was attached to him when transferring the blame of the war from the State at large to the cupidity of a few. After a speech of varied character, in which he sometimes refuted the charges which had been brought, at other times admitted some, lest by imprudently denying what was manifestly true their forgiveness might be the more difficult; and then, even admonishing the conscript fathers to be guided by the rules of decorum and moderation in their prosperity, he said that if the Carthaginians had listened to himself and Hanno, and had been disposed to make a proper use of circumstances, they would themselves have dictated terms of peace, instead of begging it as they now did. That it rarely happened that good fortune and a sound judgment were bestowed upon men at the same time. That the Roman people were therefore invincible, because when successful they forgot not the maxims of wisdom and prudence; and indeed it would have been matter of astonishment did they act otherwise. That those persons to whom success was a new and uncommon thing proceeded to a pitch of madness in their ungoverned transports in consequence of their not being accustomed to it. That to the Roman people the joy arising from victory was a matter of common occurrence, and was now almost become old-fashioned. That they had extended their empire more by sparing the vanquished than by conquering.

The language employed by the others was of a nature more calculated to excite compassion; they represented from what a height of power the Carthaginian affairs had fallen. That nothing besides the walls of Carthage remained to those who a little time ago held almost the whole world in subjection by their arms; that shut up within these, they could see nothing anywhere on sea or land which owned their authority. That they would retain possession of their city itself and their household gods only in case the Roman people should refrain from venting their indignation upon these, which is all that remains for them to do. When it was manifest that the fathers were moved by compassion, it is said that one of the senators, violently incensed at the perfidy of the Carthaginians, immediately asked with a loud voice by what gods they would swear in striking the league, since they had broken their faith with those by whom they swore in striking the former one? By those same, replied Hasdrubal, who have shown such determined hostility to the violators of treaties.

The minds of all being disposed to peace, Cneius Lentulus, whose province the fleet was, protested against the decree of the senate. Upon this, Manius Acilius and Quintus Minucius, tribunes of the people, put the question to the people whether they willed and ordered that the senate should decree that peace should be made with the Carthaginians? whom they ordered to grant that peace, and whom to conduct the army out of Africa? All the tribes ordered respecting the peace according as the question had been put. That Publius Scipio should grant the peace, and that he also should conduct the army home. Agreeably to this order, the senate decreed that Publius Scipio, acting according to the opinion of the ten deputies, should make peace with the Carthaginian people on what terms he pleased. The Carthaginians then returned thanks to the senate, and requested that they might be allowed to enter the city and converse with their countrymen who had been made prisoners and were in custody of the State; observing that some of them were their relations and friends, and men of rank, and some, persons to whom they were charged with messages from their relations.

Having obtained these requests, they again asked permission to ransom such of them as they pleased; when they were desired to give in their names. Having given in a list of about two hundred, a decree of the senate was passed to the effect that the Carthaginian ambassadors should be allowed to take away into Africa to Publius Cornelius Scipio two hundred of the Carthaginian prisoners, selecting whom they pleased; and that they should convey to him a message that if the peace were concluded he should restore them to the Carthaginians without ransom. The heralds being ordered to go into Africa to strike the league, at their own desire the senate passed a decree that they should take with them flint stones of their own and vervain of their own; that the Roman prætor should command them to strike the league, and that they should demand of him herbs. The description of herb usually given to the heralds is taken from the Capitol. Thus the Carthaginians being allowed to depart from Rome, when they had gone into Africa to Scipio concluded the peace on the terms before mentioned. They delivered up their men-of-war, their elephants, deserters, fugitives, and four thousand prisoners, among whom was Quintus Terentius Culleo, a senator. The ships he ordered to be taken out into the main and burned. Some say there were five hundred of every description of those which are worked with oars, and that the sudden sight of these when burning occasioned as deep a sensation of grief to the Carthaginians as if Carthage had been in flames. The measures adopted respecting the deserters were more severe than those respecting the fugitives. Those who were of the Latin confederacy were decapitated; the Romans were crucified.

The last peace with the Carthaginians was made forty years before this in the consulate of Quintus Lutatius and Aulus Manlius. The war commenced twenty-three years afterward in the consulate of Publius Cornelius and Tiberius Sempronius. It was concluded in the seventeenth year, in the consulate of Cneius Cornelius and Publius Ælius Pætus. It is related that Scipio frequently said afterward, that first the ambition of Tiberius Claudius, and afterward of Cneius Cornelius, were the causes which prevented his terminating the war by the destruction of Carthage.

The Carthaginians finding difficulty in raising the first sum of money to be paid, as their finances were exhausted by a protracted war, and in consequence great lamentation and grief arising in the senate house, it is said that Hannibal was observed laughing, and when Hasdrubal Hædus rebuked him for laughing amid the public grief, when he himself was the occasion of the tears which were shed, he said: "If, as the expression of the countenance is discerned by the sight, so the inward feelings of the mind could be distinguished, it would clearly appear to you that that laughter which you censure came from a heart not elated with joy, but frantic with misfortunes. And yet it is not so ill-timed as those absurd and inconsistent tears of yours. Then you ought to have wept when our arms were taken from us, our ships burned, and we were forbidden to engage in foreign wars, for that was the wound by which we fell. Nor is it just that you should suppose that the measures which the Romans have adopted toward you have been dictated by animosity. No great state can remain at rest long together. If it has no enemy abroad it finds one at home in the same manner as over-robust bodies seem secure from external causes, but are encumbered with their own strength. So far, forsooth, we are affected with the public calamities as they reach our private affairs; nor is there any circumstance attending them which is felt more acutely than the loss of money. Accordingly, when the spoils were torn down from vanquished Carthage, when you beheld her left unarmed and defenceless amid so many armed nations of Africa, none heaved a sigh. Now, because a tribute is to be levied from private property you lament with one accord, as though at the funeral of the State.

How much do I dread lest you should soon be made sensible
that you have shed tears this day for the lightest of your misfortunes!"

Such were the sentiments which Hannibal delivered to the
Carthaginians. Scipio, having summoned an assembly, presented Masinissa, in addition to his paternal dominions, with
the town of Cirta, and the other cities and territories which
had passed from the kingdom of Syphax into the possession of
the Romans. He ordered Cneius Octavius to conduct the
fleet to Sicily and deliver it to Cneius Cornelius the consul,
and directed the Carthaginian ambassadors to go to Rome, that
the arrangements he had made with the advice of the ten
deputies might be ratified by the sanction of the fathers and
the order of the people.

Peace having been established by sea and land, he embarked
his troops and crossed over to Lilybæum in Sicily, whence,
having sent a great part of his soldiers by ships, he himself proceeded through Italy, which was rejoicing not less on account
of the peace than the victory; while not only the inhabitants
of the cities poured out to show him honor, but crowds of rustics thronged the roads. He arrived at Rome and entered the
city in a triumph of unparalleled splendor. He brought into
the treasury one hundred and twenty-three thousand pounds
of silver. He distributed to each of his soldiers four hundred
asses out of the spoils. By the death of Syphax, which took
place but a short time before at Tibur, whither he had been removed from Alba, a diminution was occasioned in the interest
of the pageant rather than in the glory of him who triumphed.
His death, however, was attended with circumstances which
produced a strong sensation, for he was buried at the public
expense. Polybius, an author by no means to be despised, as-
serts that this King was led in the triumph. Quintus Terentius Culleo followed Scipio in his triumph with a cap of liberty
on his head, and during the remainder of his life treated him
with the respect due to him as the author of his freedom. I
have not been able to ascertain whether the partiality of the
soldiers or the favor of the people fixed upon him the surname
of Africanus, or whether in the same manner as Felix was applied to Sulla, and Magnus to Pompey, in the memory of our

fathers, it originated in the flattery of his friends. He was doubtless the first general who was distinguished by a name derived from the nation which he had conquered. Afterward, in imitation of his example, some, by no means his equals in his victories, affixed splendid inscriptions on their statues and gave honorable surnames to their families.

JUDAS MACCABÆUS LIBERATES JUDEA

B.C. 165

JOSEPHUS

The noble-minded Judas Maccabæus was the hero of Jewish independence—the deliverer of Judea and Judaism during the bloody persecutions of the Syrian king Antiochus Epiphanes, in the second century
B.C. This King was attempting to destroy in Palestine the national
religion. For this purpose pagan altars were set up among the Jews
and pagan sacrifices enjoined upon the worshippers of Jehovah. Many
Jews fled from their own towns and villages into the uninhabited wilderness, in order that they might have liberty to worship the God of their
fathers; but a few conformed to the ordinances of Antiochus. Soon,
however, open resistance to the decrees of the pagan ruler began to
manifest itself among the faithful.

The first protest in the shape of active opposition was made by Mattathias, a priest living at Modin. When the servants of Antiochus
came to that retired village and commanded Mattathias to do sacrifice to
the heathen gods, he refused; he went so far as to strike down at the
altar a Jew who was preparing to offer such a sacrifice. Then he escaped
to the mountains with his five sons and a band of followers. These followers grew in numbers and activity, overthrowing pagan altars, circum-
cising heathen children, and putting to the sword both apostates and
unbelievers. When Mattathias died, in B.C. 166, he was succeeded as
leader by his son Judas, called Maccabæus, " the Hammer "; as Charles,
who defeated the Saracens at Tours, is called Martel or hammer.

The successes of Judas were uninterrupted, and culminated B.C. 165
in the repulse of Lysias, the general of Antiochus, at Bethzur, where a
large Syrian force gathered in the expectation of crushing the patriotic
army of Judas. After this victory Judas led his followers into Jerusalem
and proceeded to restore the Temple and the worship of the national
religion, and to cleanse the Temple from all traces of pagan worship.
The great altar was rebuilt; new sacred vessels provided; and an
eight-days' dedication festival begun on the very day when, three years
before, the altar of Jehovah had been desecrated by a heathen sacrifice.
This Feast of the Dedication was ever afterward observed in the Temple
at Jerusalem and is mentioned in the gospels (John x. 22). Judas
established a dynasty of priest-kings, which lasted until supplanted by

Herod, with the aid of the Romans, in B.C. 40; and gave by his gen-
uinely heroic bearing his name to this whole glorious epoch of Jewish history.

NOW at this time there was one whose name was Mattathias, who dwelt at Modin, the son of John, the son of
Simeon, the son of Asamoneus, a priest of the order of Joarib,
and a citizen of Jerusalem. He had five sons: John, who was
called Gaddis, and Simon, who was called Matthes, and Judas,
who was called Maccabæus,[1] and Eleazar, who was called
Auran, and Jonathan, who was called Apphus. Now this Mattathias lamented to his children the sad state of their affairs,
and the ravage made in the city, and the plundering of the Temple, and the calamities the multitude were under; and he told
them that it was better for them to die for the laws of their
country than to live so ingloriously as they then did.

But when those that were appointed by the King were come
to Modin that they might compel the Jews to do what they
were commanded, and to enjoin those that were there to offer
sacrifice, as the King had commanded, they desired that Mattathias, a person of the greatest character among them, both
on other accounts and particularly on account of such a numerous and so deserving a family of children, would begin the sacrifice, because his fellow-citizens would follow his example, and
because such a procedure would make him honored by the King.
But Mattathias said that he would not do it, and that if all the
other nations would obey the commands of Antiochus, either
out of fear or to please him, yet would not he nor his sons
leave the religious worship of their country; but as soon as he
had ended his speech there came one of the Jews into the
midst of them and sacrificed as Antiochus had commanded.
At which Mattathias had great indignation, and ran upon him
violently with his sons, who had swords with them, and slew

[1] That this appellation of Maccabee was not first of all given to Judas
Maccabæus, nor was derived from any initial letters of the Hebrew words
on his banner, *Mi Kamoka Be Elim, Jehovah ?* (" Who is like unto thee
among the gods, O Jehovah ? "), Exod. xv. 11, as the modern rabbins
vainly pretend, see *Authent. Rec.*, part i., pp. 205, 206. Only we may
note, by the way, that the original name of these Maccabees and their
posterity was Asamoneans, which was derived from Asamoneus, the
great-grandfather of Mattathias, as Josephus here informs us.

both the man himself that sacrificed and Apelles, the King's general who compelled him to sacrifice, with a few of his soldiers.

He also overthrew the idol altar and cried out, "If," said he, "anyone be zealous for the laws of his country and for the worship of God, let him follow me"; and when he had said this he made haste into the desert with his sons, and left all his substance in the village.   Many others did the same also, and fled with their children and wives into the desert and dwelt in caves; but when the King's generals heard this, they took all the forces they then had in the citadel at Jerusalem, and pursued the Jews into the desert; and when they had overtaken them, they in the first place endeavored to persuade them to repent, and to choose what was most for their advantage and not put them to the necessity of using them according to the law of war; but when they would not comply with their persuasions, but continued to be of a different mind, they fought against them on the Sabbath day, and they burned them as they were in the caves, without resistance, and without so much as stopping up the entrances of the caves.   And they avoided to defend themselves on that day because they were not willing to break in upon the honor they owed the Sabbath, even in such distresses; for our law requires that we rest upon that day.

There were about a thousand, with their wives and children, who were smothered and died in these caves; but many of those that escaped joined themselves to Mattathias and appointed him to be their ruler, who taught them to fight even on the Sabbath day, and told them that unless they would do so they would become their own enemies by observing the law [so rigorously] while their adversaries would still assault them on this day, and they would not then defend themselves; and that nothing could then hinder but they must all perish without fighting.   This speech persuaded them, and this rule continues among us to this day, that if there be a necessity we may fight on Sabbath days.   So Mattathias got a great army about him and overthrew their idol altars and slew those that broke the laws, even all that he could get under his power; for many of them were dispersed among the nations round about them for fear of him.   He also commanded that those boys who were not yet circumcised should be circumcised now; and he drove those away that were appointed to hinder such their circumcision.

But when he had ruled one year and was fallen into a distemper, he called for his sons and set them round about him, and said: "O my sons, I am going the way of all the earth; and I recommend to you my resolution and beseech you not to be negligent in keeping it, but to be mindful of the desires of him who begat you and brought you up, and to preserve the customs of your country, and to recover your ancient form of government which is in danger of being overturned, and not to be carried away with those that either by their own inclination or out of necessity betray it, but to become such sons as are worthy of me; to be above all force and necessity, and so to dispose your souls as to be ready when it shall be necessary to die for your laws, as sensible of this, by just reasoning, that if God see that you are so disposed he will not overlook you, but will have a great value for your virtue, and will restore to you again what you have lost and will return to you that freedom in which you shall live quietly and enjoy your own customs.

"Your bodies are mortal and subject to fate; but they receive a sort of immortality by the remembrance of what actions they have done; and I would have you so in love with this immortality that you may pursue after glory, and that when you have undergone the greatest difficulties you may not scruple for such things to lose your lives. I exhort you especially to agree one with another, and in what excellency any one of you exceeds another, to yield to him so far, and by that means to reap the advantage of everyone's own virtues. Do you then esteem Simon as your father because he is a man of extraordinary prudence, and be governed by him in what counsels he gives you. Take Maccabæus for the general of your army, because of his courage and strength, for he will avenge your nation and will bring vengeance on your enemies. Admit among you the righteous and religious, and augment their power."

When Mattathias had thus discoursed to his sons and had prayed to God to be their assistant and to recover to the people their former constitution, he died a little afterward, and was buried at Modin, all the people making great lamentation for him. Whereupon his son Judas took upon him the administration of public affairs, in the hundred and forty-sixth year; and thus, by the ready assistance of his brethren and of others, Judas cast their enemies cut of the country and put those of their own country to death who had transgressed its laws, and purified the land of all the pollutions that were in it.

When Apollonius, the general of the Samaritan forces, heard this he took his army and made haste to go against Judas, who met him and joined battle with him, and beat him and slew many of his men, and among them Apollonius himself, their general, whose sword, being that which he happened then to wear, he seized upon and kept for himself; but he wounded more than he slew, and took a great deal of prey from the enemy's camp, and went his way; but when Seron, who was general of the army of Celesyria, heard that many had joined themselves to Judas, and that he had about him an army sufficient for fighting and for making war, he determined to make an expedition against him, as thinking it became him to endeavor to punish those that transgressed the King's injunctions. He then got together an army as large as he was able, and joined to it the runagate and wicked Jews, and came against Judas.

He then came as far as Bethoron, a village of Judea, and there pitched his camp; upon which Judas met him, and when he intended to give him battle he saw that his soldiers were backward to fight because their number was small and because they wanted food, for they were fasting. He encouraged them and said to them that victory and conquest of enemies are not derived from the multitude in armies, but in the exercise of piety toward God; and that they had the plainest instances in their forefathers, who, by their righteousness and exerting themselves on behalf of their own laws and their own children, had frequently conquered many ten thousands, for innocence is the strongest army. By this speech he induced his men to contemn the multitude of the enemy, and to fall upon Seron; and upon joining battle with him he beat the Syrians; and when their general fell among the rest they all ran away with speed, as thinking that to be their best way of escaping. So he pursued them unto the plain and slew about eight hundred of the enemy, but the rest escaped to the region which lay near to the sea.

When king Antiochus heard of these things he was very angry at what had happened; so he got together all his own army, with many mercenaries whom he had hired from the islands, and took them with him, and prepared to break into Judea about the beginning of the spring; but when, upon his mustering his soldiers, he perceived that his treasures were deficient, and there was a want of money in them, for all the taxes were not paid, by reason of the seditions there had been among the nations, he having been so magnanimous and so liberal that what he had was not sufficient for him, he therefore resolved first to go into Persia and collect the taxes of that country. Hereupon he left one whose name was Lysias, who was in great repute with him, governor of the kingdom, as far as the bounds of Egypt and of the Lower Asia and reaching from the river Euphrates, and committed to him a certain part of his forces and of his elephants and charged him to bring up his son Antiochus with all possible care until he came back; and that he should conquer Judea and take its inhabitants for slaves and utterly destroy Jerusalem, and abolish the whole nation; and when king Antiochus had given these things in charge to Lysias, he went into Persia, and in the hundred and forty-seventh year he passed over Euphrates and went to the superior provinces.

Upon this Lysias chose Ptolemy the son of Dorymenes, and Nicanor, and Gorgias, very potent men among the King's friends, and delivered to them forty thousand foot-soldiers and seven thousand horsemen, and sent them against Judea, who came as far as the city Emmaus and pitched their camp in the plain country. There came also to them auxiliaries out of Syria and the country round about, as also many of the runagate Jews; and besides these came some merchants to buy those that should be carried captives—having bonds with them to bind those that should be made prisoners—with that silver and gold which they were to pay for their price; and when Judas saw their camp and how numerous their enemies were,

he persuaded his own soldiers to be of good courage, and exhorted them to place their hopes of victory in God and to
make supplication to him, according to the custom of their
country, clothed in sackcloth, and to show what was their
usual habit of supplication in the greatest dangers, and thereby
to prevail with God to grant them the victory over their enemies.   So he set them in their ancient order of battle used by
their forefathers, under their captains of thousands, and other
officers, and dismissed such as were newly married, as well as
those that had newly gained possessions, that they might not
fight in a cowardly manner out of an inordinate love of life, in
order to enjoy those blessings.

When he had thus disposed his soldiers he encouraged
them to fight by the following speech, which he made to them:
" O my fellow-soldiers, no other time remains more opportune
than the present for courage and contempt of dangers; for if
you now fight manfully you may recover your liberty, which,
as it is a thing of itself agreeable to all men, so it proves to be
to us much more desirable, by its affording us the liberty of
worshipping God.   Since, therefore, you are in such circumstances at present, you must either recover that liberty and so
regain a happy and blessed way of living, which is that according to our laws and the customs of our country, or to submit
to the most opprobrious sufferings; nor will any seed of your
nation remain if you be beat in this battle.   Fight therefore
manfully, and suppose that you must die though you do not
fight; but believe that besides such glorious rewards as those
of the liberty of your country, of your laws, of your religion,
you shall then obtain everlasting glory.   Prepare yourselves,
therefore, and put yourselves into such an agreeable posture
that you may be ready to fight with the enemy as soon as it is
day to-morrow morning."

And this was the speech which Judas made to encourage
them.   But when the enemy sent Gorgias with five thousand
foot and one thousand horse, that he might fall upon Judas by
night, and had for that purpose certain of the runagate Jews
as guides, the son of Mattathias perceived it and resolved to
fall upon those enemies that were in their camp, now their
forces were divided.   When they had therefore supped in good

time and had left many fires in their camp he marched all night to those enemies that were at Emmaus; so that when Gorgias found no enemy in their camp, but suspected that they were retired and had hidden themselves among the mountains, he resolved to go and seek them wheresoever they were.

But about break of day Judas appeared to those enemies that were at Emmaus, with only three thousand men, and those ill-armed by reason of their poverty; and when he saw the enemy very well and skilfully fortified in their camp he encouraged the Jews and told them that they ought to fight, though it were with their naked bodies, for that God had sometimes of old given such men strength, and that against such as were more in number, and were armed also, out of regard to their great courage. So he commanded the trumpeters to sound for the battle, and by thus falling upon the enemy when they did not expect it, and thereby astonishing and disturbing their minds, he slew many of those that resisted him and went on pursuing the rest as far as Gadara and the plains of Idumea, and Ashdod, and Jamnia; and of these there fell about three thousand. Yet did Judas exhort his soldiers not to be too desirous of the spoils, for that still they must have a contest and battle with Gorgias and the forces that were with him, but that when they had once overcome them then they might securely plunder the camp because they were the only enemies remaining, and they expected no others.

And just as he was speaking to his soldiers, Gorigas' men looked down into that army which they left in their camp and saw that it was overthrown and the camp burned; for the smoke that arose from it showed them, even when they were a great way off, what had happened. When, therefore, those that were with Gorgias understood that things were in this posture, and perceived that those that were with Judas were ready to fight them, they also were affrighted and put to flight; but then Judas, as though he had already beaten Gorgias' soldiers without fighting, returned and seized on the spoils. He took a great quantity of gold and silver and purple and blue, and then returned home with joy, and singing hymns to God for their good success; for this victory greatly contributed to the recovery of their liberty.

Hereupon Lysias was confounded at the defeat of the army which he had sent, and the next year he got together sixty thousand chosen men. He also took five thousand horsemen and fell upon Judea, and he went up to the hill country of Bethsur, a village of Judea, and pitched his camp there, where Judas met him with ten thousand men; and when he saw the great number of his enemies, he prayed to God that he would assist him, and joined battle with the first of the enemy that appeared and beat them and slew about five thousand of them, and thereby became terrible to the rest of them. Nay, indeed, Lysias observing the great spirit of the Jews, how they were prepared to die rather than lose their liberty, and being afraid of their desperate way of fighting, as if it were real strength, he took the rest of the army back with him and returned to Antioch.

When, therefore, the generals of Antiochus' armies had been beaten so often, Judas assembled the people together, and told them that after these many victories which God had given them, they ought to go up to Jerusalem and purify the Temple and offer the appointed sacrifices. But as soon as he with the whole multitude was come to Jerusalem and found the Temple deserted and its gates burned down and plants growing in the Temple of their own accord on account of its desertion, he and those that were with him began to lament and were quite confounded at the sight of the Temple; so he chose out some of his soldiers and gave them orders to fight against those guards that were in the citadel until he should have purified the Temple. When therefore he had carefully purged it and had brought in new vessels, the candlestick, the table [of shew-bread], and the altar [of incense], which were made of gold, he hung up the veils at the gates and added doors to them.

He also took down the altar [of burnt-offering], and built a new one of stones that he gathered together and not of such as were hewn with iron tools. So on the five-and-twentieth day of the month of Casleu, which the Macedonians call Apelleus, they lighted the lamps that were on the candlestick and offered incense upon the altar [of incense], and laid the loaves upon the table [of shew-bread], and offered burnt-offerings upon the new altar [of burnt-offering]. Now it so fell out

that these things were done on the very same day on which
their divine worship had fallen off and was reduced to a pro
fane and common use after three years' time; for so it was,
that the Temple was made desolate by Antiochus, and so continued for three years. This desolation happened to the Temple in the hundred forty and fifth year, on the twenty-fifth day
of the month Apelleus, and on the hundred and fifty-third
Olympiad; but it was dedicated anew, on the same day, the
twenty-fifth of the month Apelleus, in the hundred and forty-
eighth year, and on the hundred and fifty-fourth Olympiad.
And this desolation came to pass according to the prophecy of
Daniel, which was given four hundred and eight years before,
for he declared that the Macedonians would dissolve that worship [for some time].

Now Judas celebrated the festival of the restoration of the
sacrifices of the Temple for eight days, and omitted no sort of
pleasures thereon; but he feasted them upon very rich and
splendid sacrifices, and he honored God and delighted them
by hymns and psalms. Nay, they were so very glad at the revival of their customs, when after a long time of intermission
they unexpectedly had regained the freedom of their worship,
that they made it a law for their posterity that they should
keep a festival, on account of the restoration of their Temple
worship, for eight days. And from that time to this we celebrate this festival and call it Lights. I suppose the reason
was, because this liberty beyond our hopes appeared to us, and
that thence was the name given to that festival. Judas also
rebuilt the walls round about the city, and reared towers of
great height against the incursions of enemies, and set guards
therein. He also fortified the city Bethsura that it might
serve as a citadel against any distresses that might come from
our enemies.

When these things were over, the nations round about the
Jews were very uneasy at the revival of their power and rose
up together and destroyed many of them, as gaining advantage
over them by laying snares for them and making secret con-
spiracies against them. Judas made perpetual expeditions
against these men, and endeavored to restrain them from those
incursions and to prevent the mischiefs they did to the Jews.

So he fell upon the Idumeans, the posterity of Esau, at Acra-battene, and slew a great many of them and took their spoils. He also shut up the sons of Bean, that laid wait for the Jews; and he sat down about them, and besieged them, and burned their towers and destroyed the men [that were in them]. After this he went thence in haste against the Ammonites who had a great and a numerous army, of which Timotheus, was the commander. And when he had subdued them he seized on the city of Jazer, and took their wives and their children captives and burned the city and then returned into Judea. But when the neighboring nations understood that he was returned they got together in great numbers in the land of Gilead and came against those Jews that were at their borders, who then fled to the garrison of Dathema, and sent to Judas to inform him that Timotheus was endeavoring to take the place whither they were fled. And as these epistles were reading, there came other messengers out of Galilee who informed him that the inhabitants of Ptolemais, and of Tyre and Sidon, and strangers of Galilee, were gotten together.

Accordingly Judas, upon considering what was fit to be done with relation to the necessity both these cases required, gave order that Simon his brother should take three thousand chosen men and go to the assistance of the Jews in Galilee, while he and another of his brothers, Jonathan, made haste into the land of Gilead with eight thousand soldiers. And he left Joseph, the son of Zacharias, and Azarias, to be over the rest of the forces, and charged them to keep Judea very carefully and to fight no battles with any persons whomsoever until his return. Accordingly Simon went into Galilee and fought the enemy and put them to flight, and pursued them to the very gates of Ptolemais, and slew about three thousand of them, and took the spoils of those that were slain and those Jews whom they had made captives, with their baggage, and then returned home.

Now as for Judas Maccabæus and his brother Jonathan, they passed over the river Jordan, and when they had gone three days' journey they lighted upon the Nabateans, who came to meet them peaceably and who told them how the affairs of those in the land of Galilee stood and how many of

them were in distress and driven into garrisons and into the
cities of Galilee, and exhorted him to make haste to go against
the foreigners, and to endeavor to save his own countrymen
out of their hands. To this exhortation Judas hearkened and
returned into the wilderness, and in the first place fell upon
the inhabitants of Bosor, and took the city, and beat the inhabitants, and destroyed all the males, and all that were able to
fight, and burned the city. Nor did he stop even when night
came on, but he journeyed in it to the garrison where the Jews
happened to be then shut up, and where Timotheus lay round
the place with his army; and Judas came upon the city in the
morning, and when he found that the enemy were making an
assault upon the walls, and that some of them brought ladders
on which they might get upon those walls, and that others
brought engines [to batter them], he bid the trumpeter to
sound his trumpet, and he encouraged his soldiers cheerfully
to undergo dangers for the sake of their brethren and kindred;
he also parted his army into three bodies and fell upon the
backs of their enemies. But when Timotheus' men perceived
that it was Maccabæus that was upon them, of both whose
courage and good success in war they had formerly had sufficient experience, they were put to flight; but Judas followed
them with his army and slew about eight thousand of them.
He then turned aside to a city of the foreigners called Malle,
and took it, and slew all the males and burned the city itself.
He then removed from thence, and overthrew Casphom and
Bosor, and many other cities of the land of Gilead.

But not long after this Timotheus prepared a great army,
and took many others as auxiliaries, and induced some of the
Arabians by the promise of rewards to go with him in this expedition, and came with his army beyond the brook over
against the city Raphon; and he encouraged his soldiers, if it
came to a battle with the Jews, to fight courageously, and to
hinder their passing over the brook; for he said to them beforehand that "if they come over it we shall be beaten."
And when Judas heard that Timotheus prepared himself to
fight he took all his own army and went in haste against
Timotheus, his enemy; and when he had passed over the brook
he fell upon his enemies, and some of them met him, whom he

slew, and others of them he so terrified that he compelled them to throw down their arms and fly, and some of them escaped; but some of them fled to what was called the temple of Carnaim, and hoped thereby to preserve themselves, but Judas took the city and slew them and burned the temple, and so used several ways of destroying his enemies.

When he had done this he gathered the Jews together with their children and wives and the substance that belonged to them, and was going to bring them back into Judea. But as soon as he was come to a certain city the name of which was Ephron, that lay upon the road—and as it was not possible for him to go any other way, so he was not willing to go back again—he then sent to the inhabitants, and desired that they would open their gates and permit them to go on their way through the city; for they had stopped up the gates with stones and cut off their passage through it. And when the inhabitants of Ephron would not agree to this proposal, he encouraged those that were with him, and encompassed the city round and besieged it, and lying round it by day and night took the city and slew every male in it and burned it all down, and so obtained a way through it; and the multitude of those that were slain was so great that they went over the dead bodies. So they came over Jordan and arrived at the great plain over against which is situate the city Bethshan, which is called by the Greeks Scythopolis.[1] And going away hastily from thence, they came into Judea, singing psalms and hymns as they went, and indulging such tokens of mirth as are usual in triumphs upon victory. They also offered thank-offerings both for their good success and for the preservation of their army, for not one of the Jews was slain in these battles.

But as to Joseph, the son of Zacharias, and Azarias, whom Judas left generals [of the rest of his forces] at the same time when Simon was in Galilee fighting against the people of Ptolemais, and Judas himself and his brother Jonathan were

[1] The reason why Bethshan was called Scythopolis is well known from Herodotus, b. i., p. 105, and Syncellus, p. 214, that the Scythians, when they overran Asia, in the days of Josiah, seized on this city, and kept it as long as they continued in Asia; from which time it retained the name of Scythopolis, or the City of the Scythians.

in the land of Gilead, did these men also affect the glory of
being courageous generals in war, in order whereto they took
the army that was under their command and came to Jamnia.
There Gorgias, the general of the forces of Jamnia, met them,
and upon joining battle with him they lost two thousand of
their army and fled away, and were pursued to the very borders of Judea. And this misfortune befell them by their dis-
obedience to what injunctions Judas had given them not to
fight with anyone before his return. For besides the rest of
Judas' sagacious counsels, one may well wonder at this concerning the misfortune that befell the forces commanded by Joseph
and Azarias, which he understood would happen if they broke
any of the injunctions he had given them. But Judas and his
brethren did not leave off fighting with the Idumeans, but
pressed upon them on all sides, and took from them the city
of Hebron, and demolished all its fortifications and set all its
towers on fire, and burned the country of the foreigners and
the city Marissa. They came also to Ashdod, and took it, and
laid it waste, and took away a great deal of the spoils and prey
that were in it and returned to Judea.

THE GRACCHI AND THEIR REFORMS

B.C. 133

THEODOR MOMMSEN

Cornelia, whose father was Scipio Africanus, preferred to be called " Mother of the Gracchi" rather than daughter of the conqueror of Numantia. Tiberius and Caius Gracchus, her sons, were born at a time when the social condition of Rome was rank with corruption. The small farmer class were deprived of holdings, the soil was being worked by slaves, and its products wasted on pleasure and debauchery by the rich; the law courts were controlled by the wealthy and powerful, while oppression, bribery, and fraud were generally rampant in the city.

On December 10, B.C. 133, Tiberius Gracchus entered upon the office of tribune, to which he had been elected, and pledged himself to the abolition of crying abuses. His first movement was in the direction of agrarian legislation. He proposed to vest all public lands in the hands of three commissioners (triumviri), who were to distribute the public lands, at that time largely monopolized by the wealthy, to all citizens in needy circumstances. The bill met with bitter opposition from the rich landholders, but was eventually passed, and Gracchus rose to the summit of popular power. He also brought forward a measure limiting the necessary period of military service; a second bill was drawn up by him for the reformation of the law courts, and a third established a right of appeal from the law courts to the popular assembly. These measures were afterward carried by his brother Caius. Tiberius Gracchus was killed in a tumult which was raised in the Forum by the nobles and their partisans, and three hundred of his followers lost their lives in the fray.

Caius Gracchus, his brother, returned to Rome B.C. 124 from Sardinia, where he had been engaged in subduing the mountaineers. For ten years he had kept aloof from public life, but was at once elected tribune, in the discharge of which office he showed distinguished powers as an orator. He brought forth the important measures known as the Sempronian Laws, the provisions of which were quite revolutionary in character. The first of these laws renewed and extended the agrarian laws of his brother and instituted new colonies in Italy and the provinces. By the second Sempronian law the State undertook to furnish corn at a low price to all Roman citizens.

Other measures aimed at diminishing the great administrative power of the senate, which had so far monopolized all judicial offices. By the law of Gracchus the administration of justice was entirely transferred to a body of three hundred persons who possessed the equestrian rate of property. The Sempronian law for the assignment of consular provinces, which hitherto had been left to the senate, made the allotment of two designated provinces to be decided by the newly elected consuls themselves. The power of the senate was also crippled by the law of Gracchus in which he transferred to the tribunes the burden of improving the roads of Italy, contracts for which had hitherto been awarded by the censor under the approval of the senate. These movements were all in the direction of increasing popular and democratic power, and the work of the Gracchi tended to the extension of political freedom. In the history of politics these social struggles are among the most important events illustrative of the gradual dawn of civil liberty among a people which had been dominated and oppressed by a selfish aristocracy.

THE power of Gracchus rested on the mercantile class and the proletariat; primarily on the latter, which in this conflict—wherein neither side had any military reserve—acted, as it were, the part of an army. It was clear that the senate was not powerful enough to wrest either from the merchants or from the proletariat their new privileges; any attempt to assail the corn laws or the new jury arrangement would have led under a somewhat grosser or somewhat more civilized form to a street riot, in presence of which the senate was utterly defenceless. But it was no less clear that Gracchus himself and these merchants and proletarians were only kept together by mutual advantage, and that the men of material interests were ready to accept their posts, and the populace, strictly so called, its bread, quite as well from any other as from Caius Gracchus.

The institutions of Gracchus stood, for the moment at least, immovably firm, with the exception of a single one—his own supremacy. The weakness of the latter lay in the fact that in the constitution of Gracchus there was no relation of allegiance subsisting at all between the chief and the army; and, while the new constitution possessed all other elements of vitality, it lacked one—the moral tie between ruler and ruled, without which every state rests on a pedestal of clay. In the rejection of the proposal to admit the Latins to the franchise it had been demonstrated with decisive clearness that the multitude in fact never voted for Gracchus, but always simply for itself. The aristocracy conceived the plan of offering battle to the author of the corn largesses and land assignations on his own ground.

As a matter of course the senate offered to the proletariat not merely the same advantages as Gracchus had already assured to it in corn and otherwise, but advantages still greater. Commissioned by the senate, the tribune of the people, Marcus Livius Drusus, proposed to relieve those who received land under the laws of Gracchus from the rent imposed on them, and to declare their allotments to be free and alienable property; and, further, to provide for the proletariat not in transmarine, but in twelve Italian, colonies, each of three thousand colonists, for the planting of which the people might nominate suitable men; only Drusus himself declined—in contrast with the family complexion of the Gracchan commission—to take part in this honorable duty. Presumably the Latins were named as those who would have to bear the costs of the plan, for there does not appear to have existed then in Italy other occupied domain land of any extent save that which was enjoyed by them.

We find isolated enactments of Drusus—such as the regulation that the punishment of scourging might only be inflicted on the Latin soldier by the Latin officer set over him, and not by the Roman officer—which were to all appearance intended to indemnify the Latins for other losses. The plan was not the most refined. The attempt at rivalry was too clear; the endeavor to draw the fair bond between the nobles and the proletariat still closer by their exercising jointly a tyranny over the Latins was too transparent; the inquiry suggested itself too readily.

In what part of the peninsula, now that the Italian domains had been mainly given away already—even granting that the whole domains assigned to the Latins were confiscated—was the occupied domain land requisite for the formation of twelve new, numerous, and compact burgess communities to be discovered? Lastly, the declaration of Drusus that he would have nothing to do with the execution of his law was so dreadfully prudent as to border on sheer folly. But the clumsy snare was quite suited to the stupid game which they wished to catch. There was the additional and perhaps decisive consideration

that Gracchus, on whose personal influence everything depended, was just then establishing the Carthaginian colony in
Africa, and that his lieutenant in the capital, Marcus Flaccus,
played into the hands of his opponents by his vehement and
maladroit acts.   The "people" accordingly ratified the Livian
laws as readily as it had before ratified the Sempronian.   It
then as usual repaid its latest by inflicting a gentle blow on
its earlier benefactor, declining to reëlect him when he stood
for the third time as a candidate for the tribunate for the year
B.C. 120.   On this occasion, however, there are alleged to have
been unjust proceedings on the part of the tribune presiding at
the election, who had been offended by Gracchus.

Thus the foundation of his despotism gave way beneath
him.   A second blow was inflicted on him by the consular
elections, which not only proved, in a general sense, adverse to
the democracy, but which placed at the head of the State Lucius Opimius, one of the least scrupulous chiefs of the strict
aristocratic party and a man firmly resolved to get rid of their
dangerous antagonist at the earliest opportunity. Such an
opportunity soon occurred.   On the 10th of December, B.C.
121, Gracchus ceased to be tribune of the people.   On the 1st
of January, B.C. 120, Opimius entered upon his office.

The first attack, as was fair, was directed against the most
useful and the most unpopular measure of Gracchus, the reës-
tablishment of Carthage, while the transmarine colonies had
hitherto been only indirectly assailed through the greater allure-
ments of the Italian.   African hyenas, it was now alleged, dug
up the newly placed boundary stones of Carthage, and the
Roman priests when requested certified that such signs and
portents ought to form an express warning against rebuilding
on a site accursed by the gods.   The senate thereby found itself in its conscience compelled to have a law proposed which
prohibited the planting of the colony of Sunonia.   Gracchus,
who with the other men nominated to establish it was just then
selecting the colonists, appeared on the day of voting at the
Capitol, whither the burgesses were convoked, with a view to
procure by means of his adherents the rejection of the law.

He wished to shun acts of violence that he might not himself supply his opponents with the pretext which they sought,

but he had not been able to prevent a great portion of his faithful partisans—who remembered the catastrophe of Tiberius, and were well acquainted with the designs of the aristocracy—from appearing in arms, fearing that, amid the immense excitement on both sides, quarrels could hardly be avoided.   The consul Lucius Opimius offered the usual sacrifice in the porch of the Capitoline temple, one of the attendants assisting at the ceremony.   Quintus Antullius, with the holy entrails in his hands, haughtily ordered the "bad citizens" to quit the porch, and seemed as though he would lay hands on Caius himself; whereupon a zealous Gracchan drew his sword and cut the man down.   A fearful tumult arose.   Gracchus vainly sought to address the people and to disclaim the responsibility for the sacrilegious murder; he only furnished his antagonists with a further formal ground of accusation, as, without being aware of it in the confusion, he interrupted a tribune in the act of speaking to the people—an offence for which an obsolete statute, originating at the time of the old dissensions between the orders (I. 353), had prescribed the severest penalty.   The consul Lucius Opimius took his measures to put down by force of arms the insurrection for the overthrow of the republican constitution, as they were fond of designating the events of this day.   He himself passed the night in the temple of Castor in the Forum.   At early dawn the Capitol was filled with Cretan archers, the senate house and Forum with the men of the government party (the senators and that section of the *equites* adhering to them), who by order of the consul had all appeared in arms, each attended by two armed slaves.   None of the aristocracy was absent; even the aged and venerable Quintus Metellus, well disposed to reform, had appeared with shield and sword.   An officer of ability and experience acquired in the Spanish wars, Decimus Brutus, was intrusted with the command of the armed force; the senate assembled in the senate house.   The bier with the corpse of Antullius was deposited in front of it, the senate as if surprised appeared *en masse* at the door in order to view the dead body, and then retired to determine what should be done.

The leaders of the democracy had gone from the Capitol to their houses; Marcus Flaccus had spent the night in preparing for the war in the streets, while Gracchus apparently disdained to strive with destiny. Next morning when they learned of the preparations made by their opponents at the Capitol and the Forum, both proceeded to the Aventine, the old stronghold of the popular party in the struggles between the patricians and the plebeians. Gracchus went thither silent and unarmed. Flaccus called the slaves to arms and intrenched himself in the temple of Diana, while he at the same time sent his younger son Quintus to the enemy's camp in order if possible to arrange a compromise. The latter returned with the announcement that the aristocracy demanded unconditional surrender. At the same time he brought a summons from the senate to Gracchus and Flaccus to appear before it and to answer for their violation of the majesty of the tribunes.

Gracchus wished to comply with the summons, but Flaccus prevented him from doing so, and repeated the equally weak and mistaken attempt to move such antagonists to a compromise. When instead of the two cited leaders the young Quintus Flaccus once more presented himself alone, the consul treated their refusal to appear as the beginning of open insurrection against the Government. He ordered the messenger to be arrested and gave the signal for attack on the Aventine, while at the same time he caused proclamations to be made in the streets that the Government would give to whomsoever should bring the head of Gracchus or of Flaccus its literal weight in gold; and that they would guarantee complete indemnity to everyone who should leave the Aventine before the beginning of the conflict. The ranks on the Aventine speedily thinned; the valiant nobility in conjunction with the Cretans and the slaves stormed the almost undefended mount, and killed all whom they found—about two hundred and fifty persons, mostly of humble rank. Marcus Flaccus fled with his eldest son to a place of concealment, where they were soon afterward hunted out and put to death. Gracchus had at the beginning of the conflict retired into the temple of Minerva and was there about to pierce himself with his sword when his friend Publius Lætorius seized his arm and besought him to preserve himself, if possible, for better times.

Gracchus was induced to make an attempt to escape to the

other bank of the Tiber, but when hastening down the hill he fell and sprained his foot. To gain time for him to escape, his two attendants turned, and facing his pursuers allowed themselves to be cut down. As Marcus Pomponius at the Porta Trigemina under the Aventine; Publius Lætorius at the bridge over the Tiber—where Horatius Cocles was said to have once withstood, singly, the Etruscan army—so Gracchus, attended only by his slave Euporus, reached the suburb on the right bank of the Tiber.

There, in the grove of Furrina, afterward were found the two dead bodies. It seemed as if the slave had put to death first his master, and then himself. The heads of the two fallen leaders were handed over to the Government as required. The stipulated price, and more, was paid to Lucius Septumuleius, a man of quality, the bearer of the head of Gracchus; while the murderers of Flaccus, persons of humble rank, were sent away with empty hands. The bodies of the dead were thrown into the river, and the houses of the leaders were abandoned to the pillage of the multitude. The warfare of prosecution against the partisans of Gracchus began on the grandest scale; as many as three thousand of them are said to have been strangled in prison, among whom was Quintus Flaccus, eighteen years of age, who had taken no part in the conflict, and was universally lamented on account of his youth and his amiable disposition. On the open space beneath the Capitol, where the altar consecrated by Camillus after the restoration of internal peace (I. 382), and other shrines—erected on similar occasions to Concord—were situated, the small chapels were pulled down, and out of the property of the killed or condemned traitors—which was confiscated, even to the portions of their wives—a new and splendid temple of Concord, with the basilica belonging to it, was erected in accordance with a decree of the senate by the consul Lucius Opimius.

Certainly it was an act in accordance with the spirit of the age to remove the memorials of the old and to inaugurate a new Concord over the remains of the three grandsons of Zama, all of whom—first, Tiberius Gracchus, then Scipio Æmilianus, and lastly the youngest and the mightiest, Caius Gracchus—had now been engulfed by the revolution. The memory of the Gracchi remained officially proscribed; Cornelia was not allowed even to put on mourning for the death of her last son; but the passionate attachment which very many had felt toward the two noble brothers, and especially toward Caius, during their life, was touchingly displayed also after their death, in the almost religious veneration which the multitude, in spite of all precautions of the police, continued to pay to their memory and to the spots where they had fallen.

CÆSAR CONQUERS GAUL[1]

B.C. 58–50

NAPOLEON III

In Cæsar's military performances the Gallic war plays the most important part, as shown in his *Commentaries*, his sole extant literary work and almost the only authority for this part of Roman history.

Cisalpine Gaul—that portion lying on the southern or Italian side of the Alps—came partly under the dominion of Rome as early as B.C. 282, when a Roman colony was founded at Sena Gallica. This division of Gaul was wholly conquered by B.C. 191; and in B.C. 43, having been made a Roman province, it became a part of Italy.

Transalpine Gaul—that part lying north and northwest of the Alps from Rome—comprised in Cæsar's day three divisions: Aquitaine to the southwest, Celtic Gaul in the middle, and Belgic Gaul to the northwest. The region was inhabited by various tribes having neither unity of race nor of customs whereby nationality becomes distinguished. Toward the close of the second century B.C. the Romans made their first settlements in Transalpine Gaul, in the southeastern part. At the time when Cæsar became proconsul in Gaul, B.C. 58, the province was in a state of tranquillity, but Fortune seemed determined that he should have great opportunities for the display of his military genius, and, when Asia had been subdued by Pompey, "conferred what remained to be done in Europe upon Cæsar." The attempt of the Helvetii to leave their homes in the Alps for new dwelling-places in Gaul served him as an occasion for war. As they were crossing the Arar (now Saone) he attacked and routed them, later defeated them again, and at last drove them back to their own country.

The story of the long war, with its various campaigns, has become familiar to the world's readers through the masterly account of Cæsar himself, known to "every schoolboy" who advances to the dignity of classical studies. In the end the country between the Pyrenees and the Rhine was subjugated, and for several centuries it remained a Roman province.

At the time when the history is taken up in the following narrative by Napoleon III, the great rebellion, B.C. 52, had sustained a heavy blow in the surrender of Alesia, and the capture of the heroic chief and leader of the insurrection, Vercingetorix, whom Cæsar exhibited in his triumph at Rome, B.C. 46, and then caused to be put to death.

[1] From Louis Napoleon's Julius Cæsar, by permission of Harper & Brothers.

The distinguished author of the article says he wrote " for the purpose of proving that when Providence raises up such men as Cæsar, Charlemagne, and Napoleon it is to trace out to peoples the path they ought to follow, to stamp with the seal of their genius a new era, and to accomplish in a few years the work of many centuries." The work was prepared [*vide Manual of Historical Literature:* Adams] with the utmost care—a care which extended in some instances to special surveys, to insure perfect accuracy in the descriptions, etc.

THE capture of Alesia and that of Vercingetorix, in spite of the united efforts of all Gaul, naturally gave Cæsar hopes of a general submission; and he therefore believed that he could leave his army during the winter to rest quietly in its quarters from the hard labors which had lasted without interruption during the whole of the past summer. But the spirit of insurrection was not extinct among the Gauls; and convinced by experience that whatever might be their number they could not in a body cope with troops inured to war, they resolved, by partial insurrections raised on all points at once, to divide the attention and the forces of the Romans as their only chance of resisting them with advantage.

Cæsar was unwilling to leave them time to realize this new plan, but gave the command of his winter quarters to his quæstor, Mark Antony; quitted Bibracte on the day before the Calends of January (the 25th of December) with an escort of cavalry, joined the Thirteenth legion, which was in winter quarters among the Bituriges, not far from the frontier of the Aldui, and called to him the Eleventh legion, which was the nearest at hand. Having left two cohorts of each legion to guard the baggage, he proceeded toward the fertile country of the Bituriges, a vast territory, where the presence of a single legion was insufficient to put a stop to the preparations for insurrection.

His sudden arrival in the midst of men without distrust, who were spread over the open country, produced the result which he expected. They were surprised before they could enter into their *oppidæ*—for Cæsar had strictly forbidden everything which might have raised their suspicion; especially the application of fire, which usually betrays the sudden presence of an enemy. Several thousands of captives were made. Those who succeeded in escaping sought in vain a refuge among the neighboring nations. Cæsar, by forced marches, came up with them everywhere and obliged each tribe to think of its own safety before that of others.

This activity held the populations in their fidelity, and through fear engaged the wavering to submit to the conditions of peace. Thus the Bituriges, seeing that Cæsar offered them an easy way to recover his protection, and that the neighboring states had suffered no other chastisement than that of having to deliver hostages, did not hesitate in submitting.

The soldiers of the Eleventh and Thirteenth legions had, during the winter, supported with rare constancy the fatigues of very difficult marches in intolerable cold. To reward them he promised to give by way of prize-money two hundred *sestertii* to each soldier and two thousand to each centurion. He then sent them into their winter quarters and returned to Bibracte after an absence of forty days. While he was there, dispensing justice, the Bituriges came to implore his support against the attacks of the Carnutes. Although it was only eighteen days since he returned, he marched again at the head of two legions—the Sixth and the Fourteenth—which had been placed on the Saone to insure the supply of provisions.

On his approach the Carnutes, taught by the fate of others, abandoned their miserable huts—which they had erected on the site of their burgs and oppida destroyed in the last campaign— and fled in every direction.

Cæsar, unwilling to expose his soldiers to the rigor of the season, established his camp at Genabum (Gien), and lodged them partly in the huts which had remained undestroyed, partly in tents under penthouses covered with straw. The cavalry and auxiliary infantry were sent in pursuit of the Carnutes, who, hunted down everywhere, and without shelter, took refuge in the neighboring counties.

After having dispersed some rebellious meetings and stifled the germs of an insurrection, Cæsar believed that the summer would pass without any serious war. He left therefore at Genabum the two legions he had with him, and gave the command of them to C. Trebonius.

Nevertheless, he learned by several intimations from the Remi that the Bellovaci and neighboring peoples, with Correus and Commius at their head, were collecting troops to make an inroad on the territory of the Suessiones, who had been placed—since the campaign of 697—under the dependence of the Remi.

He considered that he regarded his interest as well as his dignity in protecting allies who had deserved so well of the republic. He again drew the Eleventh legion from its winter quarters, sent written orders to C. Fabius, who was encamped in the country of the Remi, to bring into that of the Suessiones the two legions under his command, and demanded one of his legions from Labienus, who was at Besançon. Thus without taking any rest himself he shared the fatigues among the legions by turns, as far as the position of the winter quarters and the necessities of the war permitted.

When this army was assembled he marched against the Bellovaci, established his camp on their territory, and sent cavalry in every direction in order to make some prisoners and learn from them the designs of the enemy. The cavalry reported that the emigration was general, and that the few inhabitants who were to be seen were not remaining behind in order to apply themselves to agriculture, but to act as spies upon the Romans.

Cæsar by interrogating the prisoners learned that all the Bellovaci able to fight had assembled on one spot, and that they had been joined by the Ambiani, the Aulerci, the Caletes, the Veliocasses, and the Atrebates. Their camp was in a forest on a height surrounded by marshes—Mont Saint Marc, in the forest of Compiègne; their baggage had been transported to more distant woods. The command was divided among several chiefs, but the greater part obeyed Correus on account of his well-known hatred of the Romans. Commius had a few days before gone to seek succor from the numerous Germans who lived in great numbers in the neighboring counties—probably those on the banks of the Meuse.

The Bellovaci resolved with one accord to give Cæsar battle, if, as report said, he was advancing with only three legions; for they would not run the risk of having afterward to encounter his entire army. If, on the contrary, the Romans were advancing with more considerable forces they proposed to keep their positions and confine themselves to intercepting, by means of ambuscades, the provisions and forage, which were very scarce at that season.

This plan, confirmed by many reports, seemed to Cæsar full of prudence and altogether contrary to the usual rashness of the barbarians. He took therefore every possible care to dissimulate as to the number of his troops. He had with him the Seventh, Eighth, and Ninth legions, composed of old soldiers of tried valor, and the Eleventh, which, formed of picked young men who had gone through eight campaigns, deserved his confidence, although it could not be compared with the others with regard to bravery and experience in war. In order to deceive the enemy by showing them only three legions—the only number they were willing to fight—he placed the Seventh, Eighth, and Ninth in one line; while the baggage, which was not very considerable, was placed behind under the protection of the Eleventh legion, which closed the march. In this order, which formed almost a square, he came unawares in sight of the Bellovaci. At the unexpected view of the legions, which advanced in order of battle and with a firm step, they lost their courage and, instead of attacking, as they had engaged to do, they confined themselves to drawing themselves up before their camp without leaving the height. A valley deeper than it was wide separated the two armies.

On account of this obstacle and the numerical superiority of the barbarians, Cæsar, though he had wished for battle, abandoned the idea of attacking them and placed his camp opposite that of the Gauls in a strong position. He caused it to be surrounded with a parapet twelve feet high, surmounted by accessory works proportioned to the importance of the retrenchment and preceded by a double fosse fifteen feet wide, with a square bottom. Towers of three stories were constructed from distance to distance and united together by covered bridges, the exterior parts of which were protected by hurdle-work. In this manner the camp was protected not only by a double fosse, but also by a double row of defenders, some of whom, placed on the bridges, could from this elevated and sheltered position throw their missiles farther and with a better aim; while the others, placed on the *vallum*, nearer to the enemy, were protected by the bridges from the missiles which showered down upon them. The entrances were defended by means of higher towers and were closed with gates.

These formidable retrenchments had a double aim—to increase the confidence of the barbarians by making them believe that they were feared, and next to allow the number of the garrison to be reduced with safety when they had to go far for provisions. For some days there were no serious engagements, but slight skirmishes in the marshy plain which extended between the two camps. The capture, however, of a few foragers did not fail to swell the presumption of the barbarians, which was still more increased by the arrival of Commius, although he had brought only five hundred German cavalry.

The enemy remained for several days shut up in its impregnable position. Cæsar judged that an assault would cost too many lives; an investment alone seemed to him opportune, but it would require a greater number of troops.

He wrote thereupon to Trebonius to send him as soon as possible the Thirteenth legion, which, under the command of T. Sextius, was in winter quarters among the Bituriges, to join it with the Sixth and the Fourteenth (which the first of these lieutenants commanded at Genabum), and to come himself with these three legions by forced marches.

During this time he employed the numerous cavalry of the Remi, the Lingones and the other allies, to protect the foragers and to prevent surprises, but this daily service, as is often the case, ended by being negligently performed. And one day the Remi, pursuing the Bellovaci with too much ardor, fell into an ambuscade. In withdrawing they were surrounded by foot-soldiers in the midst of whom Vertiscus, their chief, met with his death. True to his Gaulish nature, he would not allow his age to exempt him from commanding and mounting on horseback, although he was hardly able to keep his seat. His death and this feeble advantage raised the self-confidence of the barbarians still more, but it rendered the Romans more circumspect.

Nevertheless, in one of the skirmishes which were continually taking place within sight of the two camps about the fordable places of the marsh, the German infantry—which Cæsar had sent for from beyond the Rhine in order to mix them with the cavalry—joined in a body, boldly crossed the marsh, and, meeting with little resistance, continued the pursuit with such impetuosity that fear seized not only the enemy who fought, but even those who were in reserve. Instead of availing themselves of the advantages of the ground, all fled in a cowardly manner. They did not stop until they were within their camp, and some even were not ashamed to fly beyond it. This defeat caused a general discouragement, for the Gauls were as easily daunted by the least reverse as they were made arrogant by the smallest success.

Day after day was passing in this manner when Cæsar was informed of the arrival of C. Trebonius and his troops, which raised the number of his legions to seven. The chiefs of the Bellovaci then feared an investment like that of Alesia, and resolved to quit their position. They sent away by night the old men, the infirm, the unarmed men, and the part of the baggage which they had kept with them. Scarcely was this confused multitude in motion—embarrassed by its own mass and its numerous chariots—when daylight surprised it, and the troops had to be drawn up in line before the camp to give the column time to move away. Cæsar saw no advantage either in giving battle to those who were in position, nor, on account of the steepness of the hill, in pursuing those who were making their retreat; he resolved, nevertheless, to make two legions advance in order to disturb the enemy in its retreat. Having observed that the mountain on which the Gauls were established was connected with another height (Mont Collet), from which it was only separated by a narrow valley, he ordered bridges to be thrown across the marsh. The legions crossed over them and soon attained the summit of the height, which was defended on both sides by abrupt declivities.

There he collected his troops and advanced in order of battle up to the extremity of the plateau, whence the engines placed in battery could reach the masses of the enemy with their missiles.

The barbarians, rendered confident by the advantage of their position, were ready to accept battle if the Romans dared to attack the mountain; besides, they were afraid to withdraw their troops successively, as, if divided, they might have been thrown into disorder. This attitude led Cæsar to resolve upon leaving twenty cohorts under arms, and on tracing a camp on this spot, and retrenching it. When the works were completed the legions were placed before the retrenchments and the cavalry distributed with their horses bridled at the outposts. The Bellovaci had recourse to a stratagem in order to effect their retreat. They passed from hand to hand the fascines and the straw on which, according to the Gaulish custom, they were in the habit of sitting, preserving at the same time their order of battle; placed them in front of the camp, and toward the close of the day, on a preconcerted signal, set fire to them. Immediately a vast flame concealed from the Romans the Gaulish troops, who fled in haste.

Although the fire prevented Cæsar from seeing the retreat of the enemy he suspected it. He ordered his legions to advance, and sent the cavalry in pursuit, but he marched slowly in fear of some stratagem, suspecting the barbarians to have formed the design of drawing the Romans to disadvantageous ground. Besides, the cavalry did not dare to ride through the smoke and flames; and thus the Bellovaci were able to pass over a distance of ten miles and halt in a place strongly fortified by nature (Mont Ganelon), where they pitched their camp. In this position they confined themselves to placing cavalry and infantry in frequent ambuscades, thus inflicting great damage on the Romans when they went to forage. After several encounters of this kind Cæsar learned by a prisoner that Correus, chief of the Bellovaci, with six thousand picked infantry and one thousand horsemen, was preparing an ambuscade in places where the abundance of corn and forage was likely to attract the Romans. In consequence of this information he sent forward the cavalry, which was always employed to protect the foragers, and joined with them some light-armed auxiliaries, while he himself, with a greater number of legions, followed them as closely as possible.

The enemy had posted themselves in a plain—that of Choisy-au-Bac—of about one thousand paces in length and the same in breadth, surrounded on one side by forests, on the other by a river which was difficult to pass (the Aisne). The cavalry becoming acquainted with the designs of the Gauls and feeling themselves supported, advanced resolutely in squadrons toward this plain, which was surrounded with ambushes on all sides.

Correus, seeing them arrive in this manner, believed the opportunity favorable for the execution of his plan and began by attacking the first squadrons with a few men. The Romans sustained the shock without concentrating themselves in a mass on the same point, " which," says Hirtius, " usually happens in cavalry engagements, and leads always to a dangerous confusion." There, on the contrary, the squadrons, remaining separated, fought in detached bodies, and when one of them advanced, its flanks were protected by the others. Correus then ordered the rest of his cavalry to issue from the woods. An obstinate combat began on all sides without any decisive result until the enemy's infantry, debouching from the forest in close ranks, forced the Roman cavalry to fall back. The lightly armed soldiers who preceded the legions placed themselves between the squadrons and restored the fortune of the combat. After a certain time the troops, animated by the approach of the legions and the arrival of Cæsar, and ambitious of obtaining alone the honor of the victory, redoubled their efforts and gained the advantage. The enemy, on the other hand, were discouraged and took to flight, but were stopped by the very obstacles which they intended to throw in the way of the Romans. A small number, nevertheless, escaped through the forest and crossed the river. Correus, who remained unshaken under this catastrophe, obstinately refused to surrender, and fell pierced with wounds. After this success Cæsar hoped that if he continued his march the enemy in dismay would abandon his camp, which was only eight miles from the field of battle. He therefore crossed the Aisne, though not without great difficulties.

The Bellovaci and their allies, informed by the fugitives of the death of Correus, of the loss of their cavalry and the flower of their infantry, and fearing every moment to see the Romans appear, convoked by sound of trumpet a general assembly and decided by acclamation to send deputies and hostages to the proconsul. The barbarians implored forgiveness, alleging that this last defeat had ruined their power, and that the death of Correus, the instigator of the war, delivered them from oppression, for, during his life, it was not the senate which governed, but an ignorant multitude. To their prayers Cæsar replied that last year the Bellovaci had revolted in concert with the other Gaulish peoples, but that *they* alone had persisted in the revolt. It was very convenient to throw their faults upon those who were dead, but how could it be believed that with nothing but the help of a weak populace a man should have had sufficient influence to raise and sustain a war contrary to the will of the chiefs, the decision of the senate, and the desire of honest people? However, the evil which they had drawn upon themselves was for him a sufficient reparation.

The following night the Bellovaci and their allies submitted, with the exception of Commius, who fled to the country from which he had but recently drawn support. He had not dared to trust the Romans for the following reason: "The year before, in the absence of Cæsar, T. Labienus, informed that Commius was conspiring and preparing an insurrection, thought that without accusing him of bad faith," says Hirtius, "he could repress his treason." ("Under pretext of an interview he sent C. Volusenus Quadratus, with some centurions, to kill him; but when they were in the presence of the Gaulish chief the centurion who was to strike him missed his blow and only wounded him; swords were drawn on both sides and Commius had time to escape.")

The most warlike tribes had been vanquished and none of them dreamed of further revolt. Nevertheless, many inhabitants of the newly conquered countries abandoned the towns and the fields in order to withdraw themselves from the Roman dominion. Cæsar, in order to put a stop to this emigration, distributed his army in different countries. He ordered the quæstor, Mark Antony, to come to him with the Twelfth legion, and sent the lieutenant Fabius with twenty-five cohorts into an opposite part of Gaul—to the country situated between the Creuse and the Vienne—where it was said that several tribes were in arms, and where the lieutenant, Caninius Rebilus, who commanded with two legions, did not appear to be sufficiently strong. Lastly, he ordered T. Labienus to join him in person and to send the Fifteenth legion, which he had under his command, into Cisalpine Gaul to protect the colonies of Roman citizens there against the sudden inroads of the barbarians, who the summer before had attacked the Tergestini (the inhabitants of Trieste).

As for Cæsar, he proceeded with four legions to the territory of the Eburones to lay it waste. As he could not secure Ambiorix, who was still wandering at large, he thought it advisable to destroy everything by fire and sword, persuaded that this chief would never dare to return to a country upon which he had brought such a terrible calamity. The legions and the auxiliaries were charged with the execution of this plan. Then he sent Labienus, with two legions, to the country of the Treviri, who, always at war with the Germans, were only kept in obedience by the presence of a Roman army.

During this time Caninius Rebilus, who had first been appointed to go into the country of the Ruteni, but who had been detained by petty insurrections in the region situated between the Creuse and the Vienne, learned that numerous hostile bands were assembling in the country of the Pictones. He was informed of this by letters from Duratius, their king, who, amid the defection of a part of his people, had remained invariably faithful to the Romans. He started immediately for Lemonum (Poitiers). On the road he learned from prisoners that Duratius was shut up there and besieged by several thousand men under the orders of Dumnacus, chief of the Andes.

Rebilus, at the head of two weak legions, did not dare to measure his strength with the enemy; he contented himself with establishing his camp in a strong position. At the news of his approach, Dumnacus raised the siege, and marched to meet the legions, but after several days of fruitless attempts to force their camp he returned to attack Lemonum.

Meanwhile, the lieutenant, Caius Fabius, occupied in pacifying several other tribes, learned from Caninius Rebilus what was going on in the country of the Pictones and marched without delay to the assistance of Duratius. The news of the march of Fabius deprived Dumnacus of all hope of opposing, at the same time, the troops shut up in Lemonum and the relieving army. He abandoned the siege again in great haste, not thinking himself safe until he had placed the Loire between himself and the Romans; but he could only pass that river where there was a bridge (at Saumur). Before he had joined Rebilus, before he had even obtained a sight of the enemy, Fabius, who came from the North, and had lost no time, doubted not, from what he heard from the people of the country, that Dumnacus, in his fear, had taken the road which led to that bridge. He therefore marched thither with his legions, preceded at a short distance by his cavalry. The latter surprised the column of Dumnacus on its march, dispersed it, and returned to the camp laden with booty.

During the night of the following day Fabius again sent his cavalry forward with orders to delay the march of the enemy so as to give time for the arrival of the infantry. The two bodies of cavalry were soon engaged, but the enemy, thinking he had to contend with only the same troops as the day before, drew up his infantry in line so as to support the squadrons, when suddenly the Roman legions appeared in order of battle. At this sight the barbarians were struck with terror, the long train of baggage thrown into confusion, and the infantry dispersed. More than twelve thousand men were killed and all the baggage fell into the hands of the Romans.

Only five thousand fugitives escaped from this rout; they were received by the Senonan, Drappes, the same who in the first revolt of the Gauls had collected a crowd of vagabonds, slaves, exiles, and robbers to intercept the convoys of the Romans.

They took the direction of the Narbonnese with the Cadurcan Lucterius who had before attempted a similar invasion.

Rebilus pursued them with two legions in order to avoid the shame of seeing the province suffering any injury from such a contemptible rabble. As for Fabius, he led the twenty-five cohorts against the Carnutes and the other tribes whose forces had already been reduced by the defeat they had suffered from Dumnacus. The Carnutes, though often beaten, had never been completely subdued. They gave hostages, and the Armoricans followed their example. Dumnacus, driven out of his own territory, went to seek a refuge in the remotest part of Gaul.

Drappes and Lucterius, when they learned that they were pursued by Rebilus and his two legions, gave up the design of penetrating into the province; they halted in the country of the Cadurci and threw themselves into the *oppidum* of Uxellodunum (Puy-d'Issolu, near Varac), an exceedingly strong place formerly under the dependence of Lucterius, who soon incited the inhabitants to revolt.

Rebilus appeared immediately before the town, which, surrounded on all sides by steep rocks, was, even without being defended, difficult of access to armed men. Knowing that there was in the oppidum so great a quantity of baggage that the besieged could not send it away secretly without being detected and overtaken by the cavalry, and even by the infantry, he divided his cohorts into three bodies and established three camps on the highest points. Next he ordered a countervallation to be made. On seeing these preparations the besieged remembered the ill-fortune of Alesia, and feared a similar fate. Lucterius, who had witnessed the horrors of famine during the investment of that town, now took especial care of the provisions.

During this time the garrison of the oppidum attacked the redoubts of Rebilus several times, which obliged him to interrupt the work of the countervallation, which, indeed, he had not sufficient forces to defend.

Drappes and Lucterius established themselves at a distance of ten miles from the oppidum, with the intention of introducing the provisions gradually. They shared the duties between them. Drappes remained with part of the troops to protect the camp. Lucterius, during the night-time, endeavored to introduce beasts of burden into the town by a narrow and wooded path. The noise of their march gave warning to the sentries. Rebilus, informed of what was going on, ordered the cohorts to sally from the neighboring redoubts, and at daybreak fell upon the convoy, the escort of which was slaughtered. Lucterius, having escaped with a small number of his followers, was unable to rejoin Drappes.

Rebilus soon learned from prisoners that the rest of the troops which had left the oppidum were with Drappes at a distance of twelve miles, and that by a fortunate chance not one fugitive had taken that direction to carry him news of the last combat. The Roman general sent in advance all the cavalry and the light German infantry; he followed them with one legion, without baggage, leaving the other as a guard to the three camps. When he came near the enemy he learned, by his scouts, that the barbarians—according to their custom of neglecting the heights—had placed their camp on the banks of a river (probably the Dordogne); that the Germans and the cavalry had surprised them, and that they were already fighting. Rebilus then advanced rapidly at the head of the legion drawn up in order of battle and took possession of the heights.

As soon as the ensigns appeared, the cavalry redoubled its ardor; the cohorts rushed forward from all sides and the Gauls were taken or killed. The booty was immense and Drappes fell into the hands of the Romans.

Rebilus, after this successful exploit, which cost him but a few wounded, returned under the walls of Uxellodunum. Fearing no longer any attack from without, he set resolutely to work to continue his circumvallation. The day after, C. Fabius arrived, followed by his troops, and shared with him the labors of the siege. While the south of Gaul was the scene of serious trouble, Cæsar left the quæstor, Mark Antony, with fifteen cohorts in the country of the Bellovaci. To deprive the Belgæ of all idea of revolt he had proceeded to the neighboring countries with two legions; had exacted hostages, and restored confidence by his conciliating speeches. When he arrived among the Carnutes—who the year before had been the first to revolt —he saw that the remembrance of their conduct kept them in great alarm, and he resolved to put an end to it by causing his vengeance to fall only upon Gutruatus, the instigator of the war.

This man was brought in and delivered up. Although Cæsar was naturally inclined to be indulgent, he could not resist the tumultuous entreaties of his soldiers, who made that chief responsible for all the dangers they had run and for all the misery they had suffered. Gutruatus died under the stripes and was afterward beheaded.

It was in the land of the Carnutes that Cæsar received news, by the letters of Rebilus, of the events which had taken place at Uxellodunum and of the resistance of the besieged. Although a handful of men shut up in a fortress was not very formidable, he judged it necessary to punish their obstinacy, for fear that the Gauls should entertain the conviction that it was not strength, but constancy, which had failed them in resisting the Romans; and lest this example might encourage the other states which possessed fortresses advantageously situated, to recover their independence.

Moreover, it was known everywhere among the Gauls that Cæsar had only one more summer to hold his command, and that after that time they would have nothing more to fear. He left therefore the lieutenant Quintus Calenus at the head of his two legions, with orders to follow him by ordinary marches, and, with his cavalry, hastened by long marches toward Uxellodunum. Cæsar, arriving unexpectedly before the town, found it completely defended at all accessible points. He judged that it could not be taken by assault (*neque ab oppugnatione recedi vidaret ulla conditione posse*), and, as it was abundantly provided with provisions, conceived the project of depriving the inhabitants of water.

The mountain was surrounded almost on every side by very low ground, but on one side there existed a valley through which a river (the Tourmente) ran. As it flowed at the foot of two precipitous mountains the disposition of the localities did not admit of turning it aside and conducting it into lower channels. It was difficult for the besieged to come down to it, and the Romans rendered the approaches to it still more dangerous. They placed posts of archers and slingers, and brought engines which commanded all the slopes which gave access to the river. The besieged had thenceforth no other means of procuring water but by carrying it from an abundant spring which arose at the foot of the wall three hundred feet from the channel of the Tourmente. Cæsar resolved to drain this spring, and for this purpose he did not hesitate to attempt a laborious undertaking. Opposite the point where it rose he ordered covered galleries to be pushed forward against the mountain, and under protection of these a terrace to be raised—labors which were carried on in the midst of continual fighting and weariness.

Although the besieged from their elevated position fought without danger and wounded many Romans, yet the latter did not yield to discouragement, but continued the work. At the same time they made a subterranean gallery, which, running from the covered galleries, was intended to lead up to the spring. This work, carried on free from all danger, was executed without being perceived by the enemy. The terrace attained a height of sixty feet and was surmounted by a tower of ten stories, which, without equalling the elevation of the wall —a result it was impossible to obtain—still commanded the fountain. Its approaches, battered by engines from the top of this tower, became inaccessible. In consequence of this, many men and animals in the place died of thirst. The besieged, terrified at this mortality, filled barrels with pitch, grease, and shavings, and rolled them flaming upon the Roman works, making at the same time a sally to prevent them from extinguishing the fire. Soon it spread to the covered galleries and the terrace, which stopped the progress of the inflammable materials.

Notwithstanding the difficult nature of the ground and the increasing danger, the Romans still persevered in their struggle. The battle took place on a height within sight of the army. Loud cries were raised on both sides. Each individual sought to rival his fellow in zeal, and the more he was exposed to view the more courageously he faced the missiles and the fire.

Cæsar, as he was sustaining great loss, determined to feign an assault. In order to create a diversion he ordered some cohorts to climb the hill on all sides, uttering loud cries. This movement terrified the besieged, who, fearing to be attacked at other points, called back to the defence of the wall those who were setting fire to the works. Then the Romans were enabled to extinguish the flames. The Gauls, although exhausted by thirst and reduced to a small number, ceased not to defend themselves vigorously. At length the subterranean gallery having reached the source of the spring, the supply was turned aside. The besieged, beholding the fountain suddenly become dry, believed in their despair that it was an intervention of the gods, and, submitting to necessity, surrendered.

Cæsar considered that the pacification of Gaul would never be completed if as strong a resistance was encountered in other towns. He thought it advisable to spread terror by a severe example—so much the more so as "the well-known mildness of his temper," says Hirtius, "would not allow this necessary rigor to be ascribed to cruelty." He ordered that all those who had borne arms should have their hands cut off, and sent them away living examples of the punishment reserved for rebels.

Drappes, who had been taken prisoner, starved himself to death; Lucterius, who had been arrested by the Arvernan Epasnactus (a friend of the Romans), was delivered up to Cæsar. While these events were taking place on the banks of the Dordogne, Labienus, in a cavalry engagement, had gained a decisive advantage over a part of the Treviri and Germans; had taken prisoner their chief, and thus subjected a people who were always ready to support any insurrection against the Romans. The Æduan Surus fell also into his hands. He was a chief distinguished for his courage and birth, and the only one of that nation who had not yet laid down his arms.

From that moment Cæsar considered Gaul to be completely pacified. He resolved, however, to go himself to Aquitaine, which he had not yet visited and which Publius Crassus had partly conquered. Arriving there at the head of two legions, he obtained the complete submission of that country without difficulty. All the tribes sent him hostages. He proceeded next to Narbonne with a detachment of cavalry and charged his lieutenants to put the army into winter quarters. Four legions, under the orders of Mark Antony, Caius Trebonius, Publius Vatinius, and Q. Tullius, were quartered in Belgium, two among the Ædui and two among the Turones on the frontier of the Carnutes, to hold in check all the countries bordering on the ocean.

These two last legions took up their winter quarters on the territory of the Lemovices, not far from the Arverni, so that no part of Gaul should be without troops. Cæsar remained but a short time in the province, presiding hastily over the assemblies, determining cases of public dispute, and rewarding those who had served him well. He had had occasion more than anyone to know their sentiments individually, because during the general revolt of Gaul the fidelity and succor of the province had aided him in triumphing over it. When these affairs were settled he returned to his legions in Belgium and took up his winter quarters at Nemetocenna (Arras).

There he was informed of the last attempts of Commius, who, continuing a partisan war at the head of a small number of cavalry, intercepted the Roman convoys. Mark Antony had charged C. Volusenus Quadratus, prefect of the cavalry, to pursue him. He had accepted the task eagerly in the hope of succeeding the second time better than the first, but Commius, taking advantage of the rash ardor with which his enemy had rushed upon him, had wounded him seriously and escaped. He was discouraged, however, and had promised Mark Antony to retire to any spot which should be appointed him on condition that he should never be compelled to appear before a Roman. This condition having been accepted, he had given hostages. Gaul was hereby subjugated. Death or slavery had carried off its principal citizens. Of all the chiefs who had fought for its independence only two survived—Commius and Ambiorix.

Banished far from their country they died in obscurity.

ROMAN INVASION AND CONQUEST OF BRITAIN

B.C. 55–A.D. 79

OLIVER GOLDSMITH

When Julius Cæsar received the province of Gaul as his government, B.C. 58, it was only a small portion of the territory inhabited by the Gauls or Celts, being almost conterminous with the mediæval Provence. It was also at peace, and there seemed no excuse for making an extension of Roman territory among the three tribes or races between which Northern and Western Gaul were divided. But the Helvetii, who occupied that part of the Alps known to-day as Switzerland, meditated an emigration into the plains of Gaul, and, as their shortest route lay across the Roman provinces, they asked leave of Cæsar to pass three hundred and sixty thousand souls in all, counting women and children, through the imperial territory.

The Roman commander, after giving them an evasive answer, met them in the territory of the Sequani and Ædui and defeated them, driving them back to their mountains. He next went to the aid of the Ædui, ancient allies of Rome, against the Arverni and Sequani, who had invaded the Æduan territory under a German chieftain, Ariovistus. The result was that Ariovistus was defeated and driven eastward across the Rhine. He then defeated the Belgæ, who, in B.C. 57, took up arms against the garrisons which he had left in the country of the Sequani (dwellers on the Seine). He continued his conquest of the Belgic territory, and subjected the three nations who occupied it, finally entering the country of the warlike Nervii, whom he only conquered after a stubborn and bloody battle. As soon as he had subjugated the whole of Gaul, he crossed the Rhine for the purpose of intimidating the Germans and teaching them to keep within their own boundaries.

He pursued the same policy with regard to the Britons, who, according to information received by him, had sent aid to the Gauls in their struggle with Rome. His ships were brought round from the Loire to that part of the French coast now known as Boulogne, and he set out for Britain, where he landed, and eventually received the submission of the British chieftains.

THE Britons in their rude and barbarous state seemed to stand in need of more polished instructors; and indeed whatever evils may attend the conquest of heroes, their success has generally produced one good effect in disseminating the

285

arts of refinement and humanity.   It ever happens when a barbarous nation is conquered by another more advanced in the
arts of peace, that it gains in elegance a recompense for what
it loses in liberty.

The Britons had long remained in this rude but independent
state, when Cæsar, having overrun Gaul with his victories, and
willing still further to extend his fame, determined upon the
conquest of a country that seemed to promise an easy triumph.
He was allured neither by the riches nor by the renown of the
inhabitants; but being ambitious rather of splendid than of
useful conquests, he was willing to carry the Roman arms into
a country the remote situation of which would add seeming
difficulty to the enterprise and consequently produce an increase of reputation.   His pretence was to punish these islanders for having sent succors to the Gauls while he waged war
against that nation, as well as for granting an asylum to such
of the enemy as had sought protection from his resentment.

The natives, informed of his intention, were sensible of the
unequal contest and endeavored to appease him by submission.
He received their ambassadors with great complacency, and
having exhorted them to continue steadfast in the same sentiments, in the mean time made preparations for the execution of
his design.   When the troops designed for the expedition were
embarked he set sail for Britain about midnight, and the
next morning arrived on the coast near Dover, where he saw
the rocks and cliffs covered with armed men to oppose his
landing.

Finding it impracticable to gain the shore where he first intended, from the agitation of the sea and the impending mountains, he resolved to choose a landing-place of greater security.
The place he chose was about eight miles farther on (some
suppose at Deal), where an inclining shore and a level country
invited his attempts.   The poor, naked, ill-armed Britons we
may well suppose were but an unequal match for the dis-
ciplined Romans who had before conquered Gaul and afterward became the conquerors of the world.   However, they
made a brave opposition against the veteran army; the conflicts between them were fierce, the losses mutual, and the success various.

The Britons had chosen Cassibelaunus for their commander-in-chief; but the petty princes under his command, either desiring his station or suspecting his fidelity, threw off their allegiance. Some of them fled with their forces into the internal parts of the kingdom, others submitted to Cæsar; till at length Cassibelaunus himself, weakened by so many desertions, resolved upon making what terms he was able while yet he had power to keep the field. The conditions offered by Cæsar and accepted by him were that he should send to the Continent double the number of hostages at first demanded and that he should acknowledge subjection to the Romans.

The Romans were pleased with the name of this new and remote conquest, and the senate decreed a supplication of twenty days in consequence of their general's success. Having therefore in this manner rather discovered than subdued the southern parts of the island, Cæsar returned into Gaul with his forces and left the Britons to enjoy their customs, religion, and laws. But the inhabitants, thus relieved from the terror of his arms, neglected the performance of their stipulations, and only two of their states sent over hostages according to the treaty. Cæsar, it is likely, was not much displeased at the omission, as it furnished him with a pretext for visiting the island once more and completing a conquest which he had only begun.

Accordingly the ensuing spring he set sail for Britain with eight hundred ships,[1] and arriving at the place of his descent

---

[1] With regard to these Roman *ships*, let not our readers be misled by a familiar notion or a pompous name. They were but little more than rowboats, as may be easily imagined from the fact that Cicero instances for its uncommon magnitude a *ship* of only fifty-six tons ! These ancient vessels were occasionally sheathed with leather or lead, and had the prow decorated with paint and gilding, while the stern was sometimes carved in the figure of a shield, elaborately adorned. Upon a staff there erected hung ribbons distinctive of the ship and serving at the same time to show the direction of the wind. There, too, stood the *tutela*, or chosen patron of the ship, to whom prayers and sacrifices were daily offered. The selection of this deity was guided by either private or professional reasons, and as merchants committed themselves to the protection of Mercury, or lovers to the care of Cupid, warriors, it will at once be surmised, made Mars the object of their pious supplication.

At a later period than the epoch to which our present note attaches, he landed without opposition.   The islanders being apprised of his invasion had assembled an army and marched down to the sea-side to oppose him, but seeing the number of his forces, and the whole sea, as it were, covered with his shipping, they were struck with consternation and retired to their places of security.   The Romans, however, pursued them to their retreats until at last common danger induced these poor barbarians to forget their former dissensions and to unite their whole strength for the mutual defence of their liberty and possessions.

Cassibelaunus was chosen to conduct the common cause, and for some time he harassed the Romans in their march and revived the desponding hopes of his countrymen.   But no opposition that undisciplined strength could make was able to repress the vigor and intrepidity of Cæsar.   He discomfited the Britons in every action; he advanced into the country, passed the Thames in the face of the enemy, took and burned the capital city of Cassibelaunus, established his ally Mandubratius as sovereign of the Trinobantes; and having obliged the inhabitants to make new submissions, he again returned with his army into Gaul, having made himself rather the nominal than the real possessor of the island.

Whatever the stipulated tribute might have been, it is more than probable, as there was no authority left to exact it, that it was but indifferently paid.   Upon the accession of Augustus, that Emperor had formed a design of visiting Britain, but was diverted from it by an unexpected revolt of the Pannonians. Some years after he resumed his design; but being met in his way by the British ambassadors, who promised the accustomed tribute and made the usual submissions, he desisted from his intention.   The year following, finding them remiss in their supplies and untrue to their former professions, he once more prepared for the invasion of the country; but a well-timed embassy again averted his indignation, and the submissions he re-

when Constantius removed from Heliopolis to Rome an enormous obelisk, weighing fifteen hundred tons, the vessel on board of which it was shipped also carried *eleven hundred and thirty-eight tons* of pulse; but such vast and unmanageable masses were regarded as monsters, and owed their existence to the absolute urgency of a remarkable purpose, backed by the despotic institutions of the times.

ceived seemed to satisfy his resentment; upon his death-bed he appeared sensible of the overgrown extent of the Roman Empire and recommended it to his successors never to enlarge their territories.

Tiberius followed the maxims of Augustus and, wisely judging the empire already too extensive, made no attempt upon Britain. Some Roman soldiers having been wrecked on the British coast the inhabitants not only assisted them with the greatest humanity, but sent them in safety back to their general. In consequence of these friendly dispositions, a constant intercourse of good offices subsisted between the two nations; the principal British nobility resorted to Rome, and many received their education there.

From that time the Britons began to improve in all the arts which contribute to the advancement of human nature. The first art which a savage people is generally taught by politer neighbors is that of war. The Britons thenceforward, though not wholly addicted to the Roman method of fighting, nevertheless adopted several of their improvements, as well in their arms as in their arrangement in the field. Their ferocity to strangers, for which they had been always remarkable, was mitigated and they began to permit an intercourse of commerce even in the internal parts of the country. They still, however, continued to live as herdsmen and hunters; a manifest proof that the country was yet but thinly inhabited. A nation of hunters can never be populous, as their subsistence is necessarily diffused over a large tract of country, while the husbandman converts every part of nature to human use, and flourishes most by the vicinity of those whom he is to support.

The wild extravagances of Caligula by which he threatened Britain with an invasion served rather to expose him to ridicule than the island to danger. The Britons therefore for almost a century enjoyed their liberty unmolested, till at length the Romans in the reign of Claudius began to think seriously of reducing them under their dominion. The expedition for this purpose was conducted in the beginning by Plautius and other commanders, with that success which usually attended the Roman arms.

Claudius himself, finding affairs sufficiently prepared for

his reception, made a journey thither and received the submission of such states as living by commerce were willing to purchase tranquillity at the expense of freedom. It is true that
many of the inland provinces preferred their native simplicity
to imported elegance and, rather than bow their necks to the
Roman yoke, offered their bosoms to the sword. But the
southern coast with all the adjacent inland country was seized
by the conquerors, who secured the possession by fortifying
camps, building fortresses, and planting colonies. The other
parts of the country, either thought themselves in no danger
or continued patient spectators of the approaching devastation.

Caractacus was the first who seemed willing, by a vigorous
effort, to rescue his country and repel its insulting and rapacious conquerors.[1] The venality and corruption of the Roman
prætors and officers, who were appointed to levy the contribu-
tions in Britain, served to excite the indignation of the natives
and give spirit to his attempts. This rude soldier, though
with inferior forces, continued for about the space of nine
years to oppose and harass the Romans; so that at length Os-
torius Scapula was sent over to command their armies. He
was more successful than his predecessors. He advanced the
Roman conquest over Britain, pierced the country of the Si-
lures, a warlike nation along the banks of the Severn, and at
length came up with Caractacus, who had taken possession of
a very advantageous post upon an almost inaccessible mountain,
washed by a deep and rapid stream.

The unfortunate British general, when he saw the enemy
approaching, drew up his army, composed of different tribes,
and going from rank to rank exhorted them to strike the last
blow for liberty, safety, and life. To these exhortations his
soldiers replied with shouts of determined valor. But what
could undisciplined bravery avail against the attack of an army
skilled in all the arts of war and inspired by a long train of conquests? The Britons were, after an obstinate resistance, totally
routed, and a few days after Caractacus himself was delivered
up to the conquerors by Cartismandua, queen of the Brigantes,
with whom he had taken refuge. The capture of this general

[1] The character of this hero has been powerfully depicted by Beau-
mont and Fletcher, in one of their noblest dramas.

was received with such joy at Rome that Claudius commanded that he should be brought from Britain in order to be exhibited as a spectacle to the Roman people. Accordingly, on the day appointed for that purpose, the Emperor, ascending his throne, ordered the captives and Caractacus among the number to be brought into his presence. The vassals of the British King, with the spoils taken in war, were first brought forward; these were followed by his family, who, with abject lamentations, were seen to implore for mercy.

Last of all came Caractacus with an undaunted air and a dignified aspect. He appeared no way dejected at the amazing concourse of spectators that were gathered upon this occasion, but, casting his eyes on the splendors that surrounded him, "Alas!" cried he, "how is it possible that a people possessed of such magnificence at home could envy me an humble cottage in Britain?" When brought into the Emperor's presence he is said to have addressed him in the following manner: "Had my moderation been equal to my birth and fortune, I had arrived in this city not as a captive, but as a friend. But my present misfortunes redound as much to your honor as to my disgrace; and the obstinacy of my opposition serves to increase the splendor of your victory. Had I surrendered myself in the beginning of the contest, neither my disgrace nor your glory would have attracted the attention of the world, and my fate would have been buried in general oblivion. I am now at your mercy; but if my life be spared, I shall remain an eternal monument of your clemency and moderation." The Emperor was affected with the British hero's misfortunes and won by his address. He ordered him to be unchained upon the spot, with the rest of the captives, and the first use they made of their liberty was to go and prostrate themselves before the empress Agrippina, who as some suppose had been an intercessor for their freedom.

Notwithstanding these misfortunes, the Britons were not subdued, and this island was regarded by the ambitious Romans as a field in which military honor might still be acquired. The Britons made one expiring effort to recover their liberty in the time of Nero, taking advantage of the absence of Paulinus, the Roman general, who was employed in subduing the isle of

Anglesey.   That small island, separated from Britain by a narrow channel, still continued the chief seat of the Druidical superstition, and constantly afforded a retreat to their defeated forces.   It was thought necessary therefore to subdue that place, in order to extirpate a religion that disdained submission to foreign laws or leaders; and Paulinus, the greatest general of his age, undertook the task.

The Britons endeavored to obstruct his landing on that last retreat of their superstitions and liberties, both by the force of their arms and the terrors of their religion.   The priests and islanders were drawn up in order of battle upon the shore, to oppose his landing.   The women, dressed like Furies, with dishevelled hair, and torches in their hands, poured forth the most terrible execrations.   Such a sight at first confounded the Romans and fixed them motionless on the spot; so that they received the first assault without opposition.   But Paulinus, exhorting his troops to despise the menaces of an absurd superstition, impelled them to the attack, drove the Britons off the field, burned the Druids in the same fires they had prepared for their captive enemies, and destroyed all their consecrated groves and altars.

In the mean time the Britons, taking advantage of his absence, resolved, by a general insurrection, to free themselves from that state of abject servitude to which they were reduced by the Romans.   They had many motives to aggravate their resentment—the greatness of their taxes, which were levied with unremitting severity; the cruel insolence of their conquerors, who reproached that very poverty which they had caused, but particularly the barbarous treatment of Boadicea, queen of the Iceni, drove them at last into open rebellion.

Prasatagus, king of the Iceni, at his death had bequeathed one-half of his dominions to the Romans, and the other to his daughters; thus hoping by the sacrifice of a part to secure the rest in his family; but it had a different effect; for the Roman procurator immediately took possession of the whole, and when Boadicea, the widow of the deceased, attempted to remonstrate, he ordered her to be scourged like a slave, and violated the chastity of her daughters.   These outrages were sufficient to produce a revolt through the whole island.   The

Iceni, being the most deeply interested in the quarrel, were the first to take arms; all the other states soon followed the example, and Boadicea, a woman of great beauty and masculine spirit, was appointed to head the common forces, which amounted to two hundred and thirty thousand fighting men.

These, exasperated by their wrongs, attacked several of the Roman settlements and colonies with success. Paulinus hastened to relieve London, which was already a flourishing colony; but found on his arrival that it would be requisite, for the general safety, to abandon that place to the merciless fury of the enemy. London was therefore soon reduced to ashes; such of the inhabitants as remained in it were massacred; and the Romans with all other strangers to the number of seventy thousand were cruelly put to the sword. Flushed with these successes the Britons no longer sought to avoid the enemy, but boldly came to the place where Paulinus awaited their arrival, posted in a very advantageous manner with a body of ten thousand men. The battle was obstinate and bloody. Boadicea herself appeared in a chariot with her two daughters and harangued her army with masculine firmness; but the irregular and undisciplined bravery of her troops was unable to resist the cool intrepidity of the Romans. They were routed with great slaughter; eighty thousand perished in the field, and an infinite number were made prisoners, while Boadicea herself, fearing to fall into the hands of the enraged victor, put an end to her life by poison. Nero soon after recalled Paulinus from a government where, by suffering and inflicting so many severities, he was judged improper to compose the angry and alarmed minds of the natives.

After an interval, Cerealis received the command from Vespasian, and by his bravery propagated the terror of the Roman arms. Julius Frontinus succeeded Cerealis both in authority and reputation. The general who finally established the dominion of the Romans in this island was Julius Agricola, who governed it during the reigns of Vespasian, Titus, and Domitian, and distinguished himself as well by his courage as humanity.

Agricola, who is considered as one of the greatest characters in history, formed a regular plan for subduing and civilizing the island, and thus rendering the acquisition useful to the conquerors. As the northern part of the country was least tractable, he carried his victorious arms thither, and defeated the undisciplined enemy in every encounter. He pierced into the formerly inaccessible forests and mountains of Caledonia; he drove onward all those fierce and intractable spirits who preferred famine to slavery, and who, rather than submit, chose to remain in perpetual hostility. Nor was it without opposition that he thus made his way into a country rude and impervious by nature.

He was opposed by Galgacus at the head of a numerous army, whom he defeated in a decisive action, in which considerable numbers were slain. Being thus successful, he did not think proper to pursue the enemy into their retreats; but embarking a body of troops on board his fleet, he ordered the commander to surround the whole coast of Britain, which had not been discovered to be an island till the preceding year. This armament, pursuant to his orders, steered to the northward, and there subdued the Orkneys; then making the tour of the whole island, it arrived in the port of Sandwich, without having met with the least disaster.

During these military enterprises, Agricola was ever attentive to the arts of peace. He attempted to humanize the fierceness of those who acknowledged his power, by introducing the Roman laws, habits, manners, and learning. He taught them to desire and raise all the conveniences of life, instructed them in the arts of agriculture, and, in order to protect them in their peaceable possessions, he drew a rampart, and fixed a train of garrisons between them and their northern neighbors, thus cutting off the ruder and more barren parts of the island and securing the Roman province from the invasion of a fierce and necessitous enemy. In this manner the Britons, being almost totally subdued, now began to throw off all hopes of recovering their former liberty, and, having often experienced the superiority of the Romans, consented to submit, and were content with safety. From that time the Romans seemed more desirous of securing what they possessed than of making new conquests, and were employed rather in repressing than punishing their restless northern invaders.

CLEOPATRA'S CONQUEST OF CÆSAR AND ANTONY

B.C. 51–30

JOHN P. MAHAFFY

Several Egyptian princesses of the line of the Ptolemies bore the name of Cleopatra, but history, romance, and tragedy are all illumined with the story of one—Cleopatra the daughter of Ptolemy Auletes. Born at Alexandria, B.C. 69, she ruled jointly with her brother Ptolemy from 51 to 48. Being then expelled by her colleague, she entered upon the performance of her part in Roman history when her cause was espoused by Julius Cæsar, whom she had captivated by her charms. Her reinstatement by the help of Cæsar, as well as all that followed in her relations with Roman rulers, was due primarily to personal considerations, rather than political or military causes; and among women whose lives have vitally influenced the conduct of great historic leaders, and thereby affected the course of events, Cleopatra holds a place at once the most conspicuous and most unique.

Like Cæsar, Mark Antony, at his first interview with Cleopatra, succumbed to the fascinations of the " Rare Egyptian," and he never after ceased to be her slave. Not long after Cæsar's death Antony had married Fulvia, whom he deserted for the "enchanting queen." From this point to its culmination in overwhelming disaster and the tragic death of this celebrated pair of lovers, the romantic drama of Cleopatra's conquests becomes even more important in literature than in history. This extraordinary voluptuary, whose beauty and witcheries have interested mankind for almost twenty centuries, has been the subject of some thirty tragedies in various languages; and in *Antony and Cleopatra*—one of his greatest plays—Shakespeare, closely following the narratives of Plutarch and other classical writers, has invested her with a potency of charm unparalleled among literary creations.

She matches Antony in qualities of intellect, while she dazzles him with her coquettish arts. " A queen, a siren," says Thomas Campbell, "a Shakespeare's Cleopatra alone could have entangled Shakespeare's Antony." And Shakespeare alone, as declared by Mrs. Jameson, " has dared to exhibit the Egyptian Queen with all her greatness and all her littleness, all her paltry arts and dissolute passions, yet awakened our pity for fallen grandeur without once beguiling us into sympathy with guilt."

Yet the plain history of this " Sorceress of the Nile," with her " infinite variety," as told by Plutarch and the other ancients, and retold, with whatever advantages gained from critical research, by the modern masters, makes the same impression of moral contrast and inscrutability as that imparted by the greatest poet who has dramatized the character of Cleopatra.

NOW at last Egypt, coming into close connection with the world's masters, becomes the stage for some of the most striking scenes in ancient history. They seem to most readers something new and strange—the pageants and passions of the fratricide Cleopatra as something unparalleled—and yet she was one of a race in which almost every reigning princess for the last two hundred years had been swayed by like storms of passion, or had been guilty of like daring violations of common humanity. What Arsinoë, what Cleopatra, from the first to the last, had hesitated to murder a brother or a husband, to assume the throne, to raise and command armies, to discard or adopt a partner of her throne from caprice in policy, or policy in caprice? But hitherto this desperate gambling with life had been carried on in Egypt and Syria; the play had been with Hellenistic pawns—Egyptian or Syrian princes; the last Cleopatra came to play with Roman pieces, easier apparently to move than the others, but implying higher stakes, greater glory in the victory, greater disaster in the defeat. Therefore is it that this last Cleopatra, probably no more than an average specimen of the beauty, talent, daring, and cruelty of her ancestors, has taken an unique place among them in the imagination of the world, and holds her own even now and forever as a familiar name throughout the world.

Ptolemy Auletes, when dying, had taken great care not to bequeath his mortgaged kingdom to his Roman creditors. In his will he had named as his heirs the elder of his two sons, and his daughter, who was the eldest of the family. Nobody thought of claiming Egypt for a heritage of the Roman Republic, when the whole world was the prize proposed in the civil conflict, for though the war of Cæsar and Pompey had not actually broken out, the political sky was lowering with blackness, and the coming tempest was muttering its thunder through the sultry air. So Cleopatra, now about sixteen or seventeen years of age, and her much younger brother (about

ten) assumed the throne as was traditional, without any tumult
or controversy.

The opening discords came from within the royal family.
The tutors and advisers of the young King, among whom Pothinos, a eunuch brought up with him as his playmate, according to the custom of the court, was the ablest and most influential, persuaded him to assume sole direction of affairs and to
depose his elder sister. Cleopatra was not able to maintain
herself in Alexandria, but went to Syria as an exile, where she
promptly collected an army, as was the wont of these Egyptian princesses, who seem to have resources always under their
control, and returned—within a few months, says Cæsar—by
way of Pelusium, to reconquer her lawful share in the throne.
This happened in the fourth year of their so-called joint reign,
B.C. 48, at the very time that Pompey and Cæsar were engaged
in their conflict for a far greater kingdom.

Cæsar expressed his opinion that the quarrel of the sovereigns in Egypt concerned the Roman people, and himself as
consul, the more so as it was in his previous consulate that the
recognition of and alliance with their father had taken place.
So he signified his decision that Ptolemy and Cleopatra should
dismiss their armies, and should discuss their claims before him
by argument and not by arms. All our authorities, except Dio
Cassius, state that he sent for Cleopatra that she might personally urge her claims; but Dio tells us, with far more detail and
I think greater probability, " that at first the quarrel with her
brother was argued for her by friends, till she, learning the
amorous character of Cæsar, sent him word that her case was
being mismanaged by her advocates, and she desired to plead
it herself. She was then in the flower of her age (about
twenty) and celebrated for her beauty. Moreover, she had the
sweetest of voices, and every charm of conversation, so that
she was likely to ensnare even the most obdurate and elderly
man. These gifts she regarded as her claims upon Cæsar.
She prayed therefore for an interview, and adorned herself in
a garb most becoming, but likely to arouse his pity, and so came
secretly by night to visit him."

If she indeed arrived secretly and was carried into the palace by one faithful follower as a bale of carpet, it was from fear

of assassination by the party of Pothinos. She knew that as soon as she had reached Cæsar's sentries she was safe; as the event proved, she was more than safe, for in the brief interval of peace, and perhaps even of apparent jollity, while the royal dispute was under discussion, she gained an influence over Cæsar which she retained till his death. Cæsar adjudicated the throne according to the will of Auletes; he even restored Cyprus to Egypt, and proposed to send the younger brother and his sister Arsinoe to govern it; but he also insisted on a repayment, in part at least, of the enormous outstanding debt of Auletes to him and his party.

A few months after Cæsar's departure from Egypt Cleopatra gave birth to a son, whom she alleged, without any immediate contradiction, to be the dictator's. The Alexandrians called him Cæsarion, and she never swerved from asserting for him royal privileges. We hear of no other lover, though it is impossible to imagine Cleopatra arriving at the age of twenty without providing herself with this luxury. She was, however, afraid to let Cæsar live far from her influence, and some time before his assassination—that is to say, some time between B.C. 48 and 44—she came with the young King her brother to Rome, where she was received in Cæsar's palace beyond the Tiber, causing by her residence there considerable scandal among the stricter Romans. Cicero confesses that he went to see her, but protests that his reasons for doing so were absolutely nonpolitical. Cicero found her haughty; he does not say she was beautiful and fascinating. We do not hear of any political activity on her part, though Cicero evidently suspects it; it is wellnigh impossible that she can have preferred her very doubtful position at Rome to her brilliant life in the East. She was suspected of urging Cæsar to move eastward the capital of his new empire, to desert Rome, and choose either Ilium, the imaginary cradle of his race, or Alexandria, as his residence. She is likely to have encouraged at all events his expedition against the Parthians, which would bring him to Syria, whence she hoped to gain new territory for her son. The whole situation is eloquently, perhaps too eloquently, described by Merivale, for he weaves in many conjectures of his own, as if they were ascertained facts.

The colors of this imitation of a hateful original [the oriental despot] were heightened by the demeanor of Cleopatra, who followed her lover to Rome at his invitation. She came with the younger Ptolemæus, who now shared her throne, and her ostensible object was to negotiate a treaty between her kingdom and the Commonwealth. While the Egyptian nation was formally admitted to the friendship and alliance of Rome, its sovereign was lodged in Cæsar's villa on the other side of the Tiber, and the statue of the most fascinating of women was erected in the temple of the Goddess of Love and Beauty. The connection which subsisted between her and the dictator was unblushingly avowed. Public opinion demanded no concessions to its delicacy; the feelings of the injured Calpurnia had been blunted by repeated outrage, and Cleopatra was encouraged to proclaim openly that her child Cæsarion was the son of her Roman admirer. A tribune, named Helvius Cinna, ventured, it is said, to assert among his friends that he was prepared to propose a law, with the dictator's sanction, to enable him to marry more wives than one, for the sake of progeny, and to disregard in his choice the legitimate qualification of Roman descent. The Romans, however, were spared this last insult to their prejudices. The queen of Egypt felt bitterly the scorn with which she was popularly regarded as the representative of an effeminate and licentious people. It is not improbable that she employed her fatal influence to withdraw her lover from the Roman capital, and urged him to schemes of oriental conquest to bring him more completely within her toils. In the mean while the haughtiness of her demeanor corresponded with the splendid anticipations in which she indulged. She held a court in the suburbs of the city, at which the adherents of the dictator's policy were not the only attendants. Even his opponents and concealed enemies were glad to bask in the sunshine of her smiles.

When Cæsar was assassinated, she was still at Rome, and had some wild hopes of having her son recognized by the Cæsareans. But failing in this she escaped secretly, and sailed to Egypt, not without causing satisfaction to cautious men like Cicero that she was gone. The passage in which he seems to allude to a rumor that she was about to have another child—

another misfortune to the State—does not bear that interpreta-
tion. As he says not a word concerning the young king Ptolemy, we may assume that the youth was already dead, and that
he died at Rome. The common belief was that Cleopatra poisoned him as soon as his increasing years made him trouble-
some to her. In her reign four years are assigned to a joint
rule with her elder brother, four more to that with her younger,
so that this latter must have died in the same year as Cæsar.

Cleopatra, watching from Egypt the great civil war which
ensued, summoned and commanded by the various leaders to
send aid in ships and money, threatened with plunder and confiscation by those who were now exhausting Asia Minor and
the islands with monstrous exactions, had ample occupation
for her talents in steering safely among these constant dangers.
Appian says she pleaded famine and pestilence in her country
in declining the demands of Cassius for subsidies. The latter
was on the point of invading Egypt, at the moment denuded of
defending forces and *wasted with famine*, when he was summoned to Philippi by Brutus.

It was not till B.C. 41, after the decisive battle of Philippi,
that the victorious Antony, turning to subdue the East to the
Cæsarean cause, held his *joyeuse entrée* into Ephesus, and then
proceeded to drain all Asia Minor of money for the satisfaction
of his greedy legionaries and his own still more greedy vices.
Reaching Cilicia, he sent an order to the queen of Egypt to
come before him and explain her conduct during the late war,
for she was reported to have sent aid to Cassius. The sequel
may be told in Plutarch's famous narrative:

"Dellius, who was sent on this message, had no sooner seen
her face, and remarked her adroitness and subtlety in speech,
than he felt convinced that Antony would not so much as
think of giving any molestation to a woman like this. On the
contrary, she would be the first in favor with him. So he set
himself at once to pay his court to the Egyptian, and gave her
his advice, ' to go,' in the Homeric style, to Cilicia, ' in her best
attire,' and bade her fear nothing from Antony, the gentlest and
kindest of soldiers. She had some faith in the words of Dellius, but more in her own attractions, which, having formerly
recommended her to Cæsar and the young Cnæus Pompey, she

did not doubt might yet prove more successful with Antony. Their acquaintance was with her when a girl, young, and ignorant of the world, but she was to meet Antony in the time of life when women's beauty is most splendid and their intellects are in full maturity. She made great preparation for her journey, of money, gifts, and ornaments of value, such as so wealthy a kingdom might afford, but she brought with her her surest hopes in her own magic arts and charms.

"She received several letters, both from Antony and from his friends, to summon her, but she took no account of these orders; and at last, as if in mockery of them, she came sailing up the river Cydnus, in a barge with gilded stern and outspread sails of purple, while oars of silver beat time to the music of flutes and fifes and harps. She herself lay all along, under a canopy of cloth of gold, dressed as Venus in a picture, and beautiful young boys, like painted cupids, stood on each side to fan her. Her maids were dressed like sea nymphs and graces, some steering at the rudder, some working at the ropes.[1] The perfumes diffused themselves from the vessel to the shore, which was covered with multitudes, part following the galley up the river on either bank, part running out of the city to see the sight. The market-place was quite emptied, and Antony at last was left alone sitting upon the tribunal, while the word went through all the multitude that Venus was come to feast with Bacchus, for the common good of Asia.[2] On her arrival, Antony sent to invite her to supper. She thought it fitter he should come to her; so, willing to show his good humor and courtesy, he complied, and went. He found the preparations to receive him magnificent beyond expression, but nothing so admirable as the great number of lights, for on a sudden there was let down altogether so great a number of branches with lights in them so ingeniously disposed, some in squares and

[1] There was no Egyptian feature in this show, which was purely Hellenistic.

[2] How easily such a belief started up in the minds of a crowd in the Asia Minor of that day appears from Acts xiv. 11 *seq.*, where the crowd at Iconium, on seeing a cripple cured, at once exclaim that the gods are come down to them in the likeness of men, and call Barnabas Jupiter, and Paul Mercurius, because he was the chief speaker, bringing sacrifices to offer to the apostles.

some in circles, that the whole thing was a spectacle that has seldom been equalled for beauty.

"The next day Antony invited her to supper, and was very desirous to outdo her as well in magnificence as contrivance; but he found he was altogether beaten in both, and was so well convinced of it that he was himself the first to jest and mock at his poverty of wit and his rustic awkwardness. She, perceiving that his raillery was broad and gross and savored more of the soldier than the courtier, rejoined in the same taste, and fell into it at once, without any sort of reluctance or reserve, for her actual beauty, it is said, was not in itself so remarkable that none could be compared with her, or that no one could see her without being struck by it, but the contact of her presence, if you lived with her, was irresistible; the attraction of her person, joining with the charm of her conversation and the character that attended all she said or did, was something bewitching. It was a pleasure merely to hear the sound of her voice, with which, like an instrument of many strings, she could pass from one language to another; so that there were few of the barbarian nations that she answered by an interpreter. To most of them she spoke herself, as to the Ethiopians, troglodytes, Hebrews, Arabians, Syrians, Medes, Parthians, and many others, whose language she had learned;[1] which was all the more surprising, because most of the kings her predecessors scarcely gave themselves the trouble to acquire the Egyptian tongue, and several of them quite abandoned the Macedonian.

"Antony was so captivated by her that, while Fulvia, his wife, maintained his quarrels in Rome against Cæsar by actual force of arms, and the Parthian troops, commanded by Labienus —the King's generals having made him commander-in-chief— were assembled in Mesopotamia, and ready to enter Syria, he could yet suffer himself to be carried away by her to Alexandria, there to keep holiday, like a boy, in play and diversion, squandering and fooling away in enjoyments that most costly, as Antiphon says, of all valuables, time. They had a sort of company, to which they gave a particular name, calling it that of the ' Inimitable Livers.' The members entertained one another daily in turn, with an extravagance of expenditure beyond

[1] We have here the usual lies of courtiers.

measure or belief.   Philotas, a physician of Amphissa, who was at that time a student of medicine in Alexandria, used to tell my grandfather Lamprias that, having some acquaintance with one of the royal cooks, he was invited by him, being a young man, to come and see the sumptuous preparations for dinner. So he was taken into the kitchen, where he admired the prodigious variety of all things, but, particularly seeing eight wild boars roasting whole, says he, ' Surely you have a great number of guests.'   The cook laughed at his simplicity, and told him there were not above twelve to dine, but that every dish was to be served up just roasted to a turn, and if anything was but one minute ill-timed it was spoiled.   ' And,' said he, ' maybe Antony will dine just now, maybe not this hour, maybe he will call for wine, or begin to talk, and will put it off.   So that,' he continued, ' it is not one, but many dinners, must be had in readiness, as it is impossible to guess at his hour.' "

Plato admits four sorts of flattery, but Cleopatra had a thousand.   Were Antony serious or disposed to mirth she had any moment some new delight or charm to meet his wishes.   At every turn she was upon him, and let him escape her neither by day nor by night.   She played at dice with him, drank with him, hunted with him, and when he exercised in arms she was there to see.   At night she would go rambling with him to joke with people at their doors and windows, dressed like a servant woman, for Antony also went in servant's disguise, and from these expeditions he always came home very scurvily answered, and sometimes even beaten severely, though most people guessed who it was.   However, the Alexandrians in general liked it all well enough, and joined good-humoredly and kindly in his frolic and play, saying they were much obliged to Antony for acting his tragic parts at Rome and keeping his comedy for them.   It would be trifling without end to be particular in relating his follies, but his fishing must not be forgotten.   He went out one day to angle with Cleopatra, and being so unfortunate as to catch nothing in the presence of his mistress, he gave secret orders to the fishermen to dive under water and put fishes that had been already taken upon his hooks, and these he drew in so fast that the Egyptian perceived it.   But feigning great admiration, she told everybody how dexterous Antony was, and invited them next day to come and see him again. So when a number of them had come on board the fishing boats, as soon as he had let down his hook, one of her servants was beforehand with his divers and fixed upon his hook a salted fish from Pontus. Antony, feeling his line taut, drew up the prey, and when, as may be imagined, great laughter ensued, "Leave," said Cleopatra, "the fishing rod, autocrat, to us poor sovereigns of Pharos and Canopus; your game is cities, kingdoms, and continents."

Plutarch does not mention the most tragic and the most characteristic proof of Cleopatra's complete conquest of Antony. Among his other crimes of obedience he sent by her orders and put to death the Princess Arsinoë, who, knowing well her danger, had taken refuge as a suppliant in the temple of Artemis Leucophryne at Miletus.

It is not our duty to follow the various complications of war and diplomacy, accompanied by the marriage with the serious and gentle Octavia, whereby the brilliant but dissolute Antony was weaned, as it were, from his follies, and persuaded to live a life of public activity. Whether the wily Octavian did not foresee the result, whether he did not even sacrifice his sister to accumulate odium against his dangerous rival, is not for us to determine. But when it was arranged (in B.C. 36) that Antony should lead an expedition against the Parthians, any man of ordinary sense must have known that he would come within the reach of the eastern siren, and was sure to be again attracted by her fatal voice. It is hard to account for her strange patience during these four years. She had borne twins to Antony, probably after the meeting in Cilicia. Though she still maintained the claims of her eldest son Cæsarion to be the divine Julius' only direct heir, we do not hear of her sending requests to Antony to support him, or that any agents were working in her interests at Rome. She was too subtle a woman to solicit his return to Alexandria. There are mistaken insinuations that she thought the chances of Sextus Pompey, with his naval supremacy, better than those of Antony, but these stories refer to his brother Cnæus, who visited Egypt before Pharsalia.

It is probably to this pause in her life, as we know it, that we may refer her activity in repairing and enlarging the national temples. The splendid edifice at Dendera, at present among the most perfect of Egyptian temples, bears no older names than those of Cleopatra and her son Cæsarion, and their portraits represent the latter as a growing lad, his mother as an essentially Egyptian figure, conventionally drawn according to the rules which had determined the figures of gods and kings for fifteen hundred years. Under these circumstances it is idle to speak of this well-known relief picture as a portrait of the Queen. It is no more so than the granite statues in the Vatican are portraits of Philadelphus and Arsinoë. The artist had probably never seen the Queen, and if he had, it would not have produced the slightest alteration in his drawing.

Plutarch expressly says that it was not in peerless beauty that her fascination lay, but in the combination of more than average beauty with many other personal attractions. The Egyptian portrait is likely to confirm in the spectator's mind the impression derived from Shakespeare's play, that Cleopatra was a swarthy Egyptian, in strong contrast to the fair Roman ladies, and suggesting a wide difference of race. She was no more an Egyptian than she was an Indian, but a pure Macedonian, of a race akin to, and perhaps fairer than, the Greeks.

No sooner had Antony reached Syria than the fell influence of the Egyptian Queen revived. In the words of Plutarch:

"But the mischief that thus long had lain still, the passion for Cleopatra, which better thoughts had seemed to have lulled and charmed into oblivion, upon his approach to Syria, gathered strength again, and broke out into a flame. And in fine, like Plato's restive and rebellious horse of the human soul, flinging off all good and wholesome counsel and breaking fairly loose, he sent Fonteius Capito to bring Cleopatra into Syria; to whom at her arrival he made no small or trifling present—Phœnicia, Cœle-Syria, Cyprus, great part of Cilicia, that side of Judea which produces balm, that part of Arabia where the Nabathæans extend to the outer sea—profuse gifts which much displeased the Romans. For although he had invested several private persons with great governments and kingdoms, and bereaved many kings of theirs, as Antigonus of Judea, whose head he caused to be struck off—the first example of that punishment being inflicted on a king—yet nothing stung the Romans like the shame of these honors paid to Cleopatra. Their dissatisfaction was augmented also by his acknowledging as his own the twin children he had by her, giving them the names of Alexander and Cleopatra, and adding, as their surnames, the titles of Sun and Moon."

After much dallying the triumvir really started for the wild East, whither it is not our business to follow him. Cleopatra he sent home to Egypt, to await his victorious return, and it was on this occasion that she came in state to Jerusalem to visit Herod the Great—probably the most brilliant scene of the kind which had taken place since the queen of Sheba came to learn the wisdom of Solomon. But it was a very different wisdom that Herod professed, and in which he was verily a high authority, nor was the subtle daughter of the Ptolemies a docile pupil, but a practised expert in the same arts of cruelty and cunning wherewith both pursued their several courses of ambition and sought to wheedle from their Roman masters cities and provinces. The reunion of Antony and Cleopatra must have greatly alarmed Herod, whose plans were directly thwarted by the freaks of Antony, and he must have been preparing at the time to make his case with Octavian, and seek from his favor protection against the new caprices of the then lord of the East.

"The scene at Herod's palace must have been inimitable. The display of counter-fascinations between these two tigers; their voluptuous natures mutually attracted; their hatred giving to each that deep interest in the other which so often turns to mutual passion while it incites to conquest; the grace and finish of their manners, concealing a ruthless ferocity; the splendor of their appointments—what more dramatic picture can we imagine in history?

"We hear that she actually attempted to seduce Herod, but failed, owing to his deep devotion to his wife Mariamne. The prosaic Josephus adds that Herod consulted his council whether he should not put her to death for this attempt upon his virtue. He was dissuaded by them on the ground that Antony would listen to no arguments, not even from the most persuasive of the world's princes, and would take awful vengeance when he heard of her death. So she was escorted with great gifts and politenesses back to Egypt.

Such, then, was the character of this notorious Queen. But her violation of temples, and even of ancient tombs, for the sake of treasure must have been a far more public and odious exhibition of that want of respect for the sentiment of others which is the essence of bad manners." [1]

As is well known, the first campaign of Antony against Armenians and Parthians was a signal failure, and it was only with great difficulty that he escaped the fate of Crassus. But Cleopatra was ready to meet him in Syria with provisions and clothes for his distressed and ragged battalions, and he returned with her to spend the winter (B.C. 36–35) at Alexandria. She thus snatched him again from his noble wife, Octavia, who had come from Rome to Athens with succors even greater than Cleopatra had brought. This at least is the word of the historians who write in the interest of the Romans, and regard the queen of Egypt with horror and with fear.

The new campaign of Antony (B.C. 34) was apparently more prosperous, but it was only carried far enough to warrant his holding a Roman triumph at Alexandria—perhaps the only novelty in pomp which the triumvir could exhibit to the Alexandrian populace, while it gave the most poignant offence at Rome. It was apparently now that he made that formal distribution of provinces which Octavian used as his chief *casus belli*.

" Nor was the division he made among his sons at Alexandria less unpopular. It seemed a theatrical piece of insolence and contempt of his country, for, assembling the people in the exercise ground, and causing two golden thrones to be placed on a platform of silver, the one for him and the other for Cleopatra, and at their feet lower thrones for their children, he proclaimed Cleopatra queen of Egypt, Cyprus, Libya, and Cœle-Syria, and with her conjointly Cæsarion, the reputed son of the former Cæsar. His own sons by Cleopatra were to have the style of ' King of Kings '; to Alexander he gave Armenia and Media, with Parthia so soon as it should be overcome; to Ptolemy Phœnicia, Syria, and Cilicia. Alexander was brought out before the people in Median costume, the tiara and upright peak, and Ptolemy in boots and mantle and Macedonian cap

[1] *The Greek World under Roman Sway.*

done about with the diadem; for this was the habit of the successors of Alexander, as the other was of the Medes and Armenians. And, as soon as they had saluted their parents, the one was received by a guard of Macedonians, the other by one of Armenians. Cleopatra was then, as at other times when she appeared in public, dressed in the habit of the goddess Isis, and gave audience to the people under the name of the New Isis.

"This over, he gave Priene to his players for a habitation, and set sail for Athens, where fresh sports and play-acting employed him. Cleopatra, jealous of the honors Octavia had received at Athens — for Octavia was much beloved by the Athenians—courted the favor of the people with all sorts of attentions. The Athenians, in requital, having decreed her public honors, deputed several of the citizens to wait upon her at her house, among whom went Antony as one, he being an Athenian citizen, and he it was that made the speech.

"The speed and extent of Antony's preparations alarmed Cæsar, who feared he might be forced to fight the decisive battle that summer, for he wanted many necessaries, and the people grudged very much to pay the taxes; freemen being called upon to pay a fourth part of their incomes, and freed slaves an eighth of their property, so that there were loud outcries against him, and disturbances throughout all Italy. And this is looked upon as one of the greatest of Antony's oversights that he did not then press the war, for he allowed time at once for Cæsar to make his preparations, and for the commotions to pass over, for while people were having their money called for they were mutinous and violent; but, having paid it, they held their peace

"Titius and Plancus, men of consular dignity and friends to Antony, having been ill-used by Cleopatra, whom they had most resisted in her design of being present in the war, came over to Cæsar, and gave information of the contents of Antony's will, with which they were acquainted. It was deposited in the hands of the vestal virgins, who refused to deliver it up, and sent Cæsar word, if he pleased, he should come and seize it himself, which he did. And, reading it over to himself, he noted those places that were most for his purpose, and, having summoned the senate, read them publicly. Many were scandalized at the proceeding, thinking it out of reason and equity to call a man to account for what was not to be until after his death. Cæsar specially pressed what Antony said in his will about his burial, for he had ordered that even if he died in the city of Rome, his body, after being carried in state through the Forum, should be sent to Cleopatra at Alexandria.

"Calvisius, a dependent of Cæsar's, urged other charges in connection with Cleopatra against Antony: that he had given her the library of Pergamus, containing two hundred thousand distinct volumes; that at a great banquet, in the presence of many guests, he had risen up and rubbed her feet, to fulfil some wager or promise; that he had suffered the Ephesians to salute her as their queen; that he had frequently at the public audience of kings and princes received amorous messages written in tablets made of onyx and crystal, and read them openly on the tribunal; that when Furnius, a man of great authority and eloquence among the Romans, was pleading, Cleopatra happening to pass by in her litter, Antony started up and left them in the middle of their cause, to follow at her side and attend her home." [1]

When war was declared, Antony sought to gain the support of the East in the conflict. He made alliance with a Median king who betrothed his daughter to Cleopatra's infant son Alexander; but he made the fatal mistake of allowing Cleopatra to accompany him to Samos, where he gathered his army, and even to Actium, where she led the way in flying from the fight, and so persuading the infatuated Antony to leave his army and join in her disgraceful escape.

Historians have regarded this act of Cleopatra as the mere cowardice of a woman who feared to look upon an armed conflict and join in the din of battle. But she was surely made of sterner stuff. She had probably computed with the utmost care the chances of the rivals, and had made up her mind that, in spite of Antony's gallantry, his cause was lost.[2] If she

[1] Plutarch: *Antony*.

[2] Dion says that Antony was of the same opinion, and went into the battle intending to fly; but this does not agree with his character or with the facts.

fought out the battle with her strong contingent of ships, she would probably fall into Octavian's hands as a prisoner, and would have no choice between suicide or death in the Roman prison, after being exhibited to the mob in Octavian's triumph. There was no chance whatever that she would have been spared, as was her sister Arsinoe after Julius Cæsar's triumph, nor would such clemency be less hateful than death. But there was still a chance, if Antony were killed or taken prisoner, that she might negotiate with the victor as queen of Egypt, with her fleet, army, and treasures intact, and who could tell what effect her charms, though now full ripe, might have upon the conqueror? Two great Romans had yielded to her, why not the third, who seemed a smaller man?

This view implies that she was already false to Antony, and it may well be asked how such a charge is compatible with the affecting scenes which followed at Alexandria, where her policy seemed defeated by her passion, and she felt her old love too strong even for her heartless ambition? I will say in answer that there is no more frequent anomaly in the psychology of female love than a strong passion coexisting with selfish ambition, so that each takes the lead in turn; nay, even the consciousness of treachery may so intensify the passion as to make a woman embrace with keener transports the lover whom she has betrayed than one whom she has no thought of surrendering. There are, moreover, in these tragedies unexpected accidents, which so affect even the hardest nature that calculations are cast aside, and the old loyalty resumes a temporary sway. Nor must we fail to insist again upon the traditions wherein this last Cleopatra was born and bred. She came from a stock whose women played with love and with life as if they were mere counters. To hesitate whether such a scion of such a house would have delayed to discard Antony and to assume another passion is to show small appreciation of the effects of heredity and of example. Dion tells us that she arrived in Alexandria before the news of her defeat, pretended a victory, and took the occasion of committing many murders, in order to get rid of secret opponents, and also to gather wealth by confiscation of their goods, for both she and Antony, who came along the coast of Libya, seem still to have thought of defending the inaccessible Egypt, and making terms for themselves and their children with the conqueror. But Antony's efforts completely failed; no one would rally to his standard. And meanwhile the false Queen had begun to send presents to Cæsar and encourage him to treat with her. But when he bluntly proposed to her to murder Antony as the price of her reconciliation with himself, and when he even declared by proxy that he was in love with her, he clearly made a rash move in this game of diplomacy, though Dion says he persuaded her of his love, and that accordingly she betrayed to him the fortress of Pelusium, the key of the country. Dion also differs from Plutarch in repeatedly ascribing to Octavian great anxiety to secure the treasures which Cleopatra had with her, and which she was likely to destroy by fire if driven to despair.

The historian may well leave to the biographer, nay, to the poet, the affecting details of the closing scenes of Cleopatra's life. In the fourth and fifth acts of *Antony and Cleopatra* Shakespeare has reproduced every detail of Plutarch's narrative, which was drawn from that of her physician Olympos. Her fascinations were not dead, for they swayed Dolabella to play false to his master so far as to warn her of his intentions, and leave her time for her dignified and royal end. But if these Hellenistic queens knew how to die, they knew not how to live. Even the penultimate scene of the tragedy, when she presents an inventory of her treasures to Octavian, and is charged by her steward with dishonesty, shows her in uncivilized violence striking the man in the face and bursting into indecent fury, such as an Athenian, still less a Roman, matron would have been ashamed to exhibit. Nor is there any reason to doubt the genuineness of this scene, though we must not be weary of cautioning ourselves against the hostile witnesses who have reported to us her life. They praise nothing in her but her bewitching presence and her majestic death.

"After her repast Cleopatra sent to Cæsar a letter which she had written and sealed, and, putting everybody out of the monument but her two women, she shut the doors. Cæsar, opening her letter, and finding pathetic prayers and entreaties that she might be buried in the same tomb with Antony, soon guessed what was doing. At first he was going himself in all

haste; but, changing his mind, he sent others to see. The
thing had been quickly done. The messengers came at full
speed, and found the guards apprehensive of nothing; but on
opening the doors they saw her stone dead, lying upon a bed of
gold, set out in all her royal ornaments.   Iras, one of her wom-
en, lay dying at her feet, and Charmion, just ready to fall, scarce
able to hold up her head, was adjusting her mistress' diadem.
And when one that came in said angrily, ' Was this well done
of your lady, Charmion ? ' ' Perfectly well,' she answered, ' and
as became the daughter of so many kings '; and as she said this
she fell down dead by the bedside."

Even the hostile accounts cannot conceal from us that both
in physique and in intellect she was a very remarkable figure,
exceptional in her own, exceptional had she been born in any
other, age. She is a speaking instance of the falsehood of a
prevailing belief, that the intermarriage of near relations invariably produces a decadence in the human race. The whole
dynasty of the Ptolemies contradicts this current theory, and
exhibits in the last of the series the most signal exception.
Cleopatra VI was descended from many generations of breed-
ing-in, of which four exhibit marriages of full brother and sister.   And yet she was deficient in no quality, physical or intellectual, which goes to make up a well-bred and well-developed
human being.   Her morals were indeed those of her ancestors,
and as bad as could be, but I am not aware that it is degeneration in this direction which is assumed by the theory in question, except as a consequence of physical decay. Physically,
however, Cleopatra was perfect. She was not only beautiful,
but prolific, and retained her vigor, and apparently her beauty,
to the time of her death, when she was nearly forty years old.

ASSASSINATION OF CÆSAR

B.C. 44

NIEBUHR   PLUTARCH

Cæsar's assassination forms the groundwork of one of Shakespeare's most notable tragedies. The "itching palm" of Cassius, Brutus' rectitude and honesty of purpose, and Mark Antony's oration will ever live while the English language endures. When the great Cæsar was struck down, the civil war was over and he was master of the world. The month of the year B.C. 100 in which he was born, Quinctilis, was afterward called in his honor, July.

Caius Julius Cæsar was one of the greatest figures in history, and early took a prominent part in the affairs of Rome. He was a rival of Cicero in forensic eloquence and highly esteemed as a writer, his *Commentaries* being universally admired. Ransomed from pirates who had captured him on his way to study philosophy at Rhodes, he attacked them in turn, took them to Pergamus, and crucified them.

After various successful engagements Cæsar marched against Pharnaces, now established in the kingdom of the Bosphorus, gaining at Zela, in Pontus, the decisive victory which he announced in the famous despatch, *Veni, vidi, vici* (" I came, I saw, I conquered ").

His unbounded affability, his liveliness and cordiality, his unaffected kindness to his friends had made him popular with the high as well as the low. His ambition began to show itself. During the wrangles over the election of Afranius as consul, Cæsar returned from his brilliant successes in Spain. The troops saluted him as imperator and the senate voted a thanksgiving in his honor. He was now strong enough to take his place as the leader of the popular party. He was elected consul in spite of the hostility of the senate.

A coalition was formed between Cæsar and Pompey. Cæsar's agrarian law added to his popularity with the people, and he gained the influence of the *equites* by relief of one-third of the farmed taxes of Asia. He now became proconsul of Illyricum and Gaul for five years. This suited his ambition. At this time Pompey was the absolute master of Rome. And now arose his duel for power with Cæsar. For a time he opposed the latter's election as consul, but later yielded.

Cæsar had achieved his brilliant success beyond the Alps. He had won victories in Gaul and Britain; but in the mean time his enemies had been active at Rome. Still believing that the senate would permit his quiet election to the consulship, he refused to strike any blow at their authority. But the senate had determined to humble Cæsar. Both Pompey and Cæsar were removed from leadership, but the Consul Marcellus refused to execute the decree. Cæsar was directed by the senate to disband his army by a fixed day, on pain of being considered a public enemy. Pompey sided with the senate. This meant civil war. Antony and Cassius fled to the camp of Cæsar, who was enthusiastically supported by his soldiers and "crossed the Rubicon."

Having become master of all Italy in three months without a battle, Cæsar reëntered Rome. Pompey had fled, and at the battle of Pharsalia was utterly routed, and took refuge in Egypt, where he was murdered a few days before the arrival of Cæsar.

Upon receipt of the news of Pompey's death Cæsar was named dictator for one year. The government was now placed without disguise in his hands. He was invested with the tribunician power for life. He was also again elected consul and named dictator.

Cæsar had now become a demi-god, and was named dictator for ten years, being awarded a fourfold triumph, and a thanksgiving being decreed for forty days. He was also made censor. This was in B.C. 46. After defeating the remnant of the Pompeians, he returned to Rome in September, B.C. 45, and was named imperator, and appointed consul for ten years and dictator for life, being hailed as *Parens Patriæ*.

All these triumphs had caused jealousies. It was thought that he aspired to become king, and this led to his fall.

NIEBUHR

IT is one of the inestimable advantages of a hereditary government commonly called the legitimate, whatever its form may be, that it may be formally inactive in regard to the state and the population—that it may reserve its interference until it is absolutely necessary, and apparently leave things to take their own course. If we look around us and observe the various constitutions, we shall scarcely perceive the interference of the government; the greater part of the time passes away without those who have the reins in their hands being obliged to pay any particular attention to what they are doing, and a very large amount of individual liberty may be enjoyed. But if the government is what we call a usurpation, the ruler has not only to take care to maintain his power, but in all that he undertakes he has to consider by what means and in what ways he can establish his right to govern, and his own personal qualifications for it. Men who are in such a position are urged on to act by a very sad necessity, from which they cannot escape, and such was the position of Cæsar at Rome.

In our European States, men have wide and extensive spheres in which they can act and move. The much-decried system of centralization has indeed many disadvantages; but it has this advantage for the ruler, that he can exert an activity which shows its influence far and wide. But what could Cæsar do, in the centre of nearly the whole of the known world? He could not hope to effect any material improvements either in Italy or in the provinces. He had been accustomed from his youth, and more especially during the last fifteen years, to an enormous activity, and idleness was intolerable to him. At the close of the civil war he would have had little or nothing to do unless he had turned his attention to some foreign enterprise. He was obliged to venture upon something that would occupy his whole soul, for he could not rest. His thoughts were therefore again directed to war, and that in a quarter where the most brilliant triumphs awaited him, where the bones of the legions of Crassus lay unavenged — to a war against the Parthians. About this time the Getæ also had spread in Thrace, and he intended to check their progress likewise. But his main problem was to destroy the Parthian empire and to extend the Roman dominion as far as India, a plan in which he would certainly have been successful; and he himself felt so sure of this that he was already thinking of what he should undertake afterward.

It is by no means incredible that, as we are told, he intended on his return to march through the passes of the Caucasus, and through ancient Scythia into the country of the Getæ, and thence through Germany and Gaul into Italy. Besides this expedition, he entertained other plans of no less gigantic dimensions. The port of Ostia was bad, and in reality little better than a mere roadstead, so that great ships could not come up the river. Accordingly it is said that Cæsar intended to dig a canal for sea-ships, from the Tiber, above or below Rome, through the Pomptine marshes as far as Terracina. He further contemplated to cut through the Isthmus of Corinth. It is not easy to see in what manner he would have accomplished this, considering the state of hydraulic architecture in those times. The Roman canals were mere *fossæ*, and canals with sluices, though not unknown to the Romans, were not constructed by them.[1]

The fact of Cæsar forming such enormous plans is not very surprising; but we can scarcely comprehend how it was possible for him to accomplish so much of what he undertook in the short time of five months preceding his death. Following the unfortunate system of Sulla, Cæsar founded throughout Italy a number of colonies of veterans. The old Sullanian colonists were treated with great severity, and many of them and their children were expelled from their lands, and were thus punished for the cruelty which they or their fathers had committed against the inhabitants of the municipia. In like manner colonies were established in Southern Gaul, Italy, Africa, and other parts; I may mention in particular the colonies founded at Carthage and Corinth. The latter, however, was a *colonia libertinorum*, and never rose to any importance. We do not know the details of its foundation, but one would imagine that Cæsar would have preferred restoring the place as a purely Greek town. This, however, he did not do. Its population was and remained a mixed one, and Corinth never rose to a state of real prosperity.

Cæsar made various new arrangements in the State, and among others he restored the full franchise, or the *jus honorum*, to the sons of those who had been proscribed in the time of Sulla. He had obtained for himself the title of imperator and the dictatorship for life and the consulship for ten years. Half of the offices of the republic to which persons had before been elected by the centuries were in his gift, and for the other half he usually recommended candidates; so that the elections were merely nominal.

The tribes seem to have retained their rights of election uncurtailed, and the last tribunes must have been elected by the people. But although Cæsar did not himself confer the consulship, yet the whole republic was reduced to a mere form and appearance. Cæsar made various new laws and regulations; for example, to lighten the burdens of debtors and the

---

[1] The first canals with sluices were executed by the Dutch in the fifteenth century.

like; but the changes he introduced in the form of the constitution were of little importance. He increased the number of
prætors, which Sulla had raised to eight, successively to ten,
twelve, fourteen, and sixteen, and the number of quæstors was
increased to forty. Hence the number of persons from whom
the senate was to be filled up became greater than that of the
vacancies, and Cæsar accordingly increased the number of senators, though it is uncertain what number he fixed upon, and
raised a great many of his friends to the dignity of senators.
In this, as in many other cases, he acted very arbitrarily; for
he elected into the senate whomsoever he pleased, and conferred the franchise in a manner equally arbitrary. These
things did not fail to create much discontent. It is a remarkable fact that, notwithstanding his mode of filling up the senate, not even the majority of senators were attached to his
cause after his death.

If we consider the changes and regulations which Cæsar introduced, it must strike us as a singular circumstance that
among all his measures there is no trace of any indicating that
he thought of modifying the constitution for the purpose of
putting an end to the anarchy, for all his changes are in reality
not essential or of great importance. Sulla felt the necessity
of remodelling the constitution, but he did not attain his end;
and the manner, too, in which he set about it was that of a
short-sighted man; but he was at least intelligent enough to
see that the constitution as it then was could not continue to
exist. In the regulations of Cæsar we see no trace of such a
conviction; and I think that he despaired of the possibility of
effecting any real good by constitutional reforms. Hence,
among all his laws there is not one that had any relation to
the constitution. The fact of his increasing the number of
patrician families had no reference to the constitution; so far
in fact were the patricians from having any advantages over
the plebeians that the office of the two *ædiles Cereales*, which
Cæsar instituted, was confined to the plebeians—a regulation
which was opposed to the very nature of the patriciate.

His raising persons to the rank of patricians was neither
more nor less than the modern practice of raising a family to
the rank of nobility; he picked out an individual and gave him

the rank of patrician for himself and his descendants, but did not elevate a whole gens. The distinction itself was merely a nominal one and conferred no privilege upon a person except that of holding certain priestly offices, which could be filled by none but patricians, and for which their number was scarcely sufficient. If Cæsar had died quietly the republic would have been in the same, nay, in a much worse, state of dissolution than if he had not existed at all. I consider it a proof of the wisdom and good sense of Cæsar that he did not, like Sulla, think an improvement in the state of public affairs so near at hand or a matter of so little difficulty. The cure of the disease lay yet at a very great distance, and the first condition on which it could be undertaken was the sovereignty of Cæsar, a condition which would have been quite unbearable even to many of his followers, who as rebels did not scruple to go along with him. But Rome could no longer exist as a republic.

It is curious to see in Cicero's work, *de Republica*, the consciousness running through it that Rome, as it then stood, required the strong hand of a king. Cicero had surely often owned this to himself; but he saw no one who would have entered into such an idea. The title of king had a great fascination for Cæsar, as it had for Cromwell—a surprising phenomenon in a practical mind like that of Cæsar. Everyone knows the fact that while Cæsar was sitting on the *suggestum*, during the celebration of the *Lupercalia*, Antony presented to him the diadem, to try how the people would take it. Cæsar saw the great alarm which the act created and declined the diadem for the sake of appearance; but had the people been silent, Cæsar would unquestionably have accepted it. His refusal was accompanied by loud shouts of acclamation, which for the present rendered all further attempts impossible. Antony then had a statue of Cæsar adorned with the diadem; but two tribunes of the people, L. Cæsetius Flavus and Epidius Marullus, took it away: and here Cæsar showed the real state of his feelings, for he treated the conduct of the tribunes as a personal insult toward himself. He had lost his self-possession and his fate carried him irresistibly onward. He wished to have the tribunes imprisoned, but was prevailed upon to be satisfied with their being stripped of their office and sent into exile.

This created a great sensation at Rome. Cæsar had also been guilty of an act of thoughtlessness, or perhaps merely of distraction, as might happen very easily to a man in his circumstances. When the senate had made its last decrees, conferring upon Cæsar unlimited powers, the senators, consuls, and prætors, or the whole senate, in festal attire, presented the decrees to him, and Cæsar at the moment forgot to show his respect for the senators; he did not rise from his *sella curulis*, but received the decrees in an unceremonious manner. This want of politeness was never forgiven by the persons who had not scrupled to make him their master; for it had been expected that he would at least behave politely and be grateful for such decrees.[1] Cæsar himself had no design in the act, which was merely the consequence of distraction or thoughtlessness; but it made the senate his irreconcilable enemies. The affair with the tribunes, moreover, had made a deep impression upon the people. We must, however, remember that the people under such circumstances are most sensible to anything affecting their honor, as we have seen at the beginning of the French Revolution.

In the year of Cæsar's death, Brutus and Cassius were prætors. Both had been generals under Pompey. Brutus' mother, Servilia, was a half-sister of Cato, for after the death of her first husband Cato's mother had married Servilius Cæpio. She was a remarkable woman, but very immoral, and unworthy of her son; not even the honor of her own daughter was sacred to her. The family of Brutus derived its origin from L. Junius Brutus, and from the time of its first appearance among the plebeians it had had few men of importance to boast of. During the period subsequent to the passing of the Licinian laws we meet with some Junii in the Fasti, but not one of them acquired any great reputation. The family had become reduced and almost contemptible. One M. Brutus in particular disgraced his family by sycophancy in the time of Sulla and was afterward killed in Gaul by Pompey. Although no Roman family belonged to a more illustrious gens,

---

[1] I have known an instance of a man of rank and influence who could never forgive another man, who was by far his superior in every respect, for having forgotten to take off his hat during a visit.

yet Brutus was not by any means one of those men who are raised by fortunate circumstances. The education, however, which he received had a great influence upon him. His uncle Cato, whose daughter Porcia he married—whether in Cato's lifetime or afterward is doubtful—had initiated him from his early youth in the Stoic philosophy, and had instilled into his mind a veneration for it, as though it had been a religion.

Brutus had qualities which Cato did not possess. The latter had something of an ascetic nature, and was, if I may say so, a scrupulously pious character; but Brutus had no such scrupulous timidity; his mind was more flexible and lovable. Cato spoke well, but could not be reckoned among the eloquent men of his time. Brutus' great talents had been developed with the utmost care, and if he had lived longer and in peace he would have become a classical writer of the highest order. He had been known to Cicero from his early age, and Cicero felt a fatherly attachment to him; he saw in him a young man who he hoped would exert a beneficial influence upon the next generation.

Cæsar too had known and loved him from his childhood; but the stories which are related to account for this attachment must be rejected as foolish inventions of idle persons; for nothing is more natural than that Cæsar should look with great fondness upon a young man of such extraordinary and amiable qualities. The absence of envy was one of the distinguishing features in the character of Cæsar, as it was in that of Cicero. In the battle of Pharsalus, Brutus served in the army of Pompey, and after the battle he wrote a letter to Cæsar, who had inquired after him; and when Cæsar heard of his safety he was delighted, and invited him to his camp. Cæsar afterward gave him the administration of Cisalpine Gaul, where Brutus distinguished himself in a very extraordinary manner by his love of justice.

Cassius was related to Brutus, and had likewise belonged to the Pompeian party, but he was very unlike Brutus; he was much older, and a distinguished military officer. After the death of Crassus he had maintained himself as quæstor in Syria against the Parthians, and he enjoyed a very great reputation in the army, but he was after all no better than an ordinary officer of Cæsar. After the battle of Pharsalus, Cæsar did not at first know whither Pompey was gone. Cassius was at the time stationed with some galleys in the Hellespont, notwithstanding which Cæsar with his usual boldness took a boat to sail across that strait, and on meeting Cassius called upon him to embrace his party. Cassius readily complied, and Cæsar forgave him, as he forgave all his adversaries: even Marcellus, who had mortally offended him, was pardoned at the request of Cicero. Cæsar thus endeavored to efface all recollections of the civil war.

Cæsar had appointed both Brutus and Cassius prætors for that year. With the exception of the office of *prætor urbanus*, which was honorable and lucrative, the prætorship was a burdensome office and conferred little distinction, since the other prætors were only the presidents of the courts. Formerly they had been elected by lot, but the office was now altogether in the gift of Cæsar. Both Brutus and Cassius had wished for the prætura urbana, and, when Cæsar gave that office to Brutus, Cassius was not only indignant at Cæsar, but began quarrelling with Brutus also. While Cassius was in this state of exasperation, a meeting of the senate was announced for the 15th of March, on which day, as the report went, a proposal was to be made to offer Cæsar the crown. This was a welcome opportunity for Cassius, who resolved to take vengeance, for he had even before entertained a personal hatred of Cæsar, and was now disappointed at not having obtained the city prætorship. He first sounded Brutus and, finding that he was safe, made direct overtures to him. During the night some one wrote on the tribunal and the house of Brutus the words, " Remember that thou art Brutus."

Brutus became reconciled to Cassius, offered his assistance, and gained over several other persons to join the conspiracy. All party differences seemed to have vanished all at once; two of the conspirators were old generals of Cæsar, C. Trebonius and Decimus Brutus, both of whom had fought with him in Gaul, and against Massilia, and had been raised to high honors by their chief. There were among the conspirators persons of all parties. Men who had fought against one another at Pharsalus now went hand-in-hand and intrusted their lives to one another. No proposals were made to Cicero, the reasons usually assigned for which are of the most calumniatory kind. It is generally said that the conspirators had no confidence in Cicero, an opinion which is perfectly contemptible. Cicero would not have betrayed them for any consideration, but what they feared were his objections. Brutus had as noble a soul as anyone, but he was passionate; Cicero, on the other hand, who was at an advanced age, had many sad experiences, and his feelings were so exceedingly delicate that he could not have consented to take away the life of him to whom he himself owed his own, who had always behaved most nobly toward him, and had intentionally drawn him before the world as his friend.

Cæsar's conduct toward those who had fought in the ranks of Pompey and afterward returned to him was extremely noble, and he regarded the reconciliation of those men as a personal favor conferred upon himself. All who knew Cicero must have been convinced that he would not have given his consent to the plan of the conspirators; and if they ever did give the matter a serious thought, they must have owned to themselves that every wise man would have dissuaded them from it; for it was in fact the most complete absurdity to fancy that the republic could be restored by Cæsar's death. Goethe says somewhere that the murder of Cæsar was the most senseless act that the Romans ever committed; and a truer word was never spoken. The result of it could not possibly be any other than that which did follow the deed.

Cæsar was cautioned by Hirtius and Pansa, both wise men of noble character, especially the former, who saw that the republic must become consolidated and not thrown into fresh convulsions. They advised Cæsar to be careful, and to take a bodyguard; but he replied that he would rather not live at all than be in constant fear of losing his life. Cæsar once expressed to some of his friends his conviction that Brutus was capable of harboring a murderous design, but he added that as he, Cæsar, could not live much longer, Brutus would wait, and not be guilty of such a crime. Cæsar's health was at that time weak, and the general opinion was that he intended to surrender his power to Brutus as the most worthy. While the conspirators were making their preparations, Porcia, the wife of Brutus, inferred from the excitement and restlessness of her husband that some fearful secret was pressing on his mind; but as he did not show her any confidence, she seriously wounded herself with a knife and was seized with a violent wound-fever. No one knew the cause of her illness; and it was not till after many entreaties of her husband that at length she revealed it to him, saying that as she had been able to conceal the cause of her illness, so she could also keep any secret that might be intrusted to her. Her entreaties induced Brutus to communicate to her the plan of the conspirators. Cæsar was also cautioned by the haruspices, by a dream of his wife, and by his own forebodings, which we have no reason for doubting. But on the morning of the 15th of March, the day fixed upon for assassinating Cæsar, Decimus Brutus treacherously enticed him to go with him to the Curia, as it was impossible to delay the deed any longer.

The conspirators were at first seized with fear lest their plan should be betrayed; but on Cæsar's entrance into the senate house, C. Tillius (not Tullius) Cimber made his way up to him, and insulted him with his importunities, and Casca gave the first stroke. Cæsar fell covered with twenty-three wounds. He was either in his fifty-sixth year or had completed it; I am not quite certain on this point, though, if we judge by the time of his first consulship, he must have been fifty-six years old. His birthday, which is not generally known, was the 11th of Quinctilis, which month was afterward called Julius, and his death took place on the 15th of March, between eleven and twelve o'clock.

PLUTARCH

At one time the senate having decreed Cæsar some extravagant honors, the consuls and prætors, attended by the whole body of patricians, went to inform him of what they had done. When they came, he did not rise to receive them, but kept his seat, as if they had been persons in a private station, and his answer to their address was, " that there was more need to retrench his honors than to enlarge them." This haughtiness gave pain not only to the senate, but the people, who thought the contempt of that body reflected dishonor upon the whole Commonwealth; for all who could decently withdraw went off greatly dejected.

Perceiving the false step he had taken, he retired immediately to his own house, and, laying his neck bare, told his friends "he was ready for the first hand that would strike." He then bethought himself of alleging his distemper as an excuse; and asserted that those who are under its influence are apt to find their faculties fail them when they speak standing, a trembling and giddiness coming upon them, which bereave them of their senses. This, however, was not really the case; for it is said he was desirous to rise to the senate; but Cornelius Balbus, one of his friends, or rather flatterers, held him, and had servility enough to say, "Will you not remember that you are Cæsar, and suffer them to pay their court to you as their superior?"

These discontents were greatly increased by the indignity with which he treated the tribunes of the people. In the Lupercalia, which, according to most writers, is an ancient pastoral feast, and which answers in many respects to the *Lycæa* among the Arcadians, young men of noble families, and indeed many of the magistrates, run about the streets naked, and, by way of diversion, strike all they meet with leathern thongs with the hair upon them. Numbers of women of the first quality put themselves in their way, and present their hands for stripes—as scholars do to a master—being persuaded that the pregnant gain an easy delivery by it, and that the barren are enabled to conceive. Cæsar wore a triumphal robe that day, and seated himself in a golden chair upon the *rostra*, to see the ceremony.

Antony ran among the rest, in compliance with the rules of the festival, for he was consul. When he came into the Forum, and the crowd had made way for him, he approached Cæsar, and offered him a diadem wreathed with laurel. Upon this some plaudits were heard, but very feeble, because they proceeded only from persons placed there on purpose. Cæsar refused it, and then the plaudits were loud and general. Antony presented it once more, and few applauded his officiousness; but when Cæsar rejected it again, the applause again was general. Cæsar, undeceived by his second trial, rose up and ordered the diadem to be consecrated in the Capitol.

A few days after, his statues were seen adorned with royal diadems; and Flavius and Marullus, two of the tribunes, went and tore them off. They also found out the persons who first saluted Cæsar king, and committed them to prison. The people followed with cheerful acclamations, and called them Brutuses, because Brutus was the man who expelled the kings and put the government in the hands of the senate and people. Cæsar, highly incensed at their behavior, deposed the tribunes, and by way of reprimand to them, as well as insult to the people, called them several times *Brutes* and *Cumæans.*

Upon this, many applied to Marcus Brutus, who, by the father's side, was supposed to be a descendant of that ancient Brutus, and whose mother was of the illustrious house of the Servilli. He was also nephew and son-in-law to Cato. No man was more inclined than he to lift his hand against monarchy, but he was withheld by the honors and favors he had received from Cæsar, who had not only given him his life after the defeat of Pompey at Pharsalia, and pardoned many of his friends at his request, but continued to honor him with his confidence. That very year he had procured him the most honorable prætorship, and he had named him for the consulship four years after, in preference to Cassius, who was his competitor; on which occasion Cæsar is reported to have said, "Cassius assigns the strongest reasons, but I cannot refuse Brutus."

Some impeached Brutus after the conspiracy was formed; but, instead of listening to them, he laid his hand on his body and said, "Brutus will wait for this skin"; intimating that though the virtue of Brutus rendered him worthy of empire, he would not be guilty of any ingratitude or baseness to obtain it. Those, however, who were desirous of a change kept their eyes upon him only, or principally at least; and as they durst not speak out plain, they put billets night after night in the tribunal and seat which he used as prætor, mostly in these terms: "Thou sleepest, Brutus," or, "Thou art not Brutus."

Cassius, perceiving his friend's ambition a little stimulated by these papers, began to ply him closer than before, and spur him on to the great enterprise; for he had a particular enmity against Cæsar. Cæsar, too, had some suspicion of him, and he even said one day to his friends: "What think you of Cassius? I do not like his pale looks." Another time, when Antony and Dolabella were accused of some designs against his person and government, he said: "I have no apprehensions from those fat and sleek men; I rather fear the pale and lean ones," meaning Cassius and Brutus.

It seems, from this instance, that fate is not so secret as it is inevitable; for we are told there were strong signs and presages of the death of Cæsar. As to the lights in the heavens, the strange noises heard in various quarters by night, and the appearance of solitary birds in the Forum, perhaps they deserve not our notice in so great an event as this. But some attention should be given to Strabo the philosopher. According to him there were seen in the air men of fire encountering each other; such a flame appeared to issue from the hand of a soldier's servant that all the spectators thought it must be burned, yet, when it was over, he found no harm; and one of the victims which Cæsar offered was found without a heart. The latter was certainly a most alarming prodigy; for, according to the rules of nature, no creature can exist without a heart. What is still more extraordinary, many report that a certain soothsayer forewarned him of a great danger which threatened him on the ides of March, and that when the day was come, as he was going to the senate house, he called to the soothsayer, and said, laughing, "The ides of March are come"; to which he answered softly, "Yes; but they are not gone."

The evening before, he supped with Marcus Lepidus, and signed, according to custom, a number of letters, as he sat at table. While he was so employed, there arose a question, "What kind of death was the best?" and Cæsar, answering before them all, cried out, "A sudden one." The same night, as he was in bed with his wife, the doors and windows of the room flew open at once. Disturbed both with the noise and the light, he observed, by moonshine, Calpurnia in a deep sleep, uttering broken words and inarticulate groans. She dreamed that she was weeping over him, as she held him, murdered, in her arms. Others say she dreamed that the pinnacle was fallen, which, as Livy tells us, the senate had ordered to be erected upon Cæsar's house by way of ornament and distinction; and that it was the fall of it which she lamented and wept for. Be that as it may, the next morning she conjured Cæsar not to go out that day if he could possibly avoid it, but to adjourn the senate; and, if he had no regard to her dreams, to have recourse to some other species of divination, or to sacrifices, for information as to his fate. This gave him some suspicion and alarm; for he had never known before, in Calpurnia, anything of the weakness or superstition of her sex, though she was now so much affected.

He therefore offered a number of sacrifices, and, as the diviners found no auspicious tokens in any of them, he sent Antony to dismiss the senate. In the mean time Decius Brutus, surnamed Albinus, came in. He was a person in whom Cæsar placed such confidence that he had appointed him his second heir, yet he was engaged in the conspiracy with the other Brutus and Cassius. This man, fearing that if Cæsar adjourned the senate to another day the affair might be discovered, laughed at the diviners, and told Cæsar he would be highly to blame if by such a slight he gave the senate an occasion of complaint against him. "For they were met," he said, "at his summons, and came prepared with one voice to honor him with the title of king in the provinces, and to grant that he should wear the diadem both by sea and land everywhere out of Italy. But if anyone go and tell them, now they have taken their places, they must go home again, and return when Calpurnia happens to have better dreams, what room will your enemies have to launch out against you? Or who will hear your friends when they attempt to show that this is not an open servitude on the one hand and tyranny on the other? If you are absolutely persuaded that this is an unlucky day, it is certainly better to go yourself and tell them you have strong reasons for putting off business till another time." So saying he took Cæsar by the hand and led him out.

He was not gone far from the door when a slave, who belonged to some other person, attempted to get up to speak to him, but finding it impossible, by reason of the crowd that was about him, he made his way into the house, and putting himself into the hands of Calpurnia desired her to keep him safe till Cæsar's return, because he had matters of great importance to communicate.

Artemidorus the Cnidian, who, by teaching the Greek eloquence, became acquainted with some of Brutus' friends, and had got intelligence of most of the transactions, approached Cæsar with a paper explaining what he had to discover. Observing that he gave the papers, as fast as he received them, to his officers, he got up as close as possible and said: "Cæsar, read this to yourself, and quickly: for it contains matters of great consequence and of the last concern to you." He took it and attempted several times to read it, but was always prevented by one application or other. He therefore kept that paper, and that only, in his hand, when he entered the house. Some say it was delivered to him by another man, Artemidorus being kept from approaching him all the way by the crowd.

These things might, indeed, fall out by chance; but as in the place where the senate was that day assembled, and which proved the scene of that tragedy, there was a statue of Pompey, and it was an edifice which Pompey had consecrated for an ornament to his theatre, nothing can be clearer than that some deity conducted the whole business and directed the execution of it to that very spot. Even Cassius himself, though inclined to the doctrines of Epicurus, turned his eye to the statue of Pompey, and secretly invoked his aid, before the great attempt. The arduous occasion, it seems, overruled his former sentiments, and laid them open to all the influence of enthusiasm. Antony, who was a faithful friend to Cæsar, and a man of great strength, was held in discourse without, by Brutus Albinus, who had contrived a long story to detain him.

When Cæsar entered the house, the senate rose to do him honor. Some of Brutus' accomplices came up behind his chair, and others before it, pretending to intercede, along with Metillius Cimber, for the recall of his brother from exile. They continued their instances till he came to his seat. When he was seated he gave them a positive denial; and as they continued their importunities with an air of compulsion, he grew angry. Cimber, then, with both hands, pulled his gown off his neck, which was the signal for the attack. Casca gave him the first blow. It was a stroke upon the neck with his sword, but the wound was not dangerous; for in the beginning of so tremendous an enterprise he was probably in some disorder. Cæsar therefore turned upon him and laid hold of his sword. At the same time they both cried out, the one in Latin, "Villain! Casca! what dost thou mean?" and the other in Greek, to his brother, "Brother, help!"

After such a beginning, those who knew nothing of the conspiracy were seized with consternation and horror, insomuch that they durst neither fly nor assist, nor even utter a word. All the conspirators now drew their swords, and surrounded him in such a manner that, whatever way he turned, he saw nothing but steel gleaming in his face, and met nothing but wounds. Like some savage beast attacked by the hunters, he found every hand lifted against him, for they all agreed to have a share in the sacrifice and a taste of his blood. Therefore Brutus himself gave him a stroke in the groin. Some say he opposed the rest, and continued struggling and crying out till he perceived the sword of Brutus; then he drew his robe over his face and yielded to his fate. Either by accident or pushed thither by the conspirators, he expired on the pedestal of Pompey's statue, and dyed it with his blood; so that Pompey seemed to preside over the work of vengeance, to tread his enemy under his feet, and to enjoy his agonies. Those agonies were great, for he received no less than three-and-twenty wounds. And many of the conspirators wounded each other as they were aiming their blows at him.

Cæsar thus despatched, Brutus advanced to speak to the senate and to assign his reasons for what he had done, but they could not bear to hear him; they fled out of the house and filled the people with inexpressible horror and dismay. Some shut up their houses; others left their shops and counters. All were in motion; one was running to see the spectacle; another running back. Antony and Lepidus, Cæsar's principal friends, withdrew, and hid themselves in other people's houses. Meantime Brutus and his confederates, yet warm from the slaughter, marched in a body with their bloody swords in their hands, from the senate house to the Capitol, not like men that fled, but with an air of gayety and confidence, calling the people to liberty, and stopping to talk with every man of consequence whom they met. There were some who even joined them and mingled with their train, desirous of appearing to have had a share in the action and hoping for one in the glory. Of this number were Caius Octavius and Lentulus Spinther, who afterward paid dear for their vanity, being put to death by Antony and young Cæsar; so that they gained not even the honor for which they lost their lives, for nobody believed that they had any part in the enterprise; and they were punished, not for the deed, but for the will.

Next day Brutus and the rest of the conspirators came down from the Capitol and addressed the people, who attended to their discourse without expressing either dislike or approbation of what was done. But by their silence it appeared that they pitied Cæsar, at the same time that they revered Brutus. The senate passed a general amnesty; and, to reconcile all parties, they decreed Cæsar divine honors and confirmed all the acts of his dictatorship; while on Brutus and his friends they bestowed governments and such honors as were suitable; so that it was generally imagined the Commonwealth was firmly established again, and all brought into the best order.

But when, upon the opening of Cæsar's will, it was found that he had left every Roman citizen a considerable legacy, and they beheld the body, as it was carried through the Forum, all mangled with wounds, the multitude could no longer be kept within bounds. They stopped the procession, and, tearing up the benches, with the doors and tables, heaped them into a pile, and burned the corpse there. Then snatching flaming brands from the pile, some ran to burn the houses of the assassins, while others ranged the city to find the conspirators themselves and tear them in pieces; but they had taken such care to secure themselves that they could not meet with one of them.

One Cinna, a friend of Cæsar's, had a strange dream the preceding night. He dreamed—as they tell us—that Cæsar invited him to supper, and, upon his refusal to go, caught him by the hand and drew him after him, in spite of all the resistance he could make. Hearing, however, that the body of Cæsar was to be burned in the Forum, he went to assist in doing him the last honors, though he had a fever upon him, the consequence of his uneasiness about his dream. On his coming up, one of the populace asked who that was? and having learned his name, told it to his next neighbor. A report immediately spread through the whole company that it was one of Cæsar's murderers; and, indeed, one of the conspirators was named Cinna. The multitude, taking this for the man, fell upon him, and tore him to pieces upon the spot. Brutus and Cassius were so terrified at this rage of the populace that a few days after they left the city. An account of their subsequent actions, sufferings, and death may be found in the life of Brutus.

Cæsar died at the age of fifty-six, and did not survive Pompey above four years. His object was sovereign power and authority, which he pursued through innumerable dangers, and by prodigious efforts he gained it at last. But he reaped no other fruit from it than an empty and invidious title. It is true the divine Power, which conducted him through life, attended him after his death as his avenger, pursued and hunted out the assassins over sea and land, and rested not till there was not a man left, either of those who dipped their hands in his blood or of those who gave their sanction to the deed.

The most remarkable of natural events relative to this affair was that Cassius, after he had lost the battle of Philippi, killed himself with the same dagger which he had made use of against Cæsar; and the most signal phenomenon in the heavens was that of a great comet, which shone very bright for seven nights after Cæsar's death, and then disappeared; to which we may add the fading of the sun's lustre; for his orb looked pale all that year; he rose not with a sparkling radiance, nor had the heat he afforded its usual strength. The air, of course, was dark and heavy, for want of that vigorous heat which clears and rarefies it; and the fruits were so crude and unconcocted that they pined away and decayed, through the chilliness of the atmosphere.

We have a proof still more striking that the assassination of Cæsar was displeasing to the gods, in the phantom that appeared to Brutus. The story of it is this: Brutus was on the point of transporting his army from Abydos to the opposite continent; and the night before, he lay in his tent awake, according to custom, and in deep thought about what might be the event of the war; for it was natural for him to watch a great part of the night, and no general ever required so little sleep. With all his senses about him, he heard a noise at the door of his tent, and looking toward the light, which was now burned very low, he saw a terrible appearance in the human form, but of prodigious stature and the most hideous aspect. At first he was struck with astonishment; but when he saw it neither did nor spoke anything to him, but stood in silence by his bed, he asked it who it was? The spectre answered: "I am thy evil genius, Brutus; thou shalt see me at Philippi." Brutus answered boldly, "I'll meet thee there"; and the spectre immediately vanished.

Some time after, he engaged Antony and Octavius Cæsar at Philippi, and the first day was victorious, carrying all before him, where he fought in person, and even pillaging Cæsar's camp. The night before he was to fight the second battle the same spectre appeared to him again, but spoke not a word. Brutus, however, understood that his last hour was near, and courted danger with all the violence of despair. Yet he did not fall in the action; but seeing all was lost, he retired to the top of a rock, where he presented his naked sword to his breast, and a friend, as they tell us, assisting the thrust, he died upon the spot.

ROME BECOMES A MONARCHY

DEATH OF ANTONY AND CLEOPATRA

B.C. 44-30

HENRY GEORGE LIDDELL

After the death of Cæsar, Rome was in confusion; consternation seized the people, and the "liberators" failed to rally them to their own support. In possession of Cæsar's treasure, Antony, the surviving consul, bided his time. His oration at Cæsar's funeral stirred the populace against the "liberators," and made him for the moment master of Rome; but his self-seeking soon turned the people against him. The young Octavius, Cæsar's heir, had become popular with the army. He returned to Rome and claimed his inheritance, demanded from Antony Cæsar's moneys, but in vain, and assumed the title of Cæsar. The rivalry between the two leaders rapidly approached a crisis. The partisans of Antony and Octavius began to clash, and civil war followed. Defeated, Antony retreated across the Alps. Octavius was elected consul, and began negotiations with Antony and Lepidus, which resulted in the three new masters constituting themselves a triumvirate—the Second Triumvirate—to settle the affairs of the Commonwealth. They divided the powers of government, and a partition of territory was made between them. Their next business was to put out of the way, by proscription, the enemies of this new order of things. Three hundred senators, including Cicero, were massacred, as well as two thousand knights.

When the terrified senate had legalized the self-assumed authority of the triumvirs, they turned their attention to Brutus and Cassius in the East, whither they had gone after the assassination of Cæsar and established and maintained themselves in power. At the battle of Philippi in Macedonia (B.C. 42) Antony and Octavius defeated Brutus and Cassius, both of whom died by their own hands. The Roman world was now in the hands of the triumvirs. Antony ruled in the East, Octavius in the West, and Lepidus in Africa, B.C. 42-36. In the latter year Lepidus was deposed by Octavius after a short conflict. And only a year after Philippi a war between Octavius and Antony was threatened because of a revolt in Italy, raised by Antony's brother Lucius and Fulvia, wife of Antony; but it was prevented by a treaty of peace, sealed by the marriage of Antony to Octavia, sister of Octavius. This peace lasted for ten years, during which time, however, there was constant friction between them.

333

At Tarsus, in B.C. 41, Antony received a visit from Cleopatra, to whose charms he had yielded years before. This was the turning-point in his career; he went with her to Alexandria. By his oppression of the people of the East, and his dalliance with Cleopatra, he made himself the object of hatred and contempt. His army met with a series of defeats. In the mean time Octavius was constantly strengthening himself. The rivalry between them finally reached the point where both prepared for war. The great sea fight near Actium, September 2d, B.C. 31, resulted in the destruction of Antony's fleet after he had followed Cleopatra in her flight. A year later occurred the death of both. This important battle established Octavius as the sole ruler of the Roman possessions, and historians regard it as marking the end of the republic and the beginning of the empire.

WHILE the conspirators were at their bloody work [of slaying Cæsar], the mass of the senators rushed in confused terror to the doors; and when Brutus turned to address his peers in defence of the deed, the hall was well-nigh empty. Cicero, who had been present, answered not, though he was called by name; Antony had hurried away to exchange his consular robes for the garb of a slave. Disappointed of obtaining the sanction of the senate, the conspirators sallied out into the Forum to win the ear of the people. But here, too, they were disappointed. Not knowing what massacre might be in store, every man had fled to his own house; and in vain the conspirators paraded the Forum, holding up their blood-stained weapons and proclaiming themselves the liberators of Rome. Disappointment was not their only feeling: they were not without fear. They knew that Lepidus, being on the eve of departure for his province of Narbonnese Gaul, had a legion encamped on the island of the Tiber: and if he were to unite with Antony against them, Cæsar would quickly be avenged. In all haste, therefore, they retired to the Capitol. Meanwhile three of Cæsar's slaves placed their master's body upon a stretcher and carried it to his house on the south side of the Forum, with one arm dangling from the unsupported corner. In this condition the widowed Calpurnia received the lifeless clay of him who had lately been sovereign of the world.

Lepidus moved his troops to the Campus Martius. But Antony had no thoughts of using force; for in that case probably Lepidus would have become master of Rome. During the night he took possession of the treasure which Cæsar had collected to defray the expenses of his Parthian campaign, and persuaded Calpurnia to put into his hands all the dictator's papers. Possessed of these securities, he barricaded his house on the Carinæ, and determined to watch the course of events.

In the evening Cicero, with other senators, visited the self-styled liberators in the Capitol. They had not communicated their plot to the orator, through fear (they said) of his irresolute counsels; but now that the deed was done, he extolled it as a godlike act. Next morning, Dolabella, Cicero's son-in-law, whom Cæsar had promised should be his successor in the consulship, assumed the consular fasces and joined the liberators; while Cinna, son of the old Marian leader and therefore brother-in-law to Cæsar, threw aside his prætorian robes, declaring he would no longer wear the tyrant's livery. Dec. Brutus, a good soldier, had taken a band of gladiators into pay, to serve as a bodyguard of the liberators. Thus strengthened, they ventured again to descend into the Forum. Brutus mounted the tribune, and addressed the people in a dispassionate speech, which produced little effect. But when Cinna assailed the memory of the dictator, the crowd broke out into menacing cries, and the liberators again retired to the Capitol.

That same night they entered into negotiations with Antony, and the result appeared next morning, the second after the murder. The senate, summoned to meet, obeyed the call in large numbers. Antony and Dolabella attended in their consular robes, and Cinna resumed his prætorian garb. It was soon apparent that a reconciliation had been effected: for Antony moved that a general amnesty should be granted, and Cicero seconded the motion in an animated speech. It was carried; and Antony next moved that all the acts of the dictator should be recognized as law. He had his own purposes here; but the liberators also saw in the motion an advantage to themselves; for they were actually in possession of some of the chief magistracies, and had received appointments to some of the richest provinces of the empire. This proposal, therefore, was favorably received; but it was adjourned to the next day, together with the important question of Cæsar's funeral.

On the next day Cæsar's acts were formally confirmed, and

among them his will was declared valid, though its provisions were yet unknown. After this, it was difficult to reject the proposal that the dictator should have a public burial. Old senators remembered the riots that attended the funeral of Clodius and shook their heads. Cassius opposed it. But Brutus, with imprudent magnanimity, decided in favor of allowing it. To seal the reconciliation, Lepidus entertained Brutus at dinner and Cassius was feasted by Mark Antony.

The will was immediately made public. Cleopatra was still in Rome, and entertained hopes that the boy Cæsarion would be declared the dictator's heir; for though he had been married thrice, there was no one of his lineage surviving. But Cæsar was too much a Roman, and knew the Romans too well, to be guilty of this folly. Young C. Octavius, his sister's son, was declared his heir. Legacies were left to all his supposed friends, among whom were several of those who had assassinated him. His noble gardens beyond the Tiber were devised to the use of the public, and every Roman citizen was to receive a donation of three hundred sesterces—between ten and fifteen dollars. The effect of this recital was electric. Devotion to the memory of the dictator and hatred for his murderers at once filled every breast.

Two or three days after this followed the funeral. The body was to be burned, and the ashes deposited in the Campus Martius, near the tomb of his daughter Julia. But it was first brought into the Forum upon a bier inlaid with ivory and covered with rich tapestries, which was carried by men high in rank and office. There Antony, as consul, rose to pronounce the funeral oration. He ran through the chief acts of Cæsar's life, recited his will, and then spoke of the death which had rewarded him. To make this more vividly present to the excitable Italians he displayed a waxen image marked with the three-and-twenty wounds, and produced the very robe which he had worn, all rent and blood-stained. Soul-stirring dirges added to the solemn horror of the scene. But to us the memorable speech which Shakespeare puts into Antony's mouth will give the liveliest notion of the art used and the impression produced. That impression was instantaneous. The senator friends of the liberators who had attended the ceremony looked on in moody silence. Soon the menacing gestures of the crowd made them look to their safety. They fled; and the multitude insisted on burning the body, as they had burned the body of Clodius, in the sacred precincts of the Forum. Some of the veterans who attended the funeral set fire to the bier; benches and firewood heaped round it soon made a sufficient pile.

From the blazing pyre the crowd rushed, eager for vengeance, to the houses of the conspirators. But all had fled betimes. One poor wretch fell a victim to the fury of the mob— Helvius Cinna, a poet who had devoted his art to the service of the dictator. He was mistaken for L. Cornelius Cinna the prætor, and was torn to pieces before the mistake could be explained.[1]

Antony was now the real master of Rome. The treasure which he had seized gave him the means of purchasing good will, and of securing the attachment of the veterans stationed in various parts of Italy. He did not, however, proceed in the course which, from the tone of his funeral harangue, might have been expected. He renewed friendly intercourse with Brutus and Cassius, who were encouraged to visit Rome once at least, if not oftener, after that day; and Dec. Brutus, with his gladiators, was suffered to remain in the city. Antony went still further. He gratified the senate by passing a law to abolish the dictatorship forever. He then left Rome to win the favor of the Italian communities and try the temper of the veterans.

Meanwhile another actor appeared upon the scene. This was young Octavius. He had been but six months in the camp at Apollonia; but in that short time he had formed a close friendship with M. Vipsanius Agrippa, a young man of his own age, who possessed great abilities for active life, but could not boast of any distinguished ancestry. As soon as the news of his uncle's assassination reached the camp, his friend Agrippa recommended him to appeal to the troops and march upon Rome. But the youth, with a wariness above his years, resisted these bold counsels. Landing near Brundusium almost

---

[1] This story is, however, rendered somewhat doubtful by the manner in which Cinna is mentioned in Vergil's ninth *Eclogue*, which was certainly written in or after the year B.C. 40.

alone, he there first heard that Cæsar's will had been published and that he was declared Cæsar's heir. He at once accepted the dangerous honor. As he travelled slowly toward the city he stayed some days at Puteoli with his mother, Atia, who was now married to L. Philippus. Both mother and stepfather attempted to dissuade him from the perilous business of claiming his inheritance. At the same place he had an interview with Cicero, who had quitted Rome in despair after the funeral, and left the orator under the impression that he might be won to what was deemed the patriotic party.

He arrived at Rome about the beginning of May, and demanded from Antony, who had now returned from his Italian tour, an account of the moneys of which the consul had taken possession, in order that he might discharge the obligations laid upon him by his uncle's will. But Antony had already spent great part of the money in bribing Dolabella and other influential persons; nor was he willing to give up any portion of his spoil. Octavius therefore sold what remained of his uncle's property, raised money on his own credit, and paid all legacies with great exactness. This act earned him much popularity. Antony began to fear this boy of eighteen, whom he had hitherto despised, and the senate learned to look on him as a person to be conciliated.

Still Antony remained in possession of all actual power. Cicero, not remarkable for political firmness, in this crisis displayed a vigor worthy of his earlier days. He had at one moment made up his mind to retire from public life and end his days at Athens in learned leisure. In the course of this summer he continued to employ himself on some of his most elaborate treatises. His works on the *Nature of the Gods* and on *Divination*, his *Offices*, his *Dialogue on Old Age*, and several other essays belong to this period and mark the restless activity of his mind. But though he twice set sail from Italy, he was driven back to port at Velia, where he found Brutus and Cassius. Here he received letters from Au. Hirtius and other friends of Cæsar, which gave him hopes that, in the name of Octavius, they might successfully oppose Antony and restore constitutional government. He determined to return, and announced his purpose to Brutus and Cassius, who commended him and took leave of him. They went their way to the east to raise armies against Antony; he repaired to Rome to fight the battles of his party in the senate house.

Meanwhile Antony had been running riot. In possession of Cæsar's papers, with no one to check him, he produced ready warrant for every measure which he wished to carry, and pleaded the vote of the senate which confirmed all the acts of Cæsar. When he could not produce a genuine paper, he interpolated or forged what was needful.

On the day after Cicero's return (September 1st) there was a meeting of the senate. But the orator did not attend, and Antony threatened to send men to drag him from his house. Next day Cicero was in his place, but now Antony was absent. The orator arose and addressed the senate in what is called his *First Philippic*. This was a measured attack upon the government and policy of Antony, but personalities were carefully eschewed: the tone of the whole speech, indeed, is such as might be delivered by a leader of opposition in parliament at the present day. But Antony, enraged at his boldness, summoned a meeting for the 19th of September, which Cicero did not think it prudent to attend. He then attacked the absent orator in the strongest language of personal abuse and menace. Cicero sat down and composed his famous *Second Philippic*, which is written as if it were delivered on the same day, in reply to Antony's invective. At present, however, he contented himself with sending a copy of it to Atticus, enjoining secrecy.

Matters quickly drew to a head between Antony and Octavius. The latter had succeeded in securing a thousand men of his uncle's veterans who had settled in Campania; and by great exertions in the different towns of Italy had levied a considerable force. Meantime four of the Epirote legions had just landed at Brundusium, and Antony hastened to attach them to his cause. But the largess which he offered them was only a hundred *denaries* a man, and the soldiers laughed in his face. Antony, enraged at their conduct, seized the ringleaders and decimated them. But this severity only served to change their open insolence into sullen anger, and emissaries from Octavius were ready to draw them over to the side of their young master. They had so far obeyed Antony as to march northward to Ariminum, while he repaired to Rome. But as he entered the senate house he heard that two of the four legions had deserted to his rival, and in great alarm he hastened to the camp just in time to keep the remainder of the troops under his standard by distributing to every man five hundred denaries.

The persons to hold the consulship for the next year had been designated by Cæsar. They were both old officers of the Gallic army, C. Vibius Pansa and Au. Hirtius, the reputed author of the Eighth Book of the *History of the Gallic War*. Cicero was ready to believe that they had become patriots, because, disgusted with the arrogance of Antony, they had declared for Octavius and the senate. Antony began to fear that all parties might combine to crush him. He determined, therefore, no longer to remain inactive; and about the end of November, having now collected all his troops at Ariminum, he marched along the Æmilian road to drive Dec. Brutus out of Cisalpine Gaul. Decimus was obliged to throw himself into Mutina (Modena), and Antony blockaded the place. As soon as his back was turned, Cicero published the famous *Second Philippic*, in which he lashed the consul with the most unsparing hand, going through the history of his past life, exaggerating the debaucheries, which were common to Antony with great part of the Roman youth, and painting in the strongest colors the profligate use he had made of Cæsar's papers. Its effect was great, and Cicero followed up the blow by the following twelve *Philippics*, which were speeches delivered in the senate house and Forum, at intervals from December (44) to April in the next year.

Cicero was anxious to break with Antony at once, by declaring him a public enemy. But the latter was still regarded by many senators as the head of the Cæsarean party, and it was resolved to treat with him. But the demands of Antony were so extravagant that negotiations were at once broken off, and nothing remained but to try the fortune of arms. The consuls proceeded to levy troops; but so exhausted was the treasury that now for the first time since the triumph of Æmilius Paullus it was found necessary to levy a property tax on the citizens of Rome.

Octavius and the consuls assembled their forces at Alba.

On the first day of the new year (43) Hirtius marched for Mutina, with Octavius under his command. The other consul, Pansa, remained at Rome to raise new levies; but by the end of March he also marched to form a junction with Hirtius. Both parties pretended to be acting in Cæsar's name.

Antony left his brother Lucius in the trenches before Mutina, and took the field against Hirtius and Octavius. For three months the opponents lay watching each other. But when Antony learned that Pansa was coming up, he made a rapid movement southward with two of his veteran legions and attacked him. A sharp conflict followed, in which Pansa's troops were defeated, and the consul himself was carried, mortally wounded, off the field. But Hirtius was on the alert, and assaulted Antony's wearied troops on their way back to their camp, with some advantage. This was on the 15th of April, and on the 27th Hirtius drew Antony from his intrenchments before Mutina. A fierce battle followed, which ended in the troops of Antony being driven back into their lines. Hirtius followed close upon the flying enemy; the camp was carried by storm, and a complete victory would have been won had not Hirtius himself fallen. Upon this disaster Octavius drew off the troops. The news of the first battle had been reported at Rome as a victory, and gave rise to extravagant rejoicings. The second battle was really a victory, but all rejoicing was damped by the news that one consul was dead and the other dying. No such fatal mischance had happened since the Second Punic War, when Marcellus and Crispinus fell in one day.

After his defeat Antony felt it impossible to maintain the siege of Mutina. With Dec. Brutus in the town behind him, and the victorious legions of Octavius before him, his position was critical. He therefore prepared to retreat, and effected this purpose like a good soldier. His destination was the province of Narbonnese Gaul, where Lepidus had assumed the government and had promised him support. But the senate also had hopes in the same quarter. L. Munatius Plancus commanded in Northern Gaul, and C. Asinius Pollio in Southern Spain. Sext. Pompeius had made good his ground in the latter country, and had almost expelled Pollio from Bætica. Plancus and Pollio, both friends and favorites of Cæsar, had as yet de-

clared neither for Antony nor Octavius.   If they would declare
for the senate, Lepidus, a feeble and fickle man, might desert
Antony; or if Octavius would join with Dec. Brutus, and pursue him, Antony might not be able to escape from Italy at all.
But these political combinations failed.   Plancus and Pollio
stood aloof, waiting for the course of events.   Dec. Brutus was
not strong enough to pursue Antony by himself, and Octavius
was unwilling, perhaps unable, to unite the veterans of Cæsar
with troops commanded by one of Cæsar's murderers.   And so
it happened that Antony effected his retreat across the Alps,
but not without extreme hardships, which he bore in common
with the meanest soldier.   It was at such times that his good
qualities always showed themselves, and his gallant endurance
of misery endeared him to every man under his command.   On
his arrival in Narbonnese Gaul he met Lepidus at Forum Julii
(Frejus), and here the two commanders agreed on a plan of
operations.

The conduct of Octavius gave rise to grave suspicions.   It
was even said that the consuls had been killed by his agents.
Cicero, who had hitherto maintained his cause, was silent.   He
had delivered his *Fourteenth* and last *Philippic* on the news of
the first victory gained by Hirtius.   But now he talked in private of "removing" the boy of whom he had hoped to make a
tool.   Octavius, however, had taken his part, and was not to be
removed.   Secretly he entered into negotiations with Antony.
After some vain efforts on the part of the senate to thwart him,
he appeared in the Campus Martius with his legions.   Cicero
and most of the senators disappeared, and the fickle populace
greeted the young heir of Cæsar with applause.   Though he
was not yet twenty he demanded the consulship, having been
previously relieved from the provisions of the *Lex Annalis* by
a decree of the senate, and he was elected to the first office in
the State, with his cousin, Q. Pedius.[1]

A curiate law passed, by which Octavius was adopted into
the patrician gens of the Julii, and was put into legal possession of the name which he had already assumed—C. Julius
Cæsar Octavianus.   We shall henceforth call him Octavian.

[1] Pedius was son of Cæsar's second sister, Julia minor, and therefore
first cousin (once removed) to Octavius.

The change in his policy was soon indicated by a law in which he formally separated himself from the senate. Pedius brought it forward. By its provisions all Cæsar's murderers were summoned to take their trial. Of course none of them appeared and they were condemned by default. By the end of September Octavian was again in Cisalpine Gaul and in close negotiation with Antony and Lepidus. The fruits of his conduct soon appeared. Plancus and Pollio declared against Cæsar's murderers. Dec. Brutus, deserted by his soldiery, attempted to escape into Macedonia through Illyricum; but he was overtaken near Aquileia and slain by order of Antony.

Italy and Gaul being now clear of the senatorial party, Lepidus, as mediator, arranged a meeting between Octavian and Antony, upon an island in a small river near Bononia (Bologna). Here the three potentates agreed that they should assume a joint and coördinate authority, under the name of "Triumvirs for settling the affairs of the Commonwealth." Antony was to have the two Gauls, except the Narbonnese district, which, with Spain, was assigned to Lepidus; Octavian received Sicily, Sardinia, and Africa. Italy was for the present to be left to the consuls of the year, and for the ensuing year Lepidus, with Plancus, received promise of this high office. In return, Lepidus gave up his military force, while Octavian and Antony, each at the head of ten legions, prepared to conquer the Eastern part of the empire, which could not yet be divided like the Western provinces, because it was in possession of Brutus and Cassius.

But before they began war, the triumvirs agreed to follow the example set by Sylla—to extirpate their opponents by a proscription, and to raise money by confiscation. They framed a list of all men's names whose death could be regarded as advantageous to any of the three, and on this list each in turn pricked a name. Antony had made many personal enemies by his proceedings at Rome, and was at no loss for victims. Octavian had few direct enemies; but the boy-despot discerned with precocious sagacity those who were likely to impede his ambitious projects, and chose his victims with little hesitation. Lepidus would not be left behind in the bloody work. The author of the *Philippics* was one of Antony's first victims; Octavian gave him up, and took as an equivalent for his late friend the life of L. Cæsar, uncle of Antony. Lepidus surrendered his brother Paullus for some similar favor. So the work went on. Not fewer than three hundred senators and two thousand knights were on the list. Q. Pedius, an honest and upright man, died in his consulship, overcome by vexation and shame at being implicated in these transactions.

As soon as their secret business was ended, the triumvirs determined to enter Rome publicly. Hitherto they had not published more than seventeen names of the proscribed. They made their entrance severally on three successive days, each attended by a legion. A law was immediately brought in to invest them formally with the supreme authority, which they had assumed. This was followed by the promulgation of successive lists, each larger than its predecessor.

Among the victims, far the most conspicuous was Cicero. With his brother Quintus, the old orator had retired to his Tusculan villa after the battle of Mutina; and now they endeavored to escape in the hope of joining Brutus in Macedonia; for the orator's only son was serving as a tribune in the liberator's army. After many changes of domicile they reached Astura, a little island near Antium, where they found themselves short of money, and Quintus ventured to Rome to procure the necessary supply. Here he was recognized and seized, together with his son. Each desired to die first, and the mournful claim to precedence was settled by the soldiers killing both at the same moment.

Meantime Cicero had put to sea. But even in this extremity he could not make up his mind to leave Italy, and put to land at Circeii. After further hesitation he again embarked, and again sought the Italian shore near Formiæ. For the night he stayed at his villa near that place, and next morning would not move, exclaiming: "Let me die in my own country—that country which I have so often saved." But his faithful slaves forced him into a litter and carried him again toward the coast. Scarcely were they gone when a band of Antony's bloodhounds reached his villa, and were put upon the track of their victim by a young man who owed everything to the Ciceros. The old orator from his litter saw the pursuers coming

up. His own followers were strong enough to have made resistance, but he desired them to set the litter down.   Then,
raising himself on his elbow, he calmly waited for the ruffians
and offered his neck to the sword.   He was soon despatched.
The chief of the band, by Antony's express orders, hewed off
the head and hands and carried them to Rome.   Fulvia, the
widow of Clodius and now the wife of Antony, drove her hair-
pin through the tongue which had denounced the iniquities of
both her husbands.   The head which had given birth to the
Second Philippic, and the hands which had written it, were
nailed to the Rostra, the home of their eloquence.   The sight
and the associations raised feelings of horror and pity in every
heart.   Cicero died in his sixty-fourth year.

Brutus and Cassius left Italy in the autumn of B.C. 44 and
repaired to the provinces which had been allotted to them,
though by Antony's influence the senate had transferred Macedonia from Brutus to his own brother Caius, and Syria from
Cassius to Dolabella.   C. Antonius was already in possession of
parts of Macedonia; but Brutus succeeded in dislodging him.
Meanwhile Cassius, already well known in Syria for his successful conduct of the Parthian War, had established himself in
that province before he heard of the approach of Dolabella.
This worthless man left Italy about the same time as Brutus
and Cassius, and at the head of several legions marched without opposition through Macedonia into Asia Minor.   Here C.
Trebonius had already arrived.   But he was unable to cope
with Dolabella; and the latter surprised him and took him
prisoner at Smyrna.   He was put to death with unseemly con-
tumely in Dolabella's presence.   This was in February, 43;
and thus two of Cæsar's murderers, in less than a year's time,
felt the blow of retributive justice.   When the news of this
piece of butchery reached Rome, Cicero, believing that Octavian was a puppet in his hands, was ruling Rome by the eloquence of his *Philippics*.   On his motion Dolabella was declared a public enemy.[1]   Cassius lost no time in marching his
legions into Asia, to execute the behest of the senate, though
he had been dispossessed of his province by the senate itself.

[1] He had divorced Tullia, the orator's daughter, before he left Italy.

Dolabella threw himself into Laodicea, where he sought a voluntary death.

By the end of B.C. 43, therefore, the whole of the East was in the hands of Brutus and Cassius. But instead of making preparations for war with Antony, the two commanders spent the early part of the year 42 in plundering the miserable cities of Asia Minor. Brutus demanded men and money of the Lycians; and, when they refused, he laid siege to Xanthus, their principal city. The Xanthians made the same brave resistance which they had offered five hundred years before to the Persian invaders. They burned their city and put themselves to death rather than submit. Brutus wept over their fate and abstained from further exactions. But Cassius showed less moderation; from the Rhodians alone, though they were allies of Rome, he demanded all their precious metals. After this campaign of plunder, the two chiefs met at Sardis and renewed the altercations which Cicero had deplored in Italy. It is probable that war might have broken out between them had not the preparations of the triumvirs waked them from their dream of security. It was as he was passing over into Europe that Brutus, who continued his studious habits amid all disquietudes, and limited his time of sleep to a period too small for the requirements of health, was dispirited by the vision which Shakespeare, after Plutarch, has made famous. It was no doubt the result of a diseased frame, though it was universally held to be a divine visitation. As he sat in his tent in the dead of night, he thought a huge and shadowy form stood by him; and when he calmly asked, " What and whence art thou?" it answered, or seemed to answer: "I am thine evil genius, Brutus: we shall meet again at Philippi."

Meantime Antony's lieutenants had crossed the Ionian Sea and penetrated without opposition into Thrace. The republican leaders found them at Philippi. The army of Brutus and Cassius amounted to at least eighty thousand infantry, supported by twenty thousand horse; but they were ill-supplied with experienced officers. For M. Valerius Messalla, a young man of twenty-eight, held the chief command after Brutus and Cassius; and Horace, who was but three-and-twenty, the son of a freedman, and a youth of feeble constitution, was appointed a legionary tribune. The forces opposed to them would have been at once overpowered had not Antony himself opportunely arrived with the second corps of the triumviral army. Octavian was detained by illness at Dyrrhachium, but he ordered himself to be carried on a litter to join his legions. The army of the triumvirs was now superior to the enemy; but their cavalry, counting only thirteen thousand, was considerably weaker than the force opposed to it. The republicans were strongly posted upon two hills, with intrenchments between: the camp of Cassius upon the left next the sea, that of Brutus inland on the right. The triumviral army lay upon the open plain before them, in a position rendered unhealthy by marshes; Antony, on the right, was opposed to Cassius; Octavian, on the left, fronted Brutus. But they were ill-supplied with provisions and anxious for a decisive battle. The republicans, however, kept to their intrenchments, and the other party began to suffer severely from famine.

Determined to bring on an action, Antony began works for the purpose of cutting off Cassius from the sea. Cassius had always opposed a general action, but Brutus insisted on putting an end to the suspense, and his colleague yielded. The day of the attack was probably in October. Brutus attacked Octavian's army, while Cassius assaulted the working parties of Antony. Cassius' assault was beaten back with loss, but he succeeded in regaining his camp in safety. Meanwhile, Messalla, who commanded the right wing of Brutus' army, had defeated the host of Octavian, who was still too ill to appear on the field, and the republican soldiers penetrated into the triumvirs' camp. Presently his litter was brought in stained with blood, and the corpse of a young man found near it was supposed to be Octavian's. But Brutus, not receiving any tidings of the movements of Cassius, became so anxious for his fate that he sent off a party of horse to make inquiries, and neglected to support the successful assaults of Messalla.

Cassius, on his part, discouraged at his ill-success, was unable to ascertain the progress of Brutus. When he saw the party of horse he hastily concluded that they belonged to the enemy, and retired into his tent with his freedman Pindarus. What passed there we know not for certain. Cassius was found dead, with the head severed from the body. Pindarus was never seen again. It was generally believed that Pindarus slew his master in obedience to orders; but many thought that he had dealt a felon blow. The intelligence of Cassius' death was a heavy blow to Brutus. He forgot his own success, and pronounced the elegy of Cassius in the well-known words, "There lies the last of the Romans." The praise was ill-deserved. Except in his conduct of the war against the Parthians, Cassius had never played a worthy part.

After the first battle of Philippi it would have still been politic in Brutus to abstain from battle. The triumviral armies were in great distress, and every day increased their losses. Reënforcements coming to their aid by sea were intercepted— a proof of the neglect of the republican leaders in not sooner bringing their fleet into action. Nor did Brutus ever hear of this success. He was ill-fitted for the life of the camp, and after the death of Cassius he only kept his men together by largesses and promises of plunder. Twenty days after the first battle he led them out again. Both armies faced one another. There was little manœuvring. The second battle was decided by numbers and force, not by skill; and it was decided in favor of the triumvirs. Brutus retired with four legions to a strong position in the rear, while the rest of his broken army sought refuge in the camp. Octavian remained to watch them, while Antony pursued the republican chief. Next day Brutus endeavored to rouse his men to another effort; but they sullenly refused to fight; and Brutus withdrew with a few friends into a neighboring wood. Here he took them aside one by one, and prayed each to do him the last service that a Roman could render to his friend. All refused with horror; till at nightfall a trusty Greek freedman named Strato held the sword, and his master threw himself upon it. Most of his friends followed the sad example. The body of Brutus was sent by Antony to his mother. His wife Portia, the daughter of Cato, refused all comfort; and being too closely watched to be able to slay herself by ordinary means, she suffocated herself by thrusting burning charcoal into her mouth. Massalla, with a number of other fugitives, sought safety in the island of Thasos, and soon after made submission to Antony.

The name of Brutus has, by Plutarch's beautiful narrative, sublimed by Shakespeare, become a byword for self-devoted patriotism. This exalted opinion is now generally confessed to be unjust. Brutus was not a patriot, unless devotion to the party of the senate be patriotism. Toward the provincials he was a true Roman, harsh and oppressive. He was free from the sensuality and profligacy of his age, but for public life he was unfit. His habits were those of a student. His application was great, his memory remarkable. But he possessed little power of turning his acquirements to account; and to the last he was rather a learned man than a man improved by learning. In comparison with Cassius, he was humane and generous; but in all respects his character is contrasted for the worse with that of the great man from whom he accepted favors and then became his murderer.

The battle of Philippi was in reality the closing scene of the republican drama. But the rivalship of the triumvirs prolonged for several years the divided state of the Roman world; and it was not till after the crowning victory of Actium that the imperial government was established in its unity. We shall, therefore, here add a rapid narrative of the events which led to that consummation.

The hopeless state of the republican or rather the senatorial party was such that almost all hastened to make submission to the conquerors: those whose sturdy spirit still disdained submission resorted to Sext. Pompeius in Sicily. Octavian, still suffering from ill-health, was anxious to return to Italy; but before he parted from Antony, they agreed to a second distribution of the provinces of the empire. Antony was to have the Eastern world; Octavian the Western provinces. To Lepidus, who was not consulted in this second division, Africa alone was left. Sext. Pompeius remained in possession of Sicily.

Antony at once proceeded to make a tour through Western Asia, in order to exact money from its unfortunate people. About midsummer (B.C. 41) he arrived at Tarsus, and here he received a visit which determined the future course of his life and influenced Roman history for the next ten yekrs.

Antony had visited Alexandria fourteen years before, and had been smitten by the charms of Cleopatra, then a girl of fifteen She became Cæsar's paramour, and from the time of the dictator's death Antony had never seen her She now came to meet him in Cilicia. The galley which carried her up the Cydnus was of more than oriental gorgeousness: the sails of purple; oars of silver, moving to the sound of music; the raised poop burnished with gold. There she lay upon a splendid couch, shaded by a spangled canopy; her attire was that of Venus; around her flitted attendant cupids and graces. At the news of her approach to Tarsus, the triumvir found his tribunal deserted by the people. She invited him to her ship, and he complied. From that moment he was her slave. He accompanied her to Alexandria, exchanged the Roman garb for the Græco-Egyptian costume of the court, and lent his power to the Queen to execute all her caprices.

Meanwhile Octavian was not without his difficulties. He was so ill at Brundusium that his death was reported at Rome. The veterans, eager for their promised rewards, were on the eve of mutiny. In a short time Octavian was sufficiently recovered to show himself. But he could find no other means of satisfying the greedy soldiery than by a confiscation of lands more sweeping than that which followed the proscription of Sylla. The towns of Cisalpine Gaul were accused of favoring Dec. Brutus, and saw nearly all their lands handed over to new possessors. The young poet, Vergil, lost his little patrimony, but was reinstated at the instance of Pollio and Mæcenas, and showed his gratitude in his *First Eclogue.* Other parts of Italy also suffered: Apulia, for example, as we learn from Horace's friend Ofellus, who became the tenant of the estate which had formerly been his own.

But these violent measures deferred rather than obviated the difficulty. The expulsion of so many persons threw thousands loose upon society, ripe for any crime. Many of the veterans were ready to join any new leader who promised them booty. Such a leader was at hand.

Fulvia, wife of Antony, was a woman of fierce passions and ambitious spirit. She had not been invited to follow her husband to the East. She saw that in his absence imperial power would fall into the hands of Octavian. Lucius, brother of Mark Antony, was consul for the year, and at her instigation he raised his standard at Præneste. But L. Antonius knew not how to use his strength; and young Agrippa, to whom Octavian intrusted the command, obliged Antonius and Fulvia to retire northward and shut themselves up in Perusia. Their store of provisions was so small that it sufficed only for the soldiery. Early in the next year Perusia surrendered, on condition that the lives of the leaders should be spared. The town was sacked; the conduct of L. Antonius alienated all Italy from his brother.

While his wife, his brother, and his friends were quitting Italy in confusion, the arms of Antony suffered a still heavier blow in the Eastern provinces, which were under his special government. After the battle of Philippi, Q. Labienus, son of Cæsar's old lieutenant Titus, sought refuge at the court of Orodes, king of Parthia. Encouraged by the proffered aid of a Roman officer, Pacorus (the King's son) led a formidable army into Syria. Antony's lieutenant was entirely routed; and while Pacorus with one army poured into Palestine and Phœnicia, Q. Labienus with another broke into Cilicia. Here he found no opposition; and, overrunning all Asia Minor even to the Ionian Sea, he assumed the name of Parthicus, as if he had been a Roman conqueror of the people whom he served.

These complicated disasters roused Antony from his lethargy. He sailed to Tyre, intending to take the field against the Parthians; but the season was too far advanced, and he therefore crossed the Ægean to Athens, where he found Fulvia and his brother, accompanied by Pollio, Plancus, and others, all discontented with Octavian's government. Octavian was absent in Gaul, and their representation of the state of Italy encouraged him to make another attempt. Late in the year (41) Antony formed a league with Sext. Pompeius; and while that chief blockaded Thurii and Consentia, Antony assailed Brundusium. Agrippa was preparing to meet this new combination; and a fresh civil war was imminent. But the soldiery was weary of war: both armies compelled their leaders to make pacific overtures, and the new year was ushered in by a general peace, which was rendered easier by the death of Fulvia. Antony and Octavian renewed their professions of amity, and entered Rome together in joint ovation to celebrate the restoration of peace. They now made a third division of the provinces, by which Scodra (Scutari) in Illyricum was fixed as the boundary of the West and East. Lepidus was still left in possession of Africa   It was further agreed that Octavian was to drive Sext. Pompeius, lately the ally of Antony, out of Sicily; while Antony renewed his pledges to recover the standards of Crassus from the Parthians. The new compact was sealed by the marriage of Antony with Octavia, his colleague's sister, a virtuous and beautiful lady, worthy of a better consort. These auspicious events were celebrated by the lofty verse of Vergil's *Fourth Eclogue.*

Sext. Pompeius had reason to complain. By the peace of Brundusium he was abandoned by his late friend to Octavian. He was not a man to brook ungenerous treatment. Of late years his possession of Sicily had given him command of the Roman corn market. During the winter which followed the peace of Brundusium (B.C. 40–39), Sextus blockaded Italy so closely that Rome was threatened with a positive dearth. Riots arose; the triumvirs were pelted with stones in the Forum, and they deemed it prudent to temporize by inviting Pompey to enter their league. He met them at Misenum, and the two chiefs went on board his ship to settle the terms of alliance. It is said that one of his chief officers, a Greek named Menas or Menodorus, suggested to him the expediency of putting to sea with the great prize, and then making his own terms. Sextus rejected the advice with the characteristic words, " You should have done it without asking me." It was agreed that Sicily, Sardinia, and Corsica should be given up to his absolute rule, and that Achaia should be added to his portion; so that the Roman world was now partitioned among four: Octavian, Antony, Lepidus, and Sext. Pompeius. On their return the triumvirs were received with vociferous applause.

Before winter, Antony sailed for Athens in company with Octavia, who for the time seems to have banished Cleopatra from his thoughts. But he disgusted all true Romans by assuming the attributes of Grecian gods and indulging in Grecian orgies.

He found the state of things in the East greatly changed since his departure. He had commissioned P. Ventidius Bassus, an officer who had followed Fulvia from Italy, to hold the Parthians in check till his return. Ventidius was son of a Picenian nobleman of Asculum, who had been brought to Rome as a captive in the Social War. In his youth he had been a contractor to supply mules for the use of the Roman commissariat. But in the civil wars which followed, men of military talent easily rose to command; and such was the lot of Ventidius. While Antony was absent in Italy, he drove Q. Labienus into the defiles of Taurus, and here that adventurer was defeated and slain. The conqueror then marched rapidly into Syria, and forced Pacorus also to withdraw to the eastern bank of the Euphrates.

In the following year (38) he repelled a fresh invasion of the Parthians, and defeated them in three battles. In the last of these engagements Pacorus himself was slain on the fifteenth anniversary of the death of Crassus. Antony found Ventidius laying siege to Samosata, and displaced him, only to abandon the siege and return to Athens. Ventidius repaired to Rome, where he was honored with a well-deserved triumph. He had left it as a mule jobber: he returned with the laurel round his brows. He was the first, and almost the last, Roman general who could claim such a distinction for victory over the Parthians.

The alliance with Sext. Pompeius was not intended to last, and it did not last. Antony refused to put him in possession of Achaia; and to avenge himself for this breach of faith Pompeius again began to intercept the Italian corn fleets. Fresh discontent appeared at Rome, and Octavain equipped a second fleet to sail against the naval chief; but after two battles of doubtful result, the fleet was destroyed by a storm, and Sextus was again left in undisputed mastery of the sea. Octavian, however, was never daunted by reverses, and he gave his favorite Agrippa full powers to conduct the war against Pompeius. This able commander set about his work with that resolution that marked a man determined not to fail. As a harbor for his fleet, he executed a plan of the great Cæsar; namely, to make a good and secure harbor on the coast of Latium, which then, as now, offered no shelter to ships. For this purpose he cut a passage through the narrow necks of land which separated

Lake Lucrinus from the sea, and Lake Avernus from **Lake** Lucrinus, and faced the outer barrier with stone. This was the famous Julian Port. In the whole of the two years B.C. 38 and 37 Agrippa was occupied in this work and in preparing a sufficient force of ships. Every dockyard in Italy was called into requisition. A large body of slaves was set free that they might be trained to serve as rowers.

On the 1st of July, B.C. 36, the fleet put to sea. Octavian himself, with one division, purposed to attack the northern coast of Sicily, while a second squadron was assembled at Ta-rentum for the purpose of assailing the eastern side. Lepidus, with a third fleet from Africa, was to assault Lilybæum. But the winds were again adverse; and, though Lepidus effected a landing on the southern coast, Octavian's two fleets were driven back to Italy with great damage. But the injured ships were refitted, and Agrippa was sent westward toward Panormus, while Octavian himself kept guard near Messana. Off Mylæ, a place famous for having witnessed the first naval victory of the Romans, Agrippa encountered the fleet of Sext. Pompeius; but Sextus, with the larger portion of his ships, gave Agrippa the slip, and sailing eastward fell suddenly upon Octavian's squadron off Tauromenium. A desperate conflict followed, which ended in the complete triumph of Sextus, and Octavian escaped to Italy with a few ships only. But Agrippa was soon upon the traces of the enemy. On the 3d of September Sextus was obliged once more to accept battle near the Straits of Messana, and suffered an irretrievable defeat. His troops on land were attacked and dispersed by an army which had been landed on the eastern coast by the indefatigable Octavian; and Sextus sailed off to Lesbos, where he had found refuge as a boy during the campaign of Pharsalia, to seek protection from the jealousy of Antony.

Lepidus had assisted in the campaign; but after the departure of Sextus he openly declared himself independent of his brother triumvirs. Octavian, with prompt and prudent boldness, entered the camp of Lepidus in person with a few attendants. The soldiers deserted in crowds, and in a few hours Lepidus was fain to sue for pardon, where he had hoped to rule. He was treated with contemptuous indifference. **Africa** was taken from him; but he was allowed to live and die at Rome in quiet enjoyment of the chief pontificate.

It was fortunate for Octavian that during this campaign Antony was on friendly terms with him. In B.C. 37 the ruler of the East again visited Italy, and a meeting between the two chiefs was arranged at Tarentum. The five years for which the triumvirs were originally appointed were now fast expiring; and it was settled that their authority should be renewed by the subservient senate and people for a second period of the same duration. They parted good friends; and Octavian undertook his campaign against Sext. Pompeius without fear from Antony. This was proved by the fate of the fugitive. From Lesbos Sextus passed over to Asia, where he was taken prisoner by Antony's lieutenants and put to death.

Hitherto Octavia had retained her influence over Antony. But presently, after his last interview with her brother, the fickle triumvir abruptly quitted a wife who was too good for him, and returned to the fascinating presence of the Egyptian Queen, whom he had not seen for three years. From this time forth he made no attempt to break the silken chain of her enchantments. During the next summer, indeed, he attempted a new Parthian campaign. But his advance was made with reckless indifference to the safety of his troops. Provisions failed; disease broke out; and after great suffering he was forced to seek safety by a precipitate retreat into the Armenian mountains. In the next year he contented himself with a campaign in Armenia, to punish the King of that country for alleged treachery in the last campaign. The King fell into his hands; and with this trophy Antony returned to Alexandria, where the Romans were disgusted to see the streets of a Græco-Egyptian town honored by a mimicry of a Roman triumph.

For the next three years he surrendered himself absolutely to the will of the enchantress. To this period belong those tales of luxurious indulgence which are known to every reader. The brave soldier, who in the perils of war could shake off all luxurious habits and could rival the commonest man in the cheerfulness with which he underwent every hardship, was seen no more. He sunk into an indolent voluptuary, pleased by childish amusements. At one time he would lounge in a boat at a fishing party, and laugh when he drew up pieces of salt fish which by the Queen's order had been attached to his hook by divers. At another time she wagered that she would consume ten million sesterces at one meal, and won her wager by dissolving in vinegar a pearl of unknown value. While Cleopatra bore the character of the goddess Isis, her lover appeared as Osiris. Her head was placed conjointly with his own on the coins which he issued as a Roman magistrate. He disposed of the kingdoms and principalities of the East by his sole word. By his influence Herod, son of Antipater, the Idumæan minister of Hyrcanus, the late sovereign of Judea, was made king to the exclusion of the rightful heir. Polemo, his own son by Cleopatra, was invested with the sceptre of Armenia. Encouraged by the absolute submission of her lover, Cleopatra fixed her eye upon the Capitol, and dreamed of winning by means of Antony that imperial crown which she had vainly sought from Cæsar.

While Antony was engaged in voluptuous dalliance, Octavian was resolutely pursuing the work of consolidating his power in the West. His patience, his industry, his attention to business, his affability, were winning golden opinions and rapidly obliterating all memory of the bloody work by which he had risen to power. He had won little glory in war; but so long as the corn fleets arrived daily from Sicily and Africa, the populace cared little whether the victory had been won by Octavian or by his generals. In Agrippa he possessed a consummate captain, in Mæcenas a wise and temperate minister. It is much to his credit that he never showed any jealousy of the men to whom he owed so much. He flattered the people with the hope that he would, when Antony had fulfilled his mission of recovering the standards of Crassus, engage him to join in putting an end to their sovereign power and restoring constitutional liberty.

In point of fidelity to his marriage vows Octavian was little better than Antony. He renounced his marriage with Clodia, the daughter of Fulvia, when her mother attempted to raise Italy against him. He divorced Scribonia, when it no longer suited him to court the favor of her kinsman. To replace this second wife, he forcibly took away Livia from her husband, Ti Claudius Nero, though she was at that time pregnant of her second son. But in this and other less pardonable immoralities there was nothing to shock the feelings of Romans.

But Octavian never suffered pleasure to divert him from business. If he could not be a successful general, he resolved at least to show that he could be a hardy soldier. While Antony in his Egyptian palace was neglecting the Parthian War, his rival led his legions in more than one dangerous campaign against the barbarous Dalmatians and Pannonians, who had been for some time infesting the province of Illyricum. In the year B.C. 33 he announced that the limits of the empire had been extended northward to the banks of the Save.

Octavian now began to feel that any appearance of friendship with Antony was a source of weakness rather than of strength at Rome. Misunderstandings had already broken out. Antony complained that Octavian had given him no share in the provinces wrested from Sext. Pompeius and Lepidus. Octavian retorted by accusing his colleague of appropriating Egypt and Armenia, and of increasing Cleopatra's power at the expense of the Roman Empire. Popular indignation rose to its height when Plancus and Titius, who had been admitted to Antony's confidence, passed over to Octavian, and disclosed the contents of their master's will. In that document Antony ordered that his body should be buried at Alexandria, in the mausoleum of Cleopatra. Men began to fancy that Cleopatra had already planted her throne upon the Capitol. These suspicions were sedulously encouraged by Octavian.

Before the close of B.C. 32, Octavian, by the authority of the senate, declared war nominally against Cleopatra. Antony, roused from his sleep by reports from Rome, passed over to Athens, issuing orders everywhere to levy men and collect ships for the impending struggle. At Athens he received news of the declaration of war, and replied by divorcing Octavia. His fleet was ordered to assemble at Corcyra; and his legions in the early spring prepared to pour into Epirus. He established his head-quarters at Patræ on the Corinthian Gulf.

But Antony, though his fleet was superior to that of Octavian, allowed Agrippa to sweep the Ionian Sea, and to take possession of Methone, in Messenia, as a station for a flying squadron to intercept Antony's communications with the East, nay, even to occupy Corcyra, which had been destined for his own place of rendezvous. Antony's fleet now anchored in the waters of the Ambracian Gulf, while his legions encamped on a spot of land which forms the northern horn of that spacious inlet. But the place chosen for the camp was unhealthy; and in the heats of early summer his army suffered greatly from disease. Agrippa lay close at hand watching his opportunity. In the course of the spring Octavian joined him in person.

Early in the season Antony had repaired from Patræ to his army, so as to be ready either to cross over into Italy or to meet the enemy if they attempted to land in Epirus. At first he showed something of his old military spirit, and the soldiers, who always loved his military frankness, warmed into enthusiasm; but his chief officers, won by Octavian or disgusted by the influence of Cleopatra, deserted him in such numbers that he knew not whom to trust, and gave up all thoughts of maintaining the contest with energy. Urged by Cleopatra, he resolved to carry off his fleet and abandon the army. All preparations were made in secret, and the great fleet put to sea on the 28th of August. For the four following days there was a strong gale from the south. Neither could Antony escape nor could Octavian put to sea against him from Corcyra. On the 2d of September, however, the wind fell, and Octavian's light vessels, by using their oars, easily came up with the unwieldy galleys of the eastern fleet. A battle was now inevitable.

Antony's ships were like impregnable fortresses to the assault of the slight vessels of Octavian; and, though they lay nearly motionless in the calm sea, little impression was made upon them. But about noon a breeze sprung up from the west; and Cleopatra, followed by sixty Egyptian ships, made sail in a southerly direction. Antony immediately sprang from his ship-of-war into a light galley and followed. Deserted by their commander, the captains of Antony's ships continued to resist desperately; nor was it till the greater part of them were set on fire that the contest was decided. Before evening closed, the whole fleet was destroyed; most of the men and all the treasure on board perished. A few days after, when the shameful flight of Antony was made known to his army, all his legions went over to the conqueror.

It was not for eleven months after the battle of Actium that Octavian entered the open gates of Alexandria. He had been employed in the interval in founding the city of Nicopolis to celebrate his victory on the northern horn of the Ambracian Gulf, in rewarding his soldiers, and settling the affairs of the provinces of the East. In the winter he returned to Italy, and it was midsummer, B.C. 30, before he arrived in Egypt.

When Antony and Cleopatra arrived off Alexandria they put a bold face upon the matter. Some time passed before the real state of the case was known; but it soon became plain that Egypt was at the mercy of the conqueror. The Queen formed all kinds of wild designs. One was to transport the ships that she had saved across the Isthmus of Suez and seek refuge in some distant land where the name of Rome was yet unknown. Some ships were actually drawn across, but they were destroyed by the Arabs, and the plan was abandoned. She now flattered herself that her powers of fascination, proved so potent over Cæsar and Antony, might subdue Octavian. Secret messages passed between the conqueror and the Queen; nor were Octavian's answers such as to banish hope.

Antony, full of repentance and despair, shut himself up in Pharos, and there remained in gloomy isolation.

In July, B.C. 30, Octavian appeared before Pelusium. The place was surrendered without a blow. Yet, at the approach of the conqueror, Antony put himself at the head of a division of cavalry and gained some advantage. But on his return to Alexandria he found that Cleopatra had given up all her ships; and no more opposition was offered. On the 1st of August (Sextilis, as it was then called) Octavian entered the open gates of Alexandria. Both Antony and Cleopatra sought to win him. Antony's messengers the conqueror refused to see; but he still used fair words to Cleopatra. The Queen had shut herself up in a sort of mausoleum built to receive her body after death, which was not approachable by any door; and it was given out that she was really dead. All the tenderness of old times revived in Antony's heart. He stabbed himself, and in a dying state ordered himself to be laid by the side of Cleopatra. The Queen, touched by pity, ordered her expiring lover to be drawn up by cords into her retreat, and bathed his temples with her tears.

After he had breathed his last, she consented to see Octavian. Her penetration soon told her that she had nothing to hope from him. She saw that his fair words were only intended to prevent her from desperate acts and reserve her for the degradation of his triumph. This impression was confirmed when all instruments by which death could be inflicted were found to have been removed from her apartments. But she was not to be so baffled. She pretended all submission; but when the ministers of Octavian came to carry her away, they found her lying dead upon her couch, attended by her faithful waiting-women, Iras and Charmion. The manner of her death was never ascertained; popular belief ascribed it to the bite of an asp which had been conveyed to her in a basket of fruit.

Thus died Antony and Cleopatra. Antony was by nature a genial, open-hearted Roman, a good soldier, quick, resolute, and vigorous, but reckless and self-indulgent, devoid alike of prudence and of principle. The corruptions of the age, the seductions of power, and the evil influence of Cleopatra paralyzed a nature capable of better things. We know him chiefly through the exaggerated assaults of Cicero in his *Philippic*, and the narratives of writers devoted to Octavian. But after all deductions for partial representation, enough remains to show that Antony had all the faults of Cæsar, with little of his redeeming greatness.

Cleopatra was an extraordinary person. At her death she was but thirty-eight years of age. Her power rested not so much on actual beauty as on her fascinating manners and her extreme readiness of wit. In her follies there was a certain magnificence which excites even a dull imagination. We may estimate the real power of her mental qualities by observing the impression her character made upon the Roman poets of the time. No meditated praises could have borne such testimony to her greatness as the lofty strain in which Horace celebrates her fall and congratulates the Roman world on its escape from the ruin which she was threatening to the Capitol.

Octavian dated the years of his imperial monarchy from the day of the battle of Actium. But it was not till two years after (the summer of B.C. 29) that he established himself in Rome as ruler of the Roman world. Then he celebrated three

magnificent triumphs, after the example of his uncle the great
dictator, for his victories in Dalmatia, at Actium, and in Egypt.
At the same time the temple of Janus was closed—notwithstanding that border wars still continued in Gaul and Spain—
for the first time since the year B.C. 235.   All men drew breath
more freely, and all except the soldiery looked forward to a time
of tranquillity.   Liberty and independence were forgotten
words.   After the terrible disorders of the last century, the
general cry was for quiet at any price.   Octavian was a person
admirably fitted to fulfil these aspirations.   His uncle Julius
was too fond of active exertion to play such a part well.   Octavian never shone in war, while his vigilant and patient mind
was well fitted for the discharge of business.   He avoided
shocking popular feeling by assuming any title savoring of roy-
alty; but he enjoyed by universal consent an authority more
than regal.

GERMANS UNDER ARMINIUS REVOLT AGAINST ROME

A.D. 9

SIR EDWARD SHEPHERD CREASY

The German race was beginning to make itself felt to a greater extent than hitherto in its efforts for freedom from the Roman rule. Research shows that from the earliest days there were two distinct peoples under this designation of *German* — the northern or Scandinavian, and the southern, being more truly the German. Both consisted of numerous tribes, the Romans giving separate names to each: from this arose the generic titles of *Franks*, *Bavarians*, *Alamanni*, and the rest.

They were great fighters and, as a natural sequence, mighty hunters. When warfare did not occupy their attention, hunting, feasting, and drinking took its place. Tacitus writes: "To drink continuously, night and day, was no shame for them." Their chief beverage was barley beer, though, in the South, wine was used to some extent.

Rome had garrisons throughout the whole land, and the fortunes of the Germans were at a low ebb. Freedom seemed stifled forever when Arminius led his forces against the Roman hosts in the forest of Teutoburgium. Rightly does Creasy rate this important battle so highly, for it meant the final uplifting of the Teuton, and with him the English-speaking races of a later time.

TO a truly illustrious Frenchman, whose reverses as a minister can never obscure his achievements in the world of letters, we are indebted for the most profound and most eloquent estimate that we possess of the importance of the Germanic element in European civilization, and of the extent to which the human race is indebted to those brave warriors who long were the unconquered antagonists, and finally became the conquerors, of imperial Rome.

Twenty-three eventful years have passed away since M. Guizot[1] delivered from the chair of modern history, at Paris, his course of lectures on the history of civilization in Europe.

[1] Guizot was minister of foreign affairs, and later (1848) prime minister, under Louis Philippe.

During those years the spirit of earnest inquiry into the germs and primary developments of existing institutions has become more and more active and universal, and the merited celebrity of M. Guizot's work has proportionally increased. Its admirable analysis of the complex political and social organizations of which the modern civilized world is made up must have led thousands to trace with keener interest the great crises of times past, by which the characteristics of the present were determined. The narrative of one of these great crises, of the epoch A.D. 9, when Germany took up arms for her independence against Roman invasion, has for us this special attraction—that it forms part of our own national history. Had Arminius been supine or unsuccessful, our Germanic ancestors would have been enslaved or exterminated in their original seats along the Eider and the Elbe. This island would never have borne the name of England, and " we, this great English nation, whose race and language are now overrunning the earth, from one end of it to the other," would have been utterly cut off from existence.

Arnold may, indeed, go too far in holding that we are wholly unconnected in race with the Romans and Britons who inhabited this country before the coming over of the Saxons; that, "nationally speaking, the history of Cæsar's invasion has no more to do with us than the natural history of the animals which then inhabited our forests." There seems ample evidence to prove that the Romanized Celts whom our Teutonic forefathers found here influenced materially the character of our nation. But the main stream of our people was, and is, Germanic. Our language alone decisively proves this. Arminius is far more truly one of our national heroes than Caractacus; and it was our own primeval fatherland that the brave German rescued when he slaughtered the Roman legions, eighteen centuries ago, in the marshy glens between the Lippe and the Ems.

Dark and disheartening, even to heroic spirits, must have seemed the prospects of Germany when Arminius planned the general rising of his countrymen against Rome. Half the land was occupied by Roman garrisons; and, what was worse, many of the Germans seemed patiently acquiescent in their state of bondage.   The braver portion, whose patriotism could be relied on, was ill-armed and undisciplined, while the enemy's troops consisted of veterans in the highest state of equipment and training, familiarized with victory and commanded by officers of proved skill and valor.   The resources of Rome seemed boundless; her tenacity of purpose was believed to be invincible.   There was no hope of foreign sympathy or aid; for "the self-governing powers that had filled the Old World had bent one after another before the rising power of Rome, and had vanished.   The earth seemed left void of independent nations."

The German chieftain knew well the gigantic power of the oppressor.   Arminius was no rude savage, fighting out of mere animal instinct or in ignorance of the might of his adversary. He was familiar with the Roman language and civilization; he had served in the Roman armies; he had been admitted to the Roman citizenship, and raised to the rank of the equestrian order.   It was part of the subtle policy of Rome to confer rank and privileges on the youth of the leading families in the nations which she wished to enslave.   Among other young German chieftains, Arminius and his brother, who were the heads of the noblest house in the tribe of the Cherusci, had been selected as fit objects for the exercise of this insidious system. Roman refinements and dignities succeeded in denationalizing the brother, who assumed the Roman name of Flavius, and adhered to Rome throughout all her wars against his country. Arminius remained unbought by honors or wealth, uncorrupted by refinement or luxury.   He aspired to and obtained from Roman enmity a higher title than ever could have been given him by Roman favor.   It is in the page of Rome's greatest historian that his name has come down to us with the proud addition of " *Liberator haud dubie Germaniæ.*"

Often must the young chieftain, while meditating the exploit which has thus immortalized him, have anxiously revolved in his mind the fate of the many great men who had been crushed in the attempt which he was about to renew—the attempt to stay the chariot wheels of triumphant Rome.   Could he hope to succeed where Hannibal and Mithradates had perished? What had been the doom of Viriathus? and what warning against vain valor was written on the desolate site where Numantia once had flourished? Nor was a caution wanting in scenes nearer home and more recent times. The Gauls had fruitlessly struggled for eight years against Cæsar; and the gallant Vercingetorix, who in the last year of the war had roused all his countrymen to insurrection, who had cut off Roman detachments, and brought Cæsar himself to the extreme of peril at Alesia—he, too, had finally succumbed, had been led captive in Cæsar's triumph, and had then been butchered in cold blood in a Roman dungeon.

It was true that Rome was no longer the great military republic which for so many ages had shattered the kingdoms of the world. Her system of government was changed, and, after a century of revolution and civil war, she had placed herself under the despotism of a single ruler. But the discipline of her troops was yet unimpaired and her warlike spirit seemed unabated. The first year of the empire had been signalized by conquests as valuable as any gained by the republic in a corresponding period. It is a great fallacy — though apparently sanctioned by great authorities — to suppose that the foreign policy pursued by Augustus was pacific; he certainly recommended such a policy to his successors (*incertum metu an per invidiam:* Tac., *Ann.,* i. 11), but he himself, until Arminius broke his spirit, had followed a very different course. Besides his Spanish wars, his generals, in a series of generally aggressive campaigns, had extended the Roman frontier from the Alps to the Danube, and had reduced into subjection the large and important countries that now form the territories of all Austria south of that river, and of East Switzerland, Lower Wuertemberg, Bavaria, the Valtelline, and the Tyrol.

While the progress of the Roman arms thus pressed the Germans from the south, still more formidable inroads had been made by the imperial legions on the west. Roman armies, moving from the province of Gaul, established a chain of fortresses along the right as well as the left bank of the Rhine, and, in a series of victorious campaigns, advanced their eagles as far as the Elbe, which now seemed added to the list of vassal rivers, to the Nile, the Rhine, the Rhone, the Danube, the Tagus, the Seine, and many more, that acknowledged the supremacy of the Tiber. Roman fleets also, sailing from the harbors of Gaul along the German coasts and up the estuaries, coöperated with the land forces of the empire, and seemed to display, even more decisively than her armies, her overwhelming superiority over the rude Germanic tribes. Throughout the territory thus invaded the Romans had with their usual military skill established fortified posts; and a powerful army of occupation was kept on foot, ready to move instantly on any spot where a popular outbreak might be attempted.

Vast, however, and admirably organized as the fabric of Roman power appeared on the frontiers and in the provinces, there was rottenness at the core. In Rome's unceasing hostilities with foreign foes, and still more in her long series of desolating civil wars, the free middle classes of Italy had almost wholly disappeared. Above the position which they had occupied, an oligarchy of wealth had reared itself; beneath that position a degraded mass of poverty and misery was fermenting. Slaves; the chance sweepings of every conquered country; shoals of Africans, Sardinians, Asiatics, Illyrians, and others made up the bulk of the population of the Italian peninsula.

The foulest profligacy of manners was general in all ranks. In universal weariness of revolution and civil war, and in consciousness of being too debased for self-government, the nation had submitted itself to the absolute authority of Augustus. Adulation was now the chief function of the senate; and the gifts of genius and accomplishments of art were devoted to the elaboration of eloquently false panegyrics upon the prince and his favorite courtiers. With bitter indignation must the German chieftain have beheld all this and contrasted with it the rough worth of his own countrymen: their bravery, their fidelity to their word, their manly independence of spirit, their love of their national free institutions, and their loathing of every pollution and meanness. Above all, he must have thought of the domestic virtues that hallowed a German home; of the respect there shown to the female character, and of the pure affection by which that respect was repaid. His soul must have burned within him at the contemplation of such a race yielding to these debased Italians.

Still, to persuade the Germans to combine, in spite of the frequent feuds among themselves, in one sudden outbreak against Rome; to keep the scheme concealed from the Romans until the hour for action arrived; and then, without possessing a single walled town, without military stores, without training, to teach his insurgent countrymen to defeat veteran armies and storm fortifications, seemed so perilous an enterprise that probably Arminius would have receded from it had not a stronger feeling even than patriotism urged him on. Among the Germans of high rank who had most readily submitted to the invaders and become zealous partisans of Roman authority was a chieftain named Segestes. His daughter, Thusnelda, was preëminent among the noble maidens of Germany. Arminius had sought her hand in marriage; but Segestes, who probably discerned the young chief's disaffection to Rome, forbade his suit, and strove to preclude all communication between him and his daughter. Thusnelda, however, sympathized far more with the heroic spirit of her lover than with the time-serving policy of her father. An elopement baffled the precautions of Segestes, who, disappointed in his hope of preventing the marriage, accused Arminius before the Roman governor of having carried off his daughter and of planning treason against Rome. Thus assailed, and dreading to see his bride torn from him by the officials of the foreign oppressor, Arminius delayed no longer, but bent all his energies to organize and execute a general insurrection of the great mass of his countrymen, who hitherto had submitted in sullen hatred to the Roman dominion.

A change of governors had recently taken place, which, while it materially favored the ultimate success of the insurgents, served, by the immediate aggravation of the Roman oppressions which it produced, to make the native population more universally eager to take arms. Tiberius, who was afterward emperor, had recently been recalled from the command in Germany and sent into Pannonia to put down a dangerous revolt which had broken out against the Romans in that province. The German patriots were thus delivered from the stern supervision of one of the most suspicious of mankind, and were also relieved from having to contend against the high military talents of a veteran commander, who thoroughly understood their national character, and also the nature of the country, which he himself had principally subdued.

In the room of Tiberius, Augustus sent into Germany Quintilius Varus, who had lately returned from the proconsulate of Syria. Varus was a true representative of the higher classes of the Romans, among whom a general taste for literature, a keen susceptibility to all intellectual gratifications, a minute acquaintance with the principles and practice of their own national jurisprudence, a careful training in the schools of the rhetoricians, and a fondness for either partaking in or watching the intellectual strife of forensic oratory had become generally diffused, without, however, having humanized the old Roman spirit of cruel indifference to human feelings and human sufferings, and without acting as the least checks on unprincipled avarice and ambition or on habitual and gross profligacy. Accustomed to govern the depraved and debased natives of Syria—a country where courage in man and virtue in woman had for centuries been unknown—Varus thought that he might gratify his licentious and rapacious passions with equal impunity among the high-minded sons and pure-spirited daughters of Germany. When the general of an army sets the example of outrages of this description, he is soon faithfully imitated by his officers, and surpassed by his still more brutal soldiery. The Romans now habitually indulged in those violations of the sanctity of the domestic shrine, and those insults upon honor and modesty, by which far less gallant spirits than those of our Teutonic ancestors have often been maddened into insurrection.

Arminius found among the other German chiefs many who sympathized with him in his indignation at their country's abasement, and many whom private wrongs had stung yet more deeply. There was little difficulty in collecting bold leaders for an attack on the oppressors, and little fear of the population not rising readily at those leaders' call. But to declare open war against Rome and to encounter Varus' army in a pitched battle would have been merely rushing upon certain destruction. Varus had three legions under him, a force which, after allowing for detachments, cannot be estimated at less than fourteen thousand Roman infantry. He had also eight or nine hundred Roman cavalry, and at least an equal number of horse and foot sent from the allied states, or raised among those provincials who had not received the Roman franchise.

It was not merely the number, but the quality of this force that made them formidable; and, however contemptible Varus might be as a general, Arminius well knew how admirably the Roman armies were organized and officered, and how perfectly the legionaries understood every manœuvre and every duty which the varying emergencies of a stricken field might require. Stratagem was, therefore, indispensable; and it was necessary to blind Varus to their schemes until a favorable opportunity should arrive for striking a decisive blow.

For this purpose, the German confederates frequented the head-quarters of Varus, which seem to have been near the centre of the modern country of Westphalia, where the Roman general conducted himself with all the arrogant security of the governor of a perfectly submissive province. There Varus gratified at once his vanity, his rhetorical tastes, and his avarice, by holding courts, to which he summoned the Germans for the settlement of all their disputes, while a bar of Roman advocates attended to argue the cases before the tribunal of Varus, who did not omit the opportunity of exacting court fees and accepting bribes. Varus trusted implicitly to the respect which the Germans pretended to pay to his abilities as a judge, and to the interest which they affected to take in the forensic eloquence of their conquerors.

Meanwhile a succession of heavy rains rendered the country more difficult for the operations of regular troops, and Arminius, seeing that the infatuation of Varus was complete, secretly directed the tribes near the Weser and the Ems to take up arms in open revolt against the Romans. This was represented to Varus as an occasion which required his prompt attendance at the spot; but he was kept in studied ignorance of its being part of a concerted national rising; and he still looked on Arminius as his submissive vassal, whose aid he might rely on in facilitating the march of his troops against the rebels and in extinguishing the local disturbance. He therefore set his army in motion, and marched eastward in a line parallel to the course of the Lippe. For some distance his route lay along a level plain; but on arriving at the tract between the curve of the upper part of that stream and the sources of the Ems, the country assumes a very different character; and here, in the

territory of the modern little principality of Lippe, it was that
Arminius had fixed the scene of his enterprise.

A wooded and hilly region intervenes between the heads
of the two rivers, and forms the water-shed of their streams.
This region still retains the name (Teutobergenwald = *Teuto-
bergiensis saltus*) which it bore in the days of Arminius. The
nature of the ground has probably also remained unaltered.
The eastern part of it, round Detmold, the modern capital of
the principality of Lippe, is described by a modern German
scholar, Dr. Plate, as being a "table-land intersected by numerous deep and narrow valleys, which in some places form small
plains, surrounded by steep mountains and rocks, and only accessible by narrow defiles. All the valleys are traversed by
rapid streams, shallow in the dry season, but subject to sudden
swellings in autumn and winter. The vast forests which cover
the summits and slopes of the hills consist chiefly of oak; there
is little underwood, and both men and horse would move with
ease in the forests if the ground were not broken by gulleys or
rendered impracticable by fallen trees." This is the district to
which Varus is supposed to have marched; and Dr. Plate adds
that "the names of several localities on and near that spot
seem to indicate that a great battle had once been fought there.
We find the names ' *das Winnefeld*' (the field of victory), '*die
Knochenbahn*' (the bone-lane), '*die Knochenleke*' (the bone-
brook), '*der Mordkessel*' (the kettle of slaughter), and others."

Contrary to the usual strict principles of Roman discipline,
Varus had suffered his army to be accompanied and impeded
by an immense train of baggage wagons and by a rabble of
camp followers, as if his troops had been merely changing their
quarters in a friendly country. When the long array quitted
the firm, level ground and began to wind its way among the
woods, the marshes, and the ravines, the difficulties of the
march, even without the intervention of an armed foe, became
fearfully apparent. In many places the soil, sodden with rain,
was impracticable for cavalry and even for infantry, until trees
had been felled and a rude causeway formed through the mo-
rass.

The duties of the engineer were familiar to all who served
in the Roman armies. But the crowd and confusion of the

columns embarrassed the working parties of the soldiery, and in the midst of their toil and disorder the word was suddenly passed through their ranks that the rear-guard was attacked by the barbarians. Varus resolved on pressing forward; but a heavy discharge of missiles from the woods on either flank taught him how serious was the peril, and he saw his best men falling round him without the opportunity of retaliation; for his light-armed auxiliaries, who were principally of Germanic race, now rapidly deserted, and it was impossible to deploy the legionaries on such broken ground for a charge against the enemy.

Choosing one of the most open and firm spots which they could force their way to, the Romans halted for the night; and, faithful to their national discipline and tactics, formed their camp amid the harassing attacks of the rapidly thronging foes with the elaborate toil and systematic skill the traces of which are impressed permanently on the soil of so many European countries, attesting the presence in the olden time of the imperial eagles.

On the morrow the Romans renewed their march, the veteran officers who served under Varus now probably directing the operations and hoping to find the Germans drawn up to meet them, in which case they relied on their own superior discipline and tactics for such a victory as should reassure the supremacy of Rome. But Arminius was far too sage a commander to lead on his followers, with their unwieldy broadswords and inefficient defensive armor, against the Roman legionaries, fully armed with helmet, cuirass, greaves, and shield, who were skilled to commence the conflict with a murderous volley of heavy javelins hurled upon the foe when a few yards distant, and then, with their short cut-and-thrust swords, to hew their way through all opposition, preserving the utmost steadiness and coolness, and obeying each word of command in the midst of strife and slaughter with the same precision and alertness as if upon parade. Arminius suffered the Romans to march out from their camp, to form first in line for action and then in column for marching, without the show of opposition.

For some distance Varus was allowed to move on, only harassed by slight skirmishes, but struggling with difficulty through the broken ground, the toil and distress of his men being aggravated by heavy torrents of rain, which burst upon the devoted legions, as if the angry gods of Germany were pouring out the vials of their wrath upon the invaders. After some little time their van approached a ridge of high wooded ground, which is one of the offshoots of the great Hercynian forest, and is situated between the modern villages of Driburg and Bielefeld. Arminius had caused barricades of hewn trees to be formed here, so as to add to the natural difficulties of the passage. Fatigue and discouragement now began to betray themselves in the Roman ranks. Their line became less steady; baggage wagons were abandoned from the impossibility of forcing them along; and, as this happened, many soldiers left their ranks and crowded round the wagons to secure the most valuable portions of their property; each was busy about his own affairs, and purposely slow in hearing the word of command from his officers.

Arminius now gave the signal for a general attack. The fierce shouts of the Germans pealed through the gloom of the forests, and in thronging multitudes they assailed the flanks of the invaders, pouring in clouds of darts on the encumbered legionaries as they struggled up the glens or floundered in the morasses, and watching every opportunity of charging through the intervals of the disjointed column, and so cutting off the communication between its several brigades. Arminius, with a chosen band of personal retainers round him, cheered on his countrymen by voice and example. He and his men aimed their weapons particularly at the horses of the Roman cavalry. The wounded animals, slipping about in the mire and their own blood, threw their riders and plunged among the ranks of the legions, disordering all round them. Varus now ordered the troops to be countermarched, in the hope of reaching the nearest Roman garrison on the Lippe.

But retreat now was as impracticable as advance; and the falling back of the Romans only augmented the courage of their assailants and caused fiercer and more frequent charges on the flanks of the disheartened army. The Roman officer who commanded the cavalry, Numonius Vala, rode off with his squadrons in the vain hope of escaping by thus abandoning his comrades. Unable to keep together or force their way across the woods and swamps, the horsemen were overpowered in detail and slaughtered to the last man. The Roman infantry still held together and resisted, but more through the instinct of discipline and bravery than from any hope of success or escape.

Varus, after being severely wounded in a charge of the Germans against his part of the column, committed suicide to avoid falling into the hands of those whom he had exasperated by his oppressions. One of the lieutenants-general of the army fell fighting; the other surrendered to the enemy. But mercy to a fallen foe had never been a Roman virtue, and those among her legions who now laid down their arms in hope of quarter, drank deep of the cup of suffering, which Rome had held to the lips of many a brave but unfortunate enemy. The infuriated Germans slaughtered their oppressors with deliberate ferocity, and those prisoners who were not hewn to pieces on the spot were only preserved to perish by a more cruel death in cold blood.

The bulk of the Roman army fought steadily and stubbornly, frequently repelling the masses of assailants, but gradually losing the compactness of their array and becoming weaker and weaker beneath the incessant shower of darts and the reiterated assaults of the vigorous and unencumbered Germans. At last, in a series of desperate attacks, the column was pierced through and through, two of the eagles captured, and the Roman host, which on the morning before had marched forth in such pride and might—now broken up into confused fragments —either fell fighting beneath the overpowering numbers of the enemy or perished in the swamps and woods in unavailing efforts at flight. Few, very few, ever saw again the left bank of the Rhine. One body of brave veterans, arraying themselves in a ring on a little mound, beat off every charge of the Germans, and prolonged their honorable resistance to the close of that dreadful day. The traces of a feeble attempt at forming a ditch and mound attested in after-years the spot where the last of the Romans passed their night of suffering and despair But on the morrow this remnant also, worn out with hunger, wounds, and toil, was charged by the victorious Germans, and either massacred on the spot or offered up in fearful rites on the altars of the deities of the old mythology of the North.

A gorge in the mountain ridge, through which runs the modern road between Paderborn and Pyrmont, leads from the spot where the heat of the battle raged to the Extersteine—a cluster of bold and grotesque rocks of sandstone—near which is a small sheet of water, overshadowed by a grove of aged trees. According to local tradition, this was one of the sacred groves of the ancient Germans, and it was here that the Roman captives were slain in sacrifice by the victorious warriors of Arminius.

Never was victory more decisive; never was the liberation of an oppressed people more instantaneous and complete. Throughout Germany the Roman garrisons were assailed and cut off; and within a few weeks after Varus had fallen, the German soil was freed from the foot of an invader.

At Rome the tidings of the battle were received with an agony of terror, the reports of which we would deem exaggerated did they not come from Roman historians themselves. They not only tell emphatically how great was the awe which the Romans felt of the prowess of the Germans if their various tribes could be brought to unite for a common purpose,[1] but they also reveal how weakened and debased the population of Italy had become. Dion Cassius says: "Then Augustus, when he heard the calamity of Varus, rent his garment, and was in great affliction for the troops he had lost, and for terror respecting the Germans and the Gauls. And his chief alarm was that he expected them to push on against Italy and Rome; and there remained no Roman youth fit for military duty that were worth speaking of, and the allied populations, that were at all serviceable, had been wasted away. Yet he prepared for the emergency as well as his means allowed; and when none of the citizens of military age were willing to enlist, he made them cast lots, and punished, by confiscation of goods and disfranchisement, every fifth man among those under thirty-five and every tenth man of those above that age. At last, when he found that not even thus could he make many come forward,

[1] It is clear that the Romans followed the policy of fomenting dissensions and wars of the Germans among themselves.

he put some of them to death. So he made a conscription of discharged veterans and of emancipated slaves, and, collecting as large a force as he could, sent it, under Tiberius, with all speed into Germany."

Dion mentions, also, a number of terrific portents that were believed to have occurred at the time, and the narration of which is not immaterial, as it shows the state of the public mind when such things were so believed in and so interpreted. The summits of the Alps were said to have fallen, and three columns of fire to have blazed up from them. In the Campus Martius, the temple of the war-god, from whom the founder of Rome had sprung, was struck by a thunderbolt. The nightly heavens glowed several times as if on fire. Many comets blazed forth together; and fiery meteors, shaped like spears, had shot from the northern quarter of the sky down into the Roman camps. It was said, too, that a statue of Victory, which had stood at a place on the frontier, pointing the way toward Germany, had of its own accord turned round, and now pointed to Italy. These and other prodigies were believed by the multitude to accompany the slaughter of Varus' legions and to manifest the anger of the gods against Rome.

Augustus himself was not free from superstition; but on this occasion no supernatural terrors were needed to increase the alarm and grief that he felt, and which made him, even months after the news of the battle had arrived, often beat his head against the wall and exclaim, " Quintilius Varus, give me back my legions." We learn this from his biographer Suetonius; and, indeed, every ancient writer who alludes to the overthrow of Varus attests the importance of the blow against the Roman power, and the bitterness with which it was felt.

The Germans did not pursue their victory beyond their own territory; but that victory secured at once and forever the independence of the Teutonic race. Rome sent, indeed, her legions again into Germany, to parade a temporary superiority, but all hopes of permanent conquests were abandoned by Augustus and his successors.

The blow which Arminius had struck never was forgotten. Roman fear disguised itself under the specious title of moderation, and the Rhine became the acknowledged boundary of the two nations until the fifth century of our era, when the Germans became the assailants, and carved with their conquering swords the provinces of imperial Rome into the kingdoms of modern Europe.

ARMINIUS

I have said above that the great Cheruscan is more truly one of our national heroes than Caractacus is. It may be added that an Englishman is entitled to claim a closer degree of relationship with Arminius than can be claimed by any German of modern Germany. The proof of this depends on the proof of four facts: First, that the Cheruscans were Old Saxons, or Saxons of the interior of Germany; secondly, that the Anglo-Saxons, or Saxons of the coast of Germany, were more closely akin than other German tribes were to the Cheruscan Saxons; thirdly, that the Old Saxons were almost exterminated by Charlemagne; fourthly, that the Anglo-Saxons are our immediate ancestors. The last of these may be assumed as an axiom in English history. The proofs of the other three are partly philological and partly historical. It may be, however, here remarked that the present Saxons of Germany are of the *High* Germanic division of the German race, whereas both the Anglo-Saxon and Old Saxon were of the *Low* Germanic.

Being thus the nearest heirs of the glory of Arminius, we may fairly devote more attention to his career than, in such a work as the present, could be allowed to any individual leader; and it is interesting to trace how far his fame survived during the Middle Ages, both among the Germans of the Continent and among ourselves.

It seems probable that the jealousy with which Maroboduus, the king of the Suevi and Marcomanni, regarded Arminius, and which ultimately broke out into open hostilities between those German tribes and the Cherusci, prevented Arminius from leading the confederate Germans to attack Italy after his first victory. Perhaps he may have had the rare moderation of being content with the liberation of his country, without seeking to retaliate on her former oppressors. When Tiberius marched into Germany in the year 10, Arminius was too cautious to attack him on ground favorable to the legions, and Tiberius was too skilful to entangle his troops in the difficult parts of the country. His march and countermarch were as unresisted as they were unproductive. A few years later, when a dangerous revolt of the Roman legions near the frontier caused their generals to find them active employment by leading them into the interior of Germany, we find Arminius again active in his country's defence. The old quarrel between him and his father-in-law, Segestes, had broken out afresh.

Segestes now called in the aid of the Roman general, Germanicus, to whom he surrendered himself; and by his contrivance, his daughter, Thusnelda, the wife of Arminius, also came into the hands of the Romans, she being far advanced in pregnancy. She showed, as Tacitus relates, more of the spirit of her husband than of her father, a spirit that could not be subdued into tears or supplications. She was sent to Ravenna, and there gave birth to a son, whose life we know, from an allusion in Tacitus, to have been eventful and unhappy; but the part of the great historian's work which narrated his fate has perished, and we only know from another quarter that the son of Arminius was, at the age of four years, led captive in a triumphal pageant along the streets of Rome.

The high spirit of Arminius was goaded almost into frenzy by these bereavements. The fate of his wife, thus torn from him, and of his babe doomed to bondage even before its birth, inflamed the eloquent invectives with which he roused his countrymen against the home-traitors, and against their invaders, who thus made war upon women and children. Germanicus had marched his army to the place where Varus had perished, and had there paid funeral honors to the ghastly relics of his predecessor's legions that he found heaped around him.[1] Arminius lured him to advance a little farther into the country, and then assailed him, and fought a battle, which, by the Roman accounts, was a drawn one.

The effect of it was to make Germanicus resolve on retreating to the Rhine. He himself, with part of his troops, embarked in some vessels on the Ems, and returned by that river,

[1] In the Museum of Rhenish Antiquities at Bonn there is a Roman sepulchral monument the inscription on which records that it was erected to the memory of M. Cœlius, who fell " *Bello Variano.*"

and then by sea; but part of his forces were intrusted to a Roman general named Cæcina, to lead them back by land to the
Rhine.   Arminius followed this division on its march, and
fought several battles with it, in which he inflicted heavy loss
on the Romans, captured the greater part of their baggage,
and would have destroyed them completely had not his skilful
system of operations been finally thwarted by the haste of In-
guiomerus, a confederate German chief, who insisted on assault-
ing the Romans in their camp, instead of waiting till they were
entangled in the difficulties of the country, and assailing their
columns on the march.

In the following year the Romans were inactive, but in the
year afterward Germanicus led a fresh invasion.   He placed
his army on shipboard and sailed to the mouth of the Ems,
where he disembarked and marched to the Weser, there encamping, probably in the neighborhood of Minden.   Arminius had collected his army on the other side of the river; and
a scene occurred, which is powerfully told by Tacitus, and which
is the subject of a beautiful poem by Praed.   It has been
already mentioned that the brother of Arminius, like himself,
had been trained up while young to serve in the Roman armies;
but, unlike Arminius, he not only refused to quit the Roman
service for that of his country, but fought against his country
with the legions of Germanicus.   He had assumed the Roman
name of Flavius, and had gained considerable distinction in the
Roman service, in which he had lost an eye from a wound in
battle.   When the Roman outposts approached the river Weser, Arminius called out to them from the opposite bank and
expressed a wish to see his brother.   Flavius stepped forward,
and Arminius ordered his own followers to retire, and requested
that the archers should be removed from the Roman bank of
the river.   This was done; and the brothers, who apparently
had not seen each other for some years, began a conversation
from the opposite sides of the stream, in which Arminius ques-
tioned his brother respecting the loss of his eye, and what battle it had been lost in, and what reward he had received for his
wound.   Flavius told him how the eye was lost, and mentioned
the increased pay that he had on account of its loss, and showed
the collar and other military decorations that had been given

him Arminius mocked at these as badges of slavery; and then each began to try to win the other over—Flavius boasting the power of Rome and her generosity to the submissive; Arminius appealing to him in the name of their country's gods, of the mother that had borne them, and by the holy names of fatherland and freedom, not to prefer being the betrayer to being the champion of his country. They soon proceeded to mutual taunts and menaces, and Flavius called aloud for his horse and his arms, that he might dash across the river and attack his brother; nor would he have been checked from doing so had not the Roman general Stertinius run up to him and forcibly detained him. Arminius stood on the other bank, threatening the renegade, and defying him to battle.

I shall not be thought to need apology for quoting here the stanzas in which Praed has described this scene—a scene among the most affecting, as well as the most striking, that history supplies. It makes us reflect on the desolate position of Arminius, with his wife and child captives in the enemy's hands, and with his brother a renegade in arms against him. The great liberator of our German race was there, with every source of human happiness denied him except the consciousness of doing his duty to his country.

> " Back, back ! he fears not foaming flood
>   Who fears not steel-clad line :
> No warrior thou of German blood,
>   No brother thou of mine.
> Go, earn Rome's chain to load thy neck,
>   Her gems to deck thy hilt ;
> And blazon honor's hapless wreck
>   With all the gauds of guilt.

> " But wouldst thou have *me* share the prey ?
>   By all that I have done,
> The Varian bones that day by day
>   Lie whitening in the sun,
> The legion's trampled panoply,
>   The eagle's shatter'd wing—
> I would not be for earth or sky
>   So scorn'd and mean a thing.

"Ho, call me here the wizard, boy,
    Of dark and subtle skill,
To agonize but not destroy,
    To torture, not to kill.
When swords are out and shriek and shout
    Leave little room for prayer,
No fetter on man's arm or heart
    Hangs half so heavy there.

"I curse him by the gifts the land
    Hath won from him and Rome,
The riving axe, the wasting brand,
    Rent forest, blazing home.
I curse him by our country's gods,
    The terrible, the dark,
The breakers of the Roman rods,
    The smiters of the bark.

"Oh, misery that such a ban
    On such a brow should be !
Why comes he not in battle's van
    His country's chief to be ?
To stand a comrade by my side,
    The sharer of my fame,
And worthy of a brother's pride
    And of a brother's name ?

"But it is past ! where heroes press
    And cowards bend the knee,
Arminius is not brotherless,
    His brethren are the free.
They come around : one hour, and light
    Will fade from turf and tide,
Then onward, onward to the fight,
    With darkness for our guide.

"To-night, to-night, when we shall meet
    In combat face to face,
Then only would Arminius greet
    The renegade's embrace.
The canker of Rome's guilt shall be
    Upon his dying name ;
And as he lived in slavery,
    So shall he fall in shame."

On the day after the Romans had reached the Weser, Germanicus led his army across that river, and a partial encounter took place, in which Arminius was successful. But on the succeeding day a general action was fought, in which Arminius was severely wounded and the German infantry routed with heavy loss. The horsemen of the two armies encountered without either party gaining the advantage. But the Roman army remained master of the ground and claimed a complete victory. Germanicus erected a trophy in the field, with a vaunting inscription that the nations between the Rhine and the Elbe had been thoroughly conquered by his army. But that army speedily made a final retreat to the left bank of the Rhine; nor was the effect of their campaign more durable than their trophy. The sarcasm with which Tacitus speaks of certain other triumphs of Roman generals over Germans may apply to the pageant which Germanicus celebrated on his return to Rome from his command of the Roman army of the Rhine. The Germans were "*triumphati potius quam victi.*"

After the Romans had abandoned their attempts on Germany, we find Arminius engaged in hostilities with Maroboduus, king of the Suevi and Marcomanni, who was endeavoring to bring the other German tribes into a state of dependency on him. Arminius was at the head of the Germans who took up arms against this home invader of their liberties. After some minor engagements a pitched battle was fought between the two confederacies (A.D. 19) in which the loss on each side was equal, but Maroboduus confessed the ascendency of his antagonist by avoiding a renewal of the engagement and by imploring the intervention of the Romans in his defence. The younger Drusus then commanded the Roman legions in the province of Illyricum, and by his mediation a peace was concluded between Arminius and Maroboduus, by the terms of which it is evident that the latter must have renounced his ambitious schemes against the freedom of the other German tribes.

Arminius did not long survive this second war of independence, which he successfully waged for his country. He was assassinated in the thirty-seventh year of his age by some of his own kinsmen, who conspired against him. Tacitus says that this happened while he was engaged in a civil war, which had been caused by his attempts to make himself king over his countrymen.   It is far more probable, as one of the best biographers [1] has observed, that Tacitus misunderstood an attempt of Arminius to extend his influence as elective war chieftain of the Cherusci and other tribes, for an attempt to obtain the royal dignity.

When we remember that his father-in-law and his brother were renegades, we can well understand that a party among his kinsmen may have been bitterly hostile to him, and have opposed his authority with the tribe by open violence, and, when that seemed ineffectual, by secret assassination.

Arminius left a name which the historians of the nation against which he combated so long and so gloriously have delighted to honor.   It is from the most indisputable source, from the lips of enemies, that we know his exploits.[2]   His countrymen made history, but did not write it.   But his memory lived among them in the days of their bards, who recorded

> " The deeds he did, the fields he won,
>   The freedom he restored."

Tacitus, writing years after the death of Arminius, says of him, " *Canitur adhuc barbaras apud gentes.*"   As time passed on, the gratitude of ancient Germany to her great deliverer grew into adoration, and divine honors were paid for centuries to Arminius by every tribe of the Low Germanic division of the Teutonic races.   The *Irmin-sul,* or the column of Herman, near Eresburgh (the modern Stadtberg), was the chosen object of worship to the descendants of the Cherusci (the Old Saxons), and in defence of which they fought most desperately against Charlemagne and his Christianized Franks.   "Irmin, in the cloudy Olympus of Teutonic belief, appears as a king and a warrior; and the pillar, the ' Irmin-sul,' bearing the statue, and considered as the symbol of the deity, was the Palladium of the Saxon nation until the temple of Eresburgh was destroyed by Charlemagne, and the column itself transferred to the monastery of Corbey, where perhaps a portion of the rude rock idol

[1] Dr. Plate, in *Biographical Dictionary.*
[2] Tacitus : *Annales.*

yet remains, covered by the ornaments of the Gothic era." [1] Traces of the worship of Arminius are to be found among our Anglo-Saxon ancestors after their settlement in this island. One of the four great highways was held to be under the protection of the deity, and was called the "Irmin street." The name *Arminius* is, of course, the mere Latinized form of *Herman*, the name by which the hero and the deity were known by every man of Low German blood on either side of the German Sea. It means, etymologically, the *War-man*, the *man of hosts*. No other explanation of the worship of the Irmin-sul, and of the name of the Irmin street, is so satisfactory as that which connects them with the deified Arminius. We know for certain of the existence of other columns of an analogous character. Thus there was the *Roland-seule* in North Germany; there was a *Thor-seule* in Sweden, and (what is more important) there was an *Athelstan-seule* in Saxon England. [2]

[1] Palgrave: *English Commonwealth.*
[2] Lappenburg: *Anglo-Saxons.*

CHRONOLOGY OF UNIVERSAL HISTORY

EMBRACING THE PERIOD COVERED IN THIS VOLUME

B.C. 450–A.D. 12

JOHN RUDD, LL.D.

CHRONOLOGY OF UNIVERSAL HISTORY

EMBRACING THE PERIOD COVERED IN THIS VOLUME

B.C. 450–A.D. 12

JOHN RUDD, LL.D.

Events treated at length are here indicated in large type; the numerals following give volume and page.

Separate chronologies of the various nations, and of the careers of famous persons, will be found in the INDEX VOLUME, with volume and page references showing where the several events are fully treated.

B.C.

450. The decemvirate instituted at Rome; the Twelve Tables of law framed. See "INSTITUTION AND FALL OF THE DECEMVIRATE IN ROME," ii, 1.

Alcibiades born.*

448. First Sacred War between the Phocians and Delphians for the possession of the temple at Delphi.

The decemvirate abolished at Rome. See "INSTITUTION AND FALL OF THE DECEMVIRATE IN ROME," ii, 1.

Athens is now the principal seat of Greek philosophy, literature, and art.

447. The Bœotians defeat the Athenians at Coronea; the conflict was brought about by Athens breaking the truce arranged between the Greek states to endure for five years, in order to combine against Persia. The result was the loss to Athens of Bœotia, Phocis, and Locris.

445.* Nehemiah begins the rebuilding of the walls of Jerusalem.

Peace of Callias between the Greeks and Persians.

Birth of Xenophon, general and historian.

444. Ascendency of Pericles at Athens.* See "PERICLES RULES IN ATHENS," ii, 12.

The military tribunes instituted at Rome. The consulship was in no sense abolished; until the passage of the Licinian Rogations (when it reappeared as a permanent annual magistracy) it alternated irregularly

* Date uncertain.

387

with the military tribunes. See "INSTITUTION AND FALL OF THE DE-CEMVIRATE IN ROME," ii, 1.

Thucydides exiled Athens.

443. An Athenian colony planted at Thurium, near Sybarius; it is accompanied by Herodotus and Lysias.

442. Pericles, guided by Phidias the sculptor, adorns Athens; the Parthenon, Propylæa, and Odeum built.

440. Samos resists the Athenian sway; is besieged by Pericles and Sophocles; Melissus defends the city, but surrenders after a siege of nine months.

Comedies prohibited performance at Athens.

439. Great famine in Rome; Sp. Mælius distributes corn to the citizens, for which he is accused of wishing to be king, and is assassinated by Servilius Ahala.

438. Spartacus becomes king of Bosporus.

Ahala impeached and exiled Rome.

437. The prohibition of comedy repealed at Athens.

Syracuse, the predominant state in Sicily, reaches the height of its prosperity. See "DEFEAT OF THE ATHENIANS AT SYRACUSE," ii, 48.

436. Commencement of the dispute between Corinth and Corcyra regarding the city of Epidamnus, in which Athens supported the latter: this led to the Peloponnesian War.

435. Naval victory over the Corinthians by the Corcyræans, near Actium.

432. Ambassadors from Corcyra implore the aid of Athens, which sends a fleet to defend the island against the Corinthian attack. Corinth incites Potidæa to revolt from Athens.

431. Beginning of the Peloponnesian War. Sparta declares on the side of Corinth and makes war on Athens. The real cause of the war—which was to be so disastrous to Greece—was that Sparta and its allies were jealous of the great power Athens had attained. Sparta was an oligarchy and a friend of the nobles everywhere; Athens was a democracy and the friend of the common people; so that the war was to some extent a struggle between these classes all over Greece.

430. "GREAT PLAGUE AT ATHENS." See ii, 34. The physician Hippocrates distinguishes himself by extraordinary cures of the sick.

Second invasion of Attica by the Spartans.

429. Death of Pericles, during the plague, at Athens.

Potidæa reduced by the Athenians.

Birth of Plato.

428. Attica invaded the third time.

Lesbos revolts from the Athenian confederacy; on this the Athenians besiege Mitylene.

427. Mitylene reduced; Athens becomes master of Lesbos. Platæa, the ally of Athens, after being besieged, surrenders to the Peloponnesians and is destroyed.

Attica again invaded.

425. Agis begins the fifth invasion of Attica; he retires on learning that the Athenians under Cleon had taken Pylos and Sapachteria.

Mount Ætna in eruption.

On the death of Artaxerxes I, his son, Xerxes II, succeeds him as ruler of Persia; he reigns only forty-five days, being slain by his brother Sogdianus, who usurps the throne.

424. The island of Cythera taken by the Athenians.   Brasidas, the Spartan general, captures Amphipolis, defeating Thucydides.

Ochus (Darius Nothus) rids himself of Sogdianus and succeeds him on the Persian throne.

423. The Athenians banish Thucydides for having suffered Amphipolis to be taken.

422. The Athenians send Cleon to recover Amphipolis; he is defeated by Brasidas; both fall in the battle.

421. Peace of Nicias between Sparta and Athens.   End of the first period of the Peloponnesian War.

420. Alcibiades negotiates an alliance between Athens and Argos. Amphipolis retained by the Spartans.

419. An Athenian expedition is led into the Peloponnesus by Alcibiades.

418. Victory of the Spartans at Mantinea.

The league between Athens and Argos dissolved.

416. The island of Melos, which had remained neutral, is conquered by the Athenians; its inhabitants are treated with extreme cruelty.

415. The Athenians send an expedition against Syracuse under Nicias, Lamachus, and Alcibiades; the latter is recalled to answer an accusation of having broken some statues of Mercury in Athens; he takes refuge in Sparta.   Andocides, the orator, implicated in the same charge, is imprisoned and exiled.

414. Syracuse is invested by the Athenians under Nicias; being hard pressed, Syracuse appeals to the other Greek states; Gylippus, the Spartan commander, comes with a fleet to the aid of the city.   See " DEFEAT OF THE ATHENIANS AT SYRACUSE," ii, 48.

The Romans capture Bolæ, an Æquian town; the division of the booty causes a mutiny among the soldiers, who slay the quæstor and the military tribune, M. Postumius.

413. On Alcibiades' advice the Spartans fortify a position at Decelea, in Attica.

" DEFEAT OF THE ATHENIANS AT SYRACUSE."   See ii, 48.

412. Alcibiades visits the Persian satrap Tissaphernes, with whose aid he negotiates an alliance between Persia and Sparta.

411. Owing to the machinations of Alcibiades a revolt is organized in Athens, by the aid of the clubs of the nobles and rich men; its object being to overthrow the democracy and establish an oligarchy.   The rising is successful and the " Reign of the Four Hundred " ensues; it lasts four months; its framer, Antipho, is put to death.   Alcibiades is recalled.

410. The Spartans are defeated by Alcibiades in a naval encounter at Cyzicus. Sparta makes overtures for peace.

409. The Carthaginians invade Sicily; they reduce Silenus and Himera.

408. Alcibiades takes Selymbria and Byzantium.

Psammeticus is king of Egypt.

Roman plebs first admitted to the quæstorship.

407. Lysander, the Spartan admiral, defeats the Athenian fleet at Notium; in consequence of this defeat, Alcibiades, who had been received with great honor, is banished, and ten generals are nominated to succeed him.

406. The Athenians vanquish the Spartan fleet under Callicratidas, at Arginusæ. The Athenian generals are executed at Athens for not saving the shattered vessels and the bodies of the slain.

Dionysius the Elder becomes ruler of Syracuse.

Anxur and other towns captured by the Romans, who now first give their soldiers a regular pay.

405. The Spartans under Lysander, who had been restored to command, annihilate the Athenian navy at Ægospotami.

Artaxerxes II succeeds Darius II on the Persian throne.

Successful revolt of the Egyptians against the Persians; the independence of Egypt secured.

404. Athens taken by Lysander and dismantled; thirty tyrants appointed by him. Lysias and other orators banished. End of the Peloponnesian War.

403. Democracy is restored in Athens by Thrasybulus; he publishes an act of amnesty. The Ionian alphabet adopted at Athens.

401. Cyrus rebels against his brother Artaxerxes, of Persia; he is defeated and slain at the battle of Cunaxa.

400. The Ten Thousand Greek auxiliaries of Cyrus effect their retreat to the sea. See " RETREAT OF THE TEN THOUSAND GREEKS," ii, 68.

399. Sparta and Persia engage in war.

" CONDEMNATION AND DEATH OF SOCRATES." See ii, 87.

396. Agesilaus, the Spartan general, begins his victorious campaigns against the Persians.

The Romans, headed by Camillus, capture Veii, after a ten years' siege.

395. Corinth, Thebes, Argos, and Athens combine against Sparta; the Spartans are defeated at Haliartus; Lysander is slain.

Tissaphernes' Persian army is defeated by Agesilaus, near Sardis.

394. The Athenian admiral Conon, in charge of the Persian fleet, crushingly defeats that of the Spartans, under Pisander, off Cnidus.

Agesilaus is recalled from Asia; commanding the Spartans, he gains a victory over the confederate Greeks at Coronea.

393. Conon undertakes the rebuilding of the walls in Athens and restores the fortifications.

392. Conon excites the jealousy of the Persians; he retires into Cyprus, where he dies.

391. Camillus banished from Rome, charged with misappropriating the booty secured at Veii, but really on account of his patrician haughtiness; he dies at Ardea, whither he had withdrawn.

389. Æschines born; he was accounted in Athens second only to Demosthenes as an orator.

388 [1] (387). Brennus, commanding the Gauls, burns Rome. See "BRENNUS BURNS ROME," ii, 110.

387. Through the mediation of Persia, Sparta compels the Greek states to accept the peace of Antalcidas, which leaves the Ionian cities and Cyprus at his mercy; this enables Sparta to maintain her supremacy in Greece.

385. * Birth of Demosthenes, the famous Greek orator and general.

384. Aristotle born.

383. War of Syracuse with Carthage.

Thebes is betrayed to Sparta, during her war against Olynthus.

379. The Olynthians are forced to submission by the Spartans. Pelopidas and his associates drive the Spartans from Thebes.

378. Athens declares in favor of Thebes against Sparta.

376. Cleombrotus leads the Spartans into Bœotia; the Spartan fleet, under Pollis, is overwhelmed off Maxos, by Chabrias.

371. Congress of Sparta, Thebes being excluded from the treaty of peace; Pelopidas and Epaminondas gain the great victory of Leuctra, in which Cleombrotus, King of Sparta, is slain. Thebes becomes the dominant power in Greece.

The Arcadian union formed. One of the first effects of the battle of Leuctra was to emancipate the Arcadians, and a plan was formed to raise them in the political affairs of Greece.

370. Epaminondas, the Theban general, heads his first expedition into the Peloponnesus; he threatens Sparta, which Agesilaus saves.

369. The Thebans advance into Laconia; they restore the independence of the Messenians. Epaminondas and Pelopidas are condemned for having retained their command beyond the term allowed by the laws of Thebes; they are pardoned and reappointed.

The Arcadians found Megalopolis, which they make the capital of the Arcadian confederacy.

368. The Thebans again enter the Peloponnesus, but retreat before the arrival of succor sent by Dionysius to the Lacedæmonians. Pelopidas, treacherously made prisoner by Alexander of Pheræ, is rescued by Epaminondas. A congress, under the mediation of Persia, is held at Delphi; it fails, because the Thebans will not abandon the Messenians.

The Carthaginians at war with Dionysius; but, after losing Selinus and other towns, they make peace.

---

[1] By the old chronological reckoning this event occurred B.C. 390.

* Date uncertain.

Camillus, more than eighty years old, appointed dictator at Rome; he persuades the patricians to assent to the demands of the plebs, and builds the temple of Concord.

A celestial globe brought into Greece from Egypt.

367. The Licinian Rogations, Rome; three bills introduced by Licinius, decreeing: 1. That interest on loans be deducted from the principal; 2. Limiting the public land held by any individual to 500 jugera (320 acres); 3. Ordering that one of the two consuls should be a plebeian. Institution of the prætorship.

364. Pelopidas attacks Alexander of Pheræ; during the battle of Cymoscephale his soldiers are alarmed at an eclipse of the sun, and he is slain.

362. The Spartans and allies defeated at Mantinea by Epaminondas; he is slain.

361 (359). Artaxerxes II of Persia succeeded by Artaxerxes III (Ochus).

359. Philip ascends the throne of Macedon; he concludes peace with the Athenians.

358.* Athens involves herself in the Social War with Cos, Rhodes, Chios, and Byzantium.

Amphipolis captured by Philip of Macedon; he loses his right eye by an arrow from Astor.

357. Outbreak of the Ten Years' Sacred War, caused by the Crissians levying grievous taxes on those who went to consult the oracle of Delphi.

356. Burning of the temple of Diana at Ephesus; this building was accounted one of the Seven Wonders of the World.

Birth of Alexander the Great.

Dion frees Syracuse from Dionysius the Younger; he is expelled from Sicily.

355. The Social War ends in Greece. Athens recognizes the independence of the confederated states.

353. Final conquest of Egypt by the Persians.

352. Philip of Macedon interferes in the Greek Sacred War; Demosthenes delivers his First Philippic encouraging the Greeks to resist the Macedonians; Philip's attempt to seize Thermopylæ is defeated.

Two thousand colonists are sent from Athens to Samos.

347. Philip of Macedon captures and destroys Olynthus.

346. Phocis occupied by Philip of Macedon; this ends the Sacred War. Dionysius the Younger again assumes power in Syracuse.

343 (340). Timoleon effects the deliverance of Syracuse from Dionysius the Younger.

Rome engages in the First Samnite War.

341 (338). End of the First Samnite War.

Invasion of China by Meha the Hun. See "TARTAR INVASION OF CHINA BY MEHA," ii, 126.*

* Date uncertain.

340. Adoption of the Publilian laws in Rome, which further restricted the power of the patricians.

The Romans make war upon the Latins; the latter are subjugated. Manlius, one of the Roman consuls, condemns his son to death for a breach of discipline.

338. Athens and Thebes form an alliance to resist Philip of Macedon, who had passed Thermopylæ and seized Elatea. The allied forces are overwhelmed at Chæronea, and Philip establishes the Macedonian dominion in Greece.

Artaxerxes III is succeeded by Arses in Persia.

337. Philip of Macedon declares himself commander of the Greeks against the Persians; he repudiates his wife Olympias; their son Alexander attends his mother into Epirus.

336. Assassination of Philip of Macedon, by Pausanias at Ægæ, while preparing to invade Persia; he is succeeded by his son, Alexander the Great.

Arses is succeeded by Darius III (Codomannus) in Persia.

335. Thebes, revolting against the Macedonian authority, is subdued and destroyed by Alexander, who, however, spares the house of Pindar the poet.

Rome concludes a peace with Gaul.

334. Alexander enters upon the conquest of Persia; he is victorious over Darius at the Granicus.

333. Lycia and Syria reduced by Alexander; Damascus captured by Parmenio, Alexander's general, and the siege of Tyre begun.

Darius is defeated at Issus; his family are among Alexander's captives.

332. "ALEXANDER REDUCES TYRE: LATER FOUNDS ALEXANDRIA." See ii, 133. He takes Gaza and occupies Egypt.

The Lucanians and Bruttians defeat and slay Alexander of Epirus, his ambitious designs in Italy having been betrayed.

331. "THE BATTLE OF ARBELA," in which Alexander the Great conquers Darius and overthrows the Persian empire. See ii, 141.

330. The Spartans, under Agis III, revolt against the Macedonians; Antipater defeats the Spartans and their allies at Megalopolis; Agis is slain.

Darius is seized and laden with chains by Bessus, a Bactrian satrap who soon after slays him.

Alexander captures Bessus and delivers him to Oxathres, the brother of Darius, by whom he is executed.

Alexander pursues his conquests in Parthia, Media, Bactria, and on the shores of the Caspian.

329. The Oxus and Jaxartes are crossed by Alexander; he drives back the Scythians; he founds new cities in the countries adjacent, and winters in Bactria.

The consuls at Rome are granted a triumph and the surname of "Privernas," for the conquest of Privernum,

328. Sogdiana, Central Asia, occupies Alexander during this, his seventh campaign, and he winters there at Nautaca.

327. Marriage of Alexander to Roxana, daughter of Oxyartes, a Bactrian ruler.

326. Alexander invades India and defeats Porus; his soldiers refuse to proceed farther.

Rome begins the Second Samnite War.

325-4. Alexander marches from the Indus to Persepolis; his fleet is sailed to the Euphrates by Nearchus.

Harpalus flees from Babylon with immense treasures, which he conveys to Athens.

323. Death of Alexander the Great at Babylon. His principal generals endeavored to obtain, each for himself, a portion of his empire. Ptolemy first secures Egypt and establishes his dynasty firmly there. Philip Aridæus, half-brother of Alexander, succeeds him on the throne of Macedon, with Perdiccas as regent. Demosthenes returns to Athens and rouses the Greek states to recover their freedom; under Leosthenes they overpower Antipater, who takes refuge in Lamia, whence this is called the Lamian War.

The Samnites sue for peace, but reject the terms on which it is offered by the Romans.

322. The body of Alexander is entombed at Alexandria.

The confederate Greeks are defeated by Antipater at Crannon; end of the Lamian War.

Demosthenes, who was accused by the Macedonians of being privy to the looting of the treasury by Harpalus, after the battle of Crannon fled to Calauria; he was captured by the Macedonian troops and thereupon poisoned himself.

321. Beginning of the wars between Alexander's successors; Perdiccas and Eumenes oppose themselves to Antipater, Craterus, Antigonus, and Ptolemy.

Perdiccas assails Ptolemy in Egypt; Perdiccas is slain in a mutiny. In Asia Minor, Eumenes triumphs over Craterus, who is killed.

Victory of the Samnites over the Romans at the Caudine Forks. These were two narrow gorges, united by a range of mountains on each side. The Romans went through the first pass, but found the second blocked up; on returning they found the first similarly obstructed. Being thus hemmed in they passed under the yoke.

320. Eumenes, defeated by Antigonus, shuts himself up in the castle of Nora, where he sustains a year's siege.

319. Polysperchon is appointed by Antipater to succeed him as regent for Philip Arrhidæus and Alexander Ægus, half-brother and son of Alexander the Great, on his, Antipater's, death.

Polysperchon's elevation to power is followed by a league against him, formed by Antipater's son Cassander, Antigonus, and Ptolemy. Eumenes lends his support to Polysperchon, after escaping from Nora.

318. The Romans and Samnites make a truce.

Polysperchon prevailed over by Cassander in the struggle for power in Greece and Macedonia. Athens he places under the rule of Phalereus.

317. Phocion, an Athenian general who wisely advised in vain for peace with Antipater, became regarded as a traitor; he fled to Phocis, entered into the intrigues of Cassander, who delivered him up to the Athenians, who condemned him to drink hemlock. Olympias, mother of Alexander the Great, aided by Polysperchon and the Epirotes, seizes Macedonia.

Olympias is put to death by Cassander. Eumenes, being betrayed to Antigonus, is put to death; Antigonus holds the supreme power in Asia.

315. The rebuilding of Thebes undertaken by Cassander.

314. Commencement of the struggle against Antigonus waged by Cassander, Ptolemy, Seleucus, and Lysimachus.

313. Tyre surrenders to Antigonus. Ptolemy engages with him and conquers Cyprus.

The Romans take Fregellæ and other towns from the Samnites.

312. Seleucus Nicator establishes the realm of the Seleucidæ, the army of Antigonus, under his son Demetrius Poliorcetes, being defeated by Ptolemy and Seleucus. Babylon is made the capital.

Ptolemy conquers Judea; he transplants many Jews to Alexandria and Cyrene, where their industry is encouraged and their religion protected.

At Rome Appius Claudius, the blind, constructs the Via Appia, the first aqueduct, and a canal through the Pontine marshes.

Zeno institutes the sect of Stoics at Athens.

311. A temporary peace among the competitors for power in Asia. Greece is declared to be free, and Ptolemy resigns Phœnicia to Antigonus.

Roxana, the widow of Alexander the Great, and her young son Alexander Ægas, are put to death by Cassander.

The Roman consul Bubulcus penetrates into Samnium, where he is surrounded, and cuts his way through with great courage.

310. Agathocles, the Syracusan ruler, defeated by the Carthaginians at Himera, passes over to Africa and carries the war into their own country.

The Etruscans take up arms in favor of the Samnites.

Civil war in the little kingdom of Bosporus; Satyrus II, king for a few months, falls in battle.

An eclipse of the sun, August 15th.

309. Hercules, a natural son of Alexander, proclaimed king of Macedon; he is murdered by Cassander.

The Romans are victorious over the Samnites and the Etruscans.

308. The Romans, under Fabius, compel the Etruscans to make peace; Fabius then turns against the Samnites, whom he defeats.

307. Demetrius Poliorcetes, son of Antigonus, arrives with a fleet at

Athens, expels Demetrius Phalereus, and restores the democracy; the Athenians throw down Phalereus' statues and condemn him to death.

306. Ptolemy's fleet is destroyed by Demetrius Poliorcetes at Salamis; but Antigonus fails in his attempt on Egypt. Antigonus assumes the title of king of Asia; Ptolemy Lagi, Lysimachus, and Seleucus, the rulers of Egypt, Thrace, and that part of Alexander's empire east of the Euphrates, likewise assume the royal title. Cassander of Macedon is hailed king by his subjects.

305. War between Seleucus and India, under Sandrocottus, ends in a treaty of amity.

Flavius reconciles all orders of the Roman state and erects a temple of Concord.

Demetrius Poliorcetes besieges Rome.

304. The Romans triumphantly end the Second Samnite War.

302. The priesthood at Rome is opened to the plebs.

300.[1] Battle of Ipsus. Seleucus and Lysimachus overwhelm the army of Antigonus and his son, Demetrius Poliorcetes; Antigonus is slain. His dominions are divided among the victors. Lysimachus takes a large portion of Asia Minor; Seleucus appropriates Upper Syria, Cappadocia, and other territory.

Seleucus Nicator builds Antioch, which he makes the capital of his kingdom of Syria.

299. Rome engages in the Third Samnite War, which becomes one of extermination, but the Samnites bravely resist in their mountain holds.

295. Pyrrhus, King of Epirus, espouses Antigone of the house of Ptolemy; he returns to his dominions, out of which he had been driven by the Molossi.

The Samnites, Etruscans, Umbrians, and Gauls unite against Rome. Q. Fabius Rullianus and P. Decimo Mus defeat the Samnites and Gauls at Sentinum.

Demetrius Poliorcetes retakes Athens; Lysimachus and Ptolemy deprive him of all he possesses.

294. The Macedonian throne is seized by Demetrius Poliorcetes; by violence or treachery the sons of Cassander are slain.

293. Many towns of the Samnites are so utterly destroyed by the Romans that their sites are unknown; a portion of the spoil is cast into a brazen colossus, and placed in front of the Roman Capitol.

The Roman census is 272,308 citizens.

The first sun-dial at Rome is placed on the temple of Quirinus.

290. The end of the Third Samnite War, which results in the submission of the Samnites to Rome.

287. Birth of Archimedes, celebrated mathematician.*

Lysimachus and Pyrrhus, King of Epirus, wrest Macedonia from Demetrius Poliorcetes; immediately after, Lysimachus expels Pyrrhus.

[1] The date is usually given as 301.

* Date uncertain.

286. The Hortensian law, passed by Q. Hortensino, affirmed the legislative power granted the plebeians B.C. 446 and 336.

285. Completion of the Septuagint, a Greek version of the Scriptures, called " the Alexandrian."

The length of the solar year first accurately determined by Dionysius, in the astronomical canon.

283. Death of Ptolemy Lagi (Ptolemy Soter); Ptolemy Philadelphus (jointly on the throne with his father since 295) succeeds him as King of Egypt. He further encourages the immigration of the Jews, who flourish exceedingly.

282. The Tarentines attack a Roman fleet and insult the ambassadors, who demand satisfaction. Rome prepares for war; the Tarentines engage Pyrrhus to assist them.

281. Lysimachus, at war with Seleucus Nicator, is defeated and slain in Phrygia.

The Roman consul Æmilius invades the territory of Tarentum.

280. Pyrrhus, King of Epirus, invades Italy; he makes the cause of Tarentum his own and wars on Rome. Lævinus, the Roman consul, is defeated. See " FIRST BATTLE BETWEEN GREEKS AND ROMANS," ii, 166.

Revival of the Achæan League. The Achæi originally inhabited the neighborhood of Argos; when driven thence by the Heraclidæ, they retired among the Ionians, expelled the natives, and seized their thirteen cities, forming the Achæan League.

279. Pyrrhus, who had tried to mediate between Tarentum and Rome, meeting with non-success, advances on Rome. He fails to make any impression and returns to Tarentum; the Romans follow him, and he gains an unimportant victory over them at Asculum. See " FIRST BATTLE BETWEEN GREEKS AND ROMANS," ii, 166.

Irruption of Gauls into Macedonia; King Ptolemy Ceraunus offers battle to them, in which he is killed.[1]

278. The Gauls under Brennus invade Greece; they are cut to pieces near Delphi.

Alliance formed between Rome and Carthage.

Pyrrhus wars against Carthage in Sicily.

277. A body of Gauls enter Northern Phrygia, of which they take possession.

Pyrrhus expels the Carthaginians from most of their possessions in Sicily.

276. Other Grecian cities join the Achæan League.

275. Pyrrhus, on the arrival of Carthaginian reënforcements, returns to Italy; he is totally defeated by M. Curius Dentatus (at Beneventum), who exhibits in his triumphs the first elephants ever seen in Rome.

273. Ptolemy Philadelphus, of Egypt, sends an embassy to congratulate the Romans on their victory and to ask an alliance with them.

---

[1] The date usually given is B.C. 280.

272. Pyrrhus attempts the siege of Sparta; he is repulsed. In an attack on Argos, Pyrrhus is slain.

Tarentum surrenders to the Romans.

Lucania and Brittium also submit to Rome.

269. The first silver coinage at Rome.

266. The Romans capture and destroy Volsinii; Rome controls all Italy.

264. War between Rome and Carthage. See "THE PUNIC WARS," ii, 179.

Gladiators first introduced into Rome.

263. Antigonus Gonatus, King of Macedon, captures Athens.

The Romans compel Hiero, King of Syracuse, to withdraw from the support of Carthage. See "THE PUNIC WARS," ii, 179.

Philetærus at his death appoints his nephew, Eumenes, King of Pergamus; the competition for books between him and Ptolemy Philadelphus causes the latter to prohibit the export of papyrus from Egypt; this leads to the invention of parchment at Pergamus, whence it takes its name.

Hiero makes peace with the Romans; he becomes their most trusted ally.

260. Ships-of-war first built by the Romans; the naval power of Rome inaugurated by the decisive victory of Duilius over the Carthaginians at Mylæ. See "THE PUNIC WARS," ii, 179.

259. The Romans invade Corsica; they carry off much rich spoil from thence and Sardinia, but make no permanent conquests. The island of Melita (Malta) is captured by the Romans.

258. Atilius, the Roman consul, surrounded by the Carthaginians in Sicily, escapes with difficulty.

257. A drawn battle between the fleets of Rome and Carthage off Tyndaris causes the Romans to prepare larger ships, in order to strike a decisive blow.

256. Total defeat of the Carthaginian fleet near Ecnomus; the victorious Roman consuls land in Africa. The Carthaginians hire troops from Greece and give the command to Xanthippus. See "THE PUNIC WARS," ii, 179.

255. Regelus and his Roman legions are vanquished by Xanthippus; Regelus is taken captive. The Romans fit out a large fleet, which gains another victory and brings off the remains of the army from Africa. Many of the ships are wrecked.

254. Another fleet consisting of 220 ships is equipped in three months by the Romans; Panormus (Palermo) is captured. See "THE PUNIC WARS," ii, 179.

253. The Romans again land in Africa and ravage many Carthaginian coast cities; on their return most of their ships are wrecked; the Romans resolve to abstain from naval warfare.

252. Birth of Philopœmen, called the "Last of the Greeks."

251. Aratus restores the freedom of Sicyon; joins the Achæan League, which becomes a powerful body.

250. Arsaceo founds the kingdom of Parthia.

The Romans begin the siege of Lilybæum; the Carthaginians successfully defend it till the close of the war. Metellus, the Roman proconsul, commanding in Sicily, gains a great victory over Hasdrubal near Panoramus; over one hundred elephants form part of his triumphal procession.

249. Naval victory of the Carthaginians over the Romans at Drepanum.

Regelus is sent to Rome to propose an exchange of prisoners; on his return the Carthaginians put him to death with the utmost cruelty.

The war between Syria and Egypt, which had been ruinous to the former, is ended by a treaty between Antiochus II and Ptolemy Philadelphus. One of the conditions was that Antiochus repudiate Laodice and marry Berenice, Ptolemy's daughter.

248. Parthia becomes an independent kingdom.

247. Birth of Hannibal, the famous Carthaginian general.

Ptolemy Euergetes succeeds his father Ptolemy Philadelphus on the throne of Egypt.

243. Corinth, delivered by Aratus from the yoke of Macedon, joins the Achæan League; other states follow the example.

241. Agis IV, of Sparta, assists the Achæans in their war against the Ætolians.

Rome, having again assembled a great fleet, under Lutatius Catalus, vanquishes the Carthaginians in a naval encounter off the Ægates. End of the First Punic War; Sicily is relinquished by Carthage to Rome.

240. The Carthaginian mercenaries in Africa revolt; Hamilcar Barca crushes it out.

237. Carthage is compelled to cede Sardinia to Rome.

236–221. Celomenes III of Sparta institutes great political reforms and engages in a struggle with the Achæan League.

236–220. Hamilcar Barca and Hasdrubal, his son-in-law, conquer a great part of Spain.

235. Rome, at peace with all the world, closes the temple of Janus, for the first time since Numa, according to legend, the second king of Rome.

234. Birth of Cato the Elder.

Scipio Africanus born.

230. Ambassadors sent by Rome to protest against the piracies of the Illyrians are murdered by the order of Queen Teuta.

229. A successful war is waged by the Romans against the Greek kingdom of Illyria; the Roman power is extended across the Adriatic.

On the death of Hamilcar, his son-in-law, Hasdrubal, takes his place in Spain; he founds Carthago Nova (Carthagena).

227. Sparta makes war with the Achæan League.

225–222. Cisalpine Gaul is conquered by the Romans.

221. Cleomenes III is crushed by Antigonus Doson, ruler of Macedon, at Sellasia; the Spartan power is utterly destroyed.

220. Social war; the war made by the Ætolian League on the Achæan League.

219. Hannibal lays siege to Saguntum, which he destroys; this is the real commencement of the Second Punic War. See "THE PUNIC WARS," ii, 179.

Philip V, of Macedon, is victorious in his campaigns against the Ætolian League.

218. Hannibal crosses the Alps into Italy; he defeats the Romans on the Ticinus and Trebia. See "THE PUNIC WARS," ii, 179.

217. Philip V continues his victorious way against the Ætolian League.

Hannibal defeats the Romans at the Trasimene Lake.

Antiochus the Great cedes Cœle-Syria and Palestine to Egypt.

216. Crushing defeat of the Romans by Hannibal at Cannæ. See "THE PUNIC WARS," ii, 179.

214. Rome has her first encounter with Macedon; Philip V allies himself with Hannibal and begins the war.

Marcellus is sent into Sicily and besieges Syracuse, which had declared against Rome.

213. Aratus, strategus of the Achæan League, is poisoned by Philip V of Macedon; this alienates from him many Greek states.

Hwangti crushes out literature in China.

212. After a two-years' siege the Romans under Marcellus take Syracuse.

The Two Scipios defeated and killed in Spain. See "THE PUNIC WARS," ii, 179.

211. Hannibal before the gates of Rome. See "THE PUNIC WARS," ii, 179.

The Ætolian League with its allies assists Rome against Macedon.

210. Ægina taken by the Romans; the inhabitants reduced to slavery.

Agrigentum, being conquered by Cævinus, places all Sicily again under Roman subjection.

Scipio, victorious in Spain, takes Carthago Nova. See "THE PUNIC WARS," ii, 179.

208. Suspension of his operations against Scipio—the future Scipio Africanus—in Spain by Hasdrubal, son of Hamilcar, who sets out to relieve his brother Hannibal in Italy.

207. Hasdrubal is defeated and slain on the Metaurus. See "BATTLE OF THE METAURUS," ii, 195.

A signal victory is achieved by Philopœmen, general of the Achæan League, with Macedon, over the Spartans at Matinea.

206. Birth of Polybius, Greek historian.

The Carthaginian power in Spain completely destroyed by Scipio.

205. End of the first Romo-Macedonian war.

204. Scipio carries the war into Africa; he defeats the Carthaginians and the Numidians.

203. Hannibal, recalled from Italy, arrives at Carthage.

202. The Carthaginian power is completely broken, ending the Second Punic War. See "Scipio Africanus Crushes Hannibal at Zama and Subjugates Carthage," ii, 224.

201. A war is begun by Rome for the resubjugation of the Boii and Insubres of Cisalpine Gaul, who had attained freedom owing to the Carthaginian invasion.

The Jews become subject to the Seleucid monarchy.

200. Declaration of war by Rome against Macedon; the second Macedonian war.

198. Antiochus the Great, of Syria, conquers Palestine and Cœle-Syria from Egypt, defeating Scopas and the Ætolian allies.

197. Decisive Roman victory over the Macedonians at Cynoscephale; Philip V of Macedon makes a humiliating peace.

196. The Roman general Flaminius proclaims the freedom of the Greeks.

195.* Birth of Terrence, Roman comic poet.

Ptolemy V, Epiphanes, King of Egypt. See i, 1, "The Rosetta Stone."

192. In concert with the Ætolians, Antiochus the Great takes up arms against Rome.

191. Antiochus is defeated by the Romans under Acilius Glabrio, at Thermopylæ, in Greece. The resubjugation of Cisalpine Gaul is completed by Rome.

All the Peloponnesus is included in the Achæan League, which attains its apogee.

190. Scipio Asiaticus takes command of the Romans in Greece, with his brother Africanus as lieutenant; Antiochus is vanquished at Magnesia and he is compelled to release his hold on the greater part of Asia Minor. Most of the conquered territory is annexed to Pergamus. Scipio Asiaticus takes his surname for the courage and ability he showed.

189. Fall of the Ætolian League.

185. Birth of Scipio Africanus the Younger.

179. Death of Philip V of Macedon. His son Perseus negotiates secretly with other states against Rome. The Celtiberians and Lusitanians lay down their arms.

177. Rome suppresses a revolt in Sardinia. A colony settled at Lucca. The Achæans contract an alliance with Rome.

Thessaly relapses under the Macedonian influence.

176. The consul Scipio dies, and C. Valerius Lævinus takes his place for the rest of the year. His colleague Petilius is slain in battle against the Ligurians. The Orchian and other sumptuary laws fail to repress the luxury of the Romans.

175. Disgraceful struggles for the high-priesthood of Jerusalem; Antiochus sells it to Jason, the brother of Onias, who is deposed.

174. Masinissa, after many encroachments, seizes the Carthaginian provinces of Tyssa, with fifty cities; Roman ambassadors sent to settle the dispute. Others deputed to ascertain the intentions of Perseus.

* Date uncertain.

Mithridates VI of the Arsacidæ begins his reign and prepares the elevation of Parthia to great power.

173. The Roman ambassadors return, Perseus having refused to receive them.

Death of Cleopatra, who, in the name of her young son, had been regent of Egypt.

172. The Ligurians are subdued and Northern Italy filled with Roman colonies. Eumenes honorably received at Rome; on his way back he is attacked by assassins near Delphi.

Menelaus, another brother, supplants Jason in the high-priesthood of Jerusalem.

171. Commencement of the Third Macedonian War; King Perseus begins his struggle with Rome.

Antiochus invades Egypt and takes Memphis.

170. Hostilius, who takes the command in Macedon, makes no progress; the Roman fleet ravages the sea-coast.

Perseus negotiates with Antiochus, Prusias, and many Greek states to form a coalition against Rome; even Eumenes begins to treat with him.

Ptolemy Physcon is associated with his brother as joint King of Egypt.

169. The manœuvres of Marcius Philippus drive Perseus from his strong position in Tempe.

Antiochus lays siege to Alexandria; the Egyptians apply to Rome for aid.

168. Battle of Pydna; complete defeat of Perseus, King of Macedon, by the Romans, under L. Ænilius Paulas. Macedon becomes a Roman province.

Antiochus, awed by the Roman ambassador Popillius and the fate of Perseus, evacuates Egypt. In his retreat he plunders Jerusalem and despoils the Temple, in which he sets up the statue of Jupiter Olympias.

167. Deportation of a thousand Achæans to Rome; among them is Polybius, the historian, who there finds patrons and friends. The first library opened in Rome, consisting of books plundered from Macedon.

Arms are taken up by the Asmoneans against Antiochus, King of Syria.

165. Judas Maccabæus enters Jerusalem; he purifies the Temple. See "JUDAS MACCABÆUS LIBERATES JUDEA," ii, 245.

160. Defeat and death of Judas Maccabæus in battle.

158. Roman citizens are almost entirely relieved of direct taxation by the revenues from Macedon and other conquests.

149. Commencement of the Third Punic War between Rome and Carthage. See "THE PUNIC WARS," ii, 179.

First Roman law against bribery at elections.

147.* Viriathus, the Lusitanian leader, has his first great victory over the Romans.

* Date uncertain.

146. Scipio Africanus the Younger completely destroys Carthage.

Mummius, commanding in Greece, defeats the Achæans at Leucopetra; he captures and destroys Corinth. The treasures of Grecian art conveyed to Rome. Greece becomes a Roman province.

Demetrius Nicator slays Alexander Bala in battle and becomes king of Syria.

141. Simon Maccabæus captures the citadel of Jerusalem.

Silanus, accused by the Macedonians of corrupt practices, is condemned by his father, Torquatus, and takes his own life.

140. The Jews proclaim Simon Maccabæus hereditary prince; with this dignity is united the office of high-priest.

*Viriathus, the Lusitanian leader against the Romans in Spain, is assassinated by order of the consul Cæpio.

135. Simon Maccabæus is assassinated; John Hyrcanus, his son, succeeds him as ruler at Jerusalem.

134-133. Antiochus Tidetes, King of Syria, besieges Jerusalem; he is repulsed.

134-132. Servile War in Sicily, caused by the inhuman treatment of the slaves by their owners; two great battles were fought before the rising was suppressed.

133. Tiberius Gracchus attempts his great political and agrarian reforms in Rome. See "THE GRACCHI AND THEIR REFORMS," ii, 259.

Scipio Africanus the Younger reduces Numantia.

Attalus III of Pergamus bequeaths his kingdom, which embraces a great part of Asia Minor, to the Romans.

125-121. The southeastern portion of Transalpine Gaul conquered by the Romans.

123-122. Caius Gracchus commences his agrarian reforms in Rome. See "THE GRACCHI AND THEIR REFORMS," ii, 259.

118. Rome extends her dominion beyond the Rhone; the colony of Narbo Martius (Narbonne) founded.

113. Hordes of the Cimbri and Teutons threaten the Rome dominion by an invasion of Illyrium.

112. Jugurtha, King of Numidia, kills Adherbal, who has been restored to the throne of Numidia after being driven thence by Jugurtha.

111. The consul Calpurnius proceeds with a Roman army into Numidia; bribed by Jugurtha, he makes a peace and withdraws his forces.

109. Jugurtha is opposed in Numidia by the Roman army headed by Metellus.

John Hyrcanus, the Jewish Prince and high-priest, defeats Ptolemy Lathyrus and captures Samaria.*

The Cimbri request an allotment of land from the Romans, whereon to settle; it is refused; they ravage the country, but are checked in Thrace by Nimicus Rufus.

108. Metellus, as proconsul, continues the war in Numidia.

The Cimbri defeat the consul Scaurus in Gaul.

* Date uncertain.

Mithridates of Pontus secretly prepares to regain by force the province of Phrygia, which the Romans took from him during his minority.

107. Marius vigorously carries on the war against Jugurtha; Marius is consul, Sylla his quæstor.

Cassius, Roman consul, is defeated and slain by the Cimbri in Gaul.

106. Birth of Cicero. Birth of Pompey the Great.

Jugurtha is betrayed by Bocchus, King of Mauretania, into the hands of the Romans, which ends the Jugurthine War.

105. The Cimbri and Teutones defeat the consul Manilius and proconsul Cæpio, near the Rhone, with great loss.

Aristobulus, son of John Hyrcanus, succeeds his father and assumes the title of king of Judea.

104. Alexander Jannæus succeeds his brother Aristobulus in Judea.

102. Marius overwhelmingly defeats the Teutones, while they were retreating from Spain, at Aquæ Sextiæ (Aix).

Another revolt of the slaves in Sicily (Second Servile War).

101. Marius utterly crushes the Cimbri on the Raudian Fields, after they had previously defeated the proconsul Lutatius Catulus.

100. The Second Servile War continues.

Birth of Julius Cæsar.

99. M. Aquilius finally crushes out the slave uprising in Sicily.

94. Mithridates makes his son king of Cappadocia.

93. Cappadocians appeal to the Romans, who give them Ariobarzanes for their king. Mithridates seizes Galatia.

92. Sulla is sent by the Romans into Cappadocia to observe Mithridates' proceedings; ambassadors from Parthia meet him there.

91. M. Livius Drussus, people's tribune, advocates giving the rights of citizenship to the Roman allies; he is assassinated.

90. Social or Marsic War, a conflict of the Italian states against Rome, begins, the cause being the refusal of the franchise by Rome. Cæsar, the consul, is unfortunate against the Samnites, and Rutilius is defeated and slain by the Marsi. Marius retrieves these disasters. Citizenship granted to the states which remain faithful to Rome.

The Roman senate promises aid to Cappadocia against Mithridates.

89. The consul Pompeius (father of Pompey the Great) gains decided victories over the Picentines; his colleague, Cato, defeats the Marsi, but is killed in the battle; Sulla takes the command, and is so successful that he is elected consul for the ensuing year. Cicero is a cadet in the army of Pompeius.

Cleopatra is put to death by her son Alexander, who is expelled from Egypt, and Ptolemy Soter restored.

88. End of the Social War. Most of the refractory states admitted to Roman citizenship.

Mithridates, King of Pontus, occupies Phrygia; he asks all Asia Minor to join him; a general massacre of the Romans occurs.

Quarrel between Sulla and Marius which causes war between them for the control of the Roman army. The first Roman civil war.

87. Sulla proceeds to Greece to conduct the war against Mithridates; Sulla besieges Athens.

The consul Cinna, deposed by the senate, calls Marius from Africa, raises an Italian army, and reinstates himself in office; bloody proscriptions by Marius and Cinna follow.

86. Death of Marius, in the beginning of his seventh consulate; Flaccus, appointed in his place, is assassinated on his march to the east, by C. Fimbria, who assumes command of the Roman army.

Sulla captures the revolted city of Athens and defeats the army of Mithridates under Archelaus.

A sedition of the Jews is quelled with merciless severity by Alexander Jannæus.

85. The Romans are successful against Mithridates in Asia.

84. End of the First Mithridatic War; Mithridates, finding himself between two victorious Roman armies, agrees to peace and relinquishes all his acquisitions.

83. Sulla makes war against the Marian party in Italy.

The Roman senate refuses to send Mithridates a formal ratification of the treaty. He retains a part of Cappadocia. The Second Mithridatic War begins.

82. Sulla becomes dictator at Rome, after crushing the Marian party; he inflicts a bloody vengeance on his enemies.

End of the Second Mithridatic War.

81. Pompey, having been successful in Africa, is granted a triumph in Rome.

80. Sertorius, the Marian leader, sets up an independent state in Spain.

Cæsar serves as a cadet at the siege of Mitylene; he receives a civic crown for saving the life of a citizen.

79. Sulla resigns the dictatorship, but remains master of Rome.

Alexander Jannæus, King of Judea, is succeeded on his death by his widow Alexandra.

78. Death of Sulla.

76. Pompey is sent into Spain to oppose Sertorius.

74. Mithridates renews hostilities; he enters into an abortive alliance with Sertorius. Third Mithridatic War. Lucullus commands the Roman forces.

73. Lucullus routs the army of Mithridates.

Rising of the gladiators; Spartacus collects, on Mount Vesuvius, a numerous army of slaves and gladiators; they overcome the forces sent against them and ravage Southern Italy. The Third Servile War.

72. Sertorius is assassinated in Spain; the Spaniards submit to Pompey.

King Mithridates is driven from his dominions by Lucullus; the King takes refuge in Armenia.

71. Crassus defeats and slays Spartacus; the gladiators are crushed.

70. Death of Alexandra, widow of Jannæus; she nominates her son,

Hyrcanus, as her successor; but his brother, Aristobulus, usurps the throne of Judea.

Pompey and Crassus, previously at variance, are reconciled during their joint consulship.

Cicero's six orations (the first only being actually delivered) against Verres, who, when governor of Sicily, had plundered the island of property, art treasures, etc.

Birth of Vergil.

69. Lucullus crosses the Euphrates, captures Tigranocerta, and defeats Tigranes, who had succored Mithridates in Armenia.

68. Lucullus defeats Tigranes and takes Nisibis.

67. A mutiny in the Roman army caused by the appointment of Glabrio to succeed Lucullus.

Pompey crushes the pirates of Cilicia and makes it a Roman province.

Julius Cæsar is quæstor in Spain.

Metellus completes the conquest of Crete for the Romans.

Mithridates makes a successful advance.

66. Pompey, after a conference with Lucullus, completely crushes Mithridates and drives him over the Cimmerian Bosporus.

65. End of the Third Mithridatic War.

Antiochus XIII is deposed by Pompey; this puts an end to the kingdom of the Seleucidæ (Syria).

Hyrcanus takes up arms against his brother Aristobulus in Judea.

64. Pompey takes possession of Syria; he is recalled thence to oppose Mithridates, who, returned to his states, prepares for further resistance.

63. Having intervened between the brothers John Hyrcanus II and Aristobulus II, and decided in favor of Hyrcanus, Pompey lays siege to Jerusalem, where Aristobulus reigns, captures it, and makes Judea a Roman province.

Mithridates, betrayed by his son, poisons himself.

Cicero frustrates the conspiracy of Catiline, having for its object the cancellation of debts, the proscription of the wealthy, and the distribution among the conspirators of all the offices of honor and emolument.

62. Catiline is defeated and slain, after having collected an army in Etruria.

Discord arises between Cæsar, now prætor, and Cato, tribune of the people.

60. First Triumvirate in Rome, formed of Pompey, Crassus, and Cæsar, equally dividing the power.

59. Consulship of Cæsar at Rome; he carries his agrarian law and ingratiates himself with the people; he is given the command in Gaul and Illyrium for five years.

58. Cæsar begins his campaigns in Gaul. See "CÆSAR CONQUERS GAUL," ii, 267.

Cicero exiled from Rome; he had saved the Republic at the time of the Catiline conspiracy, but had broken the constitution, which forbade capital punishment without the sentence of the assembly of the people.